CALCULUS Made Simple

H. Mulholland, MSc

MADE SIMPLE
BOOKS

Made Simple Books
An imprint of Heinemann Professional Publishing Ltd
Halley Court, Jordan Hill, Oxford OX2 8EJ

OXFORD LONDON MELBOURNE AUCKLAND SINGAPORE
IBADAN NAIROBI GABORONE KINGSTON

First edition 1976
Reprinted 1979
Reprinted 1981
Reprinted 1982
Reprinted 1985
Reprinted 1987
Reprinted 1990

British Library Cataloguing in Publication Data
Mulholland, H.
Calculus made simple.—(Made simple books, ISSN 0265–0541)
1. Calculus
I. Title II. Series
515 QA303

ISBN 0 434 98461 2

Made and printed in Great Britain by
Richard Clay Ltd, Bungay, Suffolk

Foreword

The principles of the Calculus have been known for more than 300 years but recently it has become more and more a common language and its techniques are being applied not only in the traditional subjects such as physics and engineering but also in chemistry, statistics, the life sciences—biology, botany, physiology—and economics. In this book use is made of these wider applications and the theory is illustrated with examples drawn from the new as well as the traditional sources. Early introduction of the growth function has meant that a comprehensive range of examples can be given throughout the book. An interest in how mathematical techniques, in particular, the Calculus, can be applied in various studies is thus maintained and the reader is motivated to undertake the necessary effort to acquire these techniques.

The initial presentation is by use of easy geometrical ideas already familiar to all students and practical examples drawn from a wide variety of studies. Thus each student is continually reminded of situations in which there is a need for a knowledge of the Calculus. At several convenient places in each chapter sets of short revision questions are included together with answers and reference to the relevant section. The answers should be covered up and revealed progressively as each question is attempted. This serves as a check on the understanding of the previous work. Students of mathematics and of engineering and physics in their preliminary years at polytechnics or senior technical colleges will need to study all the topics. Chemistry or life science students in polytechnics or on introductory courses in universities will find that a suitable course of study is Chapters One, Two, Three and sections 4.1 to 4.8, Chapters Five and Six and any relevant applications in Chapter Seven together with sections 10.1, 10.2, 10.4 and 11.1 to 11.4.

The ideas follow the modern trends. The definition of a function allows it to be applied widely from a probability function, which can consist of four ordered pairs of numbers, to a well behaved continuous function. While mathematical exactness has not been neglected, in order to avoid disturbing the logical flow of ideas, rigorous justification has sometimes been left to an appendix, or a note made that a particular result may need more rigorous treatment.

It is impossible to acknowledge my indebtedness to all the different sources. During a lifetime teaching and lecturing in technical colleges, polytechnics and university to students of all disciplines, I have benefited from many textbooks and standard works as well as from discussions with my colleagues. I should, however, like to acknowledge my indebtedness to my family for their choice of a wide-ranging set of subjects from astronomy through economics, environmental studies, civil and mechanical engineering to physics, which made me aware that mathematics—in particular the Calculus—is becoming more and more a common language; and to my wife for her unfailing support and patience.

The presentation of some of the early chapters was discussed with Mr J. P. Parke, and Mr D. Catterall undertook the arduous task of working through the examples and exercises; both made some helpful suggestions for which I am very grateful. Nevertheless any omissions or errors are the responsibility of the author, and I should be very grateful for any suggestions or corrections from those who use this book.

I should also like to express my thanks to to my typist, Mrs R. Marshall, for coping so admirably with the mathematical symbols and my handwritten manuscripts. Finally, my thanks to the publishers and my editor, Mr R. C. Postema, for his help and suggestions regarding the form of the book.

By the same author

Applied Mathematics for Advanced Level (with J. H. G. Phillips), Butterworths
Fundamentals of Statistics (with C. R. Jones), Butterworths
Pure Mathematics for Advanced Level (with B. D. Bunday), Butterworths

Guide to Eire's 3000-Foot Mountains—The Irish Munros, Mulholland Wirral
Guide to Wales' 3000-Foot Mountains—The Welsh Munros, Mulholland Wirral
Guide to Self-Publishing, Mulholland, Wirral

Contents

CHAPTER ONE

BASIC IDEAS OF THE DIFFERENTIAL CALCULUS

1.1 Related Changes

Related quantities are commonplace. The pressure on an underwater swimmer varies with the depth; the volume of a gas with the pressure and temperature; the wingspan of a bird with its body weight. The list of such related quantities is large. In most cases we are interested in how the change

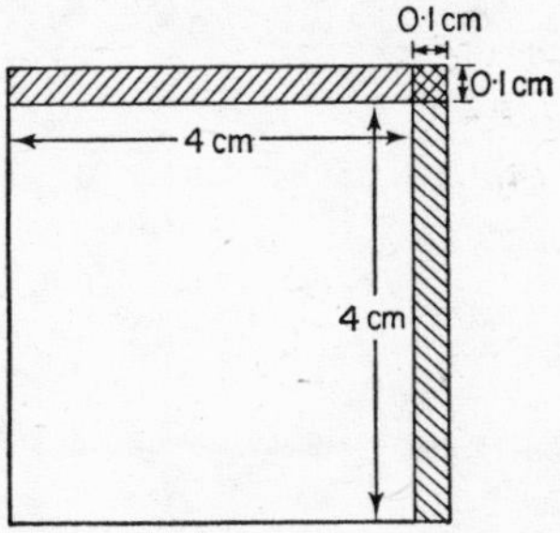

Fig. 1.1

in one quantity affects the other quantity. If the pressure on a mass of gas is halved what happens to the volume? If the number of articles produced is trebled what happens to the cost of each article? If we climb a thousand feet higher how much does the air pressure decrease? Calculus is the branch of mathematics which deals with the relation between such changes; that is, it deals with the **relative change.**

One easy way of introducing a new branch of mathematics is to consider its geometrical aspects and to introduce progressively the necessary algebra together with any new symbols required. Areas and volumes are universally understood and will serve for our initial examples.

Example 1. Consider Fig. 1.1, where a square of side 4 cm has had its sides increased by 0·1 cm. The shaded sections represent

$$\begin{aligned}\text{the increase in area} &= 4 \times 0{\cdot}1 + 4 \times 0{\cdot}1 + (0{\cdot}1)^2\\ &= 0{\cdot}81\ \text{cm}^2\end{aligned}$$

In this example we have automatically combined the arithmetical quantities, and the general relation between the increase in the length of the side and the corresponding increase in the area is totally obscured. However, the geometry of the figure does indicate what happens generally. Let us rework the example using a square of side x cm. From Fig. 1.2 we see that

$$\begin{aligned}\text{Increase in area} &= x \times 0{\cdot}1 + x \times 0{\cdot}1 + (0{\cdot}1)^2\\ &= 2x \times 0{\cdot}1 + (0{\cdot}1)^2\end{aligned}$$

Notice that the geometry of Fig. 1.2 is identical with that of Fig. 1.1 but that now, by using an unknown x, the algebraic expression indicates what happens generally to the area when the side increases.

If the length of the side of the square is *decreased* by 0·1 cm the change in the area is $-2x \times 0{\cdot}1 + (0{\cdot}1)^2$.

1.2 New Notation

We shall be referring continually to increases or decreases—that is, to changes in x or to changes in the area A and many other symbols—and it is convenient to use a shorthand for these phrases. We shall write

δx (read as delta x), meaning a small part of x
δy as meaning a small part of y
δA as meaning a small part of A
. . . .

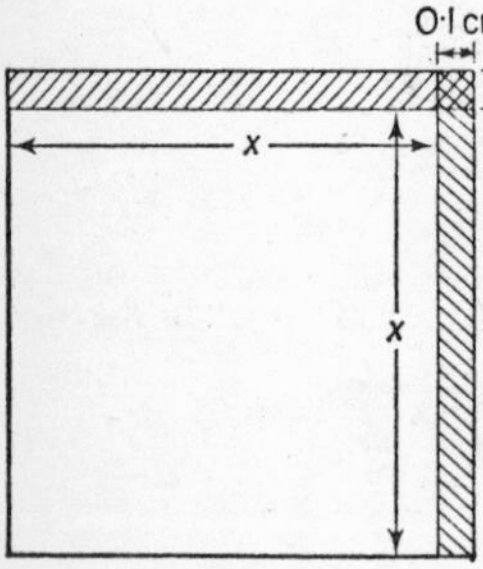

Fig. 1.2

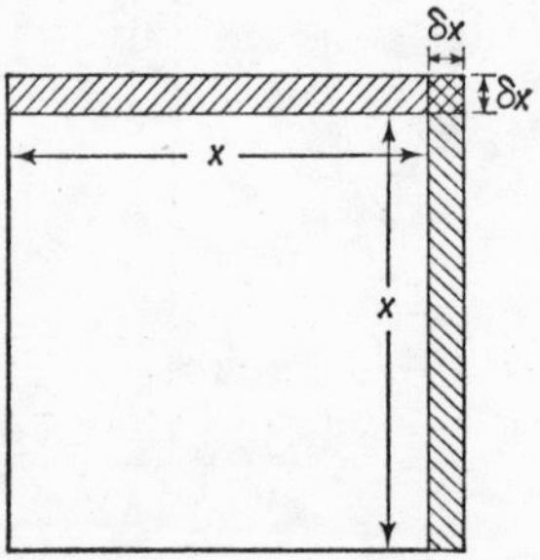

Fig. 1.3

Note (i) δx does **not** mean $\delta \times x$.
(ii) δx, δy, . . . can be positive (that is, an increase in x, y, . . .) or negative (that is, a decrease in x, y, . . .).

Example 2. Find the change in the area A cm² of a square of side x cm when the side changes by an amount δx cm.

Referring to Fig. 1.3, which we note is geometrically the same as Figs. 1.1 and 1.2

$$\text{Change in the area} = x \,.\, \delta x + x \,.\, \delta x + \delta x \,.\, \delta x$$

Two points arise here: (i) we can use our new notation δA for the change in the area; (ii) $\delta x \,.\, \delta x$ must be written as $(\delta x)^2$ because δx^2 means a small change in x^2.

Hence
$$\delta A = 2x \,.\, \delta x + (\delta x)^2 \qquad (1.1)$$

Alternatively, since

$$A = x^2$$
$$\delta A = \delta(x^2) = 2x \,.\, \delta x + (\delta x)^2$$

This result is true whether δx is positive or negative, as may be easily seen.

Consider Fig. 1.4 where δx has been taken as a decrease in x. The change in the area is measured by the new area A_2 minus the original area A_1

$$A_2 - A_1 = (x - \delta x)^2 - x^2$$

or
$$\delta A = x^2 - 2x\delta x + (\delta x)^2 - x^2$$
$$= -2x\delta x + (\delta x)^2$$
$$= 2x(-\delta x) + (-\delta x)^2 \qquad [\text{note } (-\delta x)^2 = (+\delta x)^2]$$

which is of the same form as equation 1.1 with $-\delta x$ in place of $+\delta x$.

We shall always let δx represent both positive and negative changes and separate results will not be obtained in future.

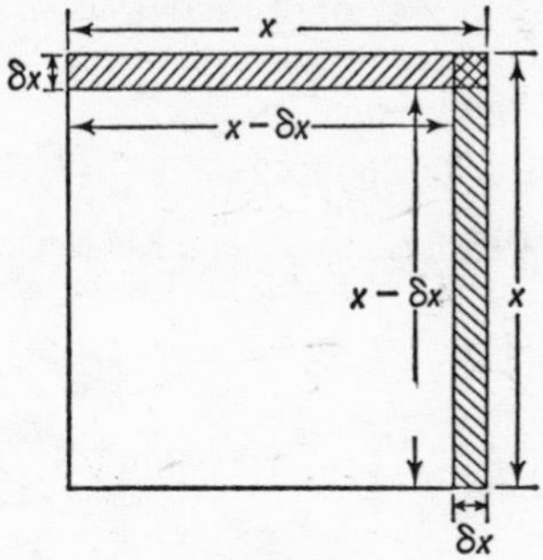

Fig. 1.4

Example 3. Find the change in area of a square of side 100 cm when the length of each side decreases by 0·3 cm.

Using the equation 1.1 with $x = 100$ and $\delta x = -0{\cdot}3$, we have

$$\delta A = 2 \times 100 \times -0{\cdot}3 + (-0{\cdot}3)^2$$
$$= -59{\cdot}91$$

1.3 Smallness

In example 3 we could ignore the term $(-0{\cdot}3)^2$ and write

$$\delta A \simeq 2 \times 100 \times (-0{\cdot}3)$$
$$\simeq -60$$

justifying this by saying 'because $(-0{\cdot}3)^2$ is so small'. This statement is imprecise. What we mean is that $(-0{\cdot}3)^2 = 0{\cdot}09$ is ignored because it is *small compared* to the -60. That is, smallness is relative.

A sum of £1 000 000 we regard as large because we automatically compare it with the amount of money we possess, but an extra interest payment of £1 million compared to an overall government spending of £4000 million would seem small.

A wait of ten minutes for a bus to take us home appears to be a long time because we compare it, unconsciously, to the total time of the journey, but ten minutes is small compared to the time to reach the planet Mars.

When we use the phrase 'δx is small' we mean that the change in x is small compared to the size of x.

1.4 Degrees of Smallness

If δx is small (compared to x), for example 1/1000 of the value of x, then the quantity $(\delta x)^2$ is $1/1000 \times 1/1000$; that is, 1/1 000 000 of the value of x and is negligible. Because $(\delta x)^2$ means $\delta x \times \delta x$, if δx is small we say that $(\delta x)^2$ is of the **second order** of smallness.

Again, $(\delta x)^3$ means $\delta x \times \delta x \times \delta x$, and if δx is small then $(\delta x)^3$ is of the **third order** of smallness and is, of course, also negligible along with higher orders of smallness.

It must be noted that where $(\delta x), (\delta x)^2, \ldots$ are multiplied by large numbers smallness and retention or rejection become a matter of judgement. In the case quoted, $(\delta x)^2 = 1/10^6$ and is negligible, but to take an extreme case, $10^8(\delta x)^2 = 10^8/10^6 = 100$, which is not negligible.

If δx is small compared to x then, neglecting second and higher orders of smallness, equation 1.1 becomes

$$\delta A \simeq 2x \, . \, \delta x$$

or

$$\delta(x^2) \simeq 2x \, . \, \delta x$$

Example 4. The volume of a right circular cylinder of height h cm and radius of base r cm is V cm^3. Find the change δV in V when r changes by a small amount δr, while h remains constant.

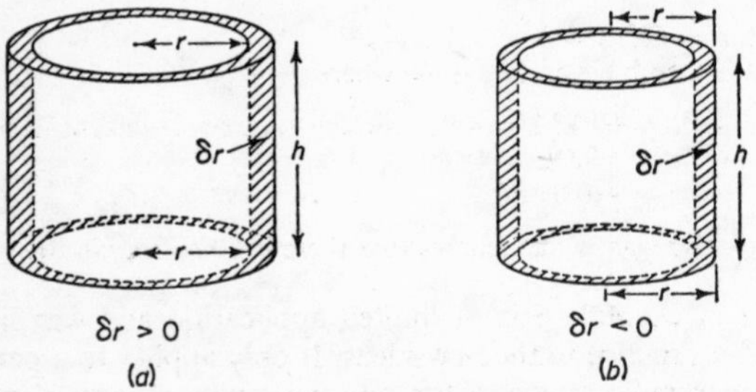

Fig. 1.5

In Fig. 1.5 the change in volume is shown shaded. Regarding this as a layer wrapped around the cylinder, we see that when unwrapped it forms a slab of thickness δr, breadth h and approximately $2\pi r$ cm long.

$$\therefore \qquad \delta V \simeq 2\pi r h \delta r$$

We notice that the geometrical picture is harder to envisage than for the square of Fig. 1.3 and that we have lost the exact expression for δV. The initial geometrical approach has been of value but will become increasingly difficult—the reader is recommended to try to draw or imagine the case of a cube the length of whose side changes from x to $(x + \delta x)$.

Example 5. Reconsider example 4 using an algebraic approach. The original volume is given by

$$V = \pi r^2 h \tag{1.2}$$

Since r changes by a small amount δr, it becomes equal to $r + \delta r$; V undergoes a corresponding change δV and becomes $V + \delta V$.

$$\therefore \qquad V + \delta V = \pi(r + \delta r)^2 h$$
$$= \pi[r^2 + 2r\delta r + (\delta r)^2]\, h$$
$$= \pi r^2 h + 2\pi r h \delta r + \pi h (\delta r)^2 \tag{1.3}$$

Note: When calculating the value of $V + \delta V$, if δr is negative the term $2\pi r h \delta r$ will have a negative value.

To find δV we subtract equation 1.2 from 1.3 and hence

$$\delta V = 2\pi rh\delta r + \pi h(\delta r)^2$$

Alternatively, since $V = \pi r^2 h$

$$\delta(\pi r^2 h) = 2\pi rh\delta r + \pi h(\delta r)^2$$

We are given that δr is small, so that $(\delta r)^2$ is of the second order of smallness, and we have as before

$$\delta V \simeq 2\pi rh\delta r \qquad (1.4)$$

or

$$\delta(\pi r^2 h) \simeq 2\pi rh\delta r$$

Example 6. The relationship between the pressure p N/m² and the volume v m³ of a given mass of gas maintained at a constant temperature is given by $pv = 60$. Find the change in volume when the pressure changes from 12 N/m² to 12·2 N/m².

$$pv = 60$$

$$\therefore \quad v = 60/p$$

when $p = 12$, $v = 60/12 = 5$
when p = 12·2, then v becomes $v + \delta v$ where

$$v + \delta v = 60/12{\cdot}2 = 4{\cdot}92 \text{ (correct to three significant figures)}$$

$$\text{subtracting } \delta v = 4{\cdot}92 - 5$$

$$= -0{\cdot}08 \text{ m}^3$$

Notice the negative sign, which shows that there is a *decrease* in the volume.

The result of example 6 is of limited application and was introduced to give the reader practice in the new ideas. It only applies to a particular mass of gas at a particular pressure for one particular change in pressure. The effort to obtain a more general result is well worth while. Therefore we shall rework the example using a general pressure change from p to $p + \delta p$.

$$pv = 60$$

$$\therefore \quad v = 60/p \qquad (1.5)$$

When p changes to $p + \delta p$, v must change and become $v + \delta v$

$$\therefore \quad v + \delta v = 60/(p + \delta p) \qquad (1.6)$$

Subtracting equation 1.5 from 1.6

$$\delta v = 60/(p + \delta p) - 60/p$$

$$= 60\left[\frac{1}{(p + \delta p)} - \frac{1}{p}\right]$$

$$= 60\left[\frac{p - (p + \delta p)}{(p + \delta p)p}\right]$$

$$= 60\left[\frac{-\delta p}{(p + \delta p)p}\right]$$

$$\therefore \quad \delta v \text{ or } \delta\left(\frac{60}{p}\right) = -60\,\delta p/(p + \delta p)p \qquad (1.7)$$

Again note the negative sign. If there is an *increase* in the pressure, δp is positive and therefore δv is negative and there is a *decrease* in the volume and vice versa.

1.5 Functions

Up to now we have always specified the relationship between the two variable quantities; for example

$$A = x^2$$
$$V = \pi r^2 h$$
$$v = 60/p$$

The ideas of mathematics are very general and of wide application and it is important to be able to talk about the relation between two variables in general without having to specify its exact nature. To do this we introduce the idea of a function. When the value of one variable, say, Y depends on the value of another variable, say, X, *and* to every value of X there corresponds *one* and *only one* value of Y we say that Y is a function of X. In the first of the above examples A is a function of x.

In the second case, if h is constant V is a function of r or if r is constant then V is a function of h. If neither is constant, the definition of a function can be extended to make V a function of the two variables r and h (discussion of this idea is postponed until later, in Chapter Eleven). Thus in the second case, either

V is a function of r (h constant)

or V is a function of h (r constant)

The third case illustrates another point: v is a function of p, but because division by zero has no meaning there is no value of v when $p = 0$, and this value has to be excluded. When defining the function we have to state the values of p, or the **domain** of p, and say

v is a function of p ($p \neq 0$)

The domain $p \neq 0$ implies that all values of p are acceptable, positive or negative, except zero.

If we do not quote a domain it is to be understood that it consists of all values.

Note also that given an expression such as $A = x^2$, where A is a function of x (the domain of x consisting of all values), it does not follow that the inverse relation $x = \pm\sqrt{A}$ gives x as a function of A. The square root of a negative quantity has no meaning and for each non-negative value of A there are two possible values of x. We could, however, define two **inverse functions**

$$x = +\sqrt{A} \qquad (A \geqslant 0)$$
$$x = -\sqrt{A} \qquad (A \geqslant 0)$$

We shall return to this point in section 2.3.

Thus for a functional relation, when a value of x (or r or p) is chosen within the particular range of values, then a unique value of A (or V or p) can be found. The quantities x, r and p are known as the **independent variables** and A, V and v as the **dependent variables.** Introducing a new mathematical shorthand, we have

$$A = f(x)$$
$$V = F(r) \qquad (h \text{ constant})$$
or
$$V = G(h) \qquad (r \text{ constant})$$
$$v = g(p) \qquad (p \neq 0)$$

The f, F or G (or even g, h, . . .) is a shorthand for 'a function of' and the (x), (r) or (p) indicates the independent variable.

The use of brackets is essential: $v = fp$ means $v = f \times p$ (one special relation between the variables v, f and p), but $v = f(p)$ means 'v is a function of p' and stands for any one of the many possibilities, such as $v = p^2/2 + 1/p$ or $v = \cos p + 3 - 7/\sqrt{p}$.

Even though the specific relationship between the two variables is not known, for example, in the relation between a manufacturer's profit £P and s pence, the selling price of one item, we can say that P is a function of s and write $P = f(s)$. The notation can be adopted to suit particular cases. If $s = 2$ then $P = f(2)$ means the profit when the items are sold for 2 pence each. If the function is known then the value of $f(2)$ can be found.

Example 7. The height reached by a shell is known to depend on the time t which has elapsed since it was fired—that is, the height can be represented by a function of t, say $h(t)$. Given that $h(t) = 29{\cdot}4t - 4{\cdot}9t^2$ $(0 \leqslant t \leqslant 6)$, find the values of $h(2)$, $h(4)$, $h(6)$, $h(a)$, $h(b^2)$, $h(2a)$.

$h(2)$ means the value of $h(t)$, in this case $29{\cdot}4t - 4{\cdot}9t^2$, when $t = 2$.

$\therefore$
$$h(2) = 29{\cdot}4(2) - 4{\cdot}9(2)^2 = 39{\cdot}2^*$$
Similarly
$$h(4) = 29{\cdot}4(4) - 4{\cdot}9(4)^2 = 39{\cdot}2^*$$
$$h(6) = 29{\cdot}4(6) - 4{\cdot}9(6)^2 = 0$$
$$h(a) = 29{\cdot}4(a) - 4{\cdot}9(a)^2 = 29{\cdot}4a - 4{\cdot}9a^2$$
$$h(b^2) = 29{\cdot}4(b^2) - 4{\cdot}9(b^2)^2 = 29{\cdot}4b^2 - 4{\cdot}9b^4$$
$$h(2a) = 29{\cdot}4(2a) - 4{\cdot}9(2a)^2 = 58{\cdot}8a - 19{\cdot}6a^2$$

* Note that the values of $h(t)$ are not necessarily all different; the important point is that any one value of t gives *only one* value of $h(t)$.

When using mathematics in practical situations the nature of the problem may place restraints on the values of the independent variable which can be considered or on the values of the dependent variable which can be used. For example, if x denotes a percentage of impurity, then only values of x between 0 and 100 can have any practical meaning. If x is the number of objects sold then only whole number values can have a meaning.

Example 8. Find the domain of values of x for which

$$f(x) = \frac{2x}{(x + 1)(x - 3)}$$

where x is the number of bacteria killed in a day, is a function consistent with physical reality.

Because x is the *number* of bacteria killed, it is restricted to the values 0, 1, 2, 3, 4, 5, . . But because division by zero is inadmissible there is another restriction due to the form of the function; that is, x cannot have the values -1 or 3. Of these only $x = 3$ has not yet been eliminated. We have finally, that x can equal zero or any positive whole number except 3.

Revision Questions 1.1

These revision questions are designed to test your understanding of the previous work. To obtain the maximum benefit from them cover up the solutions on the right-hand side of the page and try to answer each question in turn. Check your answers by uncovering each solution in turn. If you answer a question incorrectly re-read the relevant section. Follow this procedure in all subsequent sets of revision questions.

Questions	*Answers*	*Refer to*
1. The volume of a room depends on its . . .	**1.** Length, breadth and height.	
2. The volume of a sphere depends on its . . .	**2.** Radius.	Section 1.1
3. The profit obtained in selling an item could depend on . . . (Name three items)	**3.** Number sold, number unsold, number written off, overheads, cost price, selling price, efficiency of salesmen . . .	Section 1.1
4. The growth of a plant could depend on . . . (Name two things)	**4.** Hours of daylight, hours of sunshine, rainfall, amount of watering, type of soil, available nutrients . . .	Section 1.1
5. When the radius of a circle is doubled its area is multiplied by . . .	**5.** Four	Section 1.1
6. When the radius of a sphere is halved its volume is divided by . . .	**6.** Eight.	Section 1.1
7. Write in symbols: (i) a small change in p^2 (ii) the square of a small change in p	**7.** (i) $\delta(p^2)$ (ii) $(\delta p)^2$	Section 1.2
8. Given that $v = 10$ and $\delta v = -1$, calculate (i) $2v \,.\, \delta v$, (ii) $(\delta v)^2$, (iii) $(v + \delta v)^2$, (iv) $v^2 + (\delta v)^2$ (v) $(v - \delta v)^2 - v^2$	**8.** (i) -20, (ii) $+1$, (iii) 81, (iv) 101, (v) 21.	Section 1.2
9. Expand: (i) $(z + \delta z)^2$ (ii) $(\delta v - \delta p)^2$	**9.** (i) $z^2 + 2z\,\delta z + (\delta z)^2$ (ii) $(\delta v)^2 - 2\,\delta v \,.\, \delta p + (\delta p)^2$	Section 1.2

Questions	*Answers*	*Refer to*
10. Write in functional notation: (i) $P = 6/r^4$ (ii) $A = 3r^2 + 5/r$ (iii) The interest I depends on the amount invested x.	**10.** (i) $P = f(r)$ or $g(r), \ldots$ (ii) $A = F(r)$ or $h(r), \ldots$ (iii) $I = g(x), \ldots$	Section 1.5
11. Arrange in ascending order of smallness: $(\delta x)^3$, $(\delta y)^2 (\delta x)^3$, $(\delta x)(\delta y)$, $(\delta y)(\delta x)^3$, δx.	**11.** δx, $(\delta x)(\delta y)$, $(\delta x)^3$, $(\delta y)(\delta x)^3$, $(\delta y)^2 (\delta x)^3$	Sections 1.3 and 1.4
12. Given that $f(x) = 3x^2 - 1$, what are the values of $f(2)$, $f(-3), f(-2), f(2b), f(y^2)$	**12.** $f(2) = 11$, $f(-3) = 26$, $f(-2) = 11$, $f(2b) = 12b^2 - 1$, $f(y^2) = 3y^4 - 1$	Section 1.5

Exercises 1.1

1. A circular tin plate of radius 300 cm expands uniformly until its radius is 300·1 cm.
   (i) Draw a diagram to show the change in the surface area.
   (ii) Deduce from your diagram the approximate change in the surface area.
   (iii) Use the formula for the area of a circle to find, algebraically, the change in the area.

2. A bale of peat is in the form of a cube the length of whose edges is 1·2 m. It is compressed uniformly until each of its sides is of length 0·9 m. Find the resulting changes δV and δA in its volume and surface area respectively. Is the change in the volume small compared to the original volume?

3. A wooden pitprop was made in the form of a right circular cylinder of length L cm and radius of cross section R cm. Originally $L = 200$ and $R = 10$. One month after being used to hold up the roof of a mine it was found that $L = 199$ and $R = 10{\cdot}01$. State the values of (i) δL, (ii) δR, (iii) $(\delta R)^2$, (iv) $\delta R \,.\, \delta L$, (v) $(\delta L)^2$, (vi) $\delta(R^2)$, (vii) δV.

4. A solid metal cube has edges of length x cm. It expands uniformly until each of its edges is of length $x + \delta x$ cm. Find the change in its surface area δA. Is this the same as $\delta(6x^2)$?

5. The lift component L on an aircraft wing moving at a speed v relative to the air is given by $L = kv^2$, where k is a constant. The speed changes by an amount δv. Show that

$$\text{(i) } \delta L = 2kv \,.\, \delta v + k(\delta v)^2$$
$$\text{(ii) } \delta(v^2) = 2v \,.\, \delta v + (\delta v)^2$$

6. Explain how the answer to question 4 can be deduced from the answer to question 5.

7. A ball of snow is made in the form of a sphere of radius R cm. Originally $R = 5$, but after being squeezed uniformly $R = 4$. Find the values of (i) $(\delta R)^2$, (ii) $(\delta R)^3$, (iii) $\delta(R^2)$, (iv) $\delta(R^3)$, (v) $\delta(4\pi R^2)$, (vi) $\delta(4\pi R^3/3)$, (vii) $4\pi\delta(R^2)$, (viii) $[4\pi\delta(R^3)]/3$.
If V and A denote the original volume and surface area respectively, state which of the quantities (i) to (viii) are equal to δA and which to δV.

8. The gain G obtained when N units of an item are sold is given by

$$G = 5N - 0{\cdot}000\,01N^3 \; (N < 600)$$

Show that when N increases by an amount δN, to the first order of smallness, the change δG in G is given by

$$\delta G = 5\,\delta N - 0{\cdot}000\,03N^2 \,.\, \delta N.$$

State a corresponding expression for δG when N decreases by an amount δN.

9. The distance s moved by a particle in time t is given by $s^2 = at + bt^3$, where a, b are constants.
Find to the first order of smallness, the change $\delta(s^2)$ in s^2 when t changes by an amount δt.

10. Can the answer to question 8 be deduced from the answer to question 9?

11. Find the domain of values of x for which

$$f(x) = \sqrt{[(1 - x)(2 - x)]}$$

where x is the percentage of impurities in a substance, is a function consistent with physical reality.

12. Evaluate

$$\frac{f(a + h) - f(a)}{h}$$

when (i) $f(x) = 2x^2 - 1$, (ii) $f(x) = 1/x$, (iii) $f(x) = 1 - 4x$.

1.6 Continuous and Discontinuous Changes

Varying quantities can alter in two main ways. Generally where counting is involved, as in the output of a car factory, the number of houses on an estate, the price per pound of a commodity, the size of a colony of bacteria

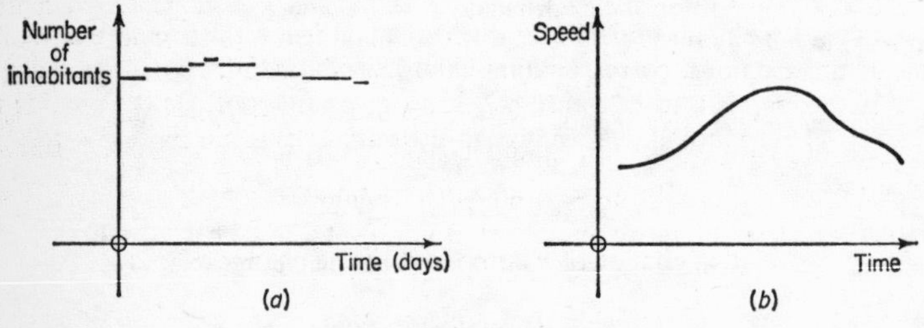

Fig. 1.6

or the population of a village, the variable can only take whole number values. Consider the last example in more detail. The number of people N living in a village can only change by steps of one. The idea of $\delta N = 0{\cdot}25$ is not practicable. δN can only be 0, ± 1, ± 2, ± 3, . . . N is an example of a **discontinuous variable** and is illustrated graphically by a discontinuous line (see Fig. 1.6(*a*)).

In other cases, such as the pressure of a gas, the current flowing in an electric circuit, the weight of concrete used in building a bridge, the percentage of ash in coal, the speed of a car, the variable can change by any amount, however small. The speed v kilometres per hour of a car cannot change suddenly from 20 to 21. It must pass, however quickly, through *all* values between 20 and 21. At some instant v must be equal, say, to 20·573, 20·689, etc., and δv can have any value, however small. The speed v is an example of a **continuous variable** and is illustrated graphically by a continuous line (see Fig. 1.6(*b*)).

Although theoretically the two types of variable are distinct, practically the distinction often becomes blurred. A continuous variable, owing to the limitations of measurement, is given only a set of discrete values—for example, to the nearest gram or 0·01 per cent, or when dealing with large quantities, say 20 000 tonnes of concrete, the mass could be to the nearest tonne. On the other hand, a variable such as the number N_b of bacteria in a colony which is discontinuous (sometimes known as discrete) can be so large that $\delta N_b = 1$ is relatively very small compared to the overall size of N_b.

To sum up, the size of a change δN must always be considered relative to the overall size of N, and while there are quantities which must always be treated as discontinuous, such as the number N_r of refineries owned by an oil company, in many practical cases the results we shall obtain by considering continuous variables can be applied practically to discontinuous variables.

1.7 Relative Change

Relative change is the comparison of one change to another, related one—for example, the change of current in a circuit compared to the change in the resistance of the circuit, the change in the lifting force on an aircraft wing compared to the change in the speed of the aircraft, the change in the time of exposure of a photographic film compared to the change in the size of the aperture. To use a more familiar term, relative change is the **ratio** of the changes. Examples of relative changes using our new notation are

(i) In the case of an underwater diver, the change in the pressure p acting on him compared to a corresponding change in the depth z is $\delta p/\delta z$.

(ii) Referring back to equation 1.7, for a given mass of gas the change in volume δv corresponding to a change in pressure δp is given by

$$\delta v = -60\ \delta p/(p + \delta p)p$$

Therefore the relative change of v compared to the change of p is

$$\delta v/\delta p = -60/(p + \delta p)p \qquad (1.8)$$

(iii) Referring back to equation 1.1, the change in the area δA of a square corresponding to a change of δx in the length of a side is given by

$$\delta A = 2x \,.\, \delta x + (\delta x)^2$$

Dividing by δx, we have

$$\delta A/\delta x = 2x + \delta x$$

or since $A = x^2$

$$\delta(x^2)/\delta x = 2x + \delta x$$

1.8 Rate of Change

The idea of a rate of change is fundamental to our study and therefore needs to be defined very carefully and precisely. It is a phrase which is often used but is not always used precisely enough. It is not always clear what is meant by, say, the rate of change of pressure of a gas. Three points need to be considered:

(i) *with respect to which quantity* we are comparing the change. Is it a rate of change of pressure with respect to volume or temperature or time, etc.

(ii) that practically the rate of change can only be found as an *average over a given interval.*

(iii) that the idea of an absolute rate of change at a particular volume, temperature, etc., is a theoretical concept which will require careful consideration.

Let us examine the first point in more detail. The phrase is misleading because by the inclusion of the word 'rate' we tend to assume that the change is compared to the time taken. This is not always so. The rate of decrease of pressure when rising from the surface of the earth is generally better compared with the height h risen, that is $\delta p/\delta h$. The rate of change of profit P is more significant if compared to the change in the price x, that is $\delta P/\delta x$. We note that the mathematical symbols leave no doubt as to what is meant, but written as a phrase 'rate of change' must always be qualified by 'with respect to . . .': thus the rate of change of pressure with respect to volume, i.e. $\delta p/\delta v$, the rate of change of pressure with respect to time, i.e. $\delta p/\delta t$, the rate of change of electric current i with respect to the applied voltage E, i.e. $\delta i/\delta E$.

With regard to the second point, if the barometric pressure at ground level is 1 010 000 dynes/cm² and at a height of 2 kilometres it is 810 000 dynes/cm², the fall in barometric pressure is 1 010 000 − 810 000 = 200 000 dynes/cm² in 2 kilometres, but it is not true to deduce that the fall is 100 000 dynes/cm² in any one kilometre or 1 dyne/cm² in any one centimetre. The average only applies, overall to the range of height from 0 to 2 kilometres above the earth, and does not in general apply to one particular height above the earth's surface. How then do we ascribe a meaning to the rate of change of pressure with respect to height at a given point?

Consider the more familiar case of 'average speed', which is the distance covered in an interval of time. A train which travels 250 kilometres in $2\frac{1}{2}$ hours is said to have an average speed of $250/2\frac{1}{2} = 100$ kilometres per hour over the whole journey. To try to find the speed at a particular instant we could measure the average speed over any one minute (which included the instant concerned) but this would still not be the speed at the particular instant. With sophisticated electronic equipment we could bring the time interval down to 5 seconds or 1 second or even 0·1 seconds, but still we would not have the speed at the particular instant. The difficulty is a practical one. In order to find the speed we have to consider the distance covered and divide by the time taken. But an instant of time has no magnitude and we cannot give a meaning to division by zero. As we shall see, the problem is resolved by considering what happens to the value of the average speed as the time and hence the distance become smaller and smaller, but first here are some more revision questions.

Revision Questions 1.2

Questions	*Answers*	*Refer to*
1. Which of the following variables are continuous and which discontinuous (discrete): (i) The distance from the earth to a comet. (ii) Number of peas in a pod. (iii) The price of butter. (iv) Size of an electric current. (v) Percentage of impurities in a chemical. (vi) Number of books sold. (vii) Thrust exerted by a jet engine. (viii) The number of bacteria in a colony of bacteria. (ix) Percentage of females in a population. (x) Growth of a tree.	**1.** Continuous (i), (iv), (v), (vii), (x). Discontinuous (ii), (iii), (vi), (viii), (ix).	Section 1.6
2. When the variables detailed in question 1 are measured at any one time, which are given discrete values?	**2.** All.	Section 1.6
3. δN is the change in a variable N. The ratio $\delta N/N$ is said to be small if $\delta N/N < 1/500$ and large if $\delta N/N > 1/50$; otherwise it is 'not known'. State whether the ratio $\delta N/N$ is small, large or not known in the following cases: N — δN (i) 10^6 — 10^2 (ii) 1·005 — 0·002 (iii) 21·6 — 0·3 (iv) 10^8 — 10^6 (v) 25·2% — 0·1% (vi) 54 — 6 (vii) 8105 — 16 (viii) 0·005 3 — 0·000 01	**3.** (i) small (ii) small (iii) not known (iv) not known (v) not known (vi) large (vii) small (viii) small	Section 1.4
4. Complete the following statements without using the word time.	**4.**	Section 1.7

Questions	*Answers*	*Refer to*
(i) The volume of a gas can vary with . . .	(i) pressure, temperature . . .	
(ii) The speed of a freely falling body can vary with . . .	(ii) distance, resistance . . .	
(iii) The price of a commodity can vary with the . . .	(iii) cost, number sold, number produced, overheads . . .	
(iv) The strength of concrete can vary with the . . .	(iv) composition, purity of the ingredients, amount of mixing . . .	

1.9 Limits

We now return to the third point referred to in section 1.8—how to give an absolute value to the speed (rate of change of distance with respect to time) at a particular time. Suppose we wished to find the speed of a train at 10 a.m. Using several measuring devices we could find the distance travelled in various intervals of time (each of which included 10.00 a.m.) and obtain a set of results as follows:

Time interval (centred around 10.00 *a.m.)*	*Distance travelled (kilometres)*	*Average speed (kilometres/hour)*
1 hour	70	70
1 minute	1·75	105
10 seconds	0·283 5	102·06
5 seconds	0·141 7	102·02
2 seconds	0·056 7	102·06

Looking at the results we cannot say exactly what the speed at 10.00 a.m. was, but reasonably we would reject the first result (70 kilometres per hour) and probably the second result (105 kilometres per hour). The last three results would incline us to say that the speed at 10.00 a.m. was most probably 102·0 or 102·1 kilometres per hour. Intuitively we would feel that if the time interval could be decreased to 1, 0·1, 0·01, . . . seconds with a corresponding increase in the accuracy with which the distance was measured, then the average speed in these time intervals centred around 10.00 a.m. would come closer and closer to some **limiting value** and that there would not be any large fluctuations as the time became vanishingly small (written as $t \to 0$). This limiting value, when it exists, we take as the value at the instant of time 10.00 a.m. Using a practical approach, we can never find the limiting value exactly, but this is not essential if we can find it with sufficient accuracy for our purposes.

A different situation arises when we can use a mathematical model to represent the problem, when much more precision is possible. The surface area of a cube can be expressed exactly in terms of x, the length of one of its sides, as $6x^2$. Instead of measuring the faces of the cube we can consider how $6x^2$ varies as x varies. Consider in particular a cube of side 3 units.

Example 9. Find the average rate of change of $6x^2$ with respect to x as x changes from: (i) 3 to 3·1, (ii) 3 to 3·01, (iii) 3 to 3·001. Deduce the limiting value of $\delta(6x^2)/\delta x$ as δx becomes vanishingly small (written as $\lim\limits_{\delta x \to 0} [\delta(6x^2)/\delta x]$) when $x = 3$.

The work is best set out in the form of a table. We first note that initially $x = 3$ and $6x^2 = 54$.

x	δx	$6x^2$	$\delta(6x^2)$	$\delta(6x^2)/\delta x$
3·1	0·1	57·66	3·66	36·6
3·01	0·01	54·360 6	0·3606	36·06
3·001	0·001	54·036 006	0·036 006	36·006

Judging by the results, the average rate of change of $6x^2$ with respect to x (when $x = 3$) is approaching the value 36, but we are not sure.

However, with the mathematical model we can use algebraic techniques and our new notation of δx as meaning a small change in x.

Example 10. Find the average rate of change of $6x^2$ as x changes from 3 to $3 + \delta x$ (remember that δx can be negative as well as positive).

As x changes from 3 to $3 + \delta x$ the change in x is δx; $6x^2$ changes from $6(3)^2$ to $6(3 + \delta x)^2$ and the change in $6x^2$ is $6(3 + \delta x)^2 - 6(3)^2$. Therefore the average rate of change

$$\delta(6x^2)/\delta x = \frac{6(3 + \delta x)^2 - 6(3)^2}{\delta x}$$

$$= \frac{54 + 36 \,.\, \delta x + 6(\delta x)^2 - 54}{\delta x}$$

$$= 36 + 6\delta x$$

It is now clear that as δx and hence $6\delta x$ become smaller and smaller, $\delta(6x^2)/\delta x$ becomes nearer and nearer to the value 36.

We could make the value of the ratio, say, 36·000 001 by taking δx equal to $+0{\cdot}000\,000\,17$, or 35·999 999 by taking δx equal to $-0{\cdot}000\,000\,17$. We cannot let $\delta x = 0$ because then the ratio $\delta(6x^2)/\delta x$ would have no meaning, but we can make the value as near to 36 as we like.

The value 36 is the limit of the average rate of change $\delta(6x^2)/\delta x$ as $\delta x \to 0$ (becomes very small), or simply is the rate of change of $6x^2$ with respect to x at the point $x = 3$.

The mathematical model of what is happening to the size of the surface area of a cube as the length of its edge changes can be used to give a more general result.

Example 11. Find the average rate of change of $6x^2$ as x changes by an amount δx and hence deduce the value of $\lim\limits_{\delta x \to 0} [\delta(6x^2)/\delta x]$.

As x changes from x to $x + \delta x$, $6x^2$ becomes $6(x + \delta x)^2$

$$\therefore \quad \delta(6x^2)/\delta x = \frac{6(x + \delta x)^2 - 6x^2}{\delta x}$$

$$= \frac{6x^2 + 12x \, . \, \delta x + 6(\delta x)^2 - 6x^2}{\delta x}$$

$$= 12x + 6\delta x$$

Now as the value of δx and hence $6\delta x$ becomes smaller and smaller, $\delta(6x^2)/\delta x$ becomes indefinitely close to the value $12x$ and we say

$$\underset{\delta x \to 0}{\text{limit}} \, [\delta(6x^2)/\delta x] = 12x$$

This is also taken as the rate of change of $6x^2$ with respect to x at any general point x (when the limit exists).

This limiting value is so well used that it is convenient to introduce another new notation, and we write

$$\underset{\delta x \to 0}{\text{limit}} \, [\delta(6x^2)/\delta x] = \frac{\mathrm{d}(6x^2)}{\mathrm{d}x}$$

(the use of the usual 'dee' indicating that the value of the limit is to be found as $\delta x \to 0$).

We note that

$$\frac{\mathrm{d}(6x^2)}{\mathrm{d}x} = 12x$$

and when $x = 3$

$$\frac{\mathrm{d}(6x^2)}{\mathrm{d}x} = 12 \times 3$$

$$= 36$$

which agrees with the result of example 9.

Example 12. Find the average rate of change of ay^3 with respect to y as y changes by an amount δy, a being constant. Deduce the value of $\mathrm{d}(ay^3)/\mathrm{d}y$ and the rate of change of the volume of a sphere with respect to its radius.

As y changes from y to $y + \delta y$, ay^3 becomes $a(y + \delta y)^3$.

$$\therefore \quad \frac{\delta(ay^3)}{\delta y} = \frac{a(y + \delta y)^3 - ay^3}{\delta y}$$

$$= \frac{ay^3 + 3ay^2\delta y + 3ay(\delta y)^2 + a(\delta y)^3 - ay^3}{\delta y}$$

$$= \frac{3ay^2\delta y + 3ay(\delta y)^2 + a(\delta y)^3}{\delta y}$$

$$= 3ay^2 + 3ay\delta y + a(\delta y)^2$$

$$\therefore \quad \frac{\mathrm{d}(ay^3)}{dy} = \underset{\delta y \to 0}{\text{limit}} \, \frac{[\delta(ay^3)]}{\delta y} = \underset{\delta y \to 0}{\text{limit}} \, [3ay^2 + 3ay\delta y + a(\delta y)^2]$$

$$= \underset{\delta y \to 0}{\text{limit}} \, 3ay^2 + \underset{\delta y \to 0}{\text{limit}} \, 3ay\delta y + \underset{\delta y \to 0}{\text{limit}} \, a(\delta y)^2$$

(assuming that the limit of a sum equals the sum of the limits).

Now as $\delta y \to 0$, $3ay\delta y \to 0$, and also $a(\delta y)^2 \to 0$. Therefore

$$\frac{d(ay^3)}{dy} = 3ay^2$$

The volume of a sphere is $4\pi r^3/3$ and therefore $d(4\pi r^3/3)/dr$ is obtained from the previous result by putting $a = 4\pi/3$ and $y = r$: that is

$$\frac{d(4\pi r^3/3)}{dr} = 3(4\pi/3)r^2 = 4\pi r^2$$

Revision Questions 1.3

Questions	*Answers*	*Refer to*
1. What is the relation between $\frac{\delta(p^3)}{\delta p}$ and $\frac{d(p^3)}{dp}$?	**1.** $\frac{d(p^3)}{dp} = \lim_{\delta p \to 0} [\delta(p^3)/\delta p]$	Section 1.9
2. Given that $\frac{d(kv^3)}{dv} = 3kv^2$, what is the value of $\frac{d(5z^3)}{dz}$?	**2.** $3(5)z^2 = 15z^2$	Section 1.9
3. Can $\frac{\delta(y^2)}{\delta x}$ be evaluated?	**3.** No, because the relation between y^2 and x is not given.	Section 1.9
4. Does a constant change in value?	**4.** No.	Section 1.9
5. What is the value of $\frac{d(k)}{dx}$, where k is a constant?	**5.** Zero.	Section 1.9
6. Does $\frac{d(x^2)}{\delta x}$ have a meaning?	**6.** No. $\frac{d(x^2)}{dx}$ is the limiting value of $\frac{\delta(x^2)}{\delta x}$ but the mixture of d and δ has no meaning.	Section 1.9

Exercises 1.2

1. The radius of a sphere is x cm. Find the average rate of change of its surface area $4\pi x^2$ when x changes from: (i) 3 to 3·1, (ii) 3 to 3·01, (iii) 3 to 3·001. Deduce the value of $\lim_{\delta x \to 0} [\delta(4\pi x^2)/\delta x]$ when $x = 3$.

2. The volume v of a gas is related to its pressure p by the relation $v = 40/p$. Find, to three places of decimals, the average rate of change of the volume with respect to the pressure when p changes from: (i) 5 to 5·1, (ii) 5 to 5·01, (iii) 5 to 5·001, (iv) explain why the results are negative, (v) can the value of $\lim_{\delta p \to 0} \delta v/\delta p$ when $p = 5$ be deduced from the results of parts (i), (ii), and (iii)?

3. The rate of capital investment I of a country is found to obey the law $I = 200t - 0{\cdot}03t^2$, where t is the time in days. Find the change δI in I when t changes from t to $t + \delta t$. Hence deduce the value of $\dfrac{dI}{dt}$.

4. Given that a variable quantity x changes to $x + \delta x$, find the corresponding change in kx^2 and hence show that $\dfrac{d(kx^2)}{dx} = 2kx$ (k being a constant).

5. The strain energy due to the bending of a simply supported beam with a distributed load of w per unit length is given by $(L^5w^2)/(240EI)$, where L is the length of the beam and E and I are constants. Using the result of question 4, state the value of $\dfrac{d}{dw}[L^5w^2/(240EI)]$.

6. Express $\dfrac{d(kz)}{dz}$, where k is a constant, as a limiting value of an average rate of change and hence obtain its value. What is the value of $\dfrac{d(z)}{dz}$?

7. Given that $\dfrac{d(y^3)}{dy} = 3y^2$ what are the values of

(i) $\dfrac{d(x+1)^3}{d(x+1)}$ (ii) $\dfrac{d(2x^3-1)^3}{d(2x^3-1)}$ (iii) $\dfrac{d(\cos^3\theta)}{d(\cos\theta)}$

1.10 The Differential Coefficient and the Derived Function

Up to now we have considered the average rate of change and its limiting value in a number of special cases where the relation between the dependent variable and the independent variable was known. Using the functional notation (refer to section 1.5), we have been given $A = f(r)$ and evaluated

$$\frac{d}{dr}[f(r)] = \lim_{\delta r \to 0}[\delta f(r)/\delta r] \quad \text{or} \quad \frac{dA}{dr} = \lim_{\delta r \to 0}[\delta A/\delta r]$$

dA/dr, the limiting value of $\delta A/\delta r$, is known as the **differential coefficient** of A with respect to r, and the process of finding this limit is known as **differentiation.** As this limiting value depends on which function of r we are concerned with, $d[f(r)]/dr$ ($= dA/dr$) is sometimes called the **derived function** and can be written as $f'(r)$.

1.11 The Derivative of ax^n

It is not practical to obtain the rate of change as a special case each time it is required. It is better to use the immense power inherent in mathematics to obtain general results. We have already seen that, knowing $d(ax^2)/dx = 2ax$, we can write down immediately that

$$\frac{d}{dr}(6\pi r^2/7) = \frac{d}{dr}[(6\pi/7)r^2] = 2(6\pi/7)r$$

(refer question 4, page 18)

or $$\frac{d}{dw}(L^5w^2/240EI) = \frac{d}{dw}[(L^5/240EI)w^2] = 2(L^5/240EI)w$$

(refer question 5, page 18).

This result, however, only applies to the case when the independent variable $x, r, w, \ldots$ is squared. Let us now generalise the power to which x is raised and consider ax^n, where a is a constant and n is a positive integer (that is, $n = +1, +2, +3, \ldots$)

As x changes to $x + \delta x$, ax^n changes to $a(x + \delta x)^n$

$$\therefore \qquad \delta(ax^n) = a(x + \delta x)^n - ax^n$$

and $$\frac{\delta(ax^n)}{\delta x} = \frac{a(x + \delta x)^n - ax^n}{\delta x}$$

Expanding $(x + \delta x)^n$ by the Binomial Theorem

$$\frac{\delta(ax^n)}{\delta x} = \frac{a\left(x^n + nx^{n-1}\delta x + \dfrac{n(n-1)}{1 . 2} . x^{n-2}(\delta x)^2 + \ldots\right) - ax^n}{\delta x}$$

$$= \frac{nax^{n-1}\delta x + \text{terms in } (\delta x)^2 \text{ or higher powers}}{\delta x}$$

$$= nax^{n-1} + \text{terms in } \delta x \text{ or higher powers}$$

In the limit as $\delta x \to 0$ all the terms other than the first one tend to zero

$$\therefore \qquad \frac{d(ax^n)}{dx} = \lim_{\delta x \to 0} \frac{\delta(ax^n)}{\delta x} = nax^{n-1} \qquad (1.9)$$

when $a = 1$

$$\frac{d(x^n)}{dx} = nx^{n-1} \qquad (1.10)$$

We note that the equation 1.10 is of wide application. For example

$$\therefore \quad \frac{d(y^n)}{dy} = ny^{n-1} \qquad \frac{d(\cos^n\theta)}{d(\cos\theta)} = \frac{d(\cos\theta)^n}{d(\cos\theta)} = n(\cos\theta)^{n-1} = n\cos^{n-1}\theta$$

$$\frac{d(az^n)}{dz} = naz^{n-1} \qquad \frac{d(3x)^n}{d(3x)} = n(3x)^{n-1}$$

This result, which we have proved when n is a positive integer, will be proved true for all values of n whether negative or fractional (refer to section 4.7). In words, to find the rate of change of ax^n with respect to x, where a is a constant, we multiply by the power of x and then reduce the power by one.

Example 13. Evaluate

(i) $\dfrac{d(x^4)}{dx}$ (ii) $\dfrac{d(y^{\frac{1}{3}})}{dy}$ (iii) $\dfrac{d(1/\sqrt{z})}{dz}$ (iv) $\dfrac{d(\cos^3\theta)}{d(\cos\theta)}$

(i) $\dfrac{d(x^4)}{dx} = 4x^{4-1} = 4x^3$

(ii) $\dfrac{d(y^{\frac{1}{3}})}{dy} = \frac{1}{3}y^{\frac{1}{3}-1} = y^{-\frac{2}{3}}/3$

(iii) $\dfrac{d(1/\sqrt{z})}{dz} = \dfrac{d(z^{-\frac{1}{2}})}{dz} = -\dfrac{1}{2} \times z^{-\frac{1}{2}-1} = -z^{-\frac{3}{2}}/2$

(iv) $\dfrac{d(\cos^3\theta)}{d(\cos\theta)} = \dfrac{d(\cos\theta)^3}{d(\cos\theta)} = 3(\cos\theta)^2 = 3\cos^2\theta$

Example 14. Boyle's Law states that $pv = C$, where C is a constant and p and v are the pressure and the volume of a given mass of gas which is maintained at constant temperature. Find the rate of change of pressure with respect to the volume.

$$pv = C$$

$$\therefore \quad p = C/v = Cv^{-1}$$

$$\therefore \quad \frac{dp}{dv} = \frac{d(Cv^{-1})}{dv} = (-1)Cv^{-2} = -C/v^2$$

Example 15. The time of oscillation T of a simple pendulum of length l is given by $T = 2\pi\sqrt{(l/g)}$. Find the differential coefficient of T with respect to g when l is constant.

$$T = 2\pi\sqrt{(l/g)}$$
$$= 2\pi l^{\frac{1}{2}}g^{-\frac{1}{2}}$$

$$\therefore \quad \frac{dT}{dg} = d(2\pi l^{\frac{1}{2}}g^{-\frac{1}{2}})/dg$$

$$= \left(-\frac{1}{2}\right) 2\pi l^{\frac{1}{2}}g^{-\frac{3}{2}}$$

$$= -\pi\sqrt{(l/g^3)}$$

1.12 The Derivative of a Constant

Because a constant C does not change in value its rate of change is always zero.

$$\frac{dC}{dx} = \frac{dC}{dp} = \frac{dC}{dy} = \ldots = 0 \qquad (1.11)$$

1.13 Differentiating the Sum or Difference of Functions

Consider two functions of x, say, $u(x)$ and $v(x)$, then

$$\frac{\delta[u(x) + v(x)]}{\delta x} = \frac{\delta[u(x)]}{\delta x} + \frac{\delta[v(x)]}{\delta x}$$

In the limit as $\delta x \to 0$

$$\lim_{\delta x \to 0} \frac{\delta[u(x) + v(x)]}{\delta x} = \lim_{\delta x \to 0} \frac{\delta[u(x)]}{\delta x} + \lim_{\delta x \to 0} \frac{\delta[v(x)]}{\delta x}$$

(assuming that the limit of a sum equals the sum of the limits).

Hence

$$\frac{d[u(x) + v(x)]}{dx} = \frac{d[u(x)]}{dx} + \frac{d[v(x)]}{dx} \qquad (1.12)$$

Similarly, if the two functions are subtracted

$$\frac{d[u(x) - v(x)]}{dx} = \frac{d[u(x)]}{dx} - \frac{d[v(x)]}{dx} \qquad (1.13)$$

Example 16. Evaluate: (i) $\frac{d}{dx}(3x + 6x^4)$; (ii) $\frac{d}{dx}(4\sqrt{x} - 5/x^2)$.

(i) $\frac{d}{dx}(3x + 6x^4) = \frac{d(3x)}{dx} + \frac{d(6x^4)}{dx}$

$= 3 + 24x^3$

(ii) $\frac{d}{dx}(4\sqrt{x} - 5/x^2) = \frac{d(4x^{\frac{1}{2}})}{dx} - \frac{d(5x^{-2})}{dx}$

$= \frac{1}{2}\,4x^{\frac{1}{2}-1} - (-2)5x^{-2-1}$

$= 2x^{-\frac{1}{2}} + 10x^{-3}$

$= 2/\sqrt{x} + 10/x^3.$

The results 1.12 and 1.13 can be extended to the sum and/or differences of three or more functions.

Example 17. An approximate expression for the drop in head (loss of pressure) h when water flows through 1 kilometre length of pipe of diameter 0·5 metres is given by $h = 8v^2 + 10v - 4$, where v is the speed of the water. Find dh/dv when $v = 2$.

$$\frac{dh}{dv} = \frac{d}{dv}(8v^2 + 10v - 4)$$

$$= \frac{d(8v^2)}{dv} + \frac{d(10v)}{dv} - \frac{d(4)}{dv}$$

$$= 16v + 10 - 0$$

$\therefore$ when $v = 2$

$$\frac{dh}{dv} = 16(2) + 10 = 42$$

1.14 Second and Higher Derivatives

First we consider the idea of repeated differentiation using the well known ideas of speed and acceleration.

The speed v of a body moving in a straight line is the rate of change of its distance s from a fixed point on the line with respect to the time t.

If
$$s = 3t^4 - 2t^2$$

$$v = \frac{ds}{dt} = \frac{d(3t^4 - 2t^2)}{dt}$$

$$= \frac{3d(t^4)}{dt} - \frac{2d(t^2)}{dt}$$

$\therefore$
$$v = 12t^3 - 4t \qquad (1.14)$$

The acceleration a of the body is the measure of how fast the speed is changing with respect to time, that is, the rate of change of v with respect to t. Therefore, from equation 1.14

$$a = \frac{dv}{dt} = \frac{d(12t^3 - 4t)}{dt}$$

$$= \frac{12d(t^3)}{dt} - 4\frac{d(t)}{dt}$$

$\therefore$
$$a = 36t^2 - 4 \qquad (1.15)$$

Acceleration is the derivative of speed with respect to time, while speed is the derivative of distance with respect to time. In terms of our notation

$$a = \frac{dv}{dt} = \frac{d}{dt}\left(\frac{ds}{dt}\right)$$

The latter expression is usually written more concisely as d^2s/dt^2, and is known as the **second derivative** of distance with respect to time, indicating that the acceleration is obtained by differentiating the distance s twice, successively, with respect to t.

The process can be repeated giving

$$\frac{d^3s}{dt^3} = \frac{d}{dt}\left(\frac{d^2s}{dt^2}\right) = \frac{d}{dt}(36t^2 - 4) = 72t$$

and
$$\frac{d^4s}{dt^4} = \frac{d}{dt}\left(\frac{d^3s}{dt^3}\right) = \frac{d}{dt}(72t) = 72$$

Further applications are possible, in this particular case giving the value zero. This is mainly an academic exercise because practically there is only occasional use for derivatives beyond the second one. If the functional notation is being used

$$s = f(t)$$

then
$$v = \frac{ds}{dt} = f'(t)$$

and
$$a = \frac{dv}{dt} = \frac{d^2s}{dt^2} = \frac{d[f'(t)]}{dt} = f''(t)$$

$f''(t)$ represents the second derivative of $f(t)$ with respect to t. Similarly, $f'''(t)$, $f^{iv}(t)$, . . ., represent the third, fourth, . . ., derivatives of $f(t)$ with respect to t.

Example 18. In the study of the forces on loaded beams it is found that if y is the deflection, M the bending moment and F the shearing force at any distance x from one end, then

$$M = EI\frac{d^2y}{dx^2} \tag{1.16}$$

and

$$F = EI\frac{d^3y}{dx^3} \tag{1.17}$$

The product EI is known as the flexural rigidity of the beam. A horizontal beam carrying a varying load is simply supported at both ends. The deflection y at a point distance x from one end is found to be given by $EIy = 19x^3 - 0{\cdot}408x^4 - 0{\cdot}0327x^5$. Find general expressions for the bending moment M and the shearing force F.

$$EI\,.\,y = 19x^3 - 0{\cdot}408x^4 - 0{\cdot}0327x^5$$

$$\therefore \quad EI\frac{dy}{dx} = 57x^2 - 1{\cdot}632x^3 - 0{\cdot}1635x^4$$

and

$$M = EI\frac{d^2y}{dx^2} = 114x - 4{\cdot}896x^2 - 0{\cdot}654x^3$$

$$F = EI\frac{d^3y}{dx^3} = 114 - 9{\cdot}792x - 1{\cdot}962x^2$$

Example 19. A particle moving in a straight line is a distance s metres from a fixed point after t seconds, where $s = t^3 - 4t^2 + 5t$. Find an expression for the speed v and the acceleration a after t seconds. For what values of t is the particle stationary and what is the acceleration at these times?

$$s = t^3 - 4t^2 + 5t$$

$$v = \frac{ds}{dt} = 3t^2 - 8t + 5$$

$$a = \frac{d^2s}{dt^2} = 6t - 8$$

The particle is stationary when $v = 0$; that is, when

$$3t^2 - 8t + 5 = 0$$

or $(3t - 5)(t - 1) = 0$, giving the times $t = 1$ or $5/3$

The body is at rest after 1 and after $1\frac{2}{3}$ seconds, when the acceleration is given by

$$t = 1 \quad a = 6 - 8 = -2 \text{ m/s}^2$$

$$t = 5/3 \quad a = 10 - 8 = +2 \text{ m/s}^2$$

In the previous examples the various rates of change have been used for such a long time that they have acquired their own names. Rate of change of distance with respect to time is always known as speed, and rate of change of speed with respect to time is always known as acceleration. In the newer applications of mathematics this is not so and the description of the quantity required indicates that it is a rate of change of a rate of change. Consider the following example.

Example 20. The total invested capital C (value of machines, buildings, land, etc.) at any time t of a combine is given by

$$C = 130 + 8t + 3t^2 - t^3/6$$

the capital C being in £ millions and the time t in months. Find the rate at which the rate of investment changes.

Investment, in which term we include disinvestment or cashing in of capital, changes the amount of capital, and

$$\text{Rate of investment} = \mathrm{d}C/\mathrm{d}t = \frac{\mathrm{d}}{\mathrm{d}t}(130 + 8t + 3t^2 - t^3/6)$$

$$= 8 + 6t - t^2/2$$

Therefore the rate at which the rate of investment changes is given by

$$\frac{\mathrm{d}^2C}{\mathrm{d}t^2} = 6 - t$$

Exercises 1.3

1. A particle moves so that its distance s metres from a fixed point after t seconds is given by $s = t^4 - 8t^3 + 18t^2$. Find its speed and acceleration after t seconds. Also find the speed of the particle when its acceleration is zero.

2. When a gas expands adiabatically (that is, without gaining or losing heat) its pressure p and volume v are connected by the equation $pv^n = C$, where n and C are constants. Show that

$$v^2\frac{\mathrm{d}^2p}{\mathrm{d}v^2} = n(n + 1)p$$

3. The deflection y at a distance x from one end of an unequally loaded beam fixed at both ends is given by $EIy = -x^5 + 300x^3 - 2000x^2$. Find the numerical values of the bending moment and the shearing force (refer to example 18) when $x = 5$.

4. The total capital C invested by a combine at any time t is given by $C = 150 + 9t + 30t^2 - t^3$, C being in £ millions and t in months. Find the value of t when the rate of change of the rate of investment is zero and the total capital invested at that time.

1.15 Problems

1. Find the first and second derivatives with respect to x of the following functions: (i) $3x^8$; (ii) $5x^{-2}$; (iii) $6x^{1/3}$; (iv) $3x - 2/x$; (v) $6/\sqrt{x} + 7$; (vi) $x^3 - 3/x^4 + 7/\sqrt{x^3}$; (vii) $3\sqrt[3]{x^2} + 5x^{-4} + 5x$.

2. Evaluate where possible:

(i) $\dfrac{\mathrm{d}(6\sqrt{y})}{\mathrm{d}y}$ (ii) $\dfrac{\mathrm{d}(6\sqrt{z})}{\mathrm{d}z}$ (iii) $\dfrac{\mathrm{d}^2(6\sqrt{p})}{\mathrm{d}p^2}$ (iv) $\dfrac{\mathrm{d}(6\sqrt{y})}{\mathrm{d}x}$

(v) $\dfrac{\mathrm{d}(\sin^3\theta)}{\mathrm{d}(\sin\theta)}$ (vi) $\dfrac{\mathrm{d}(3x)^{1/3}}{\mathrm{d}(3x)}$ (vii) $\dfrac{\mathrm{d}(3x-2)^{1/3}}{\mathrm{d}(3x-2)}$

(viii) $\dfrac{\mathrm{d}(3x-2)^{1/3}}{\mathrm{d}x}$ (ix) $\dfrac{\mathrm{d}(x+2)^{-2}}{\mathrm{d}(x+2)}$ (x) $\dfrac{\mathrm{d}^2(x+2)^{-2}}{\mathrm{d}x^2}$

3. The diameter D of a shaft required to transmit power P is given by the formula $D = \sqrt[3]{(320P/NS)}$. Given that $N = 100$ and $S = 4000$ find $\dfrac{\mathrm{d}D}{\mathrm{d}P}$ in terms of P.

4. In time t a moving body covers a distance s given by $s = 300t + 16t^{\frac{5}{2}}$. Find the speed v of the body after time t. From your answer find the acceleration (rate of change of speed with respect to time) of the body at time t.

5. The potential V at a distance r from a point charge q is given by $V = q/(4\pi\varepsilon \,.\, r)$ where q and ε are constants. Find the value of the field strength E at a distance r from the point charge, given that $E = -\dfrac{\mathrm{d}V}{\mathrm{d}r}$.

6. The deflection y at a distance x from one end of an unequally loaded beam fixed at both ends is given by $y = -kx^5 + 3kL^2x^3 - 2kL^3x^2$, where k is a constant and L its length which is also constant. Find the derivative of y with respect to x.

7. The opacity of plasma K is given by $K = C/\sqrt{T^7}$, where C is a constant and T is the absolute temperature. Find $\dfrac{\mathrm{d}K}{\mathrm{d}T}$.

8. The basic metabolic rate for vertebrates is given by $B = 1{\cdot}7W^{0{\cdot}73}$, where W is the body weight. Find $\dfrac{\mathrm{d}B}{\mathrm{d}W}$.

9. The power P dissipated along a blood vessel of radius r and length L is given by $P = f^2k/r^4 + K\pi r^2L$, where f, k and K are constants. Find (i) for a fixed length of blood vessel the rate of change of P with respect to the radius r, and (ii) for a given blood vessel of fixed radius the rate of change of P with respect to the length L.

10. A statistical distribution is defined by the equation $y = 4(x - x^3)$, where x has a value between 0 and 1. The modal value is such that $\dfrac{\mathrm{d}y}{\mathrm{d}x} = 0$. Find the modal value.

11. The relation between the supply x and the price p of a commodity is given by $x = 300 - p - p^2/50$. Find the value of the 'elasticity of supply', which is defined as $\dfrac{p}{x} \cdot \dfrac{\mathrm{d}x}{\mathrm{d}p}$, when (i) $p = 0{\cdot}15$ and (ii) $p = 0{\cdot}20$.

12. In a second-order chemical reaction the concentration c after time t is given by $c = a/(1 + akt)$, where a is the initial concentration and k is the rate constant. Rearrange this equation to express t in terms of c, k and a. Hence show that $\dfrac{\mathrm{d}t}{\mathrm{d}c} = -1/kc^2$, a and k being constant.

13. The profit P obtained from selling N articles is given by $P = -0{\cdot}01N^3 + 900NM^2$, where M is the cost of producing each article, presumed constant. Find in terms of M the value of N when $\dfrac{\mathrm{d}P}{\mathrm{d}N} = 0$.

14. The deflection y at a distance x from the end of a freely supported, loaded beam of length L is given by

$$y = 6kx^5 + 15kx^4L - 50kx^3L^2 + 29kxL^4$$

The following relations apply: the slope $s = \mathrm{d}y/\mathrm{d}x$, the bending moment $M = EI\dfrac{\mathrm{d}s}{\mathrm{d}x}$, and the shearing force $S = \dfrac{\mathrm{d}M}{\mathrm{d}x}$, where E and I are constants. Find the values of the slope s, the bending moment M and the shearing force S at the mid-point of the beam.

15. A cylindrical hot-water tank has a volume V and the rate of loss of heat from its surface is H, where $V = \pi r^2 h$ and $H = 2\pi kr(r + h)$, the radius and height of the cylinder being r and h respectively. Express H in terms of k, V and r (i.e. eliminate h), and hence show that $\frac{dH}{dr} = 0$ when $2r = h$.

16. The adiabatic gas law is $pv^\gamma = K$, where p is the pressure, v is the volume and K is a constant for a given mass of gas. In a particular case $\gamma = 1{\cdot}4$, and $p = 40$ N/cm² when $v = 2{\cdot}5 \times 10^6$ cm³. Evaluate K and find the rate of change of pressure with respect to volume when $v = 2 \times 10^6$ cm³.

17. The elasticity of volume of a gas is defined as $-v\frac{dp}{dv}$, where v is the volume and p the pressure of the gas. Show that:

(a) If the gas expands isothermally ($pv = k$) the elasticity of volume is equal to p.
(b) If the gas expands adiabatically ($pv^\gamma = k$) the elasticity of volume is equal to γp, both γ and k being constants.

CHAPTER TWO

NATURAL LAWS OF GROWTH AND THE EXPONENTIAL FUNCTION

2.1 The Translation of Laws from Words into Mathematical Symbols

In Chapter One we stated that the idea of rate of change is fundamental to our study and proceeded to develop a concise mathematical notation to represent this idea. We shall now investigate laws of growth in physics, chemistry, engineering, biology, etc., to show that it is indeed of fundamental importance. Also the use of the new mathematical symbols will bring out the theme which is common to most laws of growth and will lead to the consideration of a new function known as the **exponential function.**

Laws of growth are usually formulated in words and very little progress can be made until they are translated into mathematical symbols (i.e. a mathematical model is made). We start by comparing the mathematical models obtained from five examples from widely different studies.*

Example 1. Express the following statement in mathematical symbols: 'The rate of decay of a radioactive substance at any time is proportional to the amount remaining at that time.'

This is our first attempt at making a mathematical model and we shall consider it in detail.

Note (i) 'at any time' we have to consider a general, unspecified time, say t.

(ii) 'the amount remaining at that time' is an unspecified quantity and we denote it by any convenient symbol, say q.

(iii) 'the rate of decay' implies a change and brings in the new notation.

(iv) As is often the case, there is nothing which details with respect to which quantity we are considering 'the rate', so we assume that it is with respect to the time t; that is, we are interested in the rate of change of q with respect to t, which we can write as $\frac{dq}{dt}$.

(v) 'decay' indicates a negative change, that is $-\frac{dq}{dt}$.

'Rate of decay is proportional to the amount remaining' now translates as

$$-\frac{dq}{dt} \propto q$$

This is the mathematical statement of the law. We generally go one step further and obtain an equality by the use of a **constant of proportionality**, say k.

$$\therefore \quad -\frac{dq}{dt} = kq \text{ (where } k \text{ is a positive constant)} \qquad (2.1)$$

* In these examples we are not proving or verifying the laws but obtaining the mathematical models assuming that the laws are true.

Example 2. Express the following statement in mathematical symbols: 'The rate of growth of a colony of bacteria is proportional to its size.' (Note that this is only correct when sufficient nutrients, etc., are available.)

This is not a case of continuous change because the smallest possible increase is one bacterium. However, we discussed this point in section 1.6 and because the size of a colony of bacteria is generally very large an increase of one is small compared to the overall number. We shall obtain useful information if we treat it as a continuous change.

Note (i) We have to consider a general time t.

(ii) The size varies as the time varies and we again use a convenient letter, say N.

(iii) 'The rate' with no qualification implies a change with respect to the time t; that is, we are interested in $\frac{dN}{dt}$.

(iv) 'of growth' indicates an increasing (positive) rate of change, that is $+\frac{dN}{dt}$.

'Rate of growth is proportional to its size' now translates as

$$+\frac{dN}{dt} \propto N$$

or as an equality $\frac{dN}{dt} = kN$ (where k is a positive constant) (2.2)

Example 3. Express the following statement in mathematical symbols: 'At any height in a compressible atmosphere of constant temperature the rate of fall of the pressure with respect to the height is proportional to the pressure.'

Note (i) 'At *any* height'—therefore we denote this general height by z.

(ii) The pressure is also a general pressure and is denoted by p.

(iii) In this case the rate of fall of pressure is defined as 'with respect to height'. Therefore we are interested in $-\frac{dp}{dz}$. Note the negative sign because of 'fall in pressure'.

'The rate of fall of the pressure with respect to the height is proportional to the pressure' translates as

$$-\frac{dp}{dz} \propto p$$

or as an equality $-\frac{dp}{dz} = kp$ (where k is a positive constant) (2.3)

Example 4. Express the following statement in mathematical symbols: 'A calorimeter containing hot water is standing in a room which has a constant temperature of 20°C. The rate of fall of the temperature of the water and the calorimeter is proportional to the difference in temperature between the calorimeter and its surroundings.' (Newton's Law of Cooling.)

Note (i) Let the time at any instant be t and θ the corresponding temperature of the calorimeter and the water.

(ii) As in examples 1 and 2 the rate of fall of the temperature is not qualified; therefore it is understood to be with respect to time, that is $-\frac{d\theta}{dt}$, the negative indicating a fall in the temperature.

(iii) This example is slightly different from examples 1, 2 and 3 because the rate of fall of the temperature is proportional to 'the difference in temperature between the calorimeter and its surroundings', that is, $\theta - 20$.

The required equation is now

$$-\frac{\mathrm{d}\theta}{\mathrm{d}t} \propto \theta - 20$$

or as an equality $$-\frac{\mathrm{d}\theta}{\mathrm{d}t} = k(\theta - 20) \text{ (where } k \text{ is a positive constant)} \qquad (2.4)$$

Example 5. The cross-sectional area of a vertical column varies so that the pressure per unit area of cross-section is constant throughout the column. It is found that the rate of increase of area with respect to the distance from the flat top is proportional to the area. Express this relationship in mathematical symbols.

We are concerned with the increase of the cross-sectional area, say A (note that A is a variable in this case), at any distance, say x, from the top of the column; that is, we are concerned with $+\frac{\mathrm{d}A}{\mathrm{d}x}$ and because this is proportional to the area then

$$+\frac{\mathrm{d}A}{\mathrm{d}x} \propto A$$

or $$\frac{\mathrm{d}A}{\mathrm{d}x} = kA \text{ (where } k \text{ is a positive constant)} \qquad (2.5)$$

Gathering together four of the results of the previous five examples (example 4 and equation 2.4 will be considered later), we have that

$$\frac{\mathrm{d}q}{\mathrm{d}t} = -kq$$

$$\frac{\mathrm{d}N}{\mathrm{d}t} = kN$$

$$\frac{\mathrm{d}p}{\mathrm{d}z} = -kp$$

$$\frac{\mathrm{d}A}{\mathrm{d}x} = kA \quad \text{(where } k \text{ is a positive constant)}$$

The choice of the variable in each case was conditioned by general usage, but they are all expressible as

$$\frac{\mathrm{d}y}{\mathrm{d}x} = ay \text{ (where } a \text{ is now a positive or a negative constant)} \qquad (2.6)$$

That is, in each case the derivative of a function is equal to a constant times that function. A surprising result considering that the four examples were drawn from widely different areas of study.

2.2 The Exponential Function

In order to proceed further with the solutions of the problems, a function $F(x)$ is needed such that

$$\frac{\mathrm{d}[F(x)]}{\mathrm{d}x} = aF(x) \qquad (2.7)$$

With our present limited knowledge we appear to have reached an impasse. We have a neat equation of wide application but none of the few functions we have met satisfies it. For example

$$\frac{\mathrm{d}(ax^n)}{\mathrm{d}x} = nax^{n-1} = a(nx^{n-1}) \neq a(ax^n)$$

To abandon our investigation at this point would mean that to investigate the laws further we should have to use an empirical approach for each particular set of conditions for each separate law. The work involved would be both repetitive and tedious. However, if the reader will take a little trouble to master a new mathematical function a neater solution is available which can be easily applied to all the many diverse situations to which these laws apply.

A relation such as equation 2.7 can be used to define a function whose properties can be obtained from that equation. We shall slightly simplify the problem by taking $a = 1$ and denoting this standard function by $E(x)$, where

$$\frac{\mathrm{d}[E(x)]}{\mathrm{d}x} = E(x)$$

or

$$E'(x) = E(x) \qquad (2.8)$$

and also making the condition that when $x = 0$, then $E(x) = 1$, that is

$$E(0) = 1 \qquad (2.9)$$

If we now assume that $E(x)$ and derivatives with respect to x of all orders exist and are continuous over the required range of x then, differentiating the equation 2.8 with respect to x

$$\frac{\mathrm{d}[E'(x)]}{\mathrm{d}x} = \frac{\mathrm{d}[E(x)]}{\mathrm{d}x}$$

or

$$E''(x) = E'(x) = E(x) \qquad \text{(from 2.8)}$$

Differentiating again with respect to x

$$\frac{\mathrm{d}[E''(x)]}{\mathrm{d}x} = \frac{\mathrm{d}[E'(x)]}{\mathrm{d}x} = \frac{\mathrm{d}[E(x)]}{\mathrm{d}x}$$

or

$$E'''(x) = E''(x) = E'(x) = E(x) \qquad \text{(from 2.8)}$$

This process can be repeated as often as we like, and in general

$$E^n(x) = \ldots = E'''(x) = E''(x) = E'(x) = E(x) \qquad (2.10)$$

When $x = 0$

$$E^n(0) = \ldots = E'''(0) = E''(0) = E'(0) = E(0) = 1 \qquad (2.11)$$

(from 2.9)

We now assume that the function $E(x)$ can be represented by an infinite series of the form 2.12 and that the derivatives of $E(x)$ are equal to the sum of the corresponding separate derivatives of each term on the right-hand side; then

$$E(x) = a_0 + a_1x + a_2x^2 + a_3x^3 + a_4x^4 + \ldots + a_nx^n + \ldots \qquad (2.12)$$

With $x = 0$

$$E(0) = a_0 + 0 + 0 + \ldots$$

and from 2.11

$$1 = a_0 \text{ and we have found the first coefficient.}$$

Differentiating both sides of equation 2.12 with respect to x

$$E'(x) = 0 + 1a_1 + 2a_2x + 3a_3x^2 + 4a_4x^3 + \ldots \qquad (2.13)$$

With $x = 0$

$$E'(0) = a_1 + 0 + 0 + \ldots$$

and from 2.11

$$1 = a_1 \text{ and we have found the second coefficient.}$$

Differentiating both sides of equation 2.13 with respect to x

$$E''(x) = 1 \,.\, 2a_2 + 2 \,.\, 3a_3x + 3 \,.\, 4a_4x^2 + \ldots$$

With $x = 0$

$$E''(0) = 1 \,.\, 2a_2 + 0 + 0 \ldots$$

and from 2.11

$$1 = 2!a_2$$

$$1/2! = a_2 \text{ and we have found the third coefficient.}$$

Repeating the procedure

$$E'''(x) = 1 \,.\, 2 \,.\, 3a_3 + 2 \,.\, 3 \,.\, 4a_4x + \ldots$$

With $x = 0$

$$E'''(0) = 3!a_3 + 0 + \ldots$$

and from 2.11

$$1 = 3!a_3$$

$$1/3! = a_3$$

Similarly

$$1/4! = a_4$$

and generally

$$1/n! = a_n$$

$$\therefore \qquad E(x) = 1 + x + \frac{x^2}{2!} + \frac{x^3}{3!} + \frac{x^4}{4!} + \ldots + \frac{x^n}{n!} + \ldots \qquad (2.14)$$

This expansion can be shown to be true for all values of x both rational and irrational. It is the **Taylor's Series** for the function $E(x)$ (refer to section 8.7).

It is interesting to verify that the series 2.14 does in fact satisfy the relations 2.8 and 2.9. Substituting $x = 0$ in equation 2.14

$E(0) = 1 + 0 + 0 + \ldots = 1$ (which agrees with 2.9)

$$\frac{d[E(x)]}{dx} = \frac{d}{dx}\left[1 + x + \frac{x^2}{2!} + \ldots + \frac{x^n}{n!} + \frac{x^{n+1}}{(n+1)!} + \ldots\right]$$

$$= 0 + 1 + \frac{2x}{2!} + \frac{3x^2}{3!} + \ldots + \frac{nx^{n-1}}{n!} + \frac{(n+1)x^n}{(n+1)!} + \ldots$$

$$= 1 + x + \frac{x^2}{2!} + \ldots + \frac{x^{n-1}}{(n-1)!} + \frac{x^n}{n!} + \ldots$$

$= E(x)$, which verifies that $E(x)$ is a solution of equation 2.8.

Example 6. Find the value of $E(1)$ correct to three decimal places.
With $x = 1$ in equation 2.14

$$\begin{aligned} E(1) &= 1 + 1 + 1/2! + 1/3! + 1/4! + \ldots \\ &= 1 + 1 + 0{\cdot}5 + 0{\cdot}1667 + 0{\cdot}0417 + 0{\cdot}0083 \\ &\quad + 0{\cdot}0014 + 0{\cdot}0002 + \ldots \\ &= 2{\cdot}718 \text{ (correct to three decimal places).} \end{aligned}$$

It can be shown that (refer to Appendix One)

$$E(x) = [E(1)]^x = e^x \qquad (2.15)$$

where e^x means the *positive* xth power of $E(1) = e$ for all rational values of x and e is the symbol introduced by Euler circa 1727.

From equations 2.14 and 2.15

$$e^x = E(x) = 1 + x + x^2/2! + x^3/3! + \ldots + x^n/n! + \ldots \qquad (2.16)$$

for all rational and irrational values of x.

Example 7. Find the value of $e^{0\cdot 1}$ correct to four decimal places.

Substituting $x = 0{\cdot}1$ in equation 2.16

$$\begin{aligned} e^{0\cdot 1} &= 1 + 0{\cdot}1 + (0{\cdot}1)^2/2! + (0{\cdot}1)^3/3! + \ldots \\ &= 1 + 0{\cdot}1 + 0{\cdot}005 + 0{\cdot}00017 + 0{\cdot}00000 \\ &= 1{\cdot}10517 \\ &= 1{\cdot}1052 \text{ (correct to four decimal places).} \end{aligned}$$

The exponential function is widely used and values of e^x are included in most books of tables. Such a table can be used to obtain the values of $y = e^x$ corresponding to various values of x. Using two mutually perpendicular axes $0x$, $0y$, with appropriate scales, these pairs of values (x, y) can be represented by points. The collection of such points is called the **graph** of e^x. In the case of e^x the points can be joined by a continuous curve and for every value of x there is a corresponding value of e^x. The graph of e^x is shown in Fig. 2.1.

Example 8. Find series for e^{4x} and e^{-2x} in ascending powers of x.

From equation 2.16, with x replaced by $4x$

$$\begin{aligned} e^{4x} &= 1 + 4x + (4x)^2/2! + (4x)^3/3! + \ldots + (4x)^n/n! + \ldots \\ &= 1 + 4x + 4^2x^2/2! + 4^3x^3/3! + \ldots + 4^nx^n/n! + \ldots \end{aligned}$$

From equation 2.16, with $x = -2x$

$$e^{-2x} = 1 + (-2x) + (-2x)^2/2! + (-2x)^3/3! + \ldots + (-2x)^n/n! + \ldots$$
$$= 1 - 2x + 2^2x^2/2! - 2^3x^3/3! + \ldots + (-)^n 2^n x^n/n! + \ldots$$

We have obtained $y = e^x$ as the solution of the equation $dy/dx = y$ with the condition that $y = 1$ when $x = 0$. Consider now the original and more general equation $dy/dx = ay$, where a is a constant, together with the condition that $y = C$ when $x = 0$, C being an arbitrary constant.

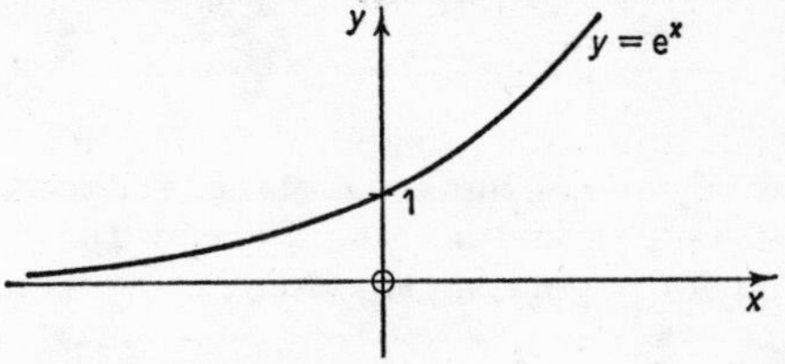

Fig. 2.1

Let $y = Ce^{ax}$, and assuming the infinite series can be differentiated term by term

$$\therefore \quad \frac{dy}{dx} = \frac{d}{dx}\left[C\left(1 + ax + \frac{a^2x^2}{2!} + \frac{a^3x^3}{3!} + \frac{a^4x^4}{4!} + \ldots + \frac{a^nx^n}{n!} + \ldots\right)\right]$$

$$= C\left(0 + a + \frac{2a^2x}{2!} + \frac{3a^3x^2}{3!} + \frac{4a^4x^3}{4!} + \ldots + \frac{na^nx^{n-1}}{n!} + \ldots\right)$$

$$= aC\left(1 + \frac{2ax}{2!} + \frac{3a^2x^2}{3!} + \frac{4a^3x^3}{4!} + \ldots + \frac{na^{n-1}x^{n-1}}{n!} + \ldots\right)$$

$$= aC\left(1 + ax + \frac{a^2x^2}{2!} + \frac{a^3x^3}{3!} + \ldots + \frac{a^{n-1}x^{n-1}}{(n-1)!} + \ldots\right)$$

$$= aCe^{ax}$$

$$= ay$$

Therefore $y = Ce^{ax}$ is the solution of the equation $dy/dx = ay$ with $y = C$ when $x = 0$ (note $e^0 = 1$) (2.17)

Example 9. Find the solution of Newton's Law of Cooling, which is $-\frac{d\theta}{dt} = k(\theta - 20)$, when the temperature of the surroundings is 20°C (refer to example 4 and equation 2.4).

Consider
$$\frac{d(\theta - 20)}{dt} = \frac{d\theta}{dt} - \frac{d(20)}{dt}$$
$$= \frac{d\theta}{dt} - 0$$
$$= \frac{d\theta}{dt}$$

Therefore the given equation can be written

$$-\frac{d(\theta - 20)}{dt} = k(\theta - 20)$$

or

$$\frac{d(\theta - 20)}{dt} = -k(\theta - 20)$$

which has the same form as equation 2.6 with $y = \theta - 20$, $-k = a$ and $x = t$. Therefore by equation 2.17, its solution is

$$\theta - 20 = Ce^{-kt}, \text{ where } C \text{ is an arbitrary constant}$$

or

$$\theta = 20 + Ce^{-kt} \tag{2.18}$$

It will be noticed that this expression for the temperature θ in terms of the time t contains two unknown constants C and k. The reason for this is that the solution is the most general one and is true whatever the shape, size, etc., of the hot body or the starting temperature. In a particular case more information will be available and values of the constants can be found to suit that case. For example, if the temperature of the water was 100°C at the start ($t = 0$), we should know that the solution had to agree with case of $\theta = 100$ when $t = 0$. Therefore substituting in equation 2.18

$$100 = 20 + Ce^0$$
$$= 20 + C$$
$$\therefore \quad 80 = C$$

and for this particular case $\theta = 20 + 80e^{-kt}$. Further discussion of this point will be found in Chapter Ten (Differential Equations).

We note that we have another standard result, namely

$$\frac{d(e^{ax})}{dx} = ae^{ax} \text{ (where } a \text{ is a constant)} \tag{2.19}$$

The unknown variable x can take a variety of forms; thus

$$\frac{d(e^{2y})}{dy} = 2e^{2y}, \quad \frac{d(e^{-5z})}{dz} = -5e^{-5z},$$

$$\frac{d(e^{2\sqrt{p}})}{d\sqrt{p}} = 2e^{2\sqrt{p}}, \quad \frac{d(e^{\cos\theta})}{d(\cos\theta)} = e^{\cos\theta},$$

$$\frac{d[e^{3(x^2-1)}]}{d(x^2-1)} = 3e^{3(x^2-1)}, \quad \frac{d(e^{5\sin\theta})}{d(\sin\theta)} = 5e^{5\sin\theta}.$$

Revision Questions 2.1

Questions	*Answers*	*Refer to*
1. If $X = 2x$ what do $3X^2$ and $-2X^3$ equal?	1. $3X^2 = 3(2x)^2 = 12x^2$ $-2X^3 = -2(2x)^3 = -16x^3$.	
2. Write in words the mathematical statement $\frac{dy}{dx} = y^2$.	2. The rate of change of y with respect to x is equal to y squared.	Section 2.1

Questions	*Answers*	*Refer to*
3. Does a negative value of the derivative of a function at a point indicate a rate of increase or a rate of decrease of the function at that point?	**3.** A rate of decrease.	Section 2.1
4. Which of the following is the correct answer to $e^{2x} \times e^{3x}$: e^{6x}, e^{5x}, or e^{6x^2}?	**4.** $e^{2x} \times e^{3x} = e^{2x+3x}$ $= e^{5x}$ ('Add the indices').	
5. State one solution of the equation $\frac{dp}{dq} = p$.	**5.** e^q or any constant multiple of it, e.g. $2e^q$, $-3e^q$, ...	Section 2.2
6. What is the most general solution of the equation $\frac{dr}{dt} = ar$, where a is a constant?	**6.** $r = Ce^{at}$, where C is any constant.	Section 2.2
7. Evaluate $\frac{d(2e^{4x})}{dx}$, $\frac{d(3e^{-x})}{dx}$, $\frac{d[e^{2\cos\theta}]}{d(\cos\theta)}$ and $\frac{d[e^{-\sin\theta}]}{d(\sin\theta)}$.	**7.** $8e^{4x}$, $-3e^{-x}$, $2e^{2\cos\theta}$, $-e^{-\sin\theta}$.	Section 2.2

Exercises 2.1

State the mathematical equations corresponding to the following four statements.

1. The rate of decrease of x with respect to z is equal to twice the value of x.

2. The rate of increase of x with respect to y is proportional to the square of x.

3. The rate of decrease of x with respect to time t is proportional to the reciprocal of x.

4. The rate of increase of x^2 with respect to time t is equal to the product of x and y.

5. In a first-order chemical reaction the rate of combination of a substance is proportional to the amount remaining. Let x represent the amount of substance remaining at any time t and write down the mathematical equation corresponding to this law. What is the most general solution of this equation?

6. A cable for a barrage balloon tapers in such a way that the stress across every section has the same value. The rate of decrease of the radius of cross section x of the cable with the distance y from the balloon is found to be proportional to the radius. Write down the mathematical equation corresponding to this law. What is the most general solution of this equation?

7. (a) Write down series of ascending powers of x for the following functions: e^{-4x}, e^{3x}, e^{x^3}.
(b) Use the series 2.16 to evaluate e^{-1}, $\sqrt[3]{e}$, $1/e^{\frac{1}{2}}$ correct to four places of decimals. Check your results from tables.

(c) If x is so small that x^5 and higher powers of x can be neglected show that

$$\text{(i)}\ \tfrac{1}{2}(e^x + e^{-x}) \simeq 1 + x^2/2! + x^4/4!$$
$$\text{(ii)}\ \tfrac{1}{2}(e^x - e^{-x}) \simeq x + x^3/3!$$

8. A falling body is moving so that the rate of decrease of the square of its speed v with respect to the distance fallen x is proportional to the square of its speed less a constant a. Write down the appropriate mathematical equation. What is the general solution of this equation?

$$\left[\textit{Hint}\text{: Remember that } \frac{dv^2}{dx} = \frac{d(v^2 - a)}{dx}\right]$$

9. An electric condenser of capacity C discharges through a resistance R of negligible inductance. The rate of decrease of the charge q on the positive plate of the condenser at any time t is proportional to that charge. Given that the constant of proportionality is $1/RC$ write down the appropriate mathematical equation. What is the most general solution of this equation?

10. When a planet P moves around a sun S the line SP is called the radius vector and its length is denoted by r. The angle which SP makes with a fixed direction SY is denoted by θ. Using Kepler's Second Law of Planetary Motion it can be shown that the rate of increase of θ is inversely proportional to the square of the radius vector. Write down the corresponding mathematical equation. Is this a case of the growth equation $\frac{dy}{dx} = ay$, where a is a constant?

11. The population of a town is P at time t years. Its rate of growth is 2 per cent of the population. Assuming this rate of growth remains constant, predict its population in 1982 to the nearest 1000, given that $P = 300\,000$ when $t = 1972$.

2.3 Log$_e$ x: The Inverse Function of e^x

When the idea of a function was discussed in section 1.5 one of the examples given was that the profit £P of a manufacturer could depend on the selling price s pence of one item—that is, P is a function of s. The values of s would be discrete values but, within limits, as s varied P would vary and would have a unique value corresponding to each value of s. The graph of the function is depicted in Fig. 2.2. Note that there is a sequence of isolated points and not a continuous curve because s is not a continuous variable.

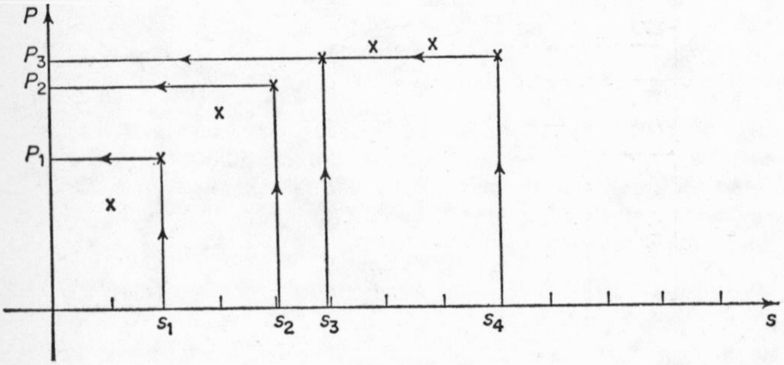

Fig. 2.2

In conformity with the idea of a function to each value of s there is a unique value of P. As shown in the figure, selling prices of s_1, s_2, and s_3 pence give rise to profits £P_1, £P_2, and £P_3. We would remind our readers that in this case s is known as the **independent variable** and P as the **dependent variable.** We might wish to consider the relation between s and P in the opposite (inverse) way and ask if the profit P is to be changed what are the corresponding values of s? That is, to consider how s varies with P. This inverse process is depicted in Fig. 2.3. There is now an important difference.

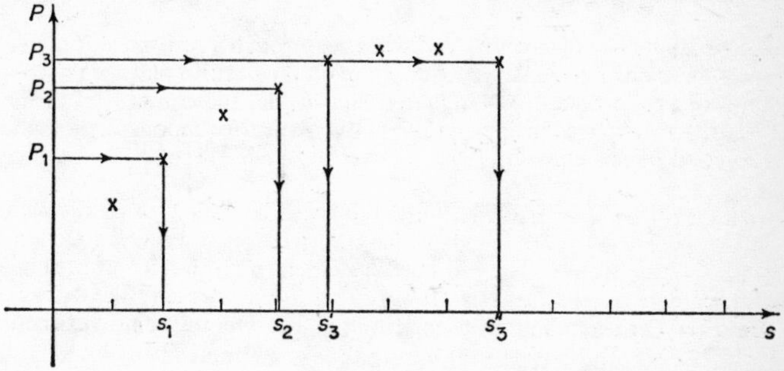

Fig. 2.3

To P_1 and P_2 there correspond unique values s_1 and s_2, but to obtain a profit of £P_3 the items can be sold either at s_3' or s_3'' pence each. There is no unique selling price corresponding to a profit of £P_3. We cannot say that s is a function of P because although to each value of P there is a corresponding value of s there is not *one* and *only one* value of s (refer to section 1.5). The inverse function to $P = f(s)$ does not exist.

Consider a second example where the exact algebraic relation is known. The area A of a rectangular piece of ground enclosed by a 40 m length of fencing is given by $A = 20x - x^2$ $(0 \leqslant x \leqslant 20)$, where x is the width of the rectangle. The graph of this function is shown in Fig. 2.4.

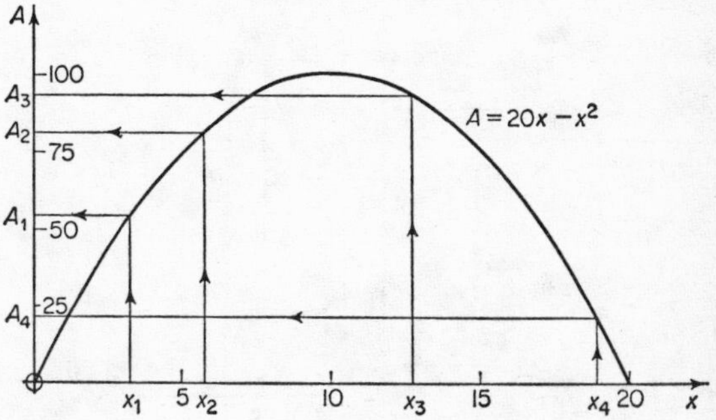

Fig. 2.4

Note that due to practical considerations x is restricted to the range $(0 \leqslant x \leqslant 20)$. For any value of x between 0 and 20 there is a corresponding unique value of A and A is a function of x. Consider the inverse relation shown in Fig. 2.5. Corresponding to each value of A such that $0 \leqslant A \leqslant 100$

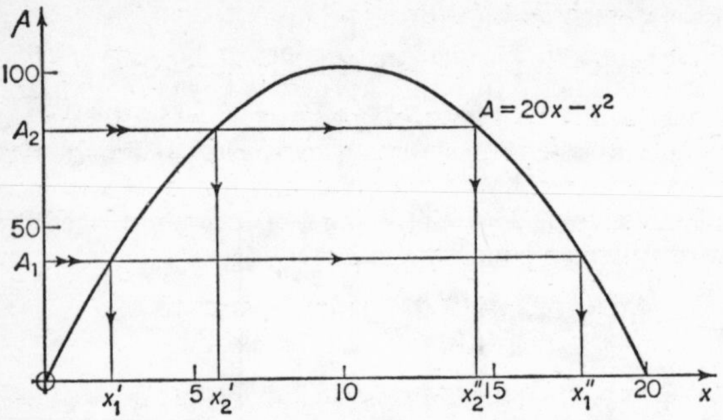

Fig. 2.5

there are two values of x; that is, there is *no unique value* (except when $A = 100$, $x = 10$) and we cannot say that x is a function of A. Although A is a function of x, the inverse function does not exist.

In the case of the function e^x, whatever value is given to x its value is always positive. For $x \geqslant 0$, the series 2.16 shows that $e^x > 0$. If $x < 0$ (say, $x = -m$) then $m > 0$ and

$$e^x = e^{-m} = \frac{1}{e^m} = \frac{1}{\text{positive}} = \text{positive}$$

Now $de^x/dx = e^x$, which is always positive; therefore the rate of change of e^x is always positive and e^x is always increasing. Its graph is repeated for convenience in Fig. 2.6. It can be seen that to each value of y there is a unique

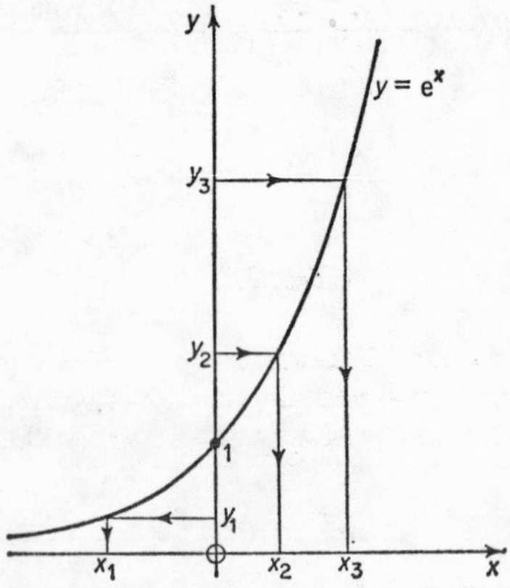

Fig. 2.6

value of x and the inverse function of the exponential function does exist. It is, moreover, a familiar function, as can be seen if we describe the relation $y = e^x$ with an inverse emphasis thus: x is the *power* to which e is raised to equal y (y is always positive), which is the definition of a logarithm to the base e. Thus logarithm (to the base e) of positive quantities is the inverse function to the exponential function.

$$\log_e x \ (x > 0) \text{ is the inverse function to } e^x$$

Readers will be familiar with logarithms to the base 10, which are used because our number system uses 10 as a base, but we should note that the definition allows for logarithms to any base and that a logarithm is a power. From a set of tables $\log_{10} 2 = 0{\cdot}3010$ and $0{\cdot}3010$ is the power to which the base 10 must be raised to equal* the number.

$$\therefore \quad \log_{10} 2 = 0{\cdot}3010 \text{ can be written as}$$
$$2 = 10^{0{\cdot}3010}$$

Example 10. Evaluate: (i) $\log_3 9$, (ii) $\log_{10} 1000$, (iii) $\log_2 16$, (iv) $\log_e 7{\cdot}389$.

(i) $9 = 3^2$; therefore the power 2 is the required logarithm and $\log_3 9 = 2$.
(ii) $1000 = 10^3$; therefore $\log_{10} 1000 = 3$.
(iii) $16 = 2^4$; therefore $\log_2 16 = 4$.
(iv) $7{\cdot}389 = e^2$; therefore $\log_e 7{\cdot}389 = 2$.

Logarithms to the base e are known as **natural logarithms** while those to the base 10 are known as **common logarithms.** It is more usual to write $\log_e x$ as $\ln x$, and we shall do so throughout this book. Tables of natural logarithms are given in most table books and can be used to plot the graph of $\ln x$ which is shown in Fig. 2.7.

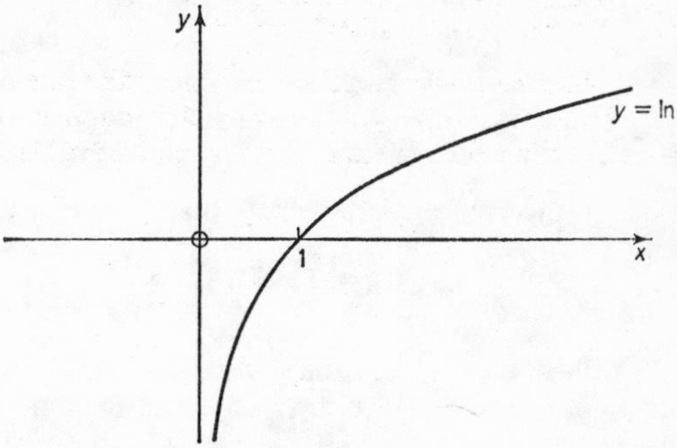

Fig. 2.7

By comparing Figs. 2.6 and 2.7 it can be seen that the graph of $\ln x$ can be obtained from that of e^x by interchanging x and y. It is also the mirror image of e^x in the line $y = x$ as shown in Fig. 2.8. There are two results which are of importance

$$e^{\ln x} = x \qquad (2.20)$$

* This and succeeding numerical values are given correct to four significant figures.

(this follows immediately from the definition of a logarithm because ln x is the power to which the base e is raised to equal the number whose logarithm is required, in this case x), and

$$\ln e^x = x \qquad (2.21)$$

because

$$\begin{aligned} \ln e^x &= x \ln e \\ &= x \log_e e \\ &= x \, . \, 1 \\ &= x \end{aligned}$$

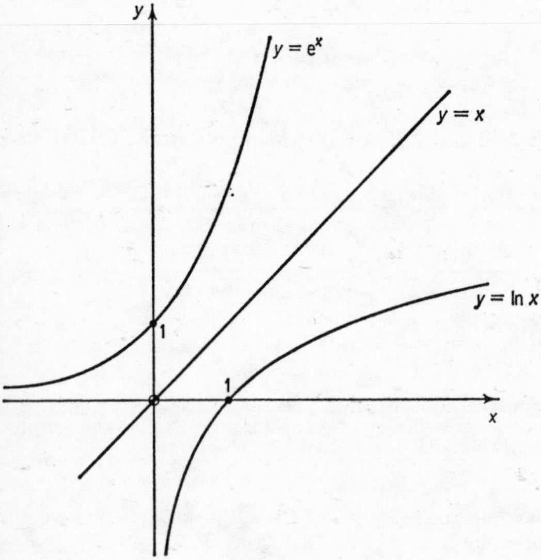

Fig. 2.8

To differentiate an inverse function we note that $\delta y \to 0$ as $\delta x \to 0$ and

$$\frac{dy}{dx} = \underset{\delta x \to 0}{\text{limit}} \frac{\delta y}{\delta x} = \underset{\delta y \to 0}{\text{limit}} \ 1/\frac{\delta x}{\delta y} = 1/\frac{dx}{dy} \left(\frac{dx}{dy} \neq 0\right)$$

where if $y = f(x)$, then $x = f^{-1}(y)$—the inverse function—and we assume that the limit of a quotient is equal to the quotient of the limits.

Let $$y = \ln x$$

then $$x = e^y$$

$\therefore$ $$\frac{dx}{dy} = \frac{d(e^y)}{dy} = e^y = x$$

$\therefore$ $$\frac{dy}{dx} = \frac{1}{x}$$

or $$\frac{d(\ln x)}{dx} = \frac{1}{x}$$

It is left as an exercise for the reader to prove that for any constant C

$$\frac{d(C \ln x)}{dx} = \frac{C}{x} \tag{2.22}$$

It is emphasised that it is only the derivative of $\ln x$ that is $1/x$; for any other base of logarithms we have to proceed as follows

$$\frac{d(\log_b x)}{dx} = \frac{d(\log_b e \,.\, \ln x)}{dx}$$

$$= \log_b e \frac{d(\ln x)}{dx} \text{ (because } \log_b e \text{ is a constant)}$$

$$= (\log_b e)/x \tag{2.23}$$

The results 2.22 and 2.23 are of wide application; for example

$$\frac{d(\ln y)}{dy} = \frac{1}{y}, \quad \frac{d(\ln q)}{dq} = \frac{1}{q}, \quad \frac{d[\ln(\cos\theta)]}{d(\cos\theta)} = \frac{1}{\cos\theta},$$

$$\frac{d[\ln(\sin 2\theta)]}{d(\sin 2\theta)} = \frac{1}{\sin 2\theta}, \quad \frac{d[\ln(3x^2-2)]}{d(3x^2-2)} = \frac{1}{(3x^2-2)}$$

$$\frac{d[\ln(\sqrt{x}+1)]}{d(\sqrt{x}+1)} = \frac{1}{(\sqrt{x}+1)}$$

Example 11. Find the derivatives with respect to x of $\log_{10} x$, $\ln^3\sqrt{x}$, $\ln(x^2/2)$.

$$\frac{d(\log_{10} x)}{dx} = \frac{d(\log_{10} e \,.\, \ln x)}{dx} = \frac{(\log_{10} e)}{x} = \frac{0{\cdot}4343}{x}$$

With functions involving logarithms the working can often be simplified as shown in the following examples.

$$\frac{d(\ln^3\sqrt{x})}{dx} = \frac{d(\ln x^{\frac{1}{3}})}{dx} = \frac{d(\frac{1}{3}\ln x)}{dx} = \frac{1}{3x}$$

$$\frac{d(\ln x^2/2)}{dx} = \frac{d(2\ln x - \ln 2)}{dx} = \frac{2}{x} - 0 = \frac{2}{x}$$

Revision Questions 2.2

Questions	*Answers*	*Refer to*
1. Given that $343 = 7^3$, what is the value of $\log_7 343$?	**1.** 3	Example 10
2. Given that $8 = 4\sqrt{4}$, what is the value of $\log_4 8$?	**2.** $1\frac{1}{2}$	Example 10
3. What are the values of $\log_4 \sqrt[3]{4}$, $\log_3 (1/243)$ and $\log_e e^3$?	**3.** $\frac{1}{3}$, -5, 3	Example 10
4. What is the derivative of $\ln y$ with respect to y?	**4.** $1/y$	Formula 2.22

Questions	*Answers*	*Refer to*
5. State the derivative of $\ln z^3$ with respect to z^3. What is the derivative of $\ln z^3$ with respect to z?	5. $1/z^3$, $3/z$	Example 11
6. Simplify $\ln e^2$ and $e^{\ln 3}$, $e^{-\ln z}$, $e^{3\ln z}$, $e^{-\ln z+\ln \sin z}$	6. 2, 3, $1/x$, x^3, $\dfrac{\sin x}{x}$	Formulae 2.20 and 2.21

Exercises 2.2

Before commencing the following exercises our readers are reminded that for logarithms to any base

$$\log AB = \log A + \log B$$
$$\log A^n = n \log A$$

Find the derivatives with respect to x of

1. $\ln(2x)$ 2. $\ln(x^n)$ 3. $\ln(5x^4)$
4. $\ln(1/x^3)$ 5. $\ln(\sqrt{x})$ 6. $\ln(6/\sqrt{x})$

Evaluate

7. (i) $\dfrac{d[\ln(\sqrt{z})]}{d(\sqrt{z})}$ (ii) $\dfrac{d[\ln(\sqrt{z})]}{dz}$

8. (i) $\dfrac{d[\ln(p^4)]}{d(p^4)}$ (ii) $\dfrac{d[\ln(p^4)]}{dp}$

9. (i) $e^{2\ln z}$, (ii) $e^{-\ln z}$, (iii) $e^{\ln z+\ln y}$, (iv) $e^{\ln z-\ln y}$.

10. A hollow cylindrical pipe is carrying steam at 105°C. The temperature θ inside the wall of the pipe at a distance r from its axis is given by

$$r\frac{d^2\theta}{dr^2} + \frac{d\theta}{dr} = 0$$

Show that

$$\theta = \frac{105 \ln\left(\dfrac{r}{r_2}\right) - 15 \ln\left(\dfrac{r}{r_1}\right)}{\ln\left(\dfrac{r_1}{r_2}\right)} \quad (r_1 \leqslant r \leqslant r_2)$$

is a solution of the equation (r_1 and r_2 are the inner and outer radii of the pipe).

CHAPTER THREE

SOME APPLICATIONS OF DIFFERENTIATION

3.1 Introduction

If a manufacturer makes more of a product, one would expect that his profit would rise. He knows, however, that the situation is not as simple as that. As the number of articles made increases, other factors have to be taken into account. His advertising and selling costs can rise, difficulties can occur over distribution and he may even saturate the market. His forecast of the profits is generally made on an empirical basis. However, if a mathematical model can be made to represent the situation, he has some very powerful techniques at his disposal. Consider what it is that interests him: it is the change (increase, he hopes) in his profit P as the number N sold increases—that is, the rate of change of P with respect to N, or $\mathrm{d}P/\mathrm{d}N$. While $\mathrm{d}P/\mathrm{d}N$ is positive (profits increasing as N increases) he will wish to step up his production but *not* if $\mathrm{d}P/\mathrm{d}N$ is negative (profits decreasing as N increases). The critical point is when $\mathrm{d}P/\mathrm{d}N$ is zero, for then his profit could be a maximum (or a minimum).

The power P transmitted by a belt does not increase indefinitely with the speed v. There is a point when a further increase in the speed leads to loss of power, the loss being due to slipping, etc.; at such a point $\mathrm{d}P/\mathrm{d}v = 0$ and the maximum power is being transmitted.

Even Nature seems to make use of the idea. The radius of a given length of blood vessel appears to be chosen to minimise the power loss.

From Van der Waal's equation, which is an extension of the simple gas law $pv = nRT$, the critical values of p, v and T can be found by considering the rate of change of the pressure with respect to the volume.

Other uses of rates of change are to calculate possible errors in a result due to uncertainties in the data used or to simplify the drawing of graphs which can be used to give an overall view of a situation.

These examples have been quoted so that the reader can see that the uses of differentiation are many and varied and that it is worthwhile spending some time learning the mathematical techniques.

In this chapter we shall consider how differentiation can be used in geometrical problems and its application to problems involving maximum and minimum values, and to the calculation of errors and approximations.

3.2 Graphical Interpretation of the Derivative of a Function

A function $f(x)$ is a new idea and can cause misgivings. It is helpful to represent it by its graph. The reader will be familiar with the graphs of the simpler functions such as $f(x) = x + 1$, which is a linear function and has a straight line graph as shown in Fig. 3.1.

The graph of the function $f(x) = x^2$ is also well known. It is smooth and continuous over any range of values for which x is given, and is shown in Fig. 3.2.

Our third example is the graph of the function $f(x) = 1/x$. When x is positive $f(x)$ is positive and when x is negative $f(x)$ is negative, and the graph lies wholly in the first and third quadrants. It can be seen that for small values of x the value of $f(x)$ is large and as x increases $f(x)$ becomes smaller. There is no value of $f(x)$ when $x = 0$ because $f(0) = 1/0$ has no meaning (division by zero is not valid). The graph is shown in Fig. 3.3. There is a

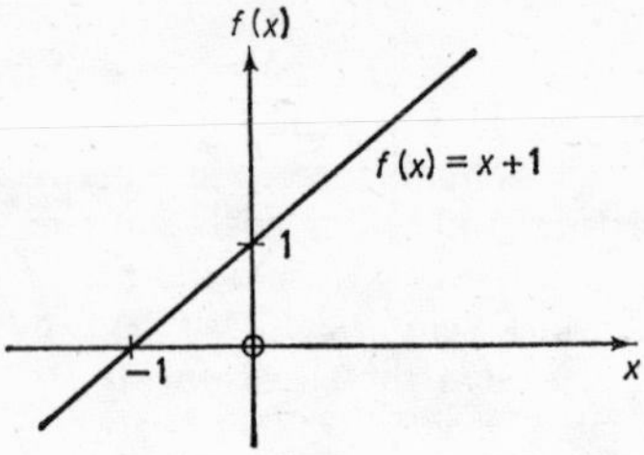

Fig. 3.1

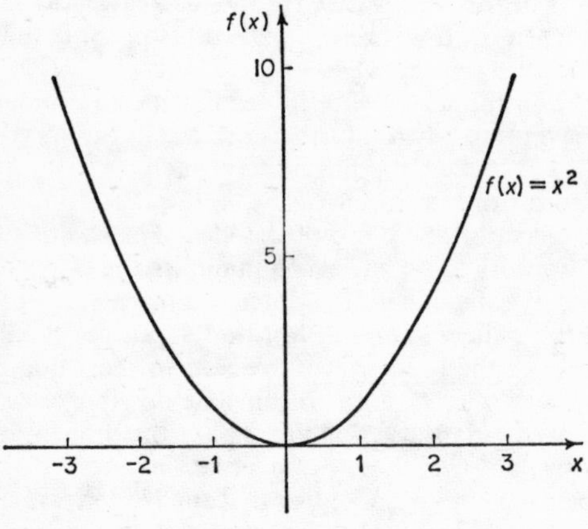

Fig. 3.2

break in the curve when $x = 0$; this is known as a **discontinuity** and the graph is **discontinuous.**

A function $f(x)$ is continuous if $\lim_{h \to 0} f(x + h) = f(x)$ for all x in its domain. In taking the limit, only values of $x + h$ in the domain are to be considered. Geometrically there is no break in its graph.

Some functions cannot be expressed as exact mathematical expressions and may have to be represented as a table of values of $f(x)$ corresponding to various values of x. This often occurs in practice, especially if a computer has been used to solve a problem. Such functions should strictly be represented by a set of points (see Fig. 2.2). Discontinuities are not just mathematical curiosities, they can occur in practice. Consider the load L on a road bridge at any time t. L is a function of t. At the instant a man steps on or off the bridge the value of L changes practically instantaneously from one value to another and the graph would be as shown in Fig. 3.4.

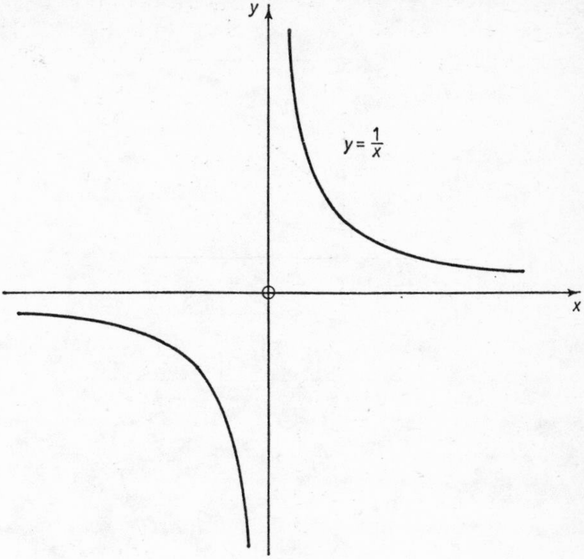

Fig. 3.3

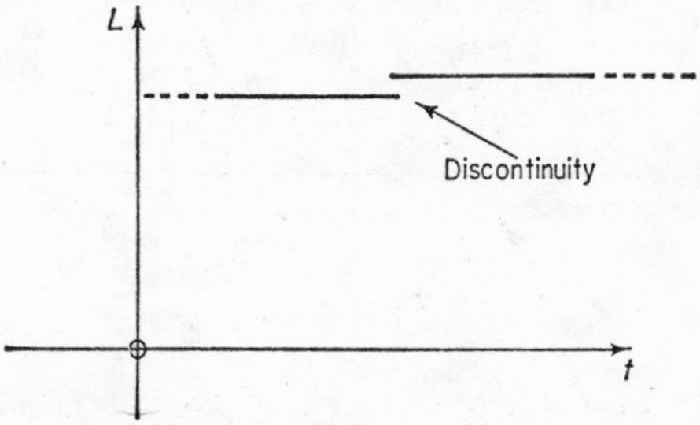

Fig. 3.4

Electrical engineers are familiar with the idea of an impulsive current and atomic physicists with the idea that an electron can only occupy certain discrete states of motion within an atom.

Whether a function is continuous or discontinuous, it is not always easy to obtain its graph from a mathematical expression. We shall now see that rates of change can be interpreted geometrically and, amongst other uses, this can be a help when drawing graphs of functions.

Consider any function $f(x)$ and let P and Q be any two points on its graph. Draw PA and QB perpendicular to the x-axis and PR perpendicular to QB, as shown in Fig. 3.5. The slope of the chord PQ is the ratio QR/PR (the tangent of the angle QPR). PR also represents the change in the value of x and QR the corresponding change in the value of $f(x)$.

$$\therefore \quad \text{The slope of the chord } PQ = \frac{QR}{PR} = \frac{\text{the change in the value of } f(x)}{\text{the change in the value of } x}$$

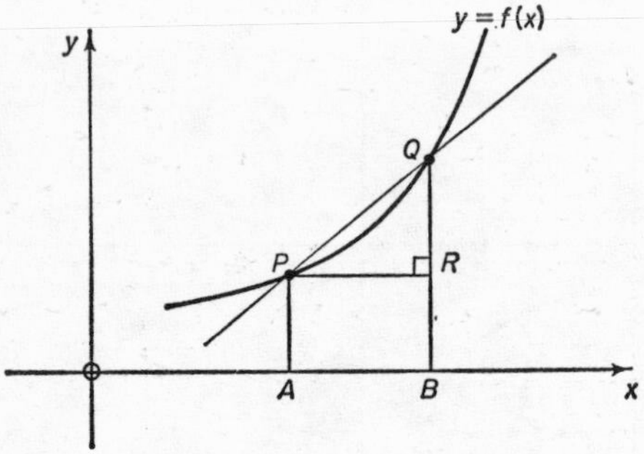

Fig. 3.5

which is the average rate of change of the function $f(x)$ with respect to x.

$$\therefore \qquad \text{The slope of the chord } PQ = \frac{\delta[f(x)]}{\delta x}$$

Consider the limiting value of this expression as $Q \to P\,(\delta x \to 0)$. The limiting value of the right-hand side is $\mathrm{d}[f(x)]/\mathrm{d}x$ or $f'(x)$. Consider the left-hand side: that is, the limiting value of the slope of the chord PQ as Q moves closer and closer to P. Let Q take positions Q_1, Q_2, Q_3, . . ., as in Fig. 3.6.

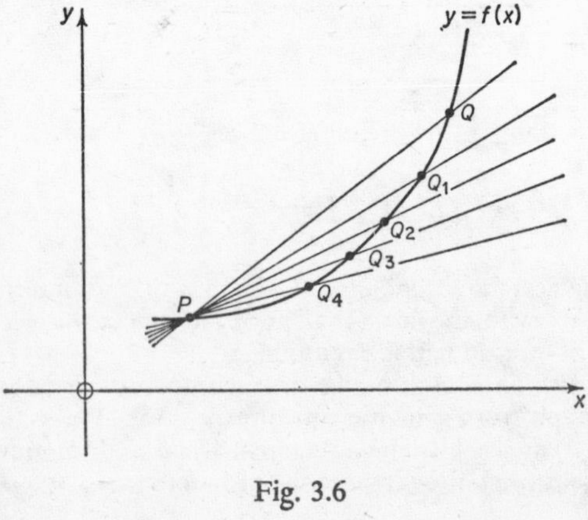

Fig. 3.6

It can be seen that as $Q \rightarrow P$ the chord QP becomes closer and closer to the tangent to the curve at P, and in the limit

Slope of the tangent to the curve at P is equal to the value of $d[f(x)]/(dx)$ at P (3.1)

Example 1. Sketch the graph of the function $f(x) = -x^2 + 5x - 6$. Find the slopes of the tangents at the points $x = 2$ and $x = 3$ and show that the tangents at these points are at right-angles.

$$\text{Let } y = f(x) = -x^2 + 5x - 6$$
$$= -(x - 2)(x - 3)$$

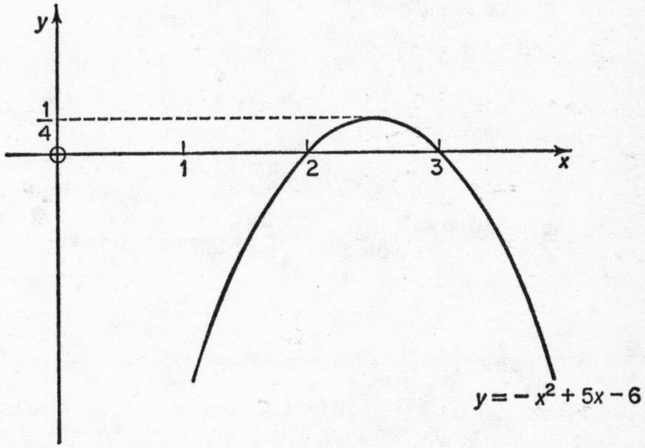

Fig. 3.7

When $x = 2$ or 3 then $y = 0$ and the graph crosses the x-axis. Midway between these two points $x = 2\frac{1}{2}$ and $y = +\frac{1}{4}$. The table for values of x between 0 and 5 is

x	0	1	2	$2\frac{1}{2}$	3	4	5
$f(x)$	−6	−2	0	$\frac{1}{4}$	0	−2	−6

and the graph is shown in Fig. 3.7. The derivative of $f(x)$ is

$$f'(x) = -2x + 5$$

at $x = 2$ $\quad f'(2) = -4 + 5 = +1$

at $x = 3$ $\quad f'(3) = -6 + 5 = -1$

Therefore the slopes of the tangents are $m_1 = +1$ and $m_2 = -1$. The product $m_1m_2 = +1 \times -1 = -1$, and the two tangents are at right-angles.

3.3 The Tangent and Normal to a Curve

The tangent to a curve at a given point is a straight line and its equation is therefore of the form $y = mx + c$. In the previous section, we found that the gradient m can be found from the derivative $f'(x)$. Also the tangent passes through the given point and the constant c can be evaluated.

Example 2. Find the equation of the tangent to the curve $y = 2x^3 - 21x + 29$ at the point (2, 3)

$$y = 2x^3 - 21x + 29$$

Therefore, differentiating

$$\frac{dy}{dx} = 6x^2 - 21$$

when $x = 2$ $$\frac{dy}{dx} = 6(2)^2 - 21 = 3$$

and the equation of the tangent is

$$y = 3x + c$$

It passes through the given point (2, 3)

$\therefore$ $$3 = 3(2) + c$$

$\therefore$ $$c = -3$$

and $y = 3x - 3$ is the required equation.

Example 3. Find the equation of the tangent to the curve $y = e^{2x} - 4x + 8$ at the point where it crosses the y-axis. Note that it is not necessary to sketch the curve in order to find the equation of a tangent.

$$y = e^{2x} - 4x + 8$$

differentiating $$\frac{dy}{dx} = 2e^{2x} - 4$$ (see equation 2.19)

The curve crosses the y-axis when $x = 0$. The slope of the tangent at that point is given by

$$\frac{dy}{dx} = 2e^0 - 4 = -2$$

and the equation of the tangent is

$$y = -2x + c$$

When $x = 0$, $y = e^0 - 0 + 8 = 9$ and the tangent passes through this point. Substituting the coordinates (0, 9) in

$$y = -2x + c$$
$$9 = 0 + c \text{ and } c = 9$$

The required equation is $y = -2x + 9$.

The normal to a curve at any point is perpendicular to the tangent at that point. The gradient of the normal is therefore the negative reciprocal of the slope of the tangent ($m_n = -1/m_t$).

Example 4. Find the equation of the normal to the curve $y = x^4 - 2x^3 + 3$ at the point (−1, 6).

$$\frac{dy}{dx} = 4x^3 - 6x^2$$

at the point $x = -1$

$$\frac{dy}{dx} = -4 - 6 = -10$$

Therefore the slope of the normal is $-\dfrac{1}{-10} = +\frac{1}{10}$, and its equation is $y = \frac{1}{10}x + c$.

It passes through the point $(-1, 6)$

$$\therefore \quad 6 = -\tfrac{1}{10} + c \quad \text{and} \quad c = 6\tfrac{1}{10}$$
$$y = \tfrac{1}{10}x + 6\tfrac{1}{10}$$

or $\quad 10y = x + 61$ is the required equation.

Example 5. Find the equation of the tangent to the curve $y = 3x^2 - 8x + 5$ which is parallel to the line $y + 2x - 3 = 0$ and passes through the point $(1, 0)$.

$$\frac{dy}{dx} = 6x - 8$$

The line $y + 2x - 3 = 0$ or $y = -2x + 3$ has a gradient of -2. Any parallel line also has a gradient of -2. Therefore

$$\frac{dy}{dx} \text{ or } 6x - 8 = -2$$

$$x = 1 \text{ and } y = 3(1)^2 - 8(1) + 5 = 0$$

The equation of the tangent is $y = -2x + c$ and it passes through the point $(1, 0)$; therefore $0 = -2 + c$ and $c = 2$. The required equation is $y = -2x + 2$.

Revision Questions 3.1

Complete the following statements	*Answers*	*Refer to*
1. The graphs of functions are either continuous or . . .	**1.** discontinuous	Section 3.2 Fig. 2.2
2. The gradient of a tangent to a curve can be obtained by . . . the appropriate function.	**2.** differentiating	Section 3.2
3. A . . . can be thought of as meeting a curve in two coincident points.	**3.** tangent	Section 3.2 Fig. 3.6
4. If the slope of a normal at any point on a curve is m then the slope of the tangent at that point is . . .	**4.** $-1/m$	Section 3.3
5. Two tangents with slopes m_1 and m_2 are at right-angles if . . .	**5.** $m_1m_2 = -1$	Section 3.3

Exercises 3.1

1. The modulus of a number x, written as $|x|$, is such that

$$|x| = x \quad \text{if } x \geqslant 0$$
$$= -x \text{ if } x < 0$$

thus $|5| = 5$, $|-2{\cdot}5| = 2{\cdot}5$, $|-\pi| = \pi$.

Sketch the graphs of the functions

(i) $f(x) = |x|$ (ii) $f(x) = |x - 3|$ (iii) $f(x) = \sin |x|$.

Are these graphs continuous or discontinuous?

2. Sketch the graphs of (i) $y = -x^2$, (ii) $y = (x - 2)(x + 1)$ for the range of values $x = -3$ to $x = +3$.

3. Find the equations of the tangents and the normals to the curve $y = x^3 - 1$ at the points (1, 0) and (−2, −9).

4. Find the equations of the tangents to the curve $y = 2x^3 + 3x^2 + 7$ which are parallel to the line $y = 12x + 7$.

5. Find the equations of the normals to the curve $y = x^2 - x - 6$ at the points where it crosses the x-axis.

6. Find the equations of the tangent and normal to the curve $y = e^{-3x} + 5x - 5$ at the point (0, −4).

7. Show that the tangents to the curve $y = x^3/3 - x^2/4 - x - 1/12$ at the points $x = 1$ and $x = 2$ are at right-angles.

8. Find the coordinates of the point at which the tangent to the curve $y = 2 \ln x - 3x^2 + 4x$ is parallel to the x-axis. Why is the value $x = -\frac{1}{3}$ inadmissible? What is the equation of the normal to the curve at that point?

9. In a chemical reaction the rate of the reaction is monitored by observing the pressure p, in centimetres of mercury, of an evolved gas at any time t. The relation between p and t is given by $\frac{dp}{dt} = k(25 - p)$.

When the reaction was carried out at 45°C the following values were obtained

t (min)	0	10	15	25	35	50	60
p (cm of mercury)	0	4·53	6·48	9·84	12·58	15·80	17·47

Draw a graph of p against t. Obtain the values of dp/dt corresponding to the values $p = 4, 8, 12, 16$ by drawing tangents to the curve and measuring their gradients. Show that the graph of dp/dt against corresponding values of $(25 - p)$ is a straight line. Find the slope of the line; this is also the value of k. (Note $dp/dt = k(25 - p) \equiv Y = kX$.)

10. Using the method of example 9 in Chapter Two, show that the general solution of the equation $dp/dt = k(25 - p)$ for which $p = 0$ when $t = 0$ is $p = 25 - 25e^{-kt}$. Find the value of k using any pair of values (other than the first) given in the table in question 9. Compare this value with your answer to question 9.

3.4 Maxima and Minima

It is important to realise that in a mathematical sense a maximum value of a continuous function* is one which is greater than the values near to it on both sides. Thus a 'maximum' is not necessarily the greatest value. In

* In this section it is assumed not only that the function is continuous but that its first and second derivatives also exist.

Fig. 3.8 the value $f(x_4)$ of the function, which is represented by the point S, is a maximum because points A and B near to it on either side represent smaller values of the function. As is easily seen, $f(x_4)$ is not the greatest value. Similarly, a minimum value of a continuous function is one which is less than the values near to it on either side. This is not necessarily the least value. Again in Fig. 3.8, the value $f(x_2)$ of the function represented by the point Q is a minimum, but $f(x_2)$ is not the least value. We sometimes talk of local maxima or local minima, or **turning points.**

The position of the points Q and S can readily be found by using the property that the tangent at such a point is parallel to the x-axis: that is, the tangent has zero slope and the derivative $f'(x)$ has a zero value at such points.

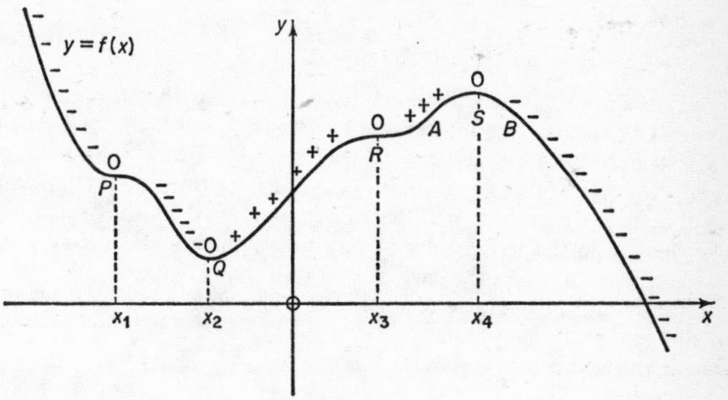

Fig. 3.8

To decide if the points are truly local maxima or minima the sign (but not the size) of the derivative is considered. In Fig. 3.8 the graph of the function $y = f(x)$ has been drawn and the sign of its derivative marked on the graph: when the value of the function is *decreasing* with increasing values of x then $f'(x)$ has a negative sign. When the value of the function is *increasing* with increasing values of x then $f'(x)$ has a positive sign. At points like P, Q, R, and S, where the value of $f'(x)$ is zero, we say that the function has a stationary value and they are known as **stationary points.** It is clear that:

(a) At a stationary point $f'(x) = 0$.
(b) At a local maximum the value of $f'(x)$ changes sign from positive to zero to negative as x increases.
(c) At a local minimum the value of $f'(x)$ changes sign from negative to zero to positive as x increases.
(d) There are stationary points where the value of $f'(x)$ does not change sign but goes from
positive to zero to positive as x increases (for example, the point R)
negative to zero to negative as x increases (for example, the point P)

At points such as P and R, if a tangent was drawn to the curve it would cross the curve and these points are generally known as **points of inflexion.** In the particular case of P and R we say they are *horizontal* points of inflexion because the tangent to the curve is horizontal. The general theory of points of inflexion will be considered later. To find the turning points, $f'(x)$ is equated to zero. Examination of the sign of $f'(x)$ on either side of these points enables us to distinguish between them.

Example 6. Find the nature of the stationary points of the function $f(x) = 3x^5 + 6x^4 - 4x^3 + 1$.

$$f(x) = 3x^5 + 6x^4 - 4x^3 + 1$$

$$\therefore \quad f'(x) = 15x^4 + 24x^3 - 12x^2$$

At the stationary points, $f'(x) = 0$; that is

$$f'(x) = 15x^4 + 24x^3 - 12x^2 = 0$$
$$3x^2 (5x^2 + 8x - 4) = 0$$
$$3x^2 (5x - 2) (x + 2) = 0$$

$$\therefore \quad x = 0, 2/5 \text{ or } -2$$

In distinguishing between these points it is stressed that the magnitude of the value of $f'(x)$ does not matter—only its sign—and that the sign of $f'(x)$ *near to* the stationary points $x = 0$, 0·4 and -2 means in the *immediate neighbourhood* of the points. While it is helpful to think of actual values—for example, in the case of $x = 0$ the values $-0{\cdot}1$, 0, 0·1—they must be small enough to exclude the value of x at any neighbouring stationary point (or point of discontinuity). In the case of $x = 0$ in the above example, the values $-0{\cdot}5$, 0, 0·5 would give a false result because they overlap $x = 0{\cdot}4$, the value of x at the next stationary point.

Consider the value $x = 0$

when $x = -0{\cdot}1$

$$f'(x) = 3(-0{\cdot}1)^2[5(-0{\cdot}1) - 2][-0{\cdot}1 + 2]$$
$$= (+\text{ve}) \quad (-\text{ve}) \quad (+\text{ve})$$
$$= -\text{ve}$$

when $x = 0$

$$f'(x) = 0$$

when $x = +0{\cdot}1$

$$f'(x) = 3(+0{\cdot}1)^2[5(+0{\cdot}1) - 2][+0{\cdot}1 + 2]$$
$$= (+\text{ve}) \quad (-\text{ve}) \quad (+\text{ve})$$
$$= -\text{ve}$$

At $x = 0$ the value of $f'(x)$ goes from negative to zero to negative and there is a horizontal point of inflexion. The shape of the curve is like that shown at point P in Fig. 3.8.

Consider the value $x = 2/5$ (0·4)

when $x = 0{\cdot}3$

$$f'(x) = 3(0{\cdot}3)^2[5(0{\cdot}3) - 2](0{\cdot}3 + 2)$$
$$= (+\text{ve}) \quad (-\text{ve}) \quad (+\text{ve})$$
$$= -\text{ve}$$

when $x = 0{\cdot}4$

$$f'(x) = 0$$

when $x = 0{\cdot}5$

$$\begin{aligned} f'(x) &= 3(0{\cdot}5)^2[5(0{\cdot}5) - 2](0{\cdot}5 + 2) \\ &= (+\text{ve}) \quad (+\text{ve}) \quad (+\text{ve}) \\ &= +\text{ve} \end{aligned}$$

At $x = 0{\cdot}4$ the value of $f'(x)$ goes from negative to zero to positive and there is a minimum value of $f(x)$ given by

$$\begin{aligned} f(0{\cdot}4) &= 3(0{\cdot}4)^5 + 6(0{\cdot}4)^4 - 4(0{\cdot}4)^3 + 1 \\ &= 0{\cdot}928 \end{aligned}$$

Consider the value $x = -2$

when $x = -2{\cdot}1$

$$\begin{aligned} f'(x) &= 3(-2{\cdot}1)^2[5(-2{\cdot}1) - 2](-2{\cdot}1 + 2) \\ &= (+\text{ve}) \quad (-\text{ve}) \quad (-\text{ve}) \\ &= +\text{ve} \end{aligned}$$

when $x = -2$

$$f'(x) = 0$$

when $x = -1{\cdot}9$

$$\begin{aligned} f'(x) &= 3(-1{\cdot}9)^2[5(-1{\cdot}9) - 2](-1{\cdot}9 + 2) \\ &= (+\text{ve}) \quad (-\text{ve}) \quad (+\text{ve}) \\ &= -\text{ve} \end{aligned}$$

At $x = -2$ the value of $f'(x)$ goes from positive to zero to negative and there is a maximum value of $f(x)$ given by

$$\begin{aligned} f(-2) &= 3(-2)^5 + 6(-2)^4 - 4(-2)^3 + 1 \\ &= 33 \end{aligned}$$

An alternative method for finding the maxima and minima of a function (but *not* horizontal inflexions) is to use the second derivative of the function. On passing through a maximum value of $f(x)$ in the direction of x increasing, the value of $f'(x)$ changes from positive to zero to negative; that is, $f'(x)$ decreases and therefore the rate of change of $f'(x)$ with respect to x—that is, $d[f'(x)]/dx$ or $f''(x)$—is negative. Similarly, on passing through a minimum value of $f(x)$ in the direction of x increasing, the value of $f'(x)$ changes from negative to zero to positive; that is, $f'(x)$ increases and its rate of change $f''(x)$ is positive. To sum up

If $f'(x) = 0$ and $f''(x)$ is negative there is a maximum
If $f'(x) = 0$ and $f''(x)$ is positive there is a minimum

It must be stressed that when $f'(x)$ and $f''(x)$ are both zero *no* conclusion can be reached without further investigation and we have to return to our first method of distinguishing between stationary points by examination of the sign of $f'(x)$.

Example 7. Find the nature of the stationary points of the function $f(x) = 2x^6 - 3x^4$

$$\begin{aligned} f(x) &= 2x^6 - 3x^4 \\ f'(x) &= 12x^5 - 12x^3 \\ f''(x) &= 60x^4 - 36x^2 \end{aligned}$$

At the stationary points $f'(x) = 0$; that is

$$f'(x) = 12x^5 - 12x^3 = 0$$
$$12x^3(x^2 - 1) = 0$$
$$12x^3(x - 1)(x + 1) = 0$$

$$\therefore \quad x = 0, 1, \text{ or } -1$$

When $x = 1$, $f''(1) = 60 - 36 = 24$, which is positive and therefore at $x = 1$ the function has a minimum value $f(1) = 2 - 3 = -1$.

When $x = -1$, $f''(x) = 60 - 36 = 24$, which is positive and therefore at $x = -1$ the function also has a minimum value $f(-1) = 2 - 3 = -1$.

When $x = 0$, $f'(x) = 0$ and also $f''(x) = 0$. We therefore proceed as in example 6

When $x = -0{\cdot}1$

$$f'(x) = 12(-0{\cdot}1)^3\,(-0{\cdot}1 - 1)(-0{\cdot}1 + 1)$$
$$= (-\text{ve}) \qquad (-\text{ve}) \qquad (+\text{ve})$$
$$= +\text{ve}$$

when $x = 0$

$$f'(x) = 0$$

when $x = +0{\cdot}1$

$$f'(x) = 12(+0{\cdot}1)^3\,(+0{\cdot}1 - 1)(+0{\cdot}1 + 1)$$
$$= (+\text{ve}) \qquad (-\text{ve}) \qquad (+\text{ve})$$
$$= -\text{ve}$$

At $x = 0$ the value of $f'(x)$ goes from positive to zero to negative and there is a maximum value of the function given by

$$f(0) = 2(0)^6 - 3(0)^4 = 0$$

The case when $f'(x) = 0$ and $f''(x) = 0$ must always be investigated further. In fact, such cases can give horizontal points of inflexion, but can also give maxima or minima points.

In each of the following three cases

$$\text{(i) } f(x) = (x - 1)^4 \quad \text{(ii) } g(x) = -(x - 1)^4 \quad \text{(iii) } h(x) = (x - 1)^5$$

$x = 1$ gives a stationary value with the value of the second derivative zero. However

at $x = 1$

$f(x)$ has a minimum value
$g(x)$ has a maximum value

and

$h(x)$ has a horizontal point of inflexion

Example 8. Using the results of example 7 sketch the graph of the function $f(x) = 2x^6 - 3x^4$.

Summarising the results obtained in example 7

when $x = -1$ $\quad f(x) = -1$ and there is a minimum value
when $x = 0$ $\quad f(x) = 0$ and there is a maximum value
when $x = +1$ $\quad f(x) = -1$ and there is a minimum value

These facts are illustrated in Fig. 3.9.

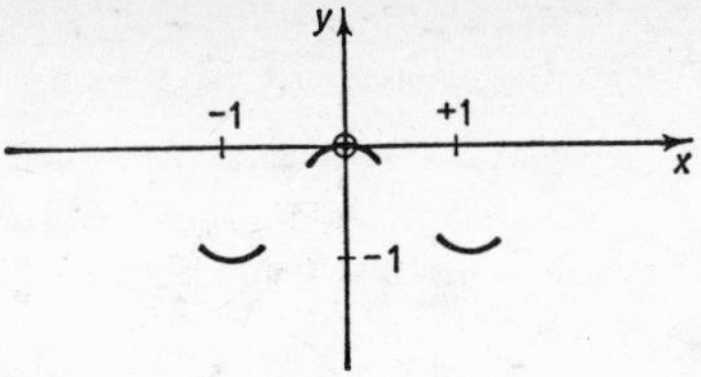

Fig. 3.9

There is one further very important deduction that we can make, namely that there are NO MORE stationary points on the graph because $f'(x) = 0$ gave only these three solutions. The evidence is not entirely sufficient as the graph could be discontinuous, as in the case of $f(x) = x/(x - 2)$, where $x = 2$ gives a zero in the denominator which is inadmissible. However, the given function is not fractional and we can complete the graph fairly confidently as shown in Fig 3.10. Note the symmetry

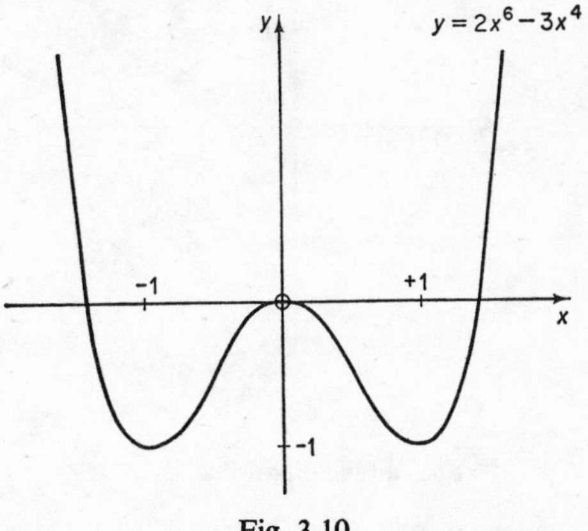

Fig. 3.10

about the y-axis because the function consists of only even powers of x. (Refer to the definition of an Even Function in section 9.6.)

Example 9. Sketch the graph of the function $f(x) = \dfrac{4x^2 + 9}{x}$.

$$f(x) = \frac{4x^2}{x} + \frac{9}{x}$$

$$= 4x + \frac{9}{x}$$

$$f'(x) = 4 - \frac{9}{x^2}$$

$$f''(x) = +\frac{18}{x^3}$$

The stationary values are given by $f'(x) = 0$

i.e. $$4 - \frac{9}{x^2} = 0$$

$$x^2 = \frac{9}{4}$$

$$x = \pm\frac{3}{2}$$

At $x = \frac{3}{2}$ $$f(\tfrac{3}{2}) = \frac{4(\frac{3}{2})^2 + 9}{\frac{3}{2}} = 12$$

and $$f''(\tfrac{3}{2}) = \frac{18}{(\frac{3}{2})^3} \text{ (which is positive)}$$

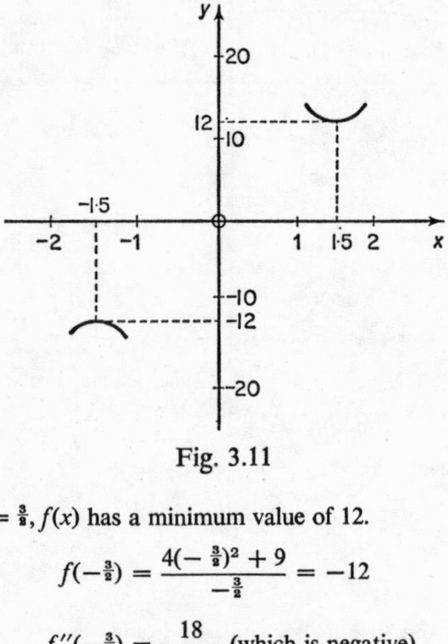

Fig. 3.11

Therefore when $x = \frac{3}{2}$, $f(x)$ has a minimum value of 12.

At $x = -\frac{3}{2}$ $$f(-\tfrac{3}{2}) = \frac{4(-\frac{3}{2})^2 + 9}{-\frac{3}{2}} = -12$$

and $$f''(-\tfrac{3}{2}) = \frac{18}{(-\frac{3}{2})^3} \text{ (which is negative)}$$

Therefore when $x = -\frac{3}{2}$, $f(x)$ has a maximum value of -12.

Also, there are only two stationary values.

These two results are illustrated in Fig. 3.11. The two pieces of graph cannot be joined without, at least, one more maximum and one more minimum point, and there are *no more* stationary values. However, again consider the function $f(x) = 4x + \frac{9}{x}$; because division by zero has no meaning $f(x)$ is not defined at $x = 0$.

Consider $x \to 0+$ (that is, x takes numerically smaller and smaller positive values, e.g. $+\frac{1}{10}$, $+\frac{1}{100}$, $+\frac{1}{1000}$, . . .); then the value of $f(x)$ becomes very large positively. Similarly, as $x \to 0-$ (that is, x takes numerically smaller and smaller negative values, e.g. $-\frac{1}{10}$, $-\frac{1}{100}$, $-\frac{1}{1000}$, . . .), the value of $f(x)$ becomes very large negatively. Finally, as x becomes numerically very large positively or negatively, $f(x) \simeq 4x$.

The graph of $f(x)$ is shown in Fig. 3.12.

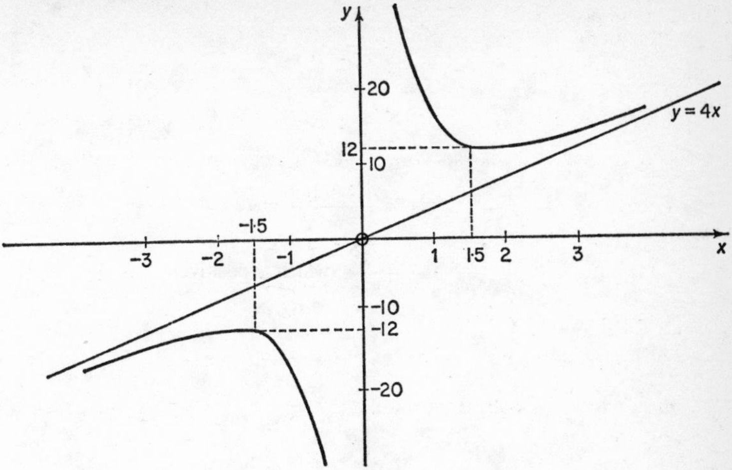

Fig. 3.12

Example 10. In a tri-molecular chemical reaction the speed of reaction v after time t is given by

$$v = k(-x^3/3 + x^2 + 35x) + C$$

k and C being positive constants and x the quantity which has reacted after time t. Find the values of x which give maximum or minimum values of v.

$$v = -kx^3/3 + kx^2 + 35kx + C$$

$$\frac{dv}{dx} = -kx^2 + 2kx + 35k$$

$$\frac{d^2v}{dx^2} = -2kx + 2k$$

At the stationary points $\dfrac{dv}{dx} = 0$

$\therefore$

$$-kx^2 + 2kx + 35k = 0$$
$$-k(x - 7)(x + 5) = 0$$
$$x = -5 \text{ or } 7$$

The negative value of x has no meaning, in a practical sense, and is therefore ignored.

When $x = 7$ $\qquad \dfrac{d^2v}{dx^2} = -2k(7) + 2k = -12k$

which is negative, k being a positive constant; therefore when $x = 7$ the speed of the reaction is a maximum.

Example 11. The profit P obtained by selling N articles is given by $P = -0{\cdot}01N^3 + 900\,NM^2$, where M is the cost of producing each article, presumed constant. Find the maximum value of P. We assume that N is large so that treating it as a continuous variable can give useful results.

$$P = -0{\cdot}01N^3 + 900NM^2$$

$$\frac{dP}{dN} = -0{\cdot}03N^2 + 900M^2$$

$$\frac{d^2P}{dN^2} = -0{\cdot}06N \qquad (M \text{ is a constant})$$

At the stationary points $\frac{dP}{dN} = 0$

$$\therefore \quad -0{\cdot}03N^2 + 900M^2 = 0$$

$$900M^2 = +0{\cdot}03N^2$$

$$N^2 = 30\,000M^2$$

$$N = \pm 100\sqrt{3}M$$

Practically, the negative value is impossible.

When $N = 100\sqrt{3}M$ $\qquad \frac{d^2P}{dN^2} = -0{\cdot}06 \times 100\sqrt{3}M$

$$= -6\sqrt{3}M \qquad \text{which is negative}$$
$$(M \text{ is given as positive})$$

Thus P has a maximum value when $N = 100\sqrt{3}M$*, given by

$$P_{max} = -0{\cdot}01(100\sqrt{3}M)^3 + 900(100\sqrt{3}M)M^2$$
$$= 100\sqrt{3}M^3(-300 + 900)$$
$$= 60\,000\sqrt{3}M^3$$

Example 12. A uniformly loaded beam of length L is freely supported at both ends The deflection y at any point distance x from one end is given by

$$EIy = \frac{w}{24}(x^4 - 2x^3L + L^3x)$$

w, E, I being positive constants. Show that the deflection at the centre of the beam is a maximum.

$$y = \frac{w}{24EI}(x^4 - 2x^3L + L^3x)$$

To simplify the working let $k = \frac{w}{24EI}$

$$\therefore \quad y = kx^4 - 2kx^3L + kL^3x$$

$$\frac{dy}{dx} = 4kx^3 - 6kx^2L + kL^3$$

$$\frac{d^2y}{dx^2} = 12kx^2 - 12kxL$$

* In practice this is rounded to the nearest whole number.

at the centre of the beam $x = L/2$

$$\frac{dy}{dx} = 4k(L/2)^3 - 6kL(L/2)^2 + kL^3$$
$$= kL^3/2 - 3kL^3/2 + kL^3$$
$$= 0$$
$$\frac{d^2y}{dx^2} = 12k(L/2)^2 - 12kL(L/2)$$
$$= 3kL^2 - 6kL^2$$
$$= -3kL^2$$

which is negative, and the deflection of the beam at its centre is a maximum given by

$$y = \frac{w}{24EI}[(L/2)^4 - 2(L/2)^3L + L^3(L/2)]$$
$$= \frac{wL^4}{24EI}\left(\frac{1}{16} - \frac{1}{4} + \frac{1}{2}\right)$$
$$= \frac{5wL^4}{384EI}$$

Revision Questions 3.2

If you complete any one of the following statements incorrectly, re-read Section 3.4.

Complete the following statements	*Answers*
1. (a) For a maximum value of the function $f(x)$, it is sufficient that $f'(x) = 0$ and $f''(x)$ is . . .	**1.** (a) negative.
(b) For a minimum value of the function $f(x)$, it is sufficient that $f'(x) = 0$ and $f''(x)$ is . . .	(b) positive.
(c) A function $f(x)$ is such that $f'(2{\cdot}9)$ is positive, $f'(3)$ is zero, $f'(3{\cdot}1)$ is positive. At $x = 3$ there is a . . .	(c) horizontal point of inflexion.
(d) $f'(x) = 0$ is found to be a quadratic equation in x; therefore the graph of the function $f(x)$ can have at the most . . . stationary points.	(d) two.
2. A function $f(x)$ is such that $f'(x_1)$ and $f''(x_1)$ are both equal to zero. At the point $x = x_1$ does $f(x)$ have (i) a maximum value (ii) a minimum value (iii) a horizontal point of inflexion?	**2.** It could be any of the three. We cannot tell without further investigation.

Exercises 3.2

1. A belt moving at a speed of v transmits a power P given by the equation $P = Tv - wv^3/g$, where T, w, g are positive constants. Find in terms of T, w, g the speed for which P is a maximum.

2. Find the stationary points of the function $f(x) = 3x^4 + 4x^3 - 12x^2 + 2$. Distinguish between them and sketch the graph.

3. Find the stationary points of the function $f(x) = x^4 - 16x^3 + 72x^2$. Distinguish between them and sketch the graph.

4. Show that the derivative of the function $f(x) = 4x^5 + 15x^4 + 20x^3 + 10x^2$ can be expressed in the form $20x(x + 1)^3$. Find the stationary points, distinguish between them and sketch the graph of the function.

5. A uniformly loaded beam of length L is fixed at both ends. The deflection y at any distance x from one end is given by $EIy = \frac{w}{24}(x^4 - 2Lx^3 + L^2x^2)$, where w, E, I are positive constants. Find the maximum deflection of the beam in terms of w, E, I, L.

6. Two consecutive integers are represented by $(x - 1)$ and x. A function $R(x)$ is defined as the ratio of the square of the first integer to the square of the second one. Make a table of values of $R(x)$ for values of x between $x = -4$ and $x = +4$ for which it is defined. Does $x = 1$ give a minimum value of $R(x)$? Would it be correct to use the first and second derivatives of $R(x)$ to find this minimum value? What is the graph of the function $R(x)$?

7. The power P dissipated along a blood vessel of radius r and length L is given by $P = f^2k/r^4 + K\pi r^2L$, where f, K, k are positive constants. Verify that for a given length of blood vessel of varying radius r there is a stationary point in the value of P when $r^6 = \frac{2f^2k}{K\pi L}$ and that this stationary point represents a minimum loss of power.

8. The gain G when N units of an item are sold is given by $G = 4{\cdot}8N - 0{\cdot}00\,001N^3$. Find the maximum value of G. Sketch the graph of G against N. Is the maximum value of G, practically, the greatest possible value of G?

9. A particle is moving in a straight line so that at time t its distance s from a fixed point P on the line is given by $s = 75t - t^3$. Find the maximum value of s.

10. Show that the maximum and minimum values of the function $f(x) = x + 1 + 9/x$ are $f(3) = 7$ (a minimum value) and $f(-3) = -5$ (a maximum value). Note that the minimum value is greater than the maximum value. Explain this apparent discrepancy by sketching the graph of the function.

3.5 Approximations and Errors

We are interested in the errors which arise due to the insensitivity or coarseness of measuring instruments—not the ones which are due to the misreading or miscopying of a figure, or the incorrect reading of an instrument. The number of tiles on a roof can generally be found with absolute accuracy as, say, 833, but the weight of a tile cannot be found with the same exactness. The weight ascribed to a tile would depend on the sensitivity of the measuring instrument. It could be given as 6·10 kg, which indicates that the weight is given to the nearest 1/100 kg, so that the possible error lies between ±0·005 kg. In calculating the mass of the tiles on the roof (833 × 6·10 = 5081·3 kg), the accuracy of the final answer would be affected by the uncertainty in the mass of a tile, but not by the number of tiles, which is exact. The possible error in the final answer is $833 \times \pm 0{\cdot}005 \simeq \pm 4$ kg and the answer would be quoted as 5081 ± 4 kg or even as 5080 kg, which is correct enough for most practical purposes.

Notice the last phrase 'correct enough for most practical purposes'. Any value whose possible error is too small to affect the required accuracy of the final result can be taken as exact. A number like π can be taken as 22/7, or if this is not sufficiently accurate as 3·1416 or 3·1415926. Because, by using a computer, it can be found to any desired number of places, it is therefore to be looked on as exact. It is quantities such as weight, length, volume, time, percentage of impurity, density, temperature, etc., which always have a margin of error in which we are interested.

More importantly, how does the use of such approximations or 'inaccurate' values affect the accuracy of our conclusions? Practically, a measurement of a length r will have a small error which can be represented by δr. A calculation of an area A using the value of r will have a corresponding error δA and we are interested in the relation between δA and δr where A depends on r or, in our notation, $A = f(r)$. Referring back to section 1.10, we saw that

$$\lim_{\delta r \to 0} \frac{\delta A}{\delta r} = \frac{dA}{dr} = f'(r)$$

If δr is small we may write

$$\frac{\delta A}{\delta r} = f'(r) + \varepsilon$$

where ε is small and tends to zero as δr tends to zero

or $$\delta A \simeq f'(r)\delta r \qquad (3.2)$$

This relation is approximately true for any small quantity δr and can be used to find the possible error in a calculation caused by errors or uncertainties in the data.

Example 13. The time T of swing of a simple pendulum was measured and found to be 2·007 s and its length L was measured to be 100 cm. The value of g, the acceleration due to gravity, was found from the formula $g = 4\pi^2 L/T^2$ to be 980·2 cm/s². It is known that there is a possible error of $\pm$ 0·2 cm in measuring L. Assuming that T is correct, find between what limits the correct value of g must lie.

From equation 3.2

$$\delta g = \frac{d(4\pi^2 L/T^2)}{dL}\,\delta L$$

$$= \frac{4\pi^2}{T^2}\,\delta L \text{ (}T\text{ being regarded as constant)}$$

$$= \frac{4\pi^2}{(2{\cdot}007)^2}(\pm 0{\cdot}2)$$

$$\therefore \quad \delta g = \pm 1{\cdot}96 \text{ cm/s}^2$$

and the correct value of g lies between $980{\cdot}2 \pm 2{\cdot}0$—that is, 978·2 and 982·2 cm/s².

If the proportional or percentage errors in both L and T are known we can find the proportional or percentage error in the calculated value of g by the use of logarithms. From equation 3.2

$$\delta(\ln x) = \frac{d(\ln x)}{dx}\delta x$$

$$= \frac{1}{x}\delta x \text{ (from equation 2.22)} \qquad (3.3)$$

which is the proportional change in x. Multiplying both sides by 100

$$100\,\delta(\ln x) = 100\delta x/x \qquad (3.4)$$

which is the percentage change in x.

Example 14. Given that the errors in measuring L and T for a simple pendulum are $\pm$ 0·2% and $\pm$ 0·1% respectively, find the possible percentage error when calculating the value of g from the formula $g = 4\pi^2L/T^2$.

$$g = 4\pi^2L/T^2$$

$$\therefore \quad \ln g = \ln 4\pi^2 + \ln L - 2\ln T$$

$$\delta(\ln g) = \delta(\ln 4\pi^2) + \delta(\ln L) - 2\delta(\ln T)$$

$$\therefore \quad \frac{d(\ln g)}{dg}\delta g = 0 + \frac{d(\ln L)}{dL}\delta L - 2\frac{d(\ln T)}{dT}\delta T$$

Note that $\delta(\ln 4\pi^2)$ is zero because there is no change in an exact value.

$$\frac{1}{g}\delta g = \frac{1}{L}\delta L - 2\frac{1}{T}\delta T \text{ (from equation 3.3)}$$

$$\therefore \quad \frac{100\,\delta g}{g} = \frac{100\,\delta L}{L} - 2\frac{100\,\delta T}{T}$$

or (% error in g) = (% error in L) $-2 \times$ (% error in T).

The maximum positive % error in g = 0·2% − 2(−0·1%)
= 0·4%

Note that we have calculated the largest possible positive error in g by using a positive error in L and a negative error in T. Similarly,

The maximum negative % error in g = −0·2% − 2(+0·1%)
= −0·4%

Example 15. An electric fire has a resistance of 22 ohms and is connected to 220-volt mains. The power P watts that it uses is given by $P = V^2/R$, where V is the voltage and R is the resistance. During a period of power cuts the voltage of the mains drops to 210 volts. Find the approximate change in the power used.

The resistance of the fire is assumed to remain constant and only the voltage to alter. Therefore we consider

$$\delta P = \frac{dP}{dV}\delta V$$

$$= \frac{d(V^2/R)}{dV}\delta V$$

$$= \frac{2V}{R}\delta V$$

$$= \frac{2 \times 220}{22}(-10)$$

$$= -200 \text{ watts}$$

The drop in the amount of power used is 0·2 kilowatts.

Exercises 3.3

1. In an adiabatic expansion the pressure p N/cm² and volume v cm³ of a gas are connected by the equation $pv^{1\cdot 4} = C$, where C is a constant. Initially, $p = 40$ and $v = 2500$. The volume is increased by 10 cm³. Using the approximate relation $\delta p = \frac{dp}{dv}\,\delta v$, find the corresponding change in p.

2. The radius r of a spherical balloon is increased from 20 cm to 20·1 cm. Find the resulting change in its surface area ($A = 4\pi r^2$).

3. The power P required to drive a ship is given by $P = kv^3L^2$, where v is its speed and L is its wetted length. Prove that a 5% increase in the speed and a 3% decrease in length will require approximately a 9% increase in power (refer to example 14).

4. The number N of bacteria in a colony at time t hours is given by $N = k\,e^{2t}$, where k is a constant. Show that an actual error of 0·03 h in the observed value of t will give a 6% error in the value of N.

5. A retailer found that his net profit P when selling a number n of a certain article per week is given by

$$P = £(750n - 0{\cdot}1n^3 - 20\,000)$$

He is selling 40 articles per week. Show that if n increases from 40 to 41 his profit will increase. Later, when he is selling 60 articles per week, show that an increase in n from 60 to 61 will cause a decrease in his profit. Give reasons why this seemingly unusual result might be true.

Revision Questions 3.3

The following questions cover the work done in the first three chapters. If you fail to answer any of these questions you are strongly advised to re-read the appropriate section before going on to Chapter Four.

Complete the following statements	*Answers*	*Refer to*
1. δx means . . .	**1.** a little bit of x. It can be either a decrease or an increase.	Section 1.2
2. Smallness is . . .	**2.** relative.	Section 1.3
3. If 0·1 is of the first degree of smallness then $(0{\cdot}1)^2$ is of the . . .	**3.** second degree of smallness.	Section 1.4
4. $V = f(r)$ is read as . . .	**4.** V is a function of r.	Section 1.5
5. In Exercises 3.3, n the number of items sold is a . . . variable.	**5.** discontinuous.	Section 1.6
6. $\delta p/\delta r$ is an . . . rate of change of p with respect to r.	**6.** average.	Section 1.8 Section 1.9

Complete the following statements	*Answers*	*Refer to*
7. $\frac{d(p^3)}{dp} = \ldots \frac{\delta(p^3)}{\delta p}$	7. $\lim_{\delta p \to 0}$	Section 1.9
8. $\frac{d(5x^3 + 3)}{dx} = \ldots$	8. $15x^2$	Section 1.11 Section 1.12
9. If $p = \frac{dy}{dx}$ then $\frac{dp}{dx} = \ldots$	9. $\frac{d^2y}{dx^2}$	Section 1.14
10. The statement 'The rate of change of current i with respect to the time t is proportional to the applied voltage v' is written in symbols as . . .	10. $\frac{di}{dt} \propto v$ or $\frac{di}{dt} = kv$	Section 2.1
11. $\frac{d(e^{ax})}{dx} = \ldots$	11. $a\,e^{ax}$	Section 2.2
12. $e^{3x} . e^{4x} = \ldots$	12. e^{7x}	Section 2.2
13. $\frac{d(\ln X)}{dX} = \ldots$	13. $1/X$	Section 2.3
14. The graph of the function $y = 1/(x + 3)$ will have a . . . at the point $x = -3$.	14. discontinuity	Sections 1.6 and 3.2
15. The slope of the tangent to the graph of the function $y = f(x)$ at any point is given by . . .	15. the value of $f'(x)$ at that point.	Section 3.3
16. If $f'(x_1) = 0$ and $f''(x_1)$ is positive then $f(x_1)$ is a . . . value of the function.	16. minimum	Section 3.4
17. If $f'(x_1) = 0$ and $f''(x_1) = 0$ then $f(x_1)$ can be . . .	17. either a maximum, minimum or a horizontal point of inflexion.	Section 3.4
18. If $y = f(x)$ then approximately $\delta y = \ldots$	18. $\frac{dy}{dx}\,\delta x$ or $\frac{d[f(x)]}{dx}\,\delta x$	Section 3.5

3.6 Problems

1. Find the third derivative of x^2, the fourth derivative of x^3, the fifth derivative of x^4 and deduce the $(n + 1)$th derivative of x^n where n is a positive integer.

2. The angle θ through which a flywheel rotates in time t is given by $\theta = 27\sqrt{t} + t^2$. Show that the angular acceleration $\dfrac{d^2\theta}{dt^2}$ is zero when $t = 2\frac{1}{4}$.

3. The distance s moved by a particle in time t is given by $s = 8t^3$. Show that its speed $v(=ds/dt)$ can be expressed as $6s^{\frac{2}{3}}$ and hence that its acceleration d^2s/dt^2 is equal to $v\,dv/ds$.

4. The pressure p and the volume v of a gas are connected by the relation $pv^{1{\cdot}4} = k$, where k is a constant. Find the elasticity of volume of the gas, defined as $-v\,dp/dv$, in terms of v and k. Hence show that the rate of change of the elasticity of volume with respect to v is equal to $-1{\cdot}96p/v$.

5. The Allometric Law in biology predicts that the relation between total metabolic rate T and body weight W for homothermic animals is $T = \alpha W^{\beta}$. From experimental data it is found that $\alpha = 50$, $\beta = 0{\cdot}75$. What is the possible error in estimating the total metabolic rate of a beef cow whose weight is given as 400 ± 5 kg?

The attention of our readers is again drawn to the fact that relationships between two variables from widely different fields often have the same type of mathematical model. In question 4 for a gas we had $p = kv^{-1{\cdot}4}$; in question 5 concerning metabolic rates in animals we had $T = \alpha W^{0{\cdot}75}$.

6. A retailer estimates that his profit P when selling x items per week is given by $P = £(7{\cdot}5x - 0{\cdot}000\,01x^3 - 2000)$. Find his maximum possible profit. Sketch a graph of P against x and estimate the range of values of x for which he makes a profit.

7. Calculate the maximum and minimum values of the function $f(x) = 2x^5 - 5x^4$ and sketch its graph.

8. Prove that the function $f(x) = x^3 + 2x^2 + 2x + 1$ has no maximum or minimum values.

9. Kramer's formula* for the opacity K (light absorption factor) of plasma for radiation passing through it is $K = K_0\rho^2T^{-3{\cdot}5}$, where K_0 is a constant, ρ is the density and T the absolute temperature. Show that for a $0{\cdot}1\%$ increase in the temperature, ρ remaining constant, K decreases by approximately $0{\cdot}35\%$.

10. Given the function $f(x) = 64 \ln x - x^4$, solve the algebraic equation $f'(x) = 0$ and explain why one of its roots cannot be taken as a turning point of the function $f(x)$.

11. The potential V at a distance r from a small constant charge q is given by $V = q/r$. Verify by differentiation and substitution that this expression is a solution of the equation

$$\frac{d^2V}{dr^2} + \frac{2}{r}\frac{dV}{dr} = 0 \text{ (Laplace's Equation)}$$

12. A number of metal tanks in the form of right circular cylinders of radius r metres and height h metres and closed at both ends, are to be made from sheet metal. They are to have a volume of 6 cubic metres and it is required to economise on the total amount of sheet metal used. Prove that the surface area S square metres of one tank is given by $S = 2\pi r^2 + 12/r$ and that when S is a minimum $h = 2r$.

* See *A Star Called the Sun*, by George Gamow, Pelican (page 109).

13. A farmer has 40 metres of movable fencing and wishes to make a rectangular pen to enclose as many sheep as possible. To do this he has to make the area A square metres of ground enclosed as large as possible. Show that if x metres is the length of the rectangle, its breadth is $(20 - x)$ metres. Hence, find an expression for A in terms of x and show that A has a maximum value of 100 when the area enclosed is a square.

14. If in question 13 the farmer was able to use a straight stretch of river as one, unfenced, side of the pen length x, show that the area enclosed would be given by $A = 20x - x^2/2$. Hence prove that the area enclosed now has a maximum value of 200 square metres.

15. A goods vehicle travels at a constant speed of x m.p.h. along a motorway. It uses fuel which costs £0·50 per gallon at a rate of $(1{\cdot}5 + x^2/450)$ gallons per hour $(10 < x < 70)$. Maintenance of the vehicle costs £0·25 per hour of use. Show that the total cost £C for a journey of N miles is given by $C = N/x + Nx/900$ and that the most economical speed is 30 m.p.h. The cost of maintaining a vehicle rises to £)·46 per hour of use. Find the new most economical speed.

16. The Post Office regulations state that they will accept only those parcels whose length and girth when added together come to less than 6 ft. There is no other constraint. Show that for a cylindrical parcel of radius r which just conforms with the regulations the volume V is given by $V = 6\pi r^2 - 2\pi^2 r^3$. Hence show that the maximum volume of a cylindrical parcel which conforms to the regulations is $8/\pi$.

17. An open rectangular box is to be made from a rectangular sheet of material 60 cm by 96 cm. Equal sized squares are removed from each of the four corners and the sides turned up. Find the largest volume which the box can contain.

18. Find a number x so that the sum of the squares of the differences between x and the five numbers 14, 11, 3, -2, -6 is a minimum. Show that in the general case with n numbers $N_1, N_2, \ldots N_n$ the value of x is the arithmetic mean of $N_1, N_2, \ldots N_n$.

19. Given that $xy = C$, where C is a constant, show that the minimum value of $x + y$ occurs when $x = y$. Deduce that the minimum value of $a \cot \theta + b \tan \theta$ where a, b are constants is $2\sqrt{(ab)}$.

20. Two ships A and B are sailing steadily with speeds u and v along courses which intersect at right angles at O. At a given instant they are both sailing towards O and $OA = a$, $OB = b$. Show that the minimum value of AB is given by $(av \sim bu)/\sqrt{(u^2 + v^2)}$. (Hint: Consider the minimum value of AB^2.)

CHAPTER FOUR

DERIVATIVES OF TRIGONOMETRICAL FUNCTIONS AND SOME THEOREMS ON DERIVATIVES

4.1 Introduction

In the previous three chapters, the usefulness of the technique of differentiation has been emphasised. With a knowledge of a limited number of derivatives $\mathrm{d}ax^n/\mathrm{d}x$, $\mathrm{d}e^{ax}/\mathrm{d}x$, and $\mathrm{d}a \ln x/\mathrm{d}x$, where a is a constant, a variety of problems have been solved. In order to widen the range of these problems, a wider knowledge of differentiation is required. We are confident that the reader will now be convinced that the time and effort spent in mastering some new techniques will be worthwhile.

In this chapter the derivatives of $\sin x$ and $\cos x$ are obtained from first principles, then some general theorems concerning derivatives are proved. These will greatly increase the number of functions which can be differentiated. There are also a number of routine exercises to give plenty of practice in the new techniques.

4.2 The Derivatives of sin x and cos x

As x changes to $x + \delta x$ then $\sin x$ changes to $\sin (x + \delta x)$. The change in $\sin x$ is equal to its new value minus its old value

or
$$\delta(\sin x) = \sin (x + \delta x) - \sin x$$

$$\therefore \quad \frac{\delta(\sin x)}{\delta x} = \frac{\sin (x + \delta x) - \sin x}{\delta x}$$

and
$$\frac{\mathrm{d}(\sin x)}{\mathrm{d}x} = \operatorname*{limit}_{\delta x \to 0} \frac{\delta(\sin x)}{\delta x} = \operatorname*{limit}_{\delta x \to 0} \frac{\sin (x + \delta x) - \sin x}{\delta x}$$

$$= \operatorname*{limit}_{\delta x \to 0} \frac{2 \cos [(x + \delta x + x)/2] \sin [(x + \delta x - x)/2]^*}{\delta x}$$

$$= \operatorname*{limit}_{\delta x \to 0} \frac{2 \cos \left(x + \dfrac{\delta x}{2}\right) \sin \left(\dfrac{\delta x}{2}\right)}{\delta x}$$

Now $\operatorname*{limit}_{\theta \to 0} \dfrac{\sin \theta}{\theta} = 1$ if the angle θ is *measured in radians.* In the above limit there is the sine of the angle $\delta x/2$; thus it is necessary to divide by $\delta x/2$ to use

* For proofs of this and any succeeding trigonometric identities which we use, refer to any standard textbook.

this result. Therefore, dividing the numerator and denominator of the fraction by 2

$$\frac{d(\sin x)}{dx} = \underset{\delta x \to 0}{\text{limit}} \frac{2\cos\left(x + \frac{\delta x}{2}\right)\sin\left(\frac{\delta x}{2}\right) \div 2}{\delta x \qquad \div 2}$$

$$= \underset{\delta x \to 0}{\text{limit}} \cos\left(x + \frac{\delta x}{2}\right) \frac{\sin\left(\frac{\delta x}{2}\right)}{\left(\frac{\delta x}{2}\right)}$$

$$= \underset{\delta x \to 0}{\text{limit}} \cos\left(x + \frac{\delta x}{2}\right) \underset{\delta x \to 0}{\text{limit}} \frac{\sin\left(\frac{\delta x}{2}\right)}{\frac{\delta x}{2}}$$

Assuming that the limiting value of a product of two functions is equal to the product of the separate limits

$$\therefore \quad \frac{d(\sin x)}{dx} = \cos x \times 1$$

$$= \cos x \text{ (where the angle } x \text{ is in radians)} \qquad (4.1)$$

Similarly, as x changes to $x + \delta x$ then $\cos x$ changes to $\cos(x + \delta x)$. The change in $\cos x$ is equal to its new value minus its old value

or $$\delta(\cos x) = \cos(x + \delta x) - \cos x$$

$$\therefore \quad \frac{\delta(\cos x)}{\delta x} = \frac{\cos(x + \delta x) - \cos x}{\delta x}$$

$$\therefore \quad \frac{d(\cos x)}{dx} = \underset{\delta x \to 0}{\text{limit}} \frac{\delta(\cos x)}{\delta x} = \underset{\delta x \to 0}{\text{limit}} \frac{\cos(x + \delta x) - \cos x}{\delta x}$$

$$= \underset{\delta x \to 0}{\text{limit}} \frac{-2\sin[(x + \delta x + x)/2]\sin[(x + \delta x - x)/2]}{\delta x}$$

$$= \underset{\delta x \to 0}{\text{limit}} \frac{-2\sin\left(x + \frac{\delta x}{2}\right)\sin\frac{\delta x}{2} \div 2}{\delta x \qquad \div 2}$$

$$= \underset{\delta x \to 0}{\text{limit}} -\sin\left(x + \frac{\delta x}{2}\right) \frac{\sin\frac{\delta x}{2}}{\frac{\delta x}{2}}$$

$$= \underset{\delta x \to 0}{\text{limit}} - \sin\left(x + \frac{\delta x}{2}\right) \underset{\delta x \to 0}{\text{limit}} \frac{\sin\frac{\delta x}{2}}{\frac{\delta x}{2}}$$

$$= -\sin x \,.\, 1$$

$$\frac{d(\cos x)}{dx} = -\sin x \text{ (where the angle } x \text{ is in radians)} \qquad (4.2)$$

The unknown variable x in formulae 4.1 and 4.2 can take a variety of forms; for example

$$\frac{d(\sin y)}{dy} = \cos y \qquad \frac{d(\cos y)}{dy} = -\sin y$$

$$\frac{d[\sin(3x)]}{d(3x)} = \cos(3x) \qquad \frac{d[\cos(5x)]}{d(5x)} = -\sin(5x)$$

$$\frac{d[\sin(p^3)]}{d(p^3)} = \cos(p^3) \qquad \frac{d[\cos(q^2)]}{d(q^2)} = -\sin(q^2)$$

$$\frac{d[\sin(2x-1)]}{d(2x-1)} = \cos(2x-1) \qquad \frac{d[\cos(3x^2-x)]}{d(3x^2-x)} = -\sin(3x^2-x)$$

It is left as an exercise for the reader to prove that when a is a constant

$$\frac{d(a \sin x)}{dx} = a \cos x \tag{4.3}$$

$$\frac{d(a \cos x)}{dx} = -a \sin x \tag{4.4}$$

The derivatives of other trigonometrical functions can be obtained from first principles, as shown in the following examples. Later in the chapter we shall develop techniques for finding derivatives of trigonometrical functions using the results of $d(\sin x)/dx$ and $d(\cos x)/dx$.

Example 1. Find from first principles the derivatives of (i) $\tan x$ ($x \neq (2n+1)\pi/2$) and (ii) $\cos^3 x$.

(i)
$$\begin{aligned}\delta(\tan x) &= \tan(x+\delta x) - \tan x \\ &= \frac{\sin(x+\delta x)}{\cos(x+\delta x)} - \frac{\sin x}{\cos x} \\ &= \frac{\sin(x+\delta x)\cos x - \cos(x+\delta x)\sin x}{\cos(x+\delta x)\cos x} \\ &= \frac{\sin[(x+\delta x) - x]}{\cos(x+\delta x)\cos x}\end{aligned}$$

$$\therefore \qquad \frac{\delta(\tan x)}{\delta x} = \frac{\sin(\delta x)}{\cos(x+\delta x)\cos x} \cdot \frac{1}{\delta x}$$

$$\therefore \qquad \frac{d(\tan x)}{dx} = \lim_{\delta x \to 0} \frac{\delta(\tan x)}{\delta x} = \lim_{\delta x \to 0} \frac{1}{\cos(x+\delta x)\cos x} \cdot \frac{\sin(\delta x)}{(\delta x)}$$

$$= \frac{1}{\cos^2 x} \cdot 1$$

$$= \sec^2 x$$

(ii) The derivative of $\cos^3 x$ is obtained by using the algebraic identity $A^3 - B^3 = (A - B)(A^2 + AB + B^2)$

$$\delta(\cos^3 x) = \cos^3 (x + \delta x) - \cos^3 x$$

$$= [\cos (x + \delta x) - \cos x][\cos^2 (x + \delta x) + \cos (x + \delta x) \cos x + \cos^2 x]$$

$$= \left[-2 \sin \left(x + \frac{\delta x}{2}\right) \sin \left(\frac{\delta x}{2}\right)\right][\cos^2 (x + \delta x) + \cos (x + \delta x) \cos x + \cos^2 x]$$

$$\therefore \quad \frac{\delta(\cos^3 x)}{\delta x} = \frac{-2 \sin \left(x + \frac{\delta x}{2}\right) \sin \frac{\delta x}{2}}{\delta x} [\cos^2 (x + \delta x) + \cos (x + \delta x) \cos x + \cos^2 x]$$

$$\therefore \quad \frac{d(\cos^3 x)}{dx} = \underset{\delta x \to 0}{\text{limit}} \frac{\delta(\cos^3 x)}{\delta x}$$

$$= \underset{\delta x \to 0}{\text{limit}} \left[-\sin \left(x + \frac{\delta x}{2}\right) \frac{\sin \frac{\delta x}{2}}{\frac{\delta x}{2}} \right] [\cos^2 (x + \delta x) + \cos (x + \delta x) \cos x + \cos^2 x]$$

$$= [-\sin x \,.\, 1][3 \cos^2 x]$$
$$= -3 \sin x \cos^2 x \text{ (refer to example 9(v))}$$

Example 2. (i) Differentiate from first principles $\cos 3x$; (ii) express $\cos^3 x$ in terms of $\cos x$ and $\cos 3x$ and hence write down the derivative of $\cos^3 x$.

(i) $$\delta[\cos (3x)] = \cos [3(x + \delta x)] - \cos (3x)$$

$$= -2 \sin \left(\frac{3x + 3\delta x + 3x}{2}\right) \sin \left(\frac{3x + 3\delta x - 3x}{2}\right)$$

$$\therefore \quad \frac{\delta[\cos (3x)]}{\delta x} = \frac{-2 \sin \left(3x + \frac{3\delta x}{2}\right) \sin \left(\frac{3\delta x}{2}\right)}{\delta x}$$

We again use the result $\underset{\theta \to 0}{\text{limit}} \frac{\sin \theta}{\theta} = 1$, where θ is in radians. We have $\sin \left(\frac{3\delta x}{2}\right)$ in the numerator and only δx in the denominator; therefore we multiply top and bottom of the fraction by 3/2

$$\frac{d[\cos (3x)]}{dx} = \underset{\delta x \to 0}{\text{limit}} \frac{\delta[\cos (3x)]}{\delta x} = \underset{\delta x \to 0}{\text{limit}} \frac{-2 \sin \left(3x + \frac{3\delta x}{2}\right) \sin \left(\frac{3\delta x}{2}\right) \cdot \frac{3}{2}}{\delta x \cdot \frac{3}{2}}$$

$$= \underset{\delta x \to 0}{\text{limit}} -3 \sin \left(3x + \frac{3\delta x}{2}\right) \cdot \frac{\sin \left(\frac{3\delta x}{2}\right)}{\left(\frac{3\delta x}{2}\right)}$$

$$= -3 \sin 3x \,.\, 1$$
$$= -3 \sin 3x$$

ii) By use of the identity $\cos(A + B) = \cos A \cos B - \sin A \sin B$ it can be shown that

$$\cos 3x = 4\cos^3 x - 3\cos x$$

Rearranging this

$$\cos^3 x = \frac{1}{4}\cos 3x + \frac{3}{4}\cos x$$

$$\therefore \quad \frac{d(\cos^3 x)}{dx} = \frac{d(\frac{1}{4}\cos 3x)}{dx} + \frac{d(\frac{3}{4}\cos x)}{dx}$$

$$= \frac{1}{4}\frac{d(\cos 3x)}{dx} + \frac{3}{4}\frac{d\cos x}{dx} \qquad \text{(by equations 4.3 and 4.4)}$$

$$= \frac{1}{4}(-3\sin 3x) - \frac{3}{4}\sin x \qquad \text{(by part (i) and the formula 4.2)}$$

$$= -\frac{3}{4}(\sin 3x + \sin x).$$

The proof that this result is equal to that obtained in example 1 (ii) is left as an exercise for our readers.

Exercises 4.1

1. Differentiate from first principles:

(i) $\cot x$ (ii) $2\tan 5x$ (iii) $\sec 3x$
(iv) $\sin^3 x$ [refer to example 1(ii)] (v) $3\sin 4x$

2. The function $f(\theta)$ is given by $f(\theta) = \sin\theta + \cos\theta$. Show that $f(\theta) = 2\sin(\pi/4)\cos(\theta - \pi/4)$. [Hint: $\cos\theta = \sin(\pi/2 - \theta)$.] Deduce the maximum and minimum values of $f(\theta)$. Verify your results by differentiation.

Evaluate the following:

3. $\dfrac{d[\cos(2x - 1)]}{d(2x - 1)}$ 4. $\dfrac{d[\sin(\sqrt{x})]}{d(\sqrt{x})}$

5. $\dfrac{d[\cos(z^2 - 1)]}{d(z^2 - 1)}$ 6. $\dfrac{d[\sin(\ln y)]}{d(\ln y)}$

7. $\dfrac{d[\sin(x^3 - 2x + 1)]}{d(x^3 - 2x + 1)}$

4.3 Differentiation of a Product

Let u and v be two functions of x, and δu, δv the changes in u and v corresponding to a change δx in x. The change in the product uv is equal to its new value $(u + \delta u)(v + \delta v)$ minus its original value uv.

$$\therefore \quad \delta(uv) = (u + \delta u)(v + \delta v) - uv$$
$$= uv + v\delta u + u\delta v + \delta u \,.\, \delta v - uv$$
$$= v\delta u + (u + \delta u)\delta v$$

$$\therefore \quad \frac{\delta(uv)}{\delta x} = v\frac{\delta u}{\delta x} + (u + \delta u)\frac{\delta v}{\delta x}$$

If $\mathrm{d}u/\mathrm{d}x$ and $\mathrm{d}v/\mathrm{d}x$ both exist, then in the limit as $\delta x \to 0$, $\delta u \to 0$ and $\delta v \to 0$, and $\delta(uv) \to 0$.

$$\therefore \quad \frac{\mathrm{d}(uv)}{\mathrm{d}x} = v\frac{\mathrm{d}u}{\mathrm{d}x} + u\frac{\mathrm{d}v}{\mathrm{d}x} \tag{4.5}$$

In words, to differentiate a product of two functions, multiply the derivative of the first by the second and the derivative of the second by the first, and add the two products.

An important result is obtained when one of the functions, say u, is a constant C. Let $u = C$

$$\therefore \quad \frac{\mathrm{d}(Cv)}{\mathrm{d}x} = v\frac{\mathrm{d}C}{\mathrm{d}x} + C\frac{\mathrm{d}v}{\mathrm{d}x}$$

$$= 0 + C\frac{\mathrm{d}v}{\mathrm{d}x}$$

$$\therefore \quad \frac{\mathrm{d}(Cv)}{\mathrm{d}x} = C\frac{\mathrm{d}v}{\mathrm{d}x} \text{ (where } C \text{ is a constant)} \tag{4.6}$$

The derivative of a constant times a function is equal to the constant times the derivative of the function.

Example 3. Differentiate with respect to x: (i) $x^2 \cos x$; (ii) $(x^3 + x)\mathrm{e}^{-x}$

(i) $x^2 \cos x$ is the product of x^2 and $\cos x$; therefore by equation 4.5

$$\frac{\mathrm{d}(x^2 \cos x)}{\mathrm{d}x} = \frac{\mathrm{d}(x^2)}{\mathrm{d}x}\cos x + x^2\frac{\mathrm{d}(\cos x)}{\mathrm{d}x}$$

$$= 2x\cos x + x^2(-\sin x)$$

$$= 2x\cos x - x^2 \sin x$$

(ii) $(x^3 + x)\mathrm{e}^{-x}$ is the product of $(x^3 + x)$ and e^{-x}; therefore by equation 4.5

$$\frac{\mathrm{d}[(x^3 + x)\mathrm{e}^{-x}]}{\mathrm{d}x} = \frac{\mathrm{d}(x^3 + x)}{\mathrm{d}x}\mathrm{e}^{-x} + (x^3 + x)\frac{\mathrm{d}\mathrm{e}^{-x}}{\mathrm{d}x}$$

$$= (3x^2 + 1)\mathrm{e}^{-x} + (x^3 + x)(-\mathrm{e}^{-x}) \quad \text{(refer to equation 2.19)}$$

$$= \mathrm{e}^{-x}(-x^3 + 3x^2 - x + 1)$$

Example 4. Differentiate (i) $(\ln x)^2$, (ii) $\ln (x^2)$, (iii) $\sin x \ln (3x)$ with respect to x.

(i) $(\ln x)^2$ is the product of $\ln x$ and $\ln x$

$$\therefore \quad \frac{\mathrm{d}(\ln x)^2}{\mathrm{d}x} = \frac{\mathrm{d}[(\ln x)(\ln x)]}{\mathrm{d}x}$$

$$= \frac{\mathrm{d}(\ln x)}{\mathrm{d}x}\ln x + \ln x\frac{\mathrm{d}(\ln x)}{\mathrm{d}x}$$

$$= \frac{1}{x}\ln x + \ln x \,.\, \frac{1}{x}$$

$$= \frac{2}{x}\ln x$$

(ii) $\ln(x^2)$ is *not* a product to differentiate: we use the fact that $\ln(x^2) = 2\ln x$

$$\therefore \quad \frac{d[\ln(x^2)]}{dx} = \frac{d[2\ln x]}{dx}$$

$$= 2\frac{d(\ln x)}{dx} \qquad \text{(refer to equation 4.6)}$$

$$= \frac{2}{x}$$

(iii) $\sin x \ln(3x)$ is the product of $\sin x$ and $\ln(3x)$. Also $\ln(3x) = \ln 3 + \ln x$

$$\therefore \quad \frac{d[\sin x \ln(3x)]}{dx} = \frac{d[\sin x(\ln 3 + \ln x)]}{dx}$$

$$= \frac{d(\sin x \ln 3)}{dx} + \frac{d(\sin x \ln x)}{dx}$$

$$= \ln 3\frac{d(\sin x)}{dx} + \frac{d\sin x}{dx}\ln x + \sin x\frac{d\ln x}{dx}$$

$$= \ln 3\cos x + \cos x \ln x + \sin x \cdot \frac{1}{x}$$

Equation 4.5 can be extended to the product of three or more functions. If u, v, w are three functions of x

$$\frac{d(uvw)}{dx} = d[(uv)w]$$

$$= \frac{d(uv)}{dx}w + uv\frac{dw}{dx}$$

$$= \left[\frac{du}{dx}v + u\frac{dv}{dx}\right]w + uv\frac{dw}{dx}$$

$$= \frac{du}{dx}vw + u\frac{dv}{dx}w + uv\frac{dw}{dx} \qquad (4.7)$$

Example 5. Differentiate $e^{-2z}\cos z \sin z$ with respect to z.

$$\frac{d(e^{-2z}\cos z\sin z)}{dz} = \frac{d(e^{-2z})}{dz}\cos z\sin z + e^{-2z}\frac{d(\cos z)}{dz}\sin z + e^{-2z}\cos z\frac{d(\sin z)}{dz}$$

$$= -2e^{-2z}\cos z\sin z + e^{-2z}(-\sin z)\sin z + e^{-2z}\cos z\cos z$$
$$= e^{-2z}(-2\cos z\sin z - \sin^2 z + \cos^2 z)$$
$$= e^{-2z}(-\sin 2z + \cos 2z)$$

Exercises 4.2

Differentiate with respect to x:

1. $(x^2 + x + 1)(x^2 - 2x + 1)$
2. $3x^2e^{2x}$
3. $x^3 \ln x$
4. $x^3 \cos x$
5. $\sqrt{x}\sin x$
6. $(x^2 + \sqrt{x} - 1)(1 - x)$
7. $e^{2x}\sin x$
8. $e^{-2x}\cos x$
9. $(x^3 - x^2 + x)\ln x$
10. $5x^2 \sin x \cos x$
11. $x\,e^x \sin x \cos x$
12. $(x^2 - 1)\,e^x \ln x$

13. A wheel is attached to the lower end of a stiff spring. The other end of the spring is fixed vertically above the wheel, which is oscillating vertically. It is found that the displacement x of the wheel from the equilibrium position is given by the equation

$$25\frac{d^2x}{dt^2} + 10\frac{dx}{dt} + 26x = 0$$

Verify that $x = Ae^{-t/5}\cos t$, where A is a constant, is a solution of the equation.

14. In an electric circuit a condenser of capacity 0·03 microfarads discharges through a resistance and an inductance. The charge q on the positive plate of the condenser at any time t is given by the equation

$$\frac{d^2q}{dt^2} + 2p\frac{dq}{dt} + (p^2 + 1)q = 0$$

where p is a constant. Verify that $q = e^{-pt}\sin t$ is a solution of this equation.

15. In a submarine cable with a core of fixed diameter the speed of signalling s is given by

$$s = \frac{k}{r^2}\ln\left(\frac{r}{2}\right)$$

where r is the radius of the covering and k is a constant. Find the radius of the covering in order that the speed of signalling is a maximum.

4.4 Differentiation of a Quotient

Let u and v be two functions of x, and δu, δv the changes in u and v corresponding to a change δx in x. The change in the quotient u/v is equal to its new value $(u + \delta u)/(v + \delta v)$ minus its original value u/v.

$$\therefore \quad \delta\left(\frac{u}{v}\right) = \frac{u + \delta u}{v + \delta v} - \frac{u}{v}$$

$$= \frac{uv + v\delta u - uv - u\delta v}{v(v + \delta v)}$$

$$= \frac{v\delta u - u\delta v}{v(v + \delta v)}$$

$$\therefore \quad \frac{\delta\left(\dfrac{u}{v}\right)}{\delta x} = \frac{v\delta u - u\delta v}{v(v + \delta v)}\,\frac{1}{\delta x}$$

$$= \frac{v\dfrac{\delta u}{\delta x} - u\dfrac{\delta v}{\delta x}}{v(v + \delta v)}$$

$$\therefore \quad \frac{d\left(\dfrac{u}{v}\right)}{dv} = \lim_{\delta x \to 0}\frac{\delta\left(\dfrac{u}{v}\right)}{\delta x} = \lim_{\delta x \to 0}\frac{v\left(\dfrac{\delta u}{\delta x}\right) - u\left(\dfrac{\delta v}{\delta x}\right)}{v(v + \delta v)}$$

If du/dx and dv/dx both exist and $v \neq 0$, then in the limit as $\delta x \to 0$, $\delta u \to 0$, $\delta v \to 0$ and $\delta(u/v) \to 0$.

$$\therefore \quad \frac{d\left(\dfrac{u}{v}\right)}{dx} = \frac{v\dfrac{du}{dx} - u\dfrac{dv}{dx}}{v^2} \tag{4.8}$$

In words, to differentiate a quotient of two functions u/v multiply the derivative of u by v, subtract the product of the derivative of v times u and divide the result by the square of v.

Example 6. Differentiate with respect to x

(i) $\dfrac{3x^2}{2x^3+1}$ (ii) $\dfrac{3\ln x}{2x^2+5x}$ (iii) $\dfrac{1}{x^3-3}$

(i) By equation 4.8

$$\frac{d}{dx}\left[\frac{3x^2}{(2x^3+1)}\right] = \frac{(2x^3+1)\dfrac{d(3x^2)}{dx} - \dfrac{d(2x^3+1)}{dx}3x^2}{(2x^3+1)^2}$$

$$= \frac{(2x^3+1)6x - (6x^2)3x^2}{(2x^3+1)^2}$$

$$= \frac{12x^4+6x-18x^4}{(2x^3+1)^2}$$

$$= \frac{6x-6x^4}{(2x^3+1)^2}$$

(ii)

$$\frac{d}{dx}\left[\frac{3\ln x}{(2x^2+5x)}\right] = \frac{(2x^2+5x)\dfrac{d(3\ln x)}{dx} - \dfrac{d(2x^2+5x)}{dx}3\ln x}{(2x^2+5x)^2}$$

$$= \frac{(2x^2+5x)(3/x) - (4x+5)3\ln x}{(2x^2+5x)^2}$$

$$= \frac{(6x+15) - 3(4x+5)\ln x}{(2x^2+5x)^2}$$

(iii)

$$\frac{d}{dx}\left[\frac{1}{(x^3-3)}\right] = \frac{(x^3-3)\dfrac{d(1)}{dx} - \dfrac{d(x^3-3)}{dx}.1}{(x^3-3)^2}$$

$$= \frac{0-3x^2}{(x^3-3)^2}$$

$$= \frac{-3x^2}{(x^3-3)^2}$$

Sometimes a combination of both 4.5 and 4.8 is required.

Example 7. Differentiate with respect to p

(i) $\dfrac{p\cos p}{(p^2-1)}$ (ii) $\dfrac{p\ln p}{e^p}$

(i) By equation 4.8

$$\frac{d}{dp}\left[\frac{p\cos p}{(p^2-1)}\right] = \frac{(p^2-1)\dfrac{d(p\cos p)}{dp} - \dfrac{d(p^2-1)}{dp}p\cos p}{(p^2-1)^2}$$

To differentiate the product $p \cos p$ we use equation 4.5

$$= \frac{(p^2 - 1)[1 \,.\, \cos p + p(-\sin p)] - (2p)\, p \cos p}{(p^2 - 1)^2}$$

$$= \frac{(p^2 - 1)(\cos p - p \sin p) - 2p^2 \cos p}{(p^2 - 1)^2}$$

(ii) By equation 4.8

$$\frac{d}{dp}\left[\frac{p \ln p}{e^p}\right] = \frac{e^p \dfrac{d(p \ln p)}{dp} - \dfrac{d(e^p)}{dp} p \ln p}{(e^p)^2}$$

To differentiate the product $p \ln p$ we use equation 4.5

$$= \frac{e^p\left(1 \,.\, \ln p + p \,.\, \dfrac{1}{p}\right) - p \ln p\, e^p}{(e^p)^2}$$

$$= \frac{e^p(\ln p + 1 - p \ln p)}{(e^p)^2}$$

$$= (\ln p + 1 - p \ln p)\, e^{-p}$$

Exercises 4.3

Differentiate with respect to x:

1. $\dfrac{x^3}{(x - 1)}$
2. $\dfrac{x^2 + 1}{x^2 - 1}$
3. $\dfrac{2 \ln x}{x}$
4. $\dfrac{5e^x}{x^2}$
5. $\dfrac{e^{2x}}{x^2 + 1}$
6. $\dfrac{3 \cos x}{x^2 - x + 1}$
7. $\dfrac{(x^3 - 2)}{(x^2 + 1)(x - 1)}$
8. $\dfrac{5 \sin x}{2 \cos x + 1}$
9. $\dfrac{x \sin x}{(x - 1)}$
10. $\dfrac{xe^x}{x^2 + 1}$
11. $\dfrac{e^x}{(\cos x + \sin x)}$
12. $\dfrac{e^x \sin x}{\cos x}$

13. The pressure p and the volume v of a given mass of gas are connected by the equation

$$\left(p + \frac{a}{v^2}\right)(v - b) = RT \quad \text{(Van der Waal's Equation)}$$

where T is the absolute temperature and a, b and R are constants. Assuming that T is constant, find dp/dv and d^2p/dv^2. Find the value of p, in terms of a and b, when $v = 3b$ and $T = 8a/27Rb$ and verify that in this case $dp/dv = 0$ and $d^2p/dv^2 = 0$.

14. A battery of 200 cells each of voltage E and internal resistance r is arranged in x rows with $200/x$ cells in each row. The cells in each row are connected in series and

the rows are connected in parallel. The battery is connected to a resistance R and the current i which flows is given by

$$i = \frac{200Ex}{Rx^2 + 200r}$$

How many rows of cells must there be for the current to be a maximum?

15. A radio valve of constant resistance R and variable impedance z has a power output P given by

$$P = \frac{kz}{(z + R)^2}$$

where k is a constant. Find the maximum value of P in terms of k and R.

4.5 Differentiation of the Trigonometrical Functions

The derivatives of $\sin x$ and $\cos x$ have already been found from first principles in section 4.2. Using these results and the formula 4.8 for the differentiation of a quotient, the derivatives of the remaining trigonometrical functions, $\tan x$, $\cot x$, $\sec x$, $\operatorname{cosec} x$ can be found.

Example 8. Differentiate with respect to x:

(i) $\tan x$ (ii) $\cot x$ (iii) $\sec x$ (iv) $\operatorname{cosec} x$

(i)

$$\frac{\mathrm{d}(\tan x)}{\mathrm{d}x} = \frac{\mathrm{d}}{\mathrm{d}x}\left(\frac{\sin x}{\cos x}\right)$$

$$= \frac{\cos x \dfrac{\mathrm{d}(\sin x)}{\mathrm{d}x} - \dfrac{\mathrm{d}(\cos x)}{\mathrm{d}x} \sin x}{\cos^2 x}$$

$$= \frac{\cos x \,.\, \cos x - (-\sin x) \sin x}{\cos^2 x}$$

$$= \frac{\cos^2 x + \sin^2 x}{\cos^2 x}$$

$$= \frac{1}{\cos^2 x}$$

$$\therefore \qquad \frac{\mathrm{d}(\tan x)}{\mathrm{d}x} = \sec^2 x \qquad (4.9)$$

(ii)

$$\frac{\mathrm{d}(\cot x)}{\mathrm{d}x} = \frac{\mathrm{d}}{\mathrm{d}x}\left(\frac{\cos x}{\sin x}\right)$$

$$= \frac{\sin x \dfrac{\mathrm{d}(\cos x)}{\mathrm{d}x} - \dfrac{\mathrm{d}(\sin x)}{\mathrm{d}x} \cos x}{\sin^2 x}$$

$$= \frac{\sin x(-\sin x) - \cos x \cos x}{\sin^2 x}$$

$$= \frac{-\sin^2 x - \cos^2 x}{\sin^2 x}$$

$$= \frac{-(\sin^2 x + \cos^2 x)}{\sin^2 x}$$

$$= \frac{-1}{\sin^2 x}$$

$$\therefore \quad \frac{d(\cot x)}{dx} = -\text{cosec}^2\, x \qquad (4.10)$$

(iii)

$$\frac{d(\sec x)}{dx} = \frac{d}{dx}\left(\frac{1}{\cos x}\right)$$

$$= \frac{\cos x \dfrac{d(l)}{dx} - \dfrac{d(\cos x)}{dx} \cdot 1}{\cos^2 x}$$

$$= \frac{0 - (-\sin x)}{\cos^2 x}$$

$$= \frac{\sin x}{\cos^2 x}$$

$$\therefore \quad \frac{d(\sec x)}{dx} = \sec x \tan x \qquad (4.11)$$

(iv)

$$\frac{d(\text{cosec}\, x)}{dx} = \frac{d}{dx}\left(\frac{1}{\sin x}\right)$$

$$= \frac{\sin x \dfrac{d(1)}{dx} - \dfrac{d(\sin x)}{dx} \cdot 1}{\sin^2 x}$$

$$= \frac{0 - \cos x}{\sin^2 x}$$

$$= \frac{-\cos x}{\sin^2 x}$$

$$\therefore \quad \frac{d(\text{cosec}\, x)}{dx} = -\text{cosec}\, x \cot x \qquad (4.12)$$

4.6 Differentiation of a Function of a Function

Many functions of a variable, say x, can be regarded as a simpler function of a function of x. Consider $f(x) = \sin(x^3 - 2x + 1)$: $f(x)$ is the sine of the function $(x^3 - 2x + 1)$ and so $f(x)$ is a function (sine) of a function $(x^3 - 2x + 1)$ of x.

Consider a second example $f(x) = \ln(x^2 + 3)$: $f(x)$ is the logarithm to the base e of the function $(x^2 + 3)$ and $f(x)$ is a function (ln) of a function $(x^2 + 3)$.

In general $\quad y = f(x)$ can be expressed as

$$y = u[v(x)]$$

or

$$y = u[z], \text{ where } z = v(x)$$

Corresponding to a change of δx in x there will be a change of δz in z, and hence a change of δy in y. Assuming that $\delta z \neq 0$ and that $\delta z \to 0$ as $\delta x \to 0$, we have that

identically $$\frac{\delta y}{\delta x} = \frac{\delta y}{\delta z} \cdot \frac{\delta z}{\delta x}$$

and hence $$\frac{dy}{dx} = \underset{\delta x \to 0}{\text{limit}} \frac{\delta y}{\delta x} = \underset{\delta x \to 0}{\text{limit}} \frac{\delta y}{\delta z} \cdot \frac{\delta z}{\delta x}$$

$$= \underset{\delta x \to 0}{\text{limit}} \frac{\delta y}{\delta z} \,.\, \underset{\delta x \to 0}{\text{limit}} \frac{\delta z}{\delta x}$$

$$= \underset{\delta z \to 0}{\text{limit}} \frac{\delta y}{\delta z} \,.\, \underset{\delta x \to 0}{\text{limit}} \frac{\delta z}{\delta x}$$

assuming that the limit of a product is equal to the product of the limits

or $$\frac{dy}{dx} = \frac{dy}{dz} \cdot \frac{dz}{dx} \tag{4.13}$$

assuming that dy/dz and dz/dx both exist.

It is not necessary actually to make the substitution $z = v(x)$. Consider the first example we quoted, $f(x) = \sin(x^3 - 2x + 1)$

$$\frac{d[f(x)]}{dx} = \frac{d \sin(x^3 - 2x + 1)}{dx}$$

$$= \frac{d \sin(x^3 - 2x + 1)}{d(x^3 - 2x + 1)} \cdot \frac{d(x^3 - 2x + 1)}{dx}$$

$$= \cos(x^3 - 2x + 1) \,.\, \frac{d(x^3 - 2x + 1)}{dx}$$ (refer to Exercises 4.1, No. 7)

$$= \cos(x^3 - 2x + 1) \,.\, (3x^2 - 2)$$
$$= (3x^2 - 2) \cos(x^3 - 2x + 1)$$

Example 9. Differentiate with respect to x:

(i) $\cos(2x - 1)$ (ii) $\sqrt{(x^2 - x + 1)}$ (iii) $e^{3(x^2-1)}$
(iv) $\ln(\cot x)$ (v) $\cos^3 x$

(i) $$\frac{d \cos(2x - 1)}{dx} = \frac{d \cos(2x - 1)}{d(2x - 1)} \cdot \frac{d(2x - 1)}{dx}$$

$$= -\sin(2x - 1) \frac{d(2x - 1)}{dx}$$ (refer to Exercises 4.1, No. 3)

$$= -\sin(2x - 1) \,.\, 2$$
$$= -2 \sin(2x - 1)$$

(ii) $$\frac{d\sqrt{(x^2 - x + 1)}}{dx} = \frac{d(x^2 - x + 1)^{\frac{1}{2}}}{dx}$$

$$= \frac{d(x^2 - x + 1)^{\frac{1}{2}}}{d(x^2 - x + 1)} \cdot \frac{d(x^2 - x + 1)}{dx}$$

$$= \frac{1}{2}(x^2 - x + 1)^{-\frac{1}{2}} \frac{d(x^2 - x + 1)}{dx}$$ (refer to formula 1.9 and the succeeding examples)

$$= \frac{1}{2}(x^2 - x + 1)^{-\frac{1}{2}}(2x - 1)$$

$$= \frac{(2x - 1)}{2\sqrt{(x^2 - x + 1)}}$$

(iii) $$\frac{d\,e^{3(x^2-1)}}{dx} = \frac{d\,e^{(3x^2-3)}}{dx}$$

$$= \frac{d\,e^{(3x^2-3)}}{d(3x^2 - 3)} \cdot \frac{d(3x^2 - 3)}{dx}$$

$$= e^{(3x^2-3)} \,.\, 6x$$

$$= 6x\,e^{(3x^2-3)}$$

(iv) $$\frac{d \ln (\cot x)}{dx} = \frac{d \ln (\cot x)}{d(\cot x)} \cdot \frac{d \cot x}{dx}$$

$$= \frac{1}{\cot x} \,.\, (-\operatorname{cosec}^2 x)$$

$$= -\tan x \operatorname{cosec}^2 x$$

$$= -\frac{\sin x}{\cos x} \cdot \frac{1}{\sin^2 x}$$

$$= -\frac{1}{\sin x \cos x}$$

(v) $$\frac{d \cos^3 x}{dx} = \frac{d(\cos x)^3}{dx}$$

$$= \frac{d(\cos x)^3}{d(\cos x)} \cdot \frac{d(\cos x)}{dx}$$

$$= 3(\cos x)^2 (-\sin x)$$

$$= -3 \sin x \cos^2 x$$ (refer to example 1(ii))

The formula 4.13 can be extended to deal with functions such as sin (e^{2x-1}), which is a function (sine) of a function (e) which it itself a function of x. The required extension is

$$\frac{dy}{dx} = \frac{dy}{dv} \cdot \frac{dv}{dw} \cdot \frac{dw}{dx} \qquad (4.14)$$

Again it is not necessary to make the actual substitutions.

Example 10. Find the derivatives with respect to x of:

(i) $\sin(e^{2x-1})$ (ii) $\sec^4(3x-1)$ (iii) $e^{\sqrt{(1-4x)}}$

(i) $$\frac{d\sin(e^{2x-1})}{dx} = \frac{d\sin(e^{(2x-1)})}{d(e^{2x-1})}\cdot\frac{d\,e^{(2x-1)}}{d(2x-1)}\cdot\frac{d(2x-1)}{dx}$$

$$= \cos(e^{(2x-1)})\,.\,e^{(2x-1)}\,.\,2$$

$$= 2\,e^{(2x-1)}\cos(e^{(2x-1)}).$$

(ii) $$\frac{d\sec^4(3x-1)}{dx} = \frac{d[\sec(3x-1)]^4}{d[\sec(3x-1)]}\cdot\frac{d\sec(3x-1)}{d(3x-1)}\cdot\frac{d(3x-1)}{dx}$$

$$= 4[\sec(3x-1)]^3\,.\,\sec(3x-1)\,.\,\tan(3x-1)\,.\,3$$

$$= 12\sec^4(3x-1)\tan(3x-1).$$

(iii) $$\frac{d\,e^{\sqrt{(1-4x)}}}{dx} = \frac{d\,e^{(1-4x)^{\frac{1}{2}}}}{dx}$$

$$= \frac{d\,e^{[(1-4x)^{\frac{1}{2}}]}}{d[(1-4x)^{\frac{1}{2}}]}\cdot\frac{d(1-4x)^{\frac{1}{2}}}{d(1-4x)}\cdot\frac{d(1-4x)}{dx}$$

$$= e^{(1-4x)^{\frac{1}{2}}}\cdot\frac{1}{2}(1-4x)^{-\frac{1}{2}}\,.\,(-4)$$

$$= -2\,e^{(1-4x)^{\frac{1}{2}}}/\sqrt{(1-4x)}$$

A useful application of the formula 4.13 occurs in the study of rectilinear motion. The speed v of a body, moving in a straight line, which has travelled a distance s in time t is given by

$$v = \frac{ds}{dt}$$

and its acceleration a is given by

$$a = \frac{dv}{dt}$$

An alternative expression for the acceleration can be obtained by regarding v as a function of s, which is a function of t

$$\therefore \qquad a = \frac{dv}{dt} = \frac{dv}{ds}\cdot\frac{ds}{dt}$$

$$= \frac{dv}{ds}\cdot v$$

Now $$\frac{d(\frac{1}{2}v^2)}{ds} = \frac{d(\frac{1}{2}v^2)}{dv}\cdot\frac{dv}{ds} = v\frac{dv}{ds}$$

$$\therefore \qquad a = v\frac{dv}{ds} = \frac{d(\frac{1}{2}v^2)}{ds} \tag{4.15}$$

Example 11. The speed v of a body is proportional to the square of the distance s it has travelled. Show that the acceleration a is proportional to the cube of the distance travelled.

$$v \propto s^2$$

$\therefore \qquad v = ks^2$ (where k is a constant)

$$\therefore \qquad \frac{dv}{ds} = 2ks$$

and $$a = v\frac{dv}{ds} = ks^2 \, . \, 2ks$$

$$= 2k^2s^3$$

$\therefore \qquad a \propto s^3$ (because $2k^2$ is a constant)

Similarly, when a body is rotating about a fixed axis its angular speed w is given by $w = d\theta/dt$, where θ is the angle turned through in time t, and

$$\text{Angular acceleration} = \frac{dw}{dt}$$

$$= \frac{dw}{d\theta} \cdot \frac{d\theta}{dt}$$

$$= \frac{dw}{d\theta} \cdot w$$

$$= \frac{d(\frac{1}{2}w^2)}{d\theta} \qquad (4.16)$$

Example 12. A jet aircraft A is flying horizontally at a height of 1500 m. It passes directly over a searchlight B at a steady speed of 0·5 km/s. Find the rate $d\theta/dt$ at which the searchlight must be rotated to keep the aircraft illuminated (θ is the angle of elevation of the aircraft at any time t).

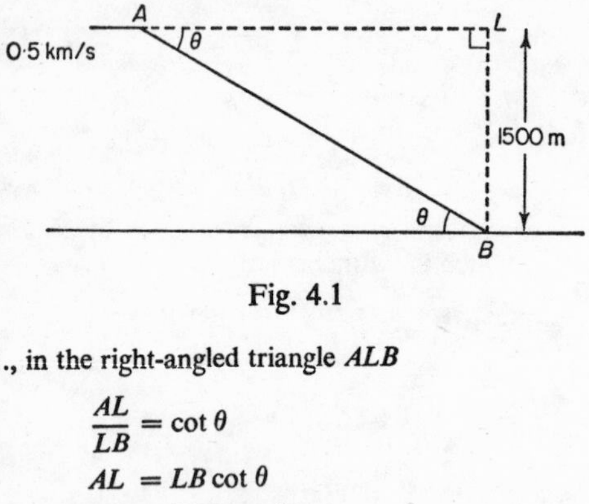

Fig. 4.1

From Fig. 4.1., in the right-angled triangle ALB

$$\frac{AL}{LB} = \cot\theta$$

$$AL = LB\cot\theta$$

$$s = 1500\cot\theta$$

$$\therefore \qquad \frac{ds}{d\theta} = -1500\,\text{cosec}^2\,\theta \qquad \text{(i)}$$

The speed of the aircraft $\dfrac{ds}{dt} = 0{\cdot}5$ km/s

$$= 500 \text{ m/s} \qquad \text{(ii)}$$

$$\frac{ds}{dt} = \frac{ds}{d\theta} \cdot \frac{d\theta}{dt}$$

$$\therefore \quad 500 = -1500 \operatorname{cosec}^2 \theta \frac{d\theta}{dt} \qquad \text{(from equations (i) and (ii))}$$

$$\therefore \quad \frac{d\theta}{dt} = -\frac{1}{3} \sin^2 \theta \text{ radians per second}$$

Example 13. The rate of increase of the area A m² of a spherical balloon is 0·3 m²/min. Find the rate of increase of (i) the radius r m, (ii) the volume V m³ at an instant when $r = 0{\cdot}2$ m. The rates of increase are understood to be with respect to the time t.

(i) It is required to find dr/dt given that

$$\frac{dA}{dt} = 0{\cdot}3 \qquad \text{(i)}$$

$$\frac{dA}{dt} = \frac{dA}{dr} \cdot \frac{dr}{dt} \qquad \text{(ii)}$$

and

$$A = 4\pi r^2$$

$$\therefore \quad \frac{dA}{dr} = 8\pi r \qquad \text{(iii)}$$

Substituting from (i) and (iii) in (ii)

$$0{\cdot}3 = 8\pi r \frac{dr}{dt}$$

$$\therefore \quad \frac{dr}{dt} = \frac{0{\cdot}3}{8\pi r}$$

when $r = 0{\cdot}2$

$$\frac{dr}{dt} = \frac{0{\cdot}3}{8\pi \times 0{\cdot}2}$$

$$= \frac{3}{16\pi} \text{ m/min} \qquad \text{(iv)}$$

(ii)

$$\frac{dV}{dt} = \frac{dV}{dr} \cdot \frac{dr}{dt} \qquad \text{(v)}$$

and

$$V = \frac{4}{3}\pi r^3$$

$$\therefore \quad \frac{dV}{dr} = 4\pi r^2 \qquad \text{(vi)}$$

Substituting from (vi) in (v)

$$\frac{dV}{dt} = 4\pi r^2 \cdot \frac{dr}{dt}$$

Now when $r = 0{\cdot}2$

$$\frac{dr}{dt} = \frac{3}{16\pi} \qquad \text{(refer to equation (iv))}$$

Therefore when $r = 0{\cdot}2$

$$\frac{dV}{dt} = 4\pi(0{\cdot}2)^2 \cdot \frac{3}{16\pi}$$

$$= 0{\cdot}03 \text{ m}^3\text{/min}$$

Revision Questions 4.1

Complete the following statements	*Answers*	*Refer to*
1. $\dfrac{d\cos\theta}{d\theta} = \ldots$	1. $-\sin\theta$ (θ in radians)	Formula 4.2
2. $\dfrac{d\cos^2\theta}{d\cos\theta} = \ldots$	2. $2\cos\theta$	Formula 1.10
3. $\dfrac{d\sin\theta}{d\theta} = \ldots$	3. $\cos\theta$ (θ in radians)	Formula 4.1
4. $\dfrac{d\tan\theta}{d\theta} = \ldots$	4. $\sec^2\theta$ (θ in radians)	Formula 4.9
5. $\dfrac{d\,\text{cosec}\,\theta}{d\theta} = \ldots$	5. $-\text{cosec}\,\theta\cot\theta$ (θ in radians)	Formula 4.12
6. $\dfrac{d\cos(2x-1)}{dx} = \dfrac{d\cos(2x-1)}{d(\,?\,)} \cdot \dfrac{d(\ldots)}{dx}$	6. $\dfrac{d\cos(2x-1)}{d(2x-1)} \cdot \dfrac{d(2x-1)}{dx}$	Example 9(i)
7. $\dfrac{d\cos^3 x}{dx} = \dfrac{d\ \ ?}{d(\cos x)} \cdot \dfrac{d(\cos x)}{dx}$	7. $\dfrac{d(\cos x)^3}{d(\cos x)} \cdot \dfrac{d(\cos x)}{dx}$	Example 9(v)
8. acceleration $= \dfrac{d(\ldots)}{ds}$	8. $a = \dfrac{d(\frac{1}{2}v^2)}{ds}$	Formula 4.15
9. acceleration $= v\dfrac{d\,?}{d\,?}$	9. $a = v\dfrac{dv}{ds}$	Formula 4.15
10. $\dfrac{d(u/v)}{dx} = \dfrac{v\frac{du}{dx} - \ldots}{\ldots}$	10. $\dfrac{v\frac{du}{dx} - u\frac{dv}{dx}}{v^2}$	Formula 4.8
11. $\dfrac{d(uv)}{dx} = v\dfrac{du}{dx} + \ldots$	11. $v\dfrac{du}{dx} + u\dfrac{dv}{dx}$	Formula 4.5
12. $\dfrac{d[C f(x)]}{dx} = \ldots$ (where C is a constant)	12. $\dfrac{d[C f(x)]}{dx} = C\dfrac{d[f(x)]}{dx}$	Formula 4.6
13. $\dfrac{d\sin\theta}{d\theta} = \cos\theta$ if and only if θ is measured in . . .	13. radians	Section 4.2
14. $\dfrac{d(\log x)}{dx} = \dfrac{1}{x}$ if and only if the logarithms are to the base . . .	14. e	Section 2.3

Exercises 4.4

Differentiate with respect to x:

1. $\sin x \cos x$
2. $e^{2x} \sin x$
3. $e^{-x} \cos x$
4. $\sec x \tan x$
5. $\operatorname{cosec} x \cot x$
6. $\sin^4 x$
7. $1/\cos^3 x$
8. $\sec^2 x$
9. $\tan^2 x$
10. $e^{\cos x}$
11. $\ln (\tan x)$
12. $\dfrac{\sin x}{\sqrt{\cos x}}$
13. $\dfrac{\cos x}{\sqrt{\sin x}}$
14. $(x^2 - x + 1)^{10}$
15. $\sqrt{(x^3 - 2x)}$
16. $\tan x^2$
17. $x \tan^2 x$
18. $x \sin x \cos x$
19. $\sin^3 \left(\dfrac{1}{x}\right)$
20. $e^{\cos 3x}$
21. $(x^2 - 1) \sin 3x$
22. $x^2 \cos (3x + 1)$
23. $\dfrac{(x^2 - 1)}{\tan x}$
24. $\dfrac{\cot 3x}{(x^2 + 1)}$
25. $\left(\dfrac{1 + x^2}{1 - x^2}\right)^3$
26. $\sin mx \cos nx$ (m, n constants)
27. $\sin^m x \cos^n x$ (m, n constants)
28. $\ln \dfrac{\sin^2 x}{1 + \cos^2 x}$
29. $x e^{\sqrt{\cos x}}$

30. Given that $y = e^{-2t} \cos 3t$ show that

$$\frac{d^2y}{dt^2} + 4\frac{dy}{dt} + 13y = 0$$

31. The pressure p and the volume v of a given mass of gas are given by the equation $pv^{1\cdot4} = C$, where C is a constant. Initially $v = 32\ \text{m}^3$ and $p = 30\ \text{N/m}^2$. If the pressure is increasing at the rate of $1\cdot5(\text{N/m}^2)/\text{min}$ find the rate at which the volume is changing when the volume is $243/32\ \text{m}^3$.

32. A man M is flying a kite K which is being carried horizontally away from him by the wind at a rate of 2·5 m/s. At what rate is the inclination of KM to the horizontal changing when the height of the kite is 25 m and the distance KM is 40 m?

33. Gas is escaping at a rate of $10\text{m}^3/\text{min}$ from a spherical balloon. At what rates are (i) the area and (ii) the radius changing at the moment when the radius is 4 m?

34. The speed v of a body is proportional to the fourth power of the distance s travelled. Show that $a \propto s^7$, where a is the acceleration.

35. The potential V at a distance r from a point charge q is given by $V = q/4\pi er$ where q and e are constants. Find an expression for the field strength E where $E = -\mathrm{d}V/\mathrm{d}r$. The distance r is increasing at a rate of 2 cm/sec. Find the rate of increase of E in terms of q and e when $r = 12$ cm.

4.7 The Derivative of x^n when n is Fractional or Negative

Let $y = x^n$ and $n = p/q$ $(q \neq 1)$, where p and q are positive integers with no factors in common. (The case of $q = 1$ has already been considered—refer to section 1.11.)

$$y = x^{p/q}$$

$$\therefore \quad y^q = x^p$$

Differentiating both sides with respect to x

$$\frac{\mathrm{d}(y^q)}{\mathrm{d}x} = px^{p-1}$$

From equation 4.13 this can be written

$$\frac{\mathrm{d}(y^q)}{\mathrm{d}y} \cdot \frac{\mathrm{d}y}{\mathrm{d}x} = px^{p-1}$$

$$\therefore \quad qy^{q-1}\frac{\mathrm{d}y}{\mathrm{d}x} = px^{p-1}$$

$$\frac{\mathrm{d}y}{\mathrm{d}x} = \frac{px^{p-1}}{qy^{q-1}}$$

Now $y = x^{p/q}$; therefore $y^{q-1} = (x^{p/q})^{q-1} = x^{p-p/q}$

$$\therefore \quad \frac{\mathrm{d}y}{\mathrm{d}x} = \frac{p}{q} \cdot \frac{x^{p-1}}{x^{p-p/q}}$$

$$\therefore \quad \frac{\mathrm{d}x^{p/q}}{\mathrm{d}x} = \frac{p}{q} \cdot x^{p/q-1}$$

$$\therefore \quad \frac{\mathrm{d}x^n}{\mathrm{d}x} = nx^{n-1} \text{ when } n = \frac{p}{q} \tag{4.17}$$

(p and q both positive integers).

Consider $y = x^n$, where $n = -m$ and m is a positive rational number

$$\frac{\mathrm{d}x^n}{\mathrm{d}x} = \frac{\mathrm{d}(x^{-m})}{\mathrm{d}x}$$

$$= \frac{\mathrm{d}\left(\frac{1}{x^m}\right)}{\mathrm{d}x}$$

$$= \frac{x^m\frac{\mathrm{d}(1)}{\mathrm{d}x} - \frac{\mathrm{d}(x^m)}{\mathrm{d}x} \,.\, 1}{x^{2m}} \qquad \text{(from equation 4.8)}$$

$$= \frac{0 - mx^{m-1}}{x^{2m}} \qquad \text{(from equation 4.17 or 1.9)}$$

$$= -mx^{-m-1}$$

$$= nx^{n-1} \qquad (4.18)$$

Thus the formula $dx^n/dx = nx^{n-1}$ is valid for all rational values of n, whether positive or negative.

4.8 Implicit Differentiation

Consider the equations

$$e^{xy} + \sin y + x = 0$$
$$x^2 + y^2 = 4$$

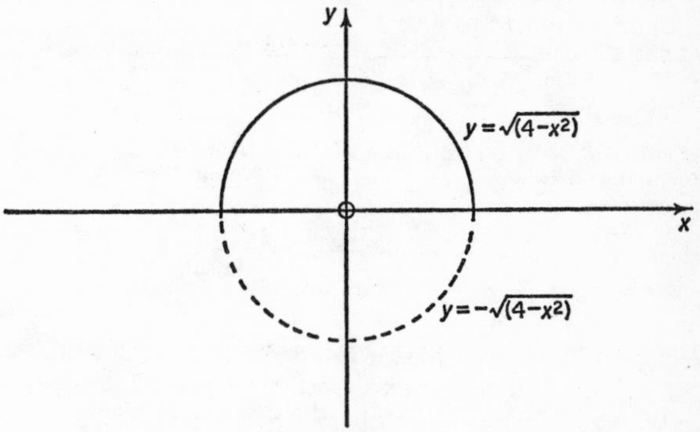

Fig. 4.2

The relation between y and x is not immediately obvious and cannot necessarily be found, as in the first equation. The second equation can be solved for y in terms of x, giving

$$y = \pm\sqrt{(4 - x^2)} \qquad (-2 \leqslant x \leqslant 2) \qquad (4.19)$$

This equation does not define a function of x, because for each value of x in the domain there are two possible values of y. We can, however, regard equation 4.19 as defining two functions

$$y = u(x) = \sqrt{(4 - x^2)} \qquad \text{(as usual, the positive sign is understood)}$$

and $\quad y = v(x) = -\sqrt{(4 - x^2)} \qquad (-2 \leqslant x \leqslant 2)$

and the graphs of these functions are shown in Fig. 4.2.

The derivatives of $u(x)$ and $v(x)$ are

$$u'(x) = \frac{d(4 - x^2)^{\frac{1}{2}}}{dx}$$

$$= \frac{d(4 - x^2)^{\frac{1}{2}}}{d(4 - x^2)} \cdot \frac{d(4 - x^2)}{dx}$$

$$= \tfrac{1}{2}(4 - x^2)^{-\frac{1}{2}} . -2x$$

$$= \frac{-x}{\sqrt{(4 - x^2)}}$$

$$= \frac{-x}{u(x)} \qquad u(x) \neq 0 \qquad (4.20)$$

Similarly

$$v'(x) = \frac{-x}{-\sqrt{(4 - x^2)}}$$

$$= \frac{-x}{v(x)} \qquad v(x) \neq 0 \qquad (4.21)$$

If y is understood to mean either $u(x)$ or $v(x)$ the results of equations 4.20 and 4.21 can be combined to give

$$y' = -\frac{x}{y} \qquad (y \neq 0) \qquad (4.22)$$

The formula 4.22 can be obtained directly from the equation $x^2 + y^2 = 4$ by differentiating both sides with respect to x; thus

$$\frac{d(x^2)}{dx} + \frac{d(y^2)}{dx} = \frac{d(4)}{dx}$$

$$2x + \frac{d(y^2)}{dy} \cdot \frac{dy}{dx} = 0$$

$$2x + 2y\frac{dy}{dx} = 0$$

$$x = -y\frac{dy}{dx}$$

$$y' = -\frac{x}{y} \qquad (y \neq 0)$$

which is in conformity with equation 4.22.

This procedure is acceptable if we are clear what we mean by dy/dx—that is, it exists only if y is a function of x, i.e. y represents either $u(x)$ or $v(x)$ $(-2 \leqslant x \leqslant 2)$.

This process is known as **implicit differentiation.** In general, it is not possible to express y explicitly in terms of x.

Example 14. Given that $e^{xy} + \sin y - x^2 = 0$, obtain an expression for dy/dx.

$$e^{xy} + \sin y - x^2 = 0$$

Differentiating with respect to x

$$\frac{d(e^{xy})}{dx} + \frac{d(\sin y)}{dx} - \frac{d(x^2)}{dx} = 0$$

$$\frac{d\,e^{(xy)}}{d(xy)} \cdot \frac{d(xy)}{dx} + \frac{d \sin (y)}{dy} \cdot \frac{dy}{dx} - 2x = 0$$

Note that xy is a product

$$\therefore \quad e^{xy}\left(1 \,.\, y + x\frac{dy}{dx}\right) + \cos y\frac{dy}{dx} - 2x = 0$$

$$\therefore \quad y\,e^{xy} + x\,e^{xy}\frac{dy}{dx} + \cos y\frac{dy}{dx} - 2x = 0$$

$$\therefore \quad \frac{dy}{dx}(x\,e^{xy} + \cos y) = 2x - y\,e^{xy}$$

$$\therefore \quad \frac{dy}{dx} = \frac{2x - y\,e^{xy}}{\cos y + x\,e^{xy}}$$

Example 15. Given that $3x^2 + 5xy + 4y^2 - 23y = 0$, obtain an expression for dy/dx. Find the values of x for which the function (or functions) defined by the equation have stationary values.

$$3x^2 + 5xy + 4y^2 - 23y = 0 \qquad \text{(i)}$$

Differentiating with respect to x

$$6x + \frac{d(5xy)}{dx} + 4\frac{d(y^2)}{dx} - 23\frac{dy}{dx} = 0$$

Note that $5xy$ is a product

$$\therefore \quad 6x + \left(5y + 5x\frac{dy}{dx}\right) + 4\frac{dy^2}{dy}\frac{dy}{dx} - 23\frac{dy}{dx} = 0$$

$$\therefore \quad 6x + 5y + 5x\frac{dy}{dx} + 8y\frac{dy}{dx} - 23\frac{dy}{dx} = 0$$

$$\therefore \quad 6x + 5y = \frac{dy}{dx}(23 - 5x - 8y)$$

$$\frac{dy}{dx} = \frac{6x + 5y}{23 - 5x - 8y}$$

Stationary values are given by $\frac{dy}{dx} = 0$, that is

$$\frac{6x + 5y}{23 - 5x - 8y} = 0$$

or

$$6x + 5y = 0 \qquad \text{(ii)}$$

To obtain the required values of x, eliminate y from equations (i) and (ii).

From (ii)

$$y = -\frac{6}{5}x$$

Substituting in equation (i)

$$3x^2 + 5x\left(-\frac{6}{5}x\right) + 4\left(-\frac{6}{5}x\right)^2 - 23\left(-\frac{6}{5}x\right) = 0$$

$$3x^2 - 6x^2 + \frac{144}{25}x^2 + \frac{138}{5}x = 0$$

$$\frac{69}{25}x^2 + \frac{138}{5}x = 0$$

$$x^2 + 10x = 0$$

$$x(x + 10) = 0$$

$$x = 0 \quad \text{or} \quad -10$$

Fig. 4.3 illustrates these results.

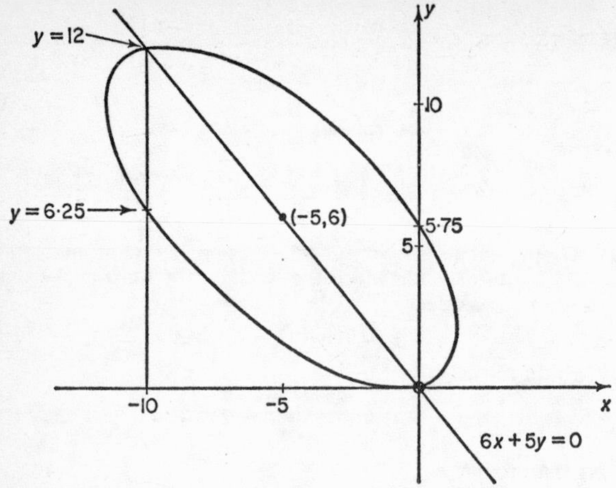

Fig. 4.3

To find d^2y/dx^2 the expression for dy/dx can be differentiated again with respect to x. This can be a lengthy process. In a practical case it could be better to proceed as follows.

Example 16. Find the values of dy/dx and d^2y/dx^2 at the point (1, 2) on the curve $5x^2 - 6xy + y^2 - 2x + 4y - 3 = 0$.

Differentiating the given equation with respect to x

$$\frac{d(5x^2)}{dx} - \frac{d(6xy)}{dx} + \frac{d(y^2)}{dx} - \frac{d(2x)}{dx} + \frac{d(4y)}{dx} - \frac{d(3)}{dx} = 0$$

Note that $6xy$ is a product

$$\therefore \qquad 10x - 6y - 6x\frac{dy}{dx} + \frac{d(y^2)}{dy}\frac{dy}{dx} - 2 + 4\frac{dy}{dx} = 0$$

$$10x - 6y - 6x\frac{dy}{dx} + 2y\frac{dy}{dx} - 2 + 4\frac{dy}{dx} = 0 \qquad \text{(i)}$$

When $x = 1, y = 2$

$$\therefore \qquad 10 - 12 - 6\frac{dy}{dx} + 4\frac{dy}{dx} - 2 + 4\frac{dy}{dx} = 0$$

$$\therefore \qquad 2\frac{dy}{dx} = 4$$

$$\frac{dy}{dx} = 2$$

Differentiating equation (i) with respect to x

$$10 - 6\frac{dy}{dx} - \frac{d}{dx}\left(6x\frac{dy}{dx}\right) + \frac{d}{dx}\left(2y\frac{dy}{dx}\right) - 0 + 4\frac{d^2y}{dx^2} = 0$$

Note that both $6x\frac{dy}{dx}$ and $2y\frac{dy}{dx}$ are products.

$$\therefore \qquad 10 - 6\frac{dy}{dx} - 6\frac{dy}{dx} - 6x\frac{d^2y}{dx^2} + 2\frac{dy}{dx}\cdot\frac{dy}{dx} + 2y\frac{d^2y}{dx^2} + 4\frac{d^2y}{dx^2} = 0$$

When $x = 1$, $y = 2$ and $\frac{dy}{dx} = 2$

$$\therefore \qquad 10 - 12 - 12 - 6\frac{d^2y}{dx^2} + 8 + 4\frac{d^2y}{dx^2} + 4\frac{d^2y}{dx^2} = 0$$

$$\therefore \qquad 2\frac{d^2y}{dx^2} = 6$$

$$\frac{d^2y}{dx^2} = 3$$

Exercises 4.5

Find $\frac{dy}{dx}$ given that:

1. $xy^2 = 1$
2. $xy^2 - x - y = 0$
3. $e^{xy} - 5y^2 + 4x = 0$
4. $\cos xy + x^2y + y = 0$
5. Find the values of dy/dx and d^2y/dx^2 at the point (1, 1) on the curve $3xy + y^2 - x - y - 2 = 0$.
6. Given the equation $4y^2 - 10xy + 4x^2 - 2y - 2x + 7 = 0$, obtain an expression for dy/dx in terms of x and y. Hence find the values of x for which the function (or functions) defined by the equation have stationary values and find these stationary values.

4.9 Differentiation of Parametric Equations

The x and y coordinates of a point P may be specified by two equations of the form

$$x = t^2 \qquad y = 2t \tag{4.23}$$

To each value of t there is a corresponding pair of values of x and y, and as t varies the point P moves along a plane curve. The variable t is known as a **parameter** and equations such as 4.23 are known as **parametric equations.** If we make a table of values of t and the corresponding values of x and y, the points (x,y) can be plotted and the curve can be drawn. For example, from the equations 4.23

t	−3	−2	−1	0	1	2	3
x	9	4	1	0	1	4	9
y	−6	−4	−2	0	2	4	6

In some cases it is possible to eliminate the parameter t and obtain an equation in x and y. Referring to equations 4.23

$$y = 2t \qquad x = t^2$$

From the second equation, we obtain the inverse relations

$$t = \pm\sqrt{x} \qquad (x \geqslant 0)$$

Substituting in the first equation

$$y = 2t = \pm 2\sqrt{x} \qquad (x \geqslant 0)$$

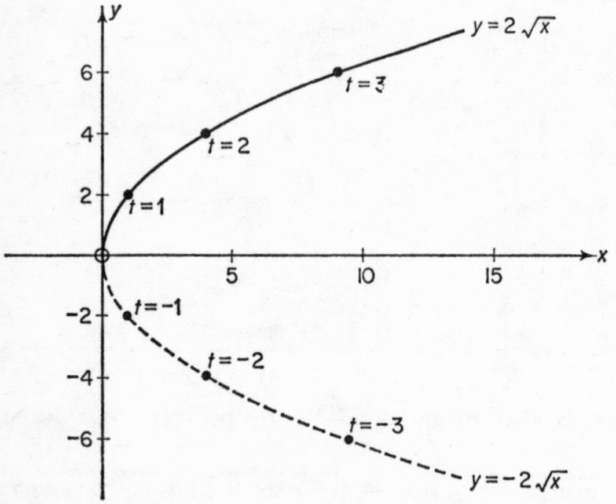

Fig. 4.4

We note that two separate functions of x are defined

$$y = u(x) = 2\sqrt{x} \quad (x \geqslant 0) \quad \text{and} \quad y = v(x) = -2\sqrt{x} \quad (x \geqslant 0)$$

These are shown in Fig. 4.4.

This is similar to the situation in section 4.8, when we differentiated implicitly.

Differentiating both $u(x)$ and $v(x)$

$$\frac{dy}{dx} = \frac{du(x)}{dx} = \frac{d2\sqrt{x}}{dx} = \frac{2}{2\sqrt{x}} = \frac{2}{u(x)} = \frac{2}{y} = \frac{1}{t} \qquad (t \neq 0)$$

$$\frac{dy}{dx} = \frac{dv(x)}{dx} = \frac{d(-2\sqrt{x})}{dx} = \frac{2}{-2\sqrt{x}} = \frac{2}{v(x)} = \frac{2}{y} = \frac{1}{t} \qquad (t \neq 0)$$

$$\therefore \qquad \frac{dy}{dx} = \frac{1}{t} \qquad (t \neq 0) \text{ in both cases}$$

In some cases the original parametric equations are simple, but elimination of the parameter gives an equation in x and y which is complicated and difficult to work with. An example is the cycloid, which is the curve traced out by a fixed point on the circumference of a circle which rolls without slipping on a fixed straight line (see Fig. 4.5).

Let the rolling circle have radius a and centre C, the fixed line be the x-axis, P be the fixed point on the circle and the origin O one of the points where P touches the x-axis. Consider the position of P when the circle has rotated through an angle θ. Referring to Fig. 4.5

$$OA = \text{arc } AP = a\theta$$

$$BA = DC \quad = a \sin \theta$$

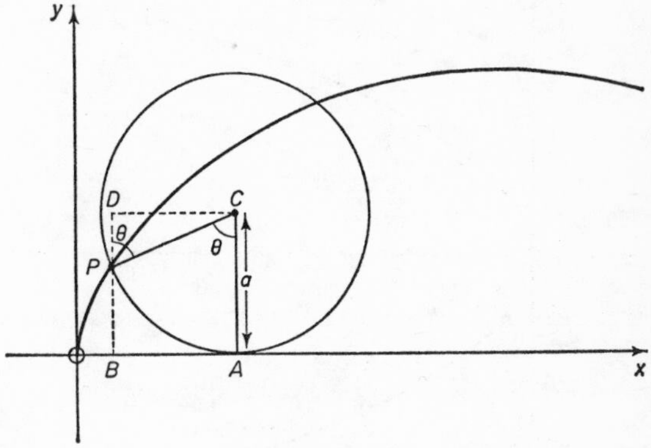

Fig. 4.5

The length of OB is the x coordinate of P

$\therefore$ $$x = OA - AB$$

$$x = a\theta - a \sin \theta$$

The length of PB is the y coordinate of P

$\therefore$ $$y = DB - DP$$

$$= a - a \cos \theta$$

Therefore the parametric equations of the cycloid are

$$x = a(\theta - \sin \theta) \qquad y = a(1 - \cos \theta) \tag{4.24}$$

(The case of $(0 \leqslant \theta \leqslant \pi/2)$ has been illustrated but the equations are true for all values of θ, as may be easily verified.)

To find an expression for $\mathrm{d}y/\mathrm{d}x$

$$\frac{\mathrm{d}y}{\mathrm{d}\theta} = \frac{\mathrm{d}y}{\mathrm{d}x} \cdot \frac{\mathrm{d}x}{\mathrm{d}\theta} \qquad \text{(from 4.13)}$$

or $$\frac{\mathrm{d}y}{\mathrm{d}x} = \frac{\mathrm{d}y}{\mathrm{d}\theta} \bigg/ \frac{\mathrm{d}x}{\mathrm{d}\theta} \tag{4.25}$$

This is acceptable, provided that (a) y and x are given explicitly as functions of θ and (b) we are clear that (i) what is meant by dy/dx is the derivative of a function of x and (ii) there may be more than one such function, as in Fig. 4.4. In the case of the cycloid*

$$\frac{dy}{dx} = \frac{da(1 - \cos\theta)}{d\theta} \bigg/ \frac{da(\theta - \sin\theta)}{d\theta}$$

$$= \frac{a \sin\theta}{a(1 - \cos\theta)}$$

$$= \frac{2 \sin\frac{\theta}{2} \cos\frac{\theta}{2}}{2 \sin^2 \frac{\theta}{2}} \qquad (\sin\theta/2 \neq 0)$$

$$= \cot\frac{\theta}{2}$$

Example 17. Find dy/dx and d^2y/dx^2 in terms of θ, given that $x = a\cos^3\theta$, $y = a\sin^3\theta$, where a is a constant. Obtain an equation in x and y by eliminating the parameter θ. Differentiate this equation implicitly and verify that the expression for dy/dx obtained earlier is correct.

$$\frac{dy}{d\theta} = \frac{d(a\sin^3\theta)}{d\theta} = a\frac{d(\sin\theta)^3}{d(\sin\theta)} \cdot \frac{d\sin\theta}{d\theta}$$

$$= 3a\sin^2\theta\cos\theta \qquad \text{(i)}$$

$$\frac{dx}{d\theta} = \frac{d(a\cos^3\theta)}{d\theta} = a\frac{d(\cos\theta)^3}{d(\cos\theta)} \cdot \frac{d\cos\theta}{d\theta}$$

$$= -3a\cos^2\theta\sin\theta \qquad \text{(ii)}$$

$$\therefore \quad \frac{dy}{dx} = \frac{dy}{d\theta}\bigg/\frac{dx}{d\theta} = \frac{3a\sin^2\theta\cos\theta}{-3a\cos^2\theta\sin\theta}$$

$$= -\tan\theta$$

Differentiating both sides with respect to θ

$$\frac{d}{d\theta}\left(\frac{dy}{dx}\right) = -\sec^2\theta$$

$$\therefore \quad \frac{d}{dx}\left(\frac{dy}{dx}\right) \cdot \frac{dx}{d\theta} = -\sec^2\theta$$

$$\therefore \quad \frac{d^2y}{dx^2} = -\sec^2\theta\bigg/\frac{dx}{d\theta}$$

$$= \frac{-\sec^2\theta}{-3a\cos^2\theta\sin\theta} \qquad \text{from equation (ii)}$$

$$= \frac{1}{3a}\sec^4\theta\,\mathrm{cosec}\,\theta$$

* For an interesting discussion of rolling curves in general refer to *Infinitesimal Calculus*, by H. Lamb, C.U.P., 1947.

To eliminate the parameter θ

$$\begin{aligned} x^{\frac{2}{3}} + y^{\frac{2}{3}} &= (a\cos^3\theta)^{\frac{2}{3}} + (a\sin^3\theta)^{\frac{2}{3}} \\ &= a^{\frac{2}{3}}\cos^2\theta + a^{\frac{2}{3}}\sin^2\theta \\ &= a^{\frac{2}{3}}(\cos^2\theta + \sin^2\theta) \end{aligned}$$

$$\therefore \qquad x^{\frac{2}{3}} + y^{\frac{2}{3}} = a^{\frac{2}{3}}$$

Differentiating the equation implicitly with respect to x

$$\frac{d(x^{\frac{2}{3}})}{dx} + \frac{d(y^{\frac{2}{3}})}{dx} = \frac{d(a^{\frac{2}{3}})}{dx}$$

$$\therefore \qquad \tfrac{2}{3}x^{-\frac{1}{3}} + \frac{d(y^{\frac{2}{3}})}{dy}\cdot\frac{dy}{dx} = 0 \quad (a \text{ is a constant})$$

$$\therefore \qquad \tfrac{2}{3}x^{-\frac{1}{3}} + \tfrac{2}{3}y^{-\frac{1}{3}}\frac{dy}{dx} = 0$$

$$\begin{aligned} \therefore \qquad \frac{dy}{dx} &= -\frac{x^{-\frac{1}{3}}}{y^{-\frac{1}{3}}} \\ &= -\frac{y^{\frac{1}{3}}}{x^{\frac{1}{3}}} \\ &= -\frac{(a\sin^3\theta)^{\frac{1}{3}}}{(a\cos^3\theta)^{\frac{1}{3}}} \\ &= -\frac{a^{\frac{1}{3}}\sin\theta}{a^{\frac{1}{3}}\cos\theta} \\ &= -\tan\theta \end{aligned}$$

which agrees with the earlier result.

The curve is known as the astroid and is shown in Fig. 4.6.

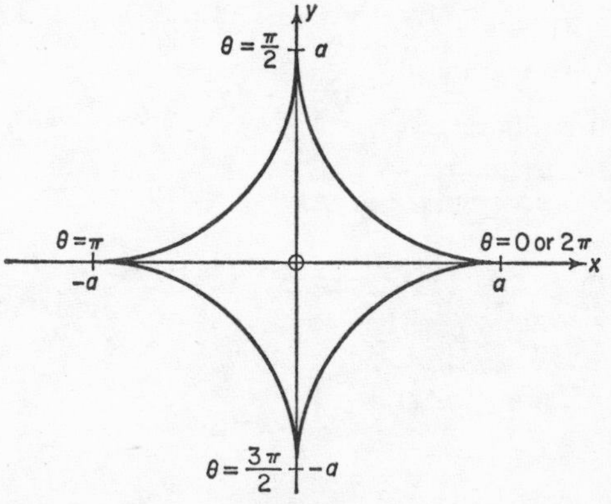

Fig. 4.6

Exercises 4.6

1. Sketch the curve whose parametric equations are $y = t^2$, $x = 3t + 1$ for values of t between -4 and $+4$. Find the values of dy/dx and d^2y/dx^2 in terms of the parameter t.

2. Sketch the curve whose parametric equations are $x = \cos\theta$, $y = \sin^2\theta$ for values of θ in the range 0 to 2π. Eliminate θ and obtain an equation in x and y. Is the curve corresponding to the x, y equation identical with the curve corresponding to the parametric equations?

3. Given the parametric equations $x = (1 - t^2)/(1 + t^2)$, $y = 2t/(1 + t^2)$ find $\mathrm{d}y/\mathrm{d}x$ in terms of t. Eliminate t and obtain an equation in x and y. Show that there are two possible functions of x. Differentiate each of these with respect to x and show that the derivatives are both equal to the value of $\mathrm{d}y/\mathrm{d}x$ obtained directly from the parametric equations.

4. A shell is fired from a point P on a horizontal plane. The coordinates of its position after time t seconds referred to horizontal and vertical axes through P are given by $x = 20t$, $y = 48t - 16t^2$. Find at what time the projectile is moving horizontally and the angle it makes with the horizontal when it hits the ground.

5. The shape of a tooth of a gear wheel is a curve whose parametric equations are $x = a(\cos\theta + \theta\sin\theta - 1)$, $y = a(\sin\theta - \theta\cos\theta)$. Sketch the curve for values of θ between 0 and $\pi/2$ and find an expression for $\mathrm{d}y/\mathrm{d}x$ in terms of θ. (The curve is an involute of a circle and is the path traced out by the end of a taut string which is being unwound from around a fixed circle.)

4.10 Logarithmic Differentiation

The logarithm of a function can sometimes be written in a different form which is easier to differentiate. Example 11 of Chapter Two gives two examples. As a further example consider the function

$$\ln\sqrt{\frac{(1 - x^2)}{(1 + x^2)}}$$

It can be written as

$$\ln\sqrt{\frac{(1 - x^2)}{(1 + x^2)}} = \frac{1}{2}\ln(1 - x^2) - \frac{1}{2}\ln(1 + x^2)$$

and its derivative with respect to x is given by

$$\frac{\mathrm{d}}{\mathrm{d}x}\left[\ln\sqrt{\frac{(1 - x^2)}{(1 + x^2)}}\right] = \frac{1}{2}\frac{\mathrm{d}}{\mathrm{d}x}[\ln(1 - x^2)] - \frac{1}{2}\frac{\mathrm{d}}{\mathrm{d}x}[\ln(1 + x^2)]$$

$$= \frac{1}{2}\frac{\mathrm{d}\ln(1 - x^2)}{\mathrm{d}(1 - x^2)}\cdot\frac{\mathrm{d}(1 - x^2)}{\mathrm{d}x} - \frac{1}{2}\frac{\mathrm{d}\ln(1 + x^2)}{\mathrm{d}(1 + x^2)}\cdot\frac{\mathrm{d}(1 + x^2)}{\mathrm{d}x}$$

$$= \frac{1}{2}\cdot\frac{-2x}{(1 - x^2)} - \frac{1}{2}\cdot\frac{2x}{(1 + x^2)}$$

$$= -\frac{x}{(1 - x^2)} - \frac{x}{(1 + x^2)}$$

$$= \frac{-2x}{(1 - x^4)}$$

In the case of some complicated functions involving roots or powers of quotients and/or products the working can be simplified by considering the logarithm of the function.

Example 18. Find dy/dx given that $y = \sqrt{\left[\frac{(1+x)x^2}{(1-x)}\right]}$.

$$y = \sqrt{\left[\frac{(1+x)x^2}{(1-x)}\right]}$$

$$\ln y = \ln \sqrt{\left[\frac{(1+x)x^2}{(1-x)}\right]}$$

$$= \tfrac{1}{2}\ln(1+x) + \tfrac{1}{2}\ln x^2 - \tfrac{1}{2}\ln(1-x)$$

$$= \tfrac{1}{2}\ln(1+x) + \ln x - \tfrac{1}{2}\ln(1-x)$$

Notice that the square root, the product and the quotient have been removed and differentiating is easier

$$\frac{d}{dx}(\ln y) = \frac{1}{2}\frac{d\ln(1+x)}{dx} + \frac{d\ln x}{dx} - \frac{1}{2}\frac{d\ln(1-x)}{dx}$$

$$\therefore \quad \frac{1}{y}\frac{dy}{dx} = \frac{1}{2}\frac{1}{(1+x)}.1 + \frac{1}{x} - \frac{1}{2}\frac{1}{(1-x)}.(-1)$$

$$= \frac{1}{1-x^2} + \frac{1}{x}$$

$$\therefore \quad \frac{dy}{dx} = y\left[\frac{1}{1-x^2} + \frac{1}{x}\right]$$

$$\therefore \quad \frac{dy}{dx} = \sqrt{\left[\frac{(1+x)x^2}{(1-x)}\right]}\left[\frac{1}{1-x^2} + \frac{1}{x}\right]$$

To differentiate functions such as 2^x, 3^x, x^x, which include a variable power, we have to understand what we mean by say 2^x.

We are familiar with the idea of 2^x when x has an integral or a rational value—for example, 2^4, 2^{-3}, $2^{3/4}$. If, however, x is a continuous variable it can take all real values, including irrational values, and what then is meant by $2^{\sqrt{2}}$, 2^π, $2^{\sqrt{3}}$?

Assuming that it exists, 2^x can be expressed in a different form as follows

Let $\quad y = 2^x$

$$\therefore \quad \ln y = \ln 2^x$$

$$\ln y = x \ln 2$$

$$\therefore \quad y \text{ or } 2^x = e^{(x \ln 2)}$$

The exponential function is defined for all powers including irrational ones; therefore $e^{(x \ln 2)}$ has a meaning and we use it to define 2^x.

Definition $\quad 2^x = e^{(x \ln 2)}$

Similarly $\quad 3^x = e^{(x \ln 3)}$

$$a^x = e^{(x \ln a)} \quad (a > 0)$$

$$x^x = e^{(x \ln x)} \quad (x > 0)$$

Example 19. Find the derivatives of: (i) 2^x, (ii) x^x $(x > 0)$.

(i) Let $\quad y = 2^x = e^{(x \ln 2)}$

$$\therefore \quad \frac{dy}{dx} = \frac{d\,e^{(x \ln 2)}}{d(x \ln 2)} \cdot \frac{d(x \ln 2)}{dx}$$

$$= e^{(x \ln 2)} \ln 2$$

$$= 2^x \ln 2$$

(ii) Let $y = x^x = e^{(x \ln x)}\ (x > 0)$

$$\therefore \quad \frac{dy}{dx} = \frac{d\,e^{(x \ln x)}}{d(x \ln x)} \cdot \frac{d(x \ln x)}{dx}$$

$$= e^{(x \ln x)}\left[1.1\text{n}\, x + x \,.\, \frac{1}{x}\right]$$

$$= x^x (\ln x + 1)$$

Revision Questions 4.2

Complete the following	*Answer*	*Refer to*
1. $\dfrac{d(x^2+1)^{12}}{dx} = \dfrac{d(x^2+1)^{12}}{d(x^2+1)} \cdot \dfrac{d\ldots}{dx}$	1. $\dfrac{d(x^2+1)^{12}}{d(x^2+1)} \cdot \dfrac{d(x^2+1)}{dx}$	Section 4.6 and formula 1.10
2. $\cos^5\theta = (\ldots)^5$	2. $(\cos\theta)^5$	
3. $\dfrac{d(\cos\theta)^5}{d(\ldots)} = 5\cos^4\theta$	3. $\dfrac{d(\cos\theta)^5}{d(\cos\theta)} = 5\cos^4\theta$	Formula 1.10
4. $\dfrac{d\cos\theta}{\ldots} = -\sin\theta$	4. $\dfrac{d\cos\theta}{d\theta} = -\sin\theta$	Formula 4.2
5. $\dfrac{d(x^2y)}{dx} = 2xy + \ldots$	5. $2xy + x^2\dfrac{dy}{dx}$	Section 4.8
6. $\dfrac{d}{dx}\left[y\dfrac{dy}{dx}\right] =$	6. $\left(\dfrac{dy}{dx}\right)^2 + y\dfrac{d^2y}{dx^2}$	Section 4.8
7. $\ln\sqrt{\dfrac{(1+x)}{(1-x)}} = \dfrac{1}{2}\ln(1+x) - \ldots$	7. $\dfrac{1}{2}\ln(1+x) - \dfrac{1}{2}\ln(1-x)$	Chapter Two Example 11
8. Given that $x = \cos\theta$ and $y = \sin\theta$, $\dfrac{dy}{dx} = \ldots$	8. $\dfrac{dy}{dx} = \dfrac{\cos\theta}{-\sin\theta} = -\cot\theta$	Section 4.9
9. Given that $f(x) = x^{2x}\ (x > 0)$, to find $f'(x)$ we first . . .	9. . . . express x^{2x} as $e^{2x \ln x}$	Section 4.10

Exercises 4.7

Find $\dfrac{dy}{dx}$ given that:

1. $y = (\cos x)^x$
2. $y = x^{\cos x}$
3. $y = x^{x-2}$
4. $y = \sqrt{\dfrac{(x+2)}{(x-2)}}$

5. $y = \left[\dfrac{(1 - x^2)}{(1 + x^2)}\right]^{\frac{3}{2}}$

6. $y = \sqrt{\dfrac{(x^2 + x + 1)}{(x^2 - x + 1)}}$

7. $y = 3^{2x+3}$

8. $y = 10^x$

9. $y = \ln(\ln x)$

10. $y = \ln(x^2 \ln x)$

4.11 Problems

The following are a set of revision exercises and are on the work done in the first four chapters.

1. The intensity of radiation at a point P at a distance r from a point source of heat S is equal to I/r^2 where I is the intensity of the source. Two point sources I_1 and I_2 are placed at points A and B respectively. Find the position of the point C on the line AB so that the intensity of radiation due to both I_1 and I_2 is a minimum.

2. In the study of vibrational spectra of diatomic molecules it is found that if r_e is the equilibrium intermolecular distance and r the distance apart when disturbed

$$\frac{\mathrm{d}^2(r - r_e)}{\mathrm{d}t^2} = -\frac{k}{\mu}(r - r_e)$$

where k is the force constant and μ is the reduced mass. Verify that $r - r_e = a \sin(2\pi V_0 t)$ is a solution of this equation where $V_0 = k^{\frac{1}{2}}/(2\pi\mu^{\frac{1}{2}})$.

3. A uniformly heavy rod of weight W is resting on a fixed smooth horizontal peg with its lower end pressing a vertical smooth wall. The rod makes an angle θ with the upward vertical. The potential energy V of the rod is given by

$$V = W\left(a - \frac{c}{\sin\theta}\right)\cos\theta$$

where a and c are constants with $c \leqslant a$. Find the value of θ for which V has a turning value and show that this gives a maximum value of V and hence an unstable system.

4. The speed of light V was found by Foucault's rotating mirror experiment. The formula from which V was calculated was $V = 8\pi n\, d_1 d/C$, where n was the number of revolutions per second performed by the revolving mirror, d_1 and d the distances from the slit to the lens and to the concave mirror and C the displacement of the image. The error in measuring d was negligible but the errors in measuring n, d_1 and C were respectively 0·05%, 0·05% and 0·5%. Find the greatest possible error in the calculation of V.

5. A uniformly loaded beam of length l is clamped horizontally at one end A; the other end B rests freely on a support. AB is horizontal. The deflection y at a distance x from A is given by

$$EIy = \frac{w}{48}(2x^4 - 5lx^3 + 3l^2x^2)$$

where E, I and w are constants. Find, correct to two places of decimals, the value of x for which y is a maximum.

6. A manufacturer sells his product at a price of £S per tonne. The monthly demand of x tonnes is given by $x = 800 - 4S$. The cost of producing x tonnes is £$(0{\cdot}025x^2 + 500)$ and the overheads are £3 per tonne. Find to the nearest whole number the value of S for which his net revenue will be a maximum.

7. A baseball 'diamond' is in the form of a square $ABCD$, the length of whose sides is 30 m. A batter stands at A and strikes the ball along the side AB at a speed of

25 m/s. How fast is the distance of the ball from second base C changing when the ball has gone (i) 10 m and (ii) 15 m? (Assume that the speed of the ball is unchanged over these distances.)

8. The position of a point $P(x,y)$ is given by the parametric equations $x = at^2$, $y = 2at$. Sketch the path of P for values of t between -3 and $+3$. Eliminate t from the equations and show that two functions of x are possible: $y = u(x)$ and $y = v(x)$. Mark these on your graph. Express $\frac{dv(x)}{dx}$, $\frac{du(x)}{dx}$ and $\frac{dy}{dt}\Big/\frac{dx}{dt}$ all in terms of t. Are the three expressions equal?

9. An alternating current i amp at any time t seconds is given by $i = 2 \sin pt + \sin 2pt$. Find the maximum and minimum values of i and the smallest positive values of t for which these occur.

10. Prove that the function $f(x) = (x^2 + 24)/(4x + 4)$ has a maximum value of -3 and a minimum value of $+2$. Note that the minimum value is greater than the maximum value and explain the apparent paradox by sketching the graph of $f(x)$.

11. Find $f'(x), f''(x), f'''(x), f^{iv}(x), f^{v}(x)$ and hence deduce the value of $f^n(x)$ when

(i) $f(x) = \dfrac{1}{(2x + 3)}$ (ii) $f(x) = x \ln x$

Are the expressions for $f^n(x)$ true for all positive integral values of n?

12. The rate of decrease of the viscosity n of glycerine with respect to the temperature θ is proportional to the viscosity. Write down the appropriate mathematical equation. What is the solution of this equation given that when $\theta = 0$, $n = 46{\cdot}0$?

13. (i) Write down the first *four* terms and the general term of the expansion of e^x in ascending powers of x. (ii) Evaluate $e^{-0\cdot1}$ correct to four places of decimals. (iii) Given that x is so small that terms in x^3 and higher powers of x may be neglected, find the values of the constants a and b such that

$$e^{-2x} e^x = 1 + ax + bx^2$$

14. The axis of a small magnet coincides with the axis of a circular conductor of radius a. When the centre of the magnet is at a distance x from the centre of the conductor the force F on it is given by $F = kx/(a^2 + x^2)^{5/2}$, where k is a constant. Find the maximum value of F.

15. The total kinetic and potential energy E of a satellite mass m moving at a uniform speed in a circular orbit of radius r about the centre of the earth is $mga^2\left(\frac{1}{a} - \frac{1}{2r}\right)$, where a is the radius of the earth and g is a constant. When the satellite is subjected to a small constant force F for one revolution, the radius of the orbit changes to $r + \delta r$ (δr small). Find an expression for the change δE in the total energy E. Equate the change in the total energy to the product of the force F and the distance for which it acted and hence show that $F = (mga^2/4\pi r^3)\delta r$.

16. By using Kepler's Third Law of Planetary Motion, the mass m of a satellite, presumed small compared to the mass of the earth, is calculated from the formula $m = a^3M/T^2$, where a is the semi-major axis of the satellite's elliptical orbit measured in astronomical units*, T is the time in years for one revolution of the satellite and M

* The semi-major axis of the earth's elliptical orbit around the sun is known as the astronomical unit of distance.

is the mass of the sun. The errors in a, T and M are each estimated to be 0·1%. Find the maximum percentage error in the calculation of the mass of the satellite.

17. The voltage E applied to the sending end of a high-pressure transmitting line is connected to the voltage e at the receiving end by the equation

$$E^2 = (e \cos \theta + a)^2 + (e \sin \theta + b)^2$$

where a and b are constants. Expand the right-hand side of this equation and by expressing $a \cos \theta + b \sin \theta$ in the form $R \cos (\theta + \alpha)$ show that the maximum and minimum values of R, as θ varies, are $e \pm \sqrt{(a^2 + b^2)}$. (Obtaining these results by differentiation is a much more difficult method and we would remind our readers that the calculus is not always the best way of solving a problem.)

18. The partition function q of a monatomic gas is given by the equation $q = KT^{5/2}$, where K is a constant and T is the absolute temperature. Find in terms of R and T the value of C_p, the heat capacity at constant pressure, where

$$C_p = R\frac{\mathrm{d}(\ln q)}{\mathrm{d}T} + \mathrm{R}\frac{\mathrm{d}^2(\ln q)}{\mathrm{d}T^2}$$

R being the gas constant.

19. In statistics the modal value of a continuous distribution is the value of the variable which gives a maximum value of the probability density function. Find the modal values of the distributions with the following probability density functions

(i) xe^{-x} (ii) x^2e^{-x} (iii) $\frac{3}{32}(4x - x^2)$

20. The speeds of light in air and in water are V_1 and V_2 respectively. A ray of light passes from a point A in air to a point B in water and meets the surface of separation of the air and water at a point P, as shown in Fig. 4.7. The rays of light AP, PB and

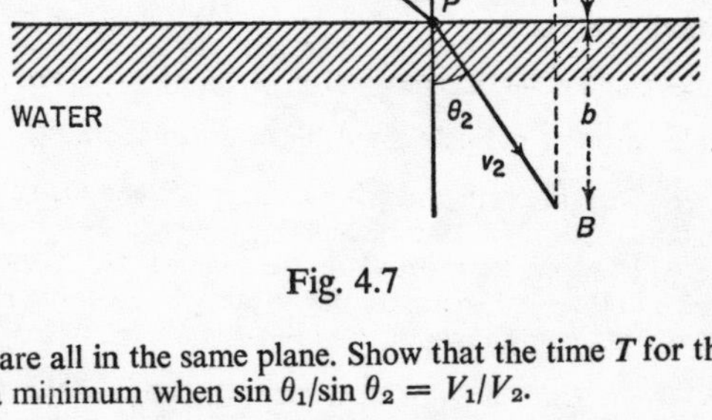

Fig. 4.7

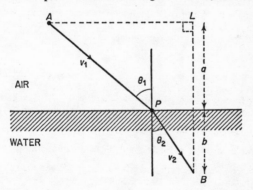

the normal at P are all in the same plane. Show that the time T for the light to pass from A to B is a minimum when $\sin \theta_1/\sin \theta_2 = V_1/V_2$.

[Hint: Show that (i) $a \tan \theta_1 + b \tan \theta_2 = AL$ (AL constant)

(ii) $T = \dfrac{a}{V_1 \cos \theta_1} + \dfrac{b}{V_2 \cos \theta_2}$

Differentiate both expressions with respect to θ_1 and eliminate $\mathrm{d}\theta_2/\mathrm{d}\theta_1$ to find $\mathrm{d}T/\mathrm{d}\theta_1$.]

21. Schrödinger's equation for the one-dimensional motion of a particle whose potential energy is zero is

$$\frac{d^2\psi}{dx^2} + \frac{2mE}{h^2}\psi = 0$$

where ψ is the wave function, m the mass of the particle, E its kinetic energy and h is Planck's constant. Show that

$$\psi = A \sin\left(\frac{2mE}{h^2}\right)^{\frac{1}{2}} x + B \cos\left(\frac{2mE}{h^2}\right)^{\frac{1}{2}} x$$

(where A and B are constants) is a solution of this equation.

Using the boundary conditions $\psi = 0$ when $x = 0$ and when $x = a$, show that

(i) the kinetic energy $E = h^2n^2/8ma^2$
(ii) the wave function $\psi = A \sin (n\pi x/a)$

where n is any integer. (Note if $\sin \theta = 0$, then $\theta = n\pi$.)

CHAPTER FIVE

INTEGRATION

5.1 Introduction

In this chapter we shall consider both indefinite and definite integration and show how the two are related. **Indefinite integration** is the reverse of differentiation; that is, given a function, say, $3x^2$, we have to find another function, say, $f(x)$ such that

$$\frac{\mathrm{d}f(x)}{\mathrm{d}x} = 3x^2 \tag{5.1}$$

One solution is $f(x) = x^3$, as may be easily verified by differentiating x^3. In general, to find the indefinite integral of a function $\phi(x)$ with respect to x we have to find a function $f(x)$ such that

$$\frac{\mathrm{d}f(x)}{\mathrm{d}x} = \phi(x) \tag{5.2}$$

This relation 5.2 is more usually written

$$f(x) = \int \phi(x)\,\mathrm{d}x \tag{5.3}$$

The reason for using an elongated 'S' to indicate the inverse operation to differentiation and the advantages of including the 'dx' will be apparent later (see paragraph after equation 5.18 and section 6.1).

Historically the process of **definite integration** was considered first and arose from the geometrical problem of finding the area under a curve. This led to an analytical definition which arose from an idea of Archimedes that because the area of a rectangle can be defined as the value obtained by multiplying its length by its breadth, an approximation to the area under a curve could be obtained by summing series of thinner and thinner rectangles. Consideration of the limiting value of this approximation as the number of rectangles increased (their widths diminishing correspondingly) leads to a value for the area under a curve. This was formally defined by Riemann in 1854. If the curve can be described analytically by $y = \phi(x)$ then the area under the curve between the two ordinates $x = a$ and $x = b$ is denoted by

$$\text{Area} = \int_a^b \phi(x)\,\mathrm{d}x \tag{5.4}$$

We note in passing that some areas have to be obtained in other ways, when $\phi(x)$ does not exist or its indefinite integral with respect to x, as in equation 5.3, cannot be found.

We shall show that the two ideas of definite and indefinite integration are connected; that is, if $f(x)$ exists where

$$\int \phi(x)\, dx = f(x)$$

then

$$\int_a^b \phi(x)\, dx = f(b) - f(a) \tag{5.5}$$

At the introductory stage it is better to consider first the solution of equation 5.3 and then, having gained some facility in solving this problem, to consider definite integration and its application to various problems.

5.2 Indefinite Integration

In the previous section x^3 was said to be *an* indefinite integral of $3x^2$ with respect to x because

$$\frac{d(x^3)}{dx} = 3x^2$$

and that the relation could be written as

$$\int 3x^2\, dx = x^3$$

Similarly, $\sin x$ is *an* indefinite integral of $\cos x$ with respect to x, written as

$$\int \cos x\, dx = \sin x$$

because

$$\frac{d(\sin x)}{dx} = \cos x$$

It will be noted that we have found '*an*' indefinite integral and not '*the*' indefinite integral. The derivative of a constant is zero and therefore $x^3 + 7$ or $x^3 - 5$ are also indefinite integrals of $3x^2$ with respect to x because

$$\frac{d(x^3 + 7)}{dx} = 3x^2 = \frac{d(x^3 - 5)}{dx}$$

In general, if C is any constant

$$\int 3x^2\, dx = x^3 + C$$

because

$$3x^2 = \frac{d(x^3 + C)}{dx}$$

Similarly

$$\int x^3\, dx = \frac{x^4}{4} + C \quad \text{because} \quad \frac{d}{dx}\left(\frac{x^4}{4} + C\right) = x^3$$

$$\int x^{-3}\, dx = \frac{x^{-2}}{-2} + C \quad \text{because} \quad \frac{d}{dx}\left(\frac{x^{-2}}{-2} + C\right) = x^{-3}$$

In general

$$\int x^n \,dx = \frac{x^{n+1}}{(n+1)} + C \qquad (n \text{ any rational value} \neq -1) \tag{5.6}$$

For example $$\int x^{\frac{1}{3}} \,dx = \frac{x^{\frac{1}{3}+1}}{\frac{1}{3}+1} + C = \frac{3x^{\frac{4}{3}}}{4} + C$$

Note that $\int 1 \,dx$ or, as it is often written, $\int dx = x + C$ because

$$\frac{d(x+C)}{dx} = 1$$

This case is included in equation 5.6 if we write 1 as x^0 because

$$\int dx = \int 1 \,dx = \int x^0 \,dx = \frac{x^{0+1}}{0+1} + C = x + C \tag{5.7}$$

Example 1. Find the indefinite integrals with respect to x of the following functions: (i) x^9, (ii) $\sqrt{x}$, (iii) $1/\sqrt[3]{x^2}$, (iv) $1/x^9$.

(i) $$\int x^9 \,dx = \frac{x^{9+1}}{9+1} + C = \frac{x^{10}}{10} + C$$

(ii) $$\int \sqrt{x} \,dx = \int x^{\frac{1}{2}} \,dx = \frac{x^{\frac{1}{2}+1}}{\frac{1}{2}+1} + C = \frac{2x^{\frac{3}{2}}}{3} + C$$

(iii) $$\int \frac{dx}{\sqrt[3]{x^2}} = \int x^{-\frac{2}{3}} \,dx = \frac{x^{-\frac{2}{3}+1}}{-\frac{2}{3}+1} + C = 3x^{\frac{1}{3}} + C$$

(iv) $$\int \frac{dx}{x^9} = \int x^{-9} \,dx = \frac{x^{-9+1}}{-9+1} + C = -\frac{x^{-8}}{8} + C$$

$$= -\frac{1}{8x^8} + C$$

Given further information C may be evaluated.

Example 2. Find the function $f(x)$ such that $d[f(x)]/dx = x^7$ and $f(1) = 5$.

$$\frac{d[f(x)]}{dx} = x^7$$

$\therefore$ $$f(x) = \int x^7 \,dx$$

$$= \frac{x^{7+1}}{7+1} + C \qquad \text{(by equation 5.6)}$$

$$= \frac{x^8}{8} + C$$

Now $$f(1) = 5 = \frac{(1)^8}{8} + C$$

$\therefore$ $$C = 4\tfrac{7}{8}$$

$\therefore$ $$f(x) = \frac{x^8}{8} + 4\tfrac{7}{8}$$

Certain integrals can be written down immediately from our knowledge of derivatives

$$\left.\begin{aligned}\int \sin x\,\mathrm{d}x &= -\cos x + C\\ \int \cos x\,\mathrm{d}x &= \sin x + C\\ \int e^{ax}\,\mathrm{d}x &= \frac{e^{ax}}{a} + C \text{ (where } a \text{ is a constant)}\end{aligned}\right\} \quad (5.8)$$

The results of equations 5.8 are of wide application. Consider the case of $\int \sin x\,\mathrm{d}x$: we can substitute y for x *throughout* and obtain

$$\int \sin y\,\mathrm{d}y = -\cos y + C$$

or even substitute $(2x + 1)$ for x *throughout* and obtain

$$\left.\begin{aligned}&\int \sin (2x + 1)\mathrm{d}(2x + 1) = -\cos (2x + 1) + C\\ \text{also} \quad &\int \cos z\,\mathrm{d}z = \sin z + C\\ &\int \cos (y^2)\,\mathrm{d}(y^2) = \sin (y^2) + C\\ &\int e^{ap}\,\mathrm{d}p = \frac{e^{ap}}{a} + C \text{ (where } a \text{ is a constant)}\\ &\int e^{2\sin x}\,\mathrm{d}(\sin x) = \tfrac{1}{2}e^{2\sin x} + C\end{aligned}\right\} \quad (5.9)$$

Referring back to the standard result of equation 5.6, we see that the case of $\int x^{-1}\,\mathrm{d}x$ (that is, $\int 1/x\,\mathrm{d}x$) is not included. From our knowledge of derivatives, it would appear that

$$\int \frac{1}{x}\,\mathrm{d}x = \ln x + C$$

However, $\ln x$ is not defined (has no meaning) for $x = 0$ or x negative, so that this result needs restricting to values of x which are positive.

However, if x is negative then $-x$ is positive and

$$\int \frac{1}{x}\,\mathrm{d}x = \ln (-x) + C$$

because

$$\frac{d[\ln(-x)]}{dx} = \frac{d[\ln(-x)]}{d(-x)} \cdot \frac{d(-x)}{dx}$$

$$= \frac{1}{-x} \cdot -1$$

$$= \frac{1}{x}$$

Neither case includes the value $x = 0$ and we write

$$\int \frac{1}{x}\,dx = \ln|x| + C \qquad (x \neq 0) \tag{5.10}$$

where $|x|$ has its usual meaning of 'the modulus of x' (refer to Exercises 3.1, No. 1). The restriction $x \neq 0$ on the range of values for which the result 5.10 holds is not uncommon, and we formally define the indefinite integral.

Definition. If $\phi(x)$ is a function of x for the range of values $a \leqslant x \leqslant b$ and $f(x)$ is a function of x, for the same range of x, such that

$$\frac{d[f(x)]}{dx} = \phi(x) \qquad (a \leqslant x \leqslant b)$$

we say that $f(x)$ is an **indefinite integral** of $\phi(x)$ with respect to x in the range $a \leqslant x \leqslant b$, and write

$$f(x) = \int \phi(x)\,dx \qquad (a \leqslant x \leqslant b) \tag{5.11}$$

The function $\phi(x)$ is known as the **integrand.**

The following four results only hold for ranges of values of x as indicated; that is, when both the integrand and the indefinite integral are defined simultaneously.

$$\left.\begin{aligned}
\int \sec^2 x\,dx &= \tan x + C && \left(x \neq n\pi + \frac{\pi}{2}\right)\\
\int \sec x \tan x\,dx &= \sec x + C && \left(x \neq n\pi + \frac{\pi}{2}\right)\\
\int \operatorname{cosec}^2 x\,dx &= -\cot x + C && (x \neq n\pi)\\
\int \operatorname{cosec} x \cot x\,dx &= -\operatorname{cosec} x && (x \neq n\pi)
\end{aligned}\right\} \tag{5.12}$$

where n is any positive or negative integer.

Revision Questions 5.1

Complete the following statements	*Answers*	*Refer to*
1. $\int x\,dx = \ldots$	1. $\frac{x^2}{2} + C$	Formula 5.6 with $n = 1$
2. $\int x^{-4}\,dx = -\frac{1}{3}x^{-3} + C$ because . . .	2. $\frac{d}{dx}\left(-\frac{1}{3}x^{-3} + C\right) = x^{-4}$	Section 5.2
3. $\frac{d[\ln(x-2)]}{dx} = \frac{1}{x-2}$; therefore $\int \frac{1}{x-2}\,dx =$ $\ln\lvert x-2\rvert + C$ when . . .	3. $x \neq 2$	Definition of an indefinite integral Section 5.2
4. $\frac{d(e^{x^2})}{dx} = 2x\,e^{x^2}$ therefore $\int 2x\,e^{x^2}\,dx = \ldots$	4. $e^{x^2} + C$	
5. $\frac{d[\sin(x^2)]}{dx} = 2x\cos(x^2)$; therefore $\int \ldots dx =$ $\sin(x^2) + C$	5. $\int 2x\cos(x^2)\,dx$	

5.3 Two Basic Rules

1. *The indefinite integral of the sum, or difference, of two functions is equal to the sum, or difference, of their separate indefinite integrals.*

This follows immediately from the definition of an indefinite integral as the reverse of differentiation. It can be extended to the sums and/or differences of any finite number of indefinite integrals.

Example 3

(i)
$$\int (x^3 - e^{3x} + \cos x)\,dx = \int x^3\,dx - \int e^{3x}\,dx + \int \cos x\,dx$$
$$= \frac{x^4}{4} - \frac{e^{3x}}{3} + \sin x + C$$

(ii)
$$\int \left(\sqrt{x} + \frac{1}{x} - \sec^2 x\right) dx = \int x^{\frac{1}{2}}\,dx + \int \frac{dx}{x} - \int \sec^2 x\,dx$$
$$= x^{\frac{3}{2}}/\tfrac{3}{2} + \ln\lvert x\rvert - \tan x + C$$
$$(x \neq 0 \textit{ and } x \neq n\pi)$$

where n is any positive integer.

2. *A* ***constant*** *factor may be brought outside the integral sign, which also follows immediately from the definition.*

Example 4

(i) $$\int 7e^{-x}\,dx = 7\int e^{-x}\,dx = -7e^{-x} + C$$

(ii) $$\int 8x^{-1}\,dx = 8\int \frac{dx}{x} = 8 \ln |x| + C \quad (x \neq 0)$$

(iii) $$\int -15\,dx = -15\int 1\,dx = -15x + C$$

Rules 1 and 2 may be combined:

Example 5

(i) $$\begin{aligned}\int (5 + 6x - 8x^3)\,dx &= \int 5\,dx + \int 6x\,dx - \int 8x^3\,dx \\ &= 5\int dx + 6\int x\,dx - 8\int x^3\,dx \\ &= 5x + \frac{6x^2}{2} - \frac{8x^4}{4} + C \\ &= 5x + 3x^2 - 2x^4 + C\end{aligned}$$

(ii) $$\begin{aligned}\int (3 \sin x - 4e^{-2x})\,dx &= \int 3 \sin x\,dx - \int 4\,e^{-2x}\,dx \\ &= 3\int \sin x\,dx - 4\int e^{-2x}\,dx \\ &= -3 \cos x - \frac{4\,e^{-2x}}{-2} + C \\ &= 2\,e^{-2x} - 3 \cos x + C\end{aligned}$$

Example 6. A particle moves in a straight line with a constant acceleration of a metres per second per second. After time t seconds its distance from a fixed point P is s metres and its speed is v metres per second. Initially it is at P and its speed is u metres per second. Given that $a = 9{\cdot}8$, obtain expressions for v and s in terms of u and t and for v in terms of u and s.

acceleration $= 9{\cdot}8$

$$\frac{dv}{dt} = 9{\cdot}8$$

$\therefore$ $v = \int 9{\cdot}8\,dt$ (from the definition of integration)

$= 9{\cdot}8t + C$ (from 5.7)

when $t = 0$, $v = u$

$\therefore$ $u = 0 + C$ and $C = u$

$$v = u + 9{\cdot}8t \qquad \text{(i)}$$

or $$\frac{ds}{dt} = u + 9{\cdot}8t$$

$\therefore \quad s = \int (u + 9{\cdot}8t)\,dt$ (from the definition of integration)

$$= ut + 9{\cdot}8\frac{t^2}{2} + C$$

$$= ut + 4{\cdot}9t^2 + C$$

when $t = 0$, $s = 0$

$$\therefore \quad 0 = 0 + 0 + C \quad \text{and} \quad C = 0$$

$$s = ut + 4{\cdot}9t^2 \qquad \text{(ii)}$$

An expression for v in terms of u and s can be obtained by eliminating t from (i) and (ii), or we may proceed as follows. Using the result 4.15

$$\text{acceleration} = \frac{d}{ds}\left(\frac{1}{2}v^2\right) = 9{\cdot}8$$

$$\therefore \quad \tfrac{1}{2}v^2 = \int 9{\cdot}8\,ds$$

$$= 9{\cdot}8s + C$$

when $s = 0$, $v = u$

$$\therefore \quad \tfrac{1}{2}u^2 = 0 + C \quad \text{and} \quad C = \tfrac{1}{2}u^2$$

$$\therefore \quad \tfrac{1}{2}v^2 = 9{\cdot}8s + \tfrac{1}{2}u^2$$

$$\text{or} \quad v^2 = u^2 + 19{\cdot}6s \qquad \text{(iii)}$$

In the theory of economics, if C is the cost of producing an amount n of a commodity then dC/dn, the rate of change of cost with respect to the amount produced, is called the 'marginal cost'. Similarly, if R is the revenue obtained from the sale of an amount n, then dR/dn is known as the 'marginal revenue'.

Example 7. A manufacturer knows that his marginal cost £M is given by $M = 300 + 2n$, where n tonnes is the amount of commodity produced. Also, before selling anything at all he has a basic cost of £10 000. Find an expression for C in terms of n (assuming n is always large, so that the use of integration yields meaningful results).

$$\text{Marginal cost } M = \frac{dC}{dn} = 300 + 2n$$

$$\therefore \quad C = \int (300 + 2n)\,dn$$

$$C = 300n + n^2 + k$$

where k is a constant. When $n = 0$, $C = 10\,000$

$$\therefore \quad 10\,000 = 0 + 0 + k$$

$$10\,000 = k$$

$$\therefore \quad C = 10\,000 + 300n + n^2$$

Exercises 5.1

Integrate the following functions with respect to x:

1. x^9, $x^{7/4}$, $x^{-\frac{1}{3}}$, $\sqrt[3]{x^2}$, $\sqrt{x^5}$

2. $1/x^2$, $4/x^5$, $2/\sqrt{x^3}$, $9/\sqrt[3]{x^4}$, $\dfrac{1}{x}$ $\quad (x \neq 0)$

3. $\sec^2 x$, $\operatorname{cosec}^2 x$, $\operatorname{cosec} x \cot x$, $\sec x \tan x$, $6/\sec x + 5/\operatorname{cosec} x$ $(0 < x < \pi/2)$

4. $(4x^3 - 2x^2 + x)/x$, $(11x^4 - 3x + 6)/x^3$ $(x \neq 0)$

5. $(3 \sec x - \sin 2x)/\cos x$ $(0 < x < \pi/2)$

6. In each of the following, find the derivative with respect to x of the given function and hence write down the indefinite integral of the second function. State the range of values of x for which your result is valid.

(i) $\dfrac{d}{dx} \ln (3 + x)$; $\displaystyle\int \frac{dx}{(3 + x)}$

(ii) $\dfrac{d}{dx} \ln (x - 5)$; $\displaystyle\int \frac{dx}{(x - 5)}$

(iii) $\dfrac{d}{dx} \ln (2x + 3)$; $\displaystyle\int \frac{dx}{3 + 2x}$

(iv) $\dfrac{d}{dx} \ln (5 - x)$; $\displaystyle\int \frac{dx}{5 - x}$

(v) $\dfrac{d[\sin (3x)]}{dx}$; $\displaystyle\int \cos 3x \, dx$

(vi) $\dfrac{d[\cos (5x)]}{dx}$; $\displaystyle\int \sin 5x \, dx$

7. A particle travels in a straight line with an acceleration at any time t of $6t - 4$. It starts from a point O with an initial speed of 6 metres per second. Find its speed and its distance from O after t seconds.

8. A particle moves along a straight line with an acceleration of $9\sqrt{s}$, where s is its distance from a fixed point O on the line. When $s = 0$ its speed v is 2 metres per second. Find an expression for v in terms of s and calculate how far it is from O when $v = 10$ metres per second. (Remember acceleration $= d(\frac{1}{2}v^2)/ds$—refer to equation 4.15.)

9. One end of a long thin wire of length l is heated to a temperature of 100°C; the other end is at a temperature of 15°C. The rate of fall of the temperature θ along the wire is proportional to e^{-x}, where x is the distance from the heated end. Find an expression for θ in terms of x assuming that l is so large that e^{-l} is negligible.

10. A uniformly loaded beam of length $2d$ is freely supported at both ends. The deflection y at any point distance x from one end is given by

$$EI\frac{d^2y}{dx^2} = \tfrac{1}{2}w(d^2 - x^2)$$

where E, I and w are constants. Given that $dy/dx = 0$ when $x = d$ and $y = 0$ when $x = 2d$, prove that at the midpoint of the beam $y = 5wd^4/24EI$.

11. A manufacturer finds that his marginal cost (see example 7) £M is given by $M = 3 + 0{\cdot}4n$, where n is the number of units produced. His basic costs before selling any items are £7000. Assuming n is always large, so that the use of integration yields meaningful results, find an expression for the cost £C of producing n units.

12. When the temperature T of a system changes, the rate of change of the entropy S with respect to T is given by

$$\frac{dS}{dT} = \frac{C}{T}$$

where C is the heat capacity of the system. When $S = S_1$, $T = T_1$ and C is independent of the temperature. Find an expression for the entropy in terms of S_1, T_1, C and T.

5.4 Definite Integration

In section 5.2 indefinite integration was defined as the reverse process to differentiation. It is this relation to derivatives which enables us to evaluate indefinite integrals. If that were all there is to integration it would be of little value except as a mathematical exercise. However, we shall show that indefinite integration can be related, through definite integration, to the limiting value of a summation and because of this it is of great value when solving many geometrical and physical problems.

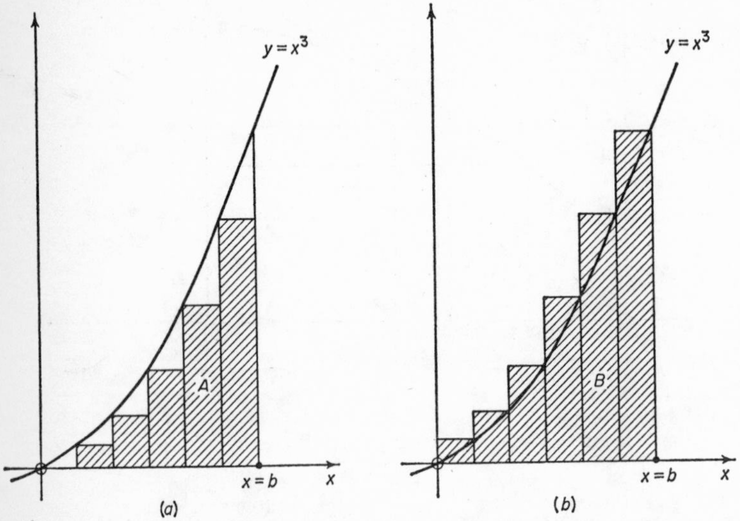

Fig. 5.1

In an introductory book it is best to rely on a geometrical approach, and the method used follows ideas first formulated by Archimedes. Consider, for example, the region under the graph of the function x^3 between $x = 0$ and $x = b$. Divide the region into n strips of equal width b/n, and using two sets of rectangles, as shown in Figs. 5.1(*a*) and 5.1(*b*), approximate to the region from below and above.

The area of a rectangle is the product of its length and breadth, and the areas of the collections of rectangles A and B can thus be calculated. The area to be ascribed to the region under the curve lies between A and B

$$A < \text{area under the curve} < B$$

As the number of divisions increases, the difference between A and B tends to become smaller and the limiting value of either sum is taken as the area* under the curve. Ingenious methods of calculating such sums have been

* We are taking for granted that every region has an 'area'.

found and one is given in Appendix Two. It is better to consider a general case and proceed as follows.

Consider a continuous function $\phi(x)$ which is always positive and increasing for values of x in the range $x = a$ to $x = b$. The graph of $\phi(x)$ is shown in Fig. 5.2. $C(a, 0)$ and $D(b, 0)$ are two points on the x-axis and the ordinates at C and D meet the graph in points L and M. Divide the line CD into n equal parts and draw the ordinates at the points of section. Consider two neighbouring ordinates PR and QS, where P and Q are the points (x, y) and $(x + \delta x, y + \delta y)$ respectively. Draw PE and QF parallel to the x-axis as shown. The size A of the region $LPRC$ depends on the position of P: that is,

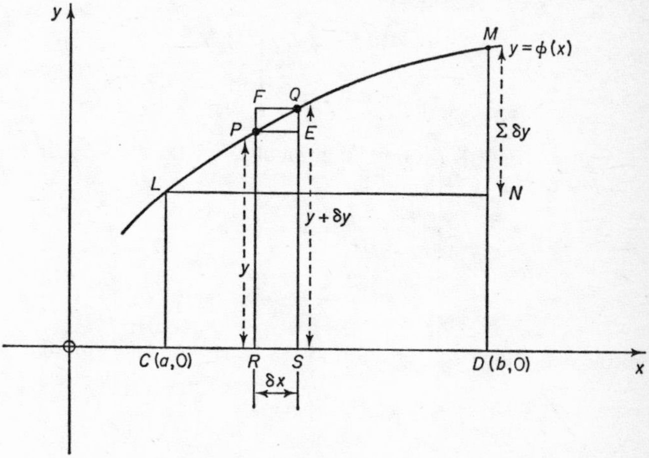

Fig. 5.2

on the value of x so that A is a function of x, say $A(x)$. Because Q is a neighbouring point to P the region $PQSR$ can be denoted by δA. From the diagram we have that

$$\text{Area of rectangle } PESR < \delta A < \text{area of rectangle } FQSR$$

$$\therefore \qquad PR \,.\, RS < \delta A < QS \,.\, RS$$

$$y\,\delta x < \delta A < (y + \delta y)\,\delta x^{*} \qquad (5.13)$$

Summing over all such strips

$$\sum_{x=a}^{x=b} y\,\delta x < \begin{array}{c}\text{Area of the}\\ \text{region } CLMD\end{array} < \sum_{x=a}^{x=b} (y + \delta y)\,\delta x \qquad (5.14)$$

The required area is squeezed between the two summations and can only have a value between them. Consider the difference between the two summations.

$$\sum_{x=a}^{x=b} (y + \delta y)\,\delta x - \sum_{x=a}^{x=b} y\,\delta x = \sum_{x=a}^{x=b} \delta y\,\delta x = \delta x \sum_{x=a}^{x=b} \delta y = \delta x\, MN \qquad \text{(see Fig. 5.2)}$$

* The student may like to consider the case when $f(x)$ decreases as x increases.

MN is of fixed length irrespective of the value of n and as n becomes large $\delta x \to 0$. Therefore the difference between the two summations tends to zero and the area of the region $CDML$, which lies between them, must be equal to the common limiting value (assuming the limit exists).

$$\therefore \quad \text{Area of } CDML = \underset{\delta x \to 0}{\text{limit}} \sum_{x=a}^{x=b} y\,\delta x$$

or

$$\text{Area of } CDML = \underset{\delta x \to 0}{\text{limit}} \sum_{x=a}^{x=b} \phi(x)\,\delta x \tag{5.15}$$

Referring back to the inequality 5.13

$$y\,\delta x < \delta A < (y + \delta y)\,\delta x$$

$$\therefore \quad y < \frac{\delta A}{\delta x} < (y + \delta y)$$

Now A and y [$= \phi(x)$] are both continuous functions of x; therefore as $\delta x \to 0$, $\delta A \to 0$ and $\delta y \to 0$

$$\therefore \quad \underset{\delta x \to 0}{\text{limit}} \frac{\delta A}{\delta x} = y = \phi(x)$$

and

$$\frac{dA}{dx} = \phi(x)$$

From the definition of integration as the inverse of differentiation

$$A(x) = \int \phi(x)\,dx$$

$$= f(x) + C$$

where $f(x)$ is a function whose derivative is $\phi(x)$.

Referring to Fig. 5.2, when PR coincides with LC, $x = a$, and the area $A(x)$ is zero

$$\therefore \quad A(a) = 0 = f(a) + C \tag{5.16}$$

and

$$C = -f(a)$$

$$\therefore \quad A(x) = f(x) - f(a)$$

When PR coincides with MD, $x = b$, and $A(x)$ gives the required area

$$\therefore \quad \text{area } CLMD = A(b) = f(b) - f(a)$$

This is often written as

$$\text{area } CLMD = \Big[f(x)\Big]_{x=a}^{x=b}$$

or because

$$f(x) = \int \phi(x)\,dx$$

$$\text{area } CLMD = \int_{x=a}^{x=b} \phi(x)\,dx$$

or simply $$\text{area } CLMD = \int_a^b \phi(x)\,dx \qquad (5.17)$$

From equations 5.15 and 5.17

$$\int_a^b \phi(x)\,dx = \text{area } CLMD = \lim_{\delta x \to 0} \sum_{x=a}^{x=b} \phi(x)\,\delta x \qquad (5.18)$$

where $\int_a^b \phi(x)\,dx$ is a definite integral and can be evaluated by finding the indefinite integral of $\phi(x)$ and subtracting the value of this indefinite integral when $x = a$ from its value when $x = b$. The relation between the definite integral and the limiting value of a summation explains why an elongated 'S' is used as an integral sign.

Example 8. Evaluate: (i) $\int_2^6 x^3\,dx$, (ii) $\int_0^2 e^{-2x}\,dx$, (iii) $\int_{-\pi/2}^{\pi/2} \cos x\,dx$.

(i)
$$\int_2^6 x^3\,dx = \Big[x^4/4\Big]_2^6$$
$$= [6^4/4] - [2^4/4]$$
$$= 324 - 4$$
$$= 320$$

(ii)
$$\int_0^2 e^{-2x}\,dx = \Big[-\tfrac{1}{2}e^{-2x}\Big]_0^2$$
$$= [-\tfrac{1}{2}e^{-4}] - [-\tfrac{1}{2}e^{0}]$$
$$= -1/2\,e^4 + 1/2$$
$$= (e^4 - 1)/2\,e^4$$

(iii)
$$\int_{-\pi/2}^{\pi/2} \cos x\,dx = \Big[\sin x\Big]_{-\pi/2}^{\pi/2}$$
$$= \left[\sin\left(\frac{\pi}{2}\right)\right] - \left[\sin\left(-\frac{\pi}{2}\right)\right]$$
$$= 1 - [-1]$$
$$= 2$$

Exercises 5.2

Evaluate the following integrals:

1. (i) $\int_0^1 x^4\,dx$ (ii) $\int_0^1 y^4\,dy$ (iii) $\int_0^1 z^4\,dz$
2. (i) $\int_0^1 e^x\,dx$ (ii) $\int_{-1}^{+1} e^{-2y}\,dy$ (iii) $\int_{-2}^{0} e^{4w}\,dw$
3. (i) $\int_1^4 \sqrt{x}\,dx$ (ii) $\int_1^2 x^{-3}\,dx$ (iii) $\int_1^2 w^{-3}\,dw$
4. (i) $\int_2^3 \frac{dx}{x}$ (ii) $\int_{-2}^{-3} \frac{dx}{x}$ (iii) $\int_{-4}^{-1} \frac{dx}{x}$
5. (i) $\int_0^{\pi/2} \sin x\,dx$ (ii) $\int_1^{\pi/2} \cos x\,dx$ (iii) $\int_{-\pi/4}^{\pi/4} \cos x\,dx$

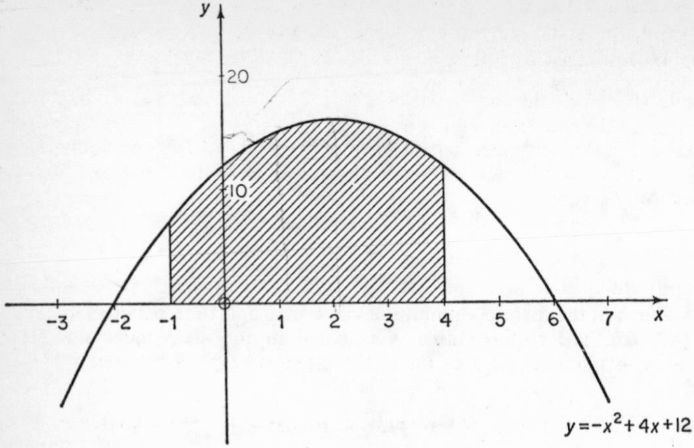

Fig. 5.3

Example 9. Find the area enclosed between the graph of the function $-x^2 + 4x + 12$, the x-axis and the ordinates $x = -1$, $x = 4$.

The graph of the function is shown in Fig. 5.3. From equation 5.17

$$\begin{aligned}\text{Required area} &= \int_{-1}^{4} (-x^2 + 4x + 12)\,dx \\ &= \Big[-x^3/3 + 2x^2 + 12x\Big]_{-1}^{4} \\ &= [-4^3/3 + 2.4^2 + 12.4] - [-(-1)^3/3 + 2(-1)^2 + 12(-1)] \\ &= (58\tfrac{2}{3}) - (-9\tfrac{2}{3}) \\ &= 68\tfrac{1}{3}\end{aligned}$$

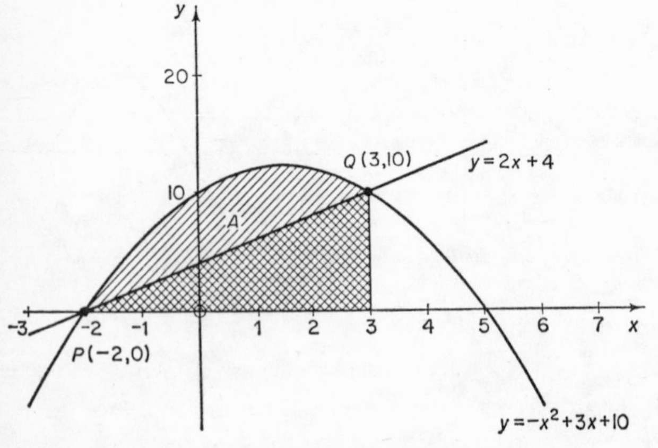

Fig. 5.4

It is stressed that the value of the definite integral gives the area between the graph, the ordinates and *the axis.* To find the area between two graphs we have to proceed as follows.

Example 10. Find the area enclosed between the graphs of the functions $-x^2 + 3x + 10$ and $2x + 4$.

The two graphs are shown in Fig. 5.4. The points P and Q lie on both graphs and therefore their coordinates satisfy both $y = 2x + 4$ and $y = -x^2 + 3x + 10$ simultaneously

$$\therefore \qquad -x^2 + 3x + 10 = y = 2x + 4$$
$$x^2 - x - 6 = 0$$
$$(x + 2)(x - 3) = 0$$

$x = -2$ or $+3$; the corresponding values of y are 0 and 10. The points are $P(-2, 0)$ and $Q(3, 10)$. The required area A is equal to the area under the graph of $-x^2 + 3x + 10$ minus the area under the graph of $2x + 4$ between $x = -2$ and $x = 3$.

$$\therefore \qquad A = \int_{-2}^{3} (-x^2 + 3x + 10)\,dx - \int_{-2}^{3} (2x + 4)\,dx^*$$
$$= \Big[-x^3/3 + 3x^2/2 + 10x\Big]_{-2}^{3} - \Big[x^2 + 4x\Big]_{-2}^{3}$$
$$= \Big[-x^3/3 + 3x^2/2 + 10x - x^2 - 4x\Big]_{-2}^{3}$$
$$= \Big[-x^3/3 + x^2/2 + 6x\Big]_{-2}^{3}$$
$$= [-27/3 + 9/2 + 18] - [8/3 + 2 - 12]$$
$$= (13\tfrac{1}{2}) - (-7\tfrac{1}{3})$$
$$= 20\tfrac{5}{6}$$

The geometrical approach, together with the assumption of an intuitive idea of 'area', has served well as an introduction but now consider the following example.

Example 11. Find the area enclosed by the graph of the function $\sin x$ and the x-axis between $x = 0$ and $x = 2\pi$. The graph is shown in Fig. 5.5.

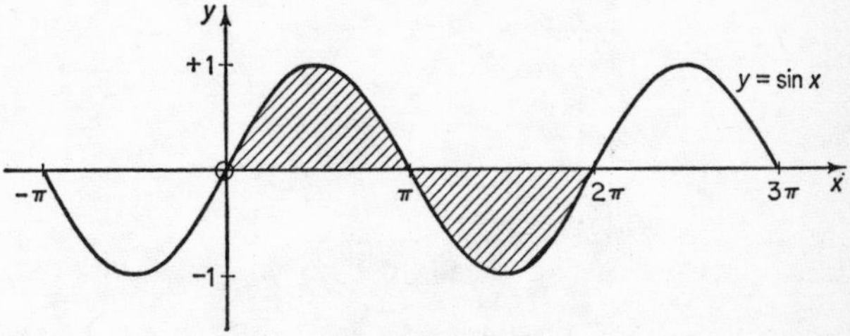

Fig. 5.5

* Note that the same result is obtained by using, in reverse, the first of the two basic rules in section 5.3 and writing

$$A = \int_{-2}^{3} [(-x^2 + 3x + 10) - (2x + 4)]\,dx = \int_{-2}^{3} (-x^2 + x + 6)\,dx, \text{ etc.}$$

By the equation 5.17

$$\begin{aligned}\text{The required area} &= \int_0^{2\pi} \sin x \, dx \\ &= \Big[-\cos x\Big]_0^{2\pi} \\ &= (-\cos 2\pi) - (-\cos 0) \\ &= (-1) - (-1) \\ &= 0\end{aligned}$$

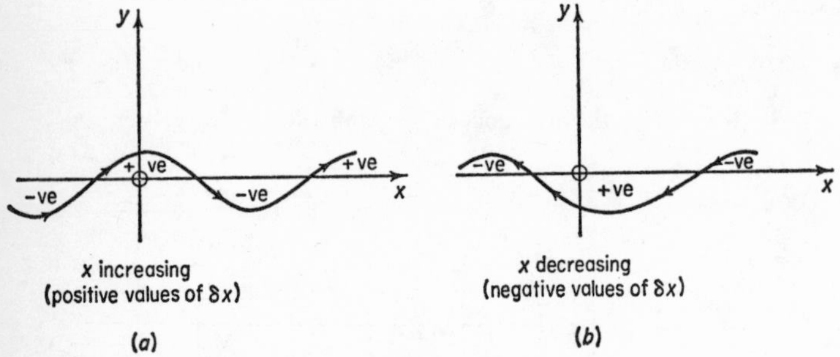

Fig. 5.6

An unexpected and unacceptable result for the 'area'. Referring back to Fig. 5.2, we see that the area of the rectangles was expressed algebraically as $y\,\delta x$, and not arithmetically. Intuitively we expect an area to be a positive number, but if the value of the function $\phi(x)$ becomes negative (δx still positive) then $\phi(x)\,\delta x$ or $y\,\delta x$ becomes negative. The introduction of the

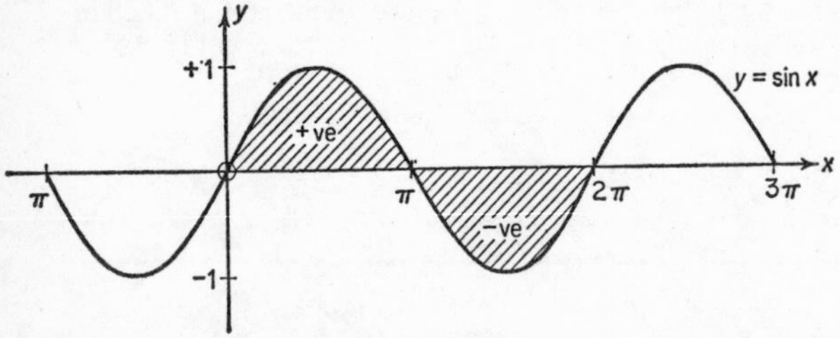

Fig. 5.7

algebraic symbols has brought in the concept of negative areas. The situation is shown in Fig. 5.6(*a*) and (*b*) for positive and negative values of both $\phi(x)$ and δx.

In order to get away from intuitive ideas of 'area' a change of emphasis is given to the relation 5.18. The definite integral is taken as the link and it is defined as the limiting value of a summation. The area, which can be either positive or negative, is then *defined* by a definite integral.

Now return to example 11: the integral gave the algebraic sum of the two areas, as shown in Fig. 5.7, and by symmetry this is zero. To find the 'area' in an intuitive or conventional sense—that is, independent of sign—we proceed as follows

$$\text{area} = \int_0^{\pi} \sin x \, dx - \int_{\pi}^{2\pi} \sin x \, dx$$

Note we *subtract* the second or *negative* area, which adds the numerical value

$$= \Big[-\cos x\Big]_0^{\pi} - \Big[-\cos x\Big]_{\pi}^{2\pi}$$

$$= [(-\cos \pi) - (-\cos 0)] - [(-\cos 2\pi) - (-\cos \pi)]$$

$$= (1 + 1) - (-1 - 1)$$

$$= 4$$

An alternative method is to use the symmetry of the curve, whence

$$\text{area} = 2 \int_0^{\pi} \sin x \, dx$$

$$= 4 \text{ (as before)}$$

In future we shall use the word 'area' in its conventional sense and allow for 'negative areas' when evaluating them.

Example 12. Find the area enclosed between the curve $y = x^3 - 5x^2 + 6x$ and the x-axis (see Fig. 5.8).

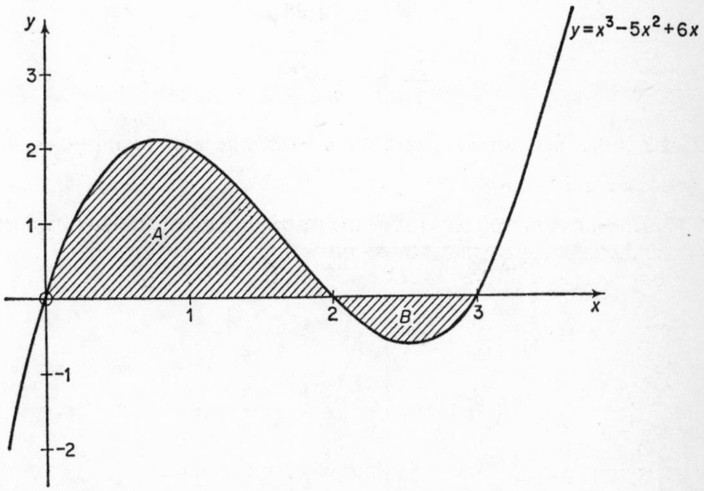

Fig. 5.8

The curve crosses the x-axis when $y = 0$; that is, when

$$x^3 - 5x^2 + 6x = 0$$
$$x(x-2)(x-3) = 0$$

at the points $x = 0$, $x = 2$, and $x = 3$

$$\text{Area } A = \int_0^2 (x^3 - 5x^2 + 6x)\,dx$$
$$= \Big[x^4/4 - 5x^3/3 + 3x^2\Big]_0^2$$
$$= (2^4/4 - 5\,.\,2^3/3 + 3\,.\,2^2) - (0)$$
$$= 2\tfrac{2}{3}$$

$$\text{Area } B = \int_2^3 (x^3 - 5x^2 + 6x)\,dx$$
$$= \Big[x^4/4 - 5x^3/3 + 3x^2\Big]_2^3$$
$$= (3^4/4 - 5\,.\,3^3/3 + 3\,.\,3^2) - (2^4/4 - 5\,.\,2^3/3 + 3\,.\,2^2)$$
$$= (2\tfrac{1}{4}) - (2\tfrac{2}{3})$$
$$= -5/12$$

$$\text{Total area} = 2\tfrac{2}{3} + 5/12$$
$$= 3\tfrac{1}{12}$$

When defining the definite integral as (refer to equation 5.18)

$$\int_a^b \phi(x)\,dx = \lim_{\delta x \to 0} \sum_{x=a}^{x=b} \phi(x)\,\delta x$$

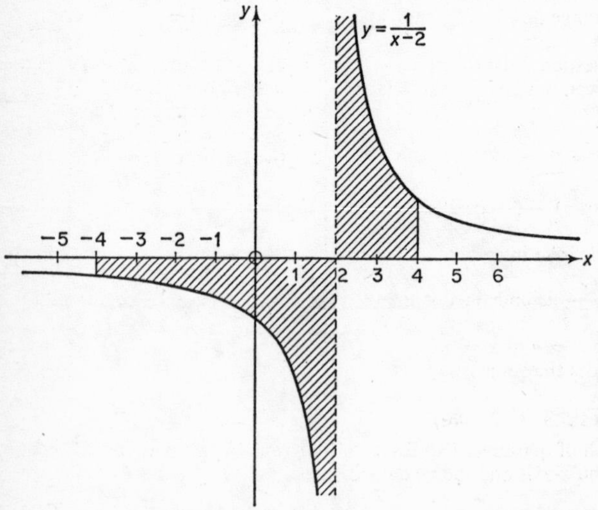

Fig. 5.9

the value of $\phi(x)$ must be finite (positive or negative) and continuous for all values of x in the range $x = a$ to $x = b$. Thus definite integrals such as

$$\int_{-4}^{4} \frac{dx}{x-2}$$

are not defined because the range of integration includes the value $x = 2$ (refer to Fig. 5.9). They will be discussed later (see section 9.8).

Revision Questions 5.2

Complete the following statements	*Answers*	*Refer to*
1. $\int_a^b \phi(x)\, dx = \underset{\delta x \to 0}{\text{limit}} \ldots$	1. $\sum_{x=a}^{x=b} \phi(x)\, \delta x$	Formula 5.18
2. The area between the graph of the function $\phi(x)$ and the x-axis can be a . . . or a . . . quantity when evaluated by a definite integral.	2. positive or a negative quantity	Fig. 5.6
3. State whether $\int_a^b \phi(x)\, dx$ is positive or negative when	3.	
(i) $\phi(x)$ is positive in the range (a, b) and x increases	(i) positive	Fig. 5.6
(ii) $\phi(x)$ is negative in the range (a, b) and x decreases	(ii) positive	
(iii) $\phi(x)$ is negative in the range (a, b) and x increases	(iii) negative	
4. In question 3 the fourth case has been omitted—what is it?	4. $\phi(x)$ is positive in the range (a, b) and x decreases. The answer to this is 'negative'.	Fig. 5.6
5. $[(-\cos \pi) - (-\cos 0)] = \ldots$	5. 2	
6. The definite integral $\int_a^b \frac{dx}{x+3}$ is undefined if the range $x = a$ to $x = b$ includes the value . . .	6. $x = -3$	Paragraph after example 12

Exercises 5.3

In each of questions 1 to 5 sketch the graph of $f(x)$ and find the area between the graph, the x-axis and the given ordinates.

1. $f(x) = -x^2 + 6x$ $\quad x = 2, x = 5$
2. $f(x) = -x^2 - 8x$ $\quad x = -6, x = -1$

3. $f(x) = x^2 - 2x - 15$ $\quad x = 0, x = 5$

4. $f(x) = \cos x$ $\quad x = -\pi/4, x = +\pi/4$

5. $f(x) = \sec^2 x$ $\quad x = -\pi/4, x = \pi/4$

6. Evaluate (i) $\int_{-5}^{-2} \frac{dx}{x}$, (ii) $\int_{2}^{5} \frac{dx}{x}$. Illustrate your results by sketching the curve $y = 1/x$.

In examples 7 to 10 'area' means area in the conventional sense.

7. Find the area enclosed between the graph of the function $x^2 - 5x + 6$, the x-axis and the ordinates $x = 1$, $x = 4$.

8. Find the area enclosed between the graphs of the functions $-x^2 + 2x + 15$ and $x + 9$.

9. Find the area enclosed between the graphs of the functions $\sqrt{(8x)}$ and $x^2/8$.

10. Find the points of intersection of the graphs of the functions $x^3 - 3x^2 + 3x$ and $13x$. Hence find the area enclosed between the two graphs.

There are other applications of the idea that the value of a definite integral is equal to the limiting value of a summation. We shall now consider simple examples of three of these. Others will be given later when some necessary techniques of integration have been considered.

5.5 Work Done when a Force Moves

Consider a variable force F whose point of application moves along a curve from A to M. Divide AM into n equal parts each of length δs by the points B, C, D, etc., as shown in Fig. 5.10.

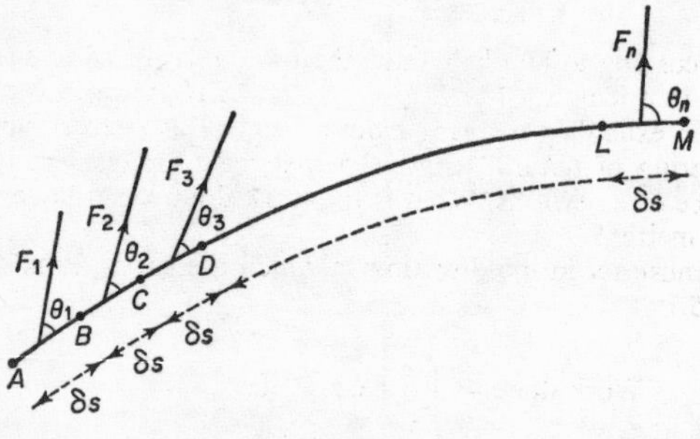

Fig. 5.10

Let the values of F at a point in each of AB, BC, CD . . . be F_1, F_2, . . . F_n, making angles of θ_1, θ_2, . . . θ_n with the directions of AB, BC, . . . LM. Then the work W done by the force F as its point of application moves from A to M is given by

$$W \simeq F_1\delta s \cos\theta_1 + F_2\delta s \cos\theta_2 + \ldots F_n\delta s \cos\theta_n$$

$$\simeq \sum_{r=1}^{r=n} F_r\delta s \cos\theta_r$$

In the limit as n becomes very large and the chords $AB, BC, \ldots LM$ tend to become very small

$$W = \lim_{n\to\infty} \sum_{r=1}^{r=n} F_r \delta s \cos \theta_r$$

$$= \int_{s_A}^{s_M} F \cos \theta \, ds^* \tag{5.19}$$

where s_A and s_M are the values of s at A and M respectively.

Example 13. A truck is pulled along a straight railway line from A to B by a force F. The distance AB is 50 metres. The force F makes a constant angle of 30° with the direction of the line and is of magnitude $(4 - s/25)$ newtons, where s is the distance from A. Find the work done by F.

By equation 5.19

$$\text{Work done} = \int_A^B F \cos \theta \, ds$$

$$= \int_0^{50} (4 - s/25) \cos 30° \, ds$$

$$= \frac{\sqrt{3}}{2}\left[4s - s^2/50\right]_0^{50}$$

$$= \frac{\sqrt{3}}{2}(200 - 50) - \frac{\sqrt{3}}{2}(0)$$

$$= 75\sqrt{3} \text{ joules}$$

Example 14. According to Hooke's Law, the force F required to stretch a spring of natural length l to a length $l + x$ is given by $F = \lambda x/l$, where λ is a constant. Find the work done in extending a spring from a length $l + x_1$ to a length $l + x_2$. It is found that a spring of natural length 0·5 metres is stretched to a length of 0·52 metres by a force of 2 newtons. What is the work done when its length is increased from 0·8 to 1·2 metres?

The force F must act in the direction in which the spring is extended; therefore from equation 5.19

$$\text{Work done} = \int_{x_1}^{x_2} F \cos 0° \, dx$$

$$= \int_{x_1}^{x_2} \frac{\lambda x}{l} \, dx$$

$$= \frac{\lambda}{l}\left[x^2/2\right]_{x_1}^{x_2} \quad (\lambda \text{ and } l \text{ are constants})$$

$$= \frac{\lambda}{2l}(x_2^2 - x_1^2) \tag{5.20}$$

* This can be written in vector notation as $\int_{s_A}^{s_M} \mathbf{F} \cdot d\mathbf{s}$.

In the case of the given spring

because $$F = \lambda x/l$$

$$2 = \frac{\lambda(0{\cdot}52 - 0{\cdot}5)}{0{\cdot}5}$$

$$\therefore \quad 2 = \lambda 0{\cdot}04$$
$$50 = \lambda$$

From equation 5.20 the work done in stretching it from 0·8 to 1·2 metres—that is from an extension of 0·3 metres to an extension of 0·7 metres—is

$$\text{Work done} = \frac{\lambda}{2l}(x_2^2 - x_1^2)$$

$$= \frac{50}{2 \times 0{\cdot}5}(0{\cdot}7^2 - 0{\cdot}3^2)$$

$$= 50 \times 0{\cdot}4$$
$$= 20 \text{ joules}$$

Example 15. A mass of gas is contained in a right cylinder by a movable piston of cross-sectional area A, its pressure and volume at any time being p and v respectively. Neglecting the work done against friction, find from first principles the work done when the volume of the gas changes from v_1 to v_2. An air compressor is working at 2 strokes per second. At each stroke it draws in 0·1 m³ of air at an atmospheric pressure of $1{\cdot}0 \times 10^5$ N/m² and compresses it isothermally to a pressure of $1{\cdot}5 \times 10^5$ N/m². Find the work done per second.

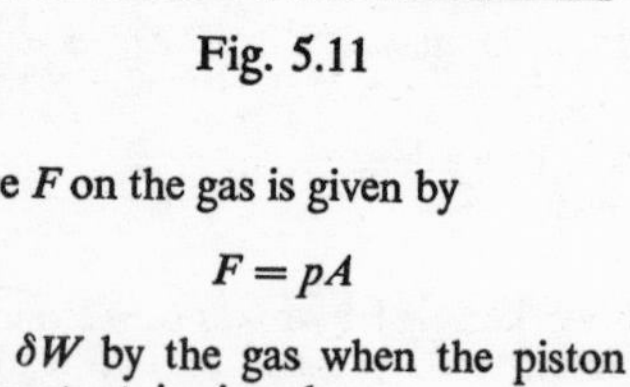

Fig. 5.11

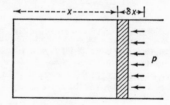

From Fig. 5.11, the force F on the gas is given by

$$F = pA$$

Therefore the work done δW by the gas when the piston moves a distance δx, assuming that F remains constant, is given by

$$\delta W \simeq F\delta x$$
$$\simeq pA\delta x$$
$$\simeq p\delta v$$

where δv is the change, in this case an increase, in the volume of the gas.

$$\therefore \quad W \simeq \sum_{v_1}^{v_2} p\delta v$$

$$\therefore \qquad W = \underset{\delta v \to 0}{\text{limit}} \sum_{v_1}^{v_2} p\delta v$$

$$W = \int_{v_1}^{v_2} p \, dv \qquad (5.21)$$

In the case of the compressor the compression is isothermal

$$\therefore \qquad pv = C \text{ (where } C \text{ is a constant)}$$
$$p = C/v$$

$$\therefore \qquad \text{Work done in one stroke} = \int_{v_1}^{v_2} \frac{C}{v} \, dv$$

$$= \Big[C \ln v\Big]_{v_1}^{v_2}$$

$$= C \ln v_2 - C \ln v_1$$
$$= C \ln (v_2/v_1) \qquad \text{(i)}$$

Let the initial and final pressures and volumes be p_1, v_1 and p_2, v_2 respectively ($v_2 < v_1$)

$$\therefore \qquad p_1v_1 = C \qquad \text{(ii)}$$

and $$p_2v_2 = C$$

dividing $$\frac{p_1}{p_2} \cdot \frac{v_1}{v_2} = 1$$

$$\frac{p_1}{p_2} = \frac{v_2}{v_1} \qquad \text{(iii)}$$

Substituting from equations (ii) and (iii) in equation (i)

$$\text{Work done per stroke} = p_1v_1 \ln (p_1/p_2) = -p_1v_1 \ln (p_2/p_1)$$

$$\therefore \qquad \text{Work done per second} = -2 \times 1{\cdot}0 \times 10^5 \times 0{\cdot}1 \ln\left(\frac{1{\cdot}5 \times 10^5}{1{\cdot}0 \times 10^5}\right)$$

$$= -2 \times 10^4 \ln (3/2) \text{ joules}$$
$$= -8100 \text{ joules}$$

(negative because work is being done on the gas).

Exercises 5.4

1. An air compressor is working at 1·5 strokes per second. At each stroke it draws in 0·08 m^3 of air at an atmospheric pressure of $1{\cdot}00 \times 10^5$ N/m^2 and compresses it isothermally to a pressure of $2{\cdot}00 \times 10^5$ N/m^2. Find the work done per second (refer to example 15).

2. The natural length of a spring is 0·4 metres. The force F newtons required to compress it by an amount x metres is given by $F = \lambda x/0{\cdot}4$, where λ is a constant (Hooke's Law). It is found that $\lambda = 24$. Calculate the work done when the spring is compressed from 0·3 to 0·25 metres (refer to example 14).

3. Two electrical charges q_1, q_2 attract one another with a force of q_1q_2/x^2, where x is the distance between them. The charge q_1 is fixed. Show that the work done against

the force of attraction when q_2 is moved from a distance a to a distance b from q_1 is given by $q_1q_2\left[\frac{1}{a}-\frac{1}{b}\right]$.

4. A truck is pulled along a straight railway line a distance of 200 metres, starting at a point A, by a force F. The force F makes a constant angle of 45° with the track and is of magnitude $(5 - s/40)$ newtons, where s is the distance from A. Find the work done by F.

5. The work done in lifting a mass m kg a distance x m against the force of gravity is mgx, where $g = 9{\cdot}8$ m/s². A pitshaft of square cross-section 3×3 m was sunk 100 m into the ground. Any material, average density 950 kg/m³, removed was spread thinly on the ground. Show that the amount of work done (δW) in bringing a horizontal layer of material thickness δx m from a depth of x m is given by $\delta W = 8550\,gx\delta x$ joules. Hence find the total work done against gravity in excavating the shaft (correct to three significant figures).

5.6 Mean Values

The mean values we shall consider are an extension of the arithmetic mean of several quantities sometimes loosely referred to as the average. The arithmetic mean $\bar{x}$ of the six numbers 5, 6, 6, 8, 11, 18 is given by

$$\bar{x} = \frac{5 + 6 + 6 + 8 + 11 + 18}{6} = 9$$

In the general case of n numbers $x_1, x_2, x_3, \ldots x_n$

$$\bar{x} = \frac{x_1 + x_2 + x_3 + \ldots + x_n}{n} \tag{5.22}$$

We extend this to find the mean value of a continuous function, $f(x)$, over a range of x, say $x = a$ to $x = b$. Divide the range (a,b) into n equal intervals each of length δx, where

$$b - a = n\delta x \tag{5.23}$$

Let $f(x_1), f(x_2), \ldots f(x_n)$ be values of the function at any points within the n equal intervals: then we define the mean value of $f(x)$ in the range (a,b) as

$$\text{Mean value } f(x) = \lim_{n\to\infty}\frac{f(x_1) + f(x_2) + \ldots + f(x_n)}{n}$$

$$= \lim_{n\to\infty}\frac{\sum_{r=1}^{r=n} f(x_r)}{n}$$

$$= \lim_{\delta x\to 0}\frac{\sum_a^b f(x)\delta x}{(b-a)} \qquad \text{(from 5.23)}$$

$$= \frac{1}{(b-a)}\lim_{\delta x\to 0}\sum_a^b f(x)\delta x$$

$$= \frac{1}{(b-a)}\int_a^b f(x)\,dx \tag{5.24}$$

The geometrical representation of this is given in Fig. 5.12, where the height CD of the rectangle $ABCD$ is equal to the mean value of $f(x)$ in the range (a,b). The area of the rectangle is equal to the area under the curve between $x = a$ and $x = b$. Also, because $f(x)$ is continuous, at one or more points in the range the value of $f(x)$ is equal to the mean value.

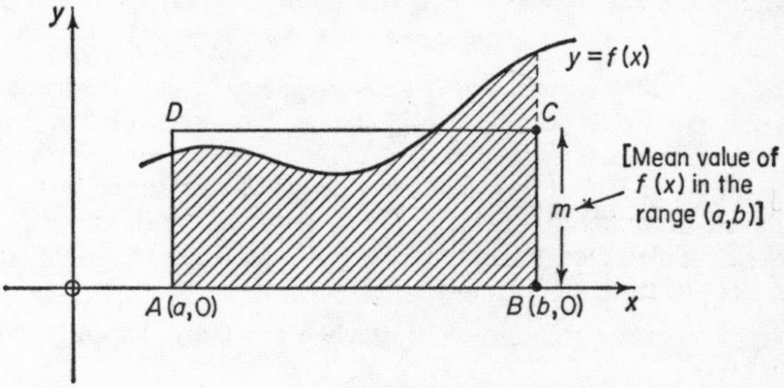

Fig. 5.12

Example 16. Find the mean value of the function $f(x) = 6/x (x \neq 0)$ in the range $x = 2$ to $x = 5$.

From equation 5.24

$$\text{Mean value} = \frac{1}{5-2}\int_2^5 6/x \, dx$$

$$= \frac{6}{3}\Big[\ln x\Big]_2^5$$

$$= 2(\ln 5) - 2(\ln 2)$$

$$= \ln 6{\cdot}25$$

In a practical example it is important to understand clearly which is the independent variable.

Example 17. A particle is falling freely from rest with a constant acceleration of $9{\cdot}8 \text{ m/s}^2$. Find its mean speed $\bar{v}$ in the first 5 seconds of its fall with respect to: (i) the time t seconds, (ii) the distance fallen s metres.

Note that because the speed v is not given as a function of a specific variable there are two possibilities

(i) $$\text{Acceleration} = \frac{dv}{dt} = 9{\cdot}8$$

$\therefore$ $$v = 9{\cdot}8t + C$$

The particle falls from rest: therefore $v = 0$ when $t = 0$ and hence $C = 0$

$\therefore$ $$v = 9{\cdot}8t \qquad \text{(i)}$$

$$\text{Mean speed with respect to time} = \frac{1}{5-0}\int_0^5 v \, dt$$

$$= \frac{1}{5}\int_0^5 9{\cdot}8t \, dt \text{ (from (i))}$$

$$= \frac{1}{5}\Big[4{\cdot}9t^2\Big]_0^5$$

$$= 24{\cdot}5 \text{ m/s}$$

(ii) Because $$v = 9{\cdot}8t$$

$$\frac{ds}{dt} = 9{\cdot}8t$$

$$s = 4{\cdot}9t^2 + C$$

when $t = 0$, $s = 0$; therefore $C = 0$

and $$s = 4{\cdot}9t^2$$

when $t = 5$ $$s = 4{\cdot}9 \times 5^2$$
$$= 122{\cdot}5 \text{ m} \qquad \text{(ii)}$$

Also $$\text{Acceleration} = \frac{1}{2}\frac{d(v^2)}{ds} = 9{\cdot}8$$

$\therefore$ $$v^2 = 19{\cdot}6s + C$$

The particle falls from rest; therefore $v = 0$ when $s = 0$ and hence $C = 0$

$\therefore$ $$v^2 = 19{\cdot}6s \qquad \text{(iii)}$$

$$\text{Mean speed with respect to distance} = \frac{1}{122{\cdot}5 - 0}\int_0^{122{\cdot}5} v\,ds$$

$$= \frac{2}{245}\int_0^{122{\cdot}5} \sqrt{(19{\cdot}6s)}\,ds \text{ (from (iii))}$$

$$= \frac{28\sqrt{10}}{2450}\int_0^{122{\cdot}5} s^{\frac{1}{2}}\,ds$$

$$= \frac{28\sqrt{10}}{2450}\left[\frac{2}{3}s^{3/2}\right]_0^{122{\cdot}5}$$

$$= \frac{28\sqrt{10}}{2450}\cdot\frac{2}{3}\cdot(122{\cdot}5)^{3/2}$$

$$= 32\tfrac{2}{3} \text{ m/s}$$

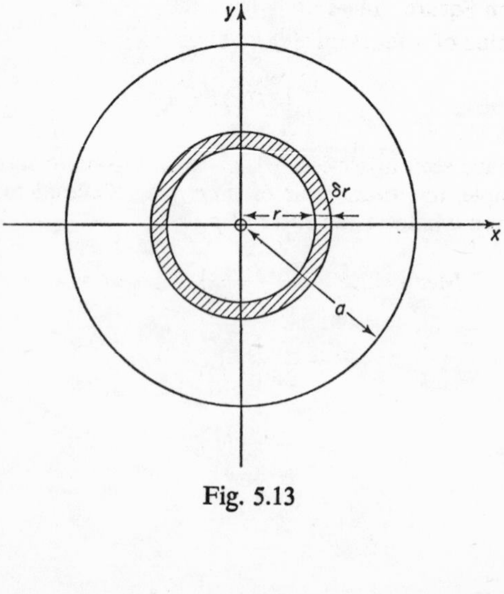

Fig. 5.13

Example 18. The planet Mars is approximately a sphere of radius a kilometres and density ρ tonnes per cubic metre, where $\rho = \rho_0(1 - 2r^2/3a^2)$, r being the distance from the centre in kilometres and ρ_0 the density at the centre of the planet. Given that the mean density is 4 tonnes per cubic metre find the value of ρ_0.

The density is a function of r, the distance from the centre; therefore we take a typical element of volume δV to be a spherical shell of radius r and thickness δr.

$$\therefore \quad \delta V \simeq 4\pi r^2 \delta r$$
$$\delta m \simeq 4\pi r^2 \delta r \rho_0 (1 - 2r^2/3a^2)$$

where m is the mass of the planet.

The mean density is the total mass divided by the total volume

$$m \simeq \sum_0^a 4\pi r^2 \delta r \rho_0 (1 - 2r^2/3a^2)$$

or

$$m = \underset{\delta r \to 0}{\text{limit}} \sum_0^a 4\pi r^2 \delta r \rho_0 (1 - 2r^2/3a^2)$$

$$m = \int_0^a 4\pi r^2 \rho_0 (1 - 2r^2/3a^2)\,\mathrm{d}r$$

$$= 4\pi\rho_0 \int_0^a (r^2 - 2r^4/3a^2)\,\mathrm{d}r$$

$$= 4\pi\rho_0 \left[r^3/3 - 2r^5/15a^2\right]_0^a$$

$$= 4\pi\rho_0[a^3/3 - 2a^3/15]$$

$$= 4\pi\rho_0 a^3/5$$

$$\therefore \quad \text{Mean density} = 4 = \frac{4\pi\rho_0 a^3/5}{4\pi a^3/3}$$

$$4 = 3\rho_0/5$$

$$6\tfrac{2}{3} = \rho_0$$

5.7 Root Mean Square Values

The mean value of a function $f(x)$ involves

$$\int_a^b f(x)\,\mathrm{d}x,$$

which, as we have seen in section 5.4, gives an algebraic sum which can be zero. For example, the mean value of $\sin pt$ over a complete period of $2\pi/p$ gives a value zero whatever the value of p

$$\text{Mean value} = \frac{1}{2\pi/p - 0} \int_0^{2\pi/p} \sin pt\,\mathrm{d}t$$

$$= \frac{p}{2\pi}\left[-(\cos pt)/p\right]_0^{2\pi/p}$$

$$= -\frac{1}{2\pi}[\cos 2\pi - \cos 0]$$

$$= 0$$

Practically this is not always convenient. When studying alternating currents in electricity the e.m.f. can be expressed in terms of periodic functions such as sine or cosine and an average value is required independent of the sign of the e.m.f. The root mean square value is used. The mean value of the square of the function is found. $[f(x)]^2$ is always positive and all values of the function contribute to the final result. This has the dimensions of a square and is square-rooted to give

$$\text{Root mean square value (r.m.s.)} = \sqrt{\left\{\frac{1}{(b-a)}\int_a^b [f(x)]^2\,dx\right\}} \qquad (5.25)$$

Example 19. An alternating current i is given by $i = I\sin(pt + \alpha)$ where I, p and α are constants. Find the root mean square value of i over a range of values of t of length $2\pi/p$.

The function $\sin(pt + \alpha)$ is periodic of period $2\pi/p$ and any range from $t = a$ to $t = b$ where $b - a = 2\pi/p$ will give the required value. We shall consider the simplest case 0 to $2\pi/p$

$$\text{Mean square value} = \frac{1}{(2\pi/p - 0)}\int_0^{2\pi/p} I^2\sin^2(pt+\alpha)\,dt$$

$$= \frac{pI^2}{2\pi}\int_0^{2\pi/p}\frac{1}{2}[1 - \cos(2pt + 2\alpha)]\,dt$$

$$= \frac{pI^2}{4\pi}\left[t - \frac{\sin(2pt + 2\alpha)}{2p}\right]_0^{2\pi/p}$$

$$= \frac{pI^2}{4\pi}\{(2\pi/p - 0) - [\sin(4\pi + 2\alpha) - \sin(2\alpha)]/2p\}$$

$$= I^2/2 \qquad [\sin(4\pi + 2\alpha) = \sin(2\alpha)]$$

$$\therefore \qquad \text{Root mean square value} = \sqrt{(I^2/2)} = I/\sqrt{2} \qquad (5.26)$$

Exercises 5.5

1. The value of the heat capacity C_v for helium is given by

$$C_v = 3{\cdot}00 + \alpha T$$

where T is the absolute temperature and α is a constant. Find, in terms of α, the mean value of C_v between 27°C and 37°C. (Degrees absolute = 273 + degrees Celsius.)

2. Calculate the mean value of the function $f(x) = x^2$ in the range $x = 2$ to $x = 5$.

3. The graph of the function $f(x) = \sqrt{(a^2 - x^2)}$ $(-a \leqslant x \leqslant a)$ is a semicircle, centre the origin and bounding diameter the portion of the x-axis between the points $A(-a, 0)$ and $B(a, 0)$. Show that the mean value with respect to x of the ordinates of the semicircle is $\pi a/4$. (This question can be done without using calculus.)

4. The semicircle in question 3 has the parametric equations

$$x = a\cos\theta,\ y = a\sin\theta \qquad (0 \leqslant \theta \leqslant \pi)$$

Show that the mean value with respect to θ of the ordinates of the semicircle is $2a/\pi(0{\cdot}64a)$.

5. To illustrate the physical significance of the difference between the answers to questions 3 and 4 draw two semicircles of suitable (equal) radius and bounding

diameters AOB. On one divide the *chord AB* into ten equal parts by nine points and draw the appropriate ordinates. On the other divide the *arc AB* into ten equal parts by nine points and draw the appropriate ordinates.

6. A stone is thrown vertically upwards with an initial speed of u. It is subject to a constant acceleration $-g$.

(i) Show that its speed v at any time t is given by $v = u - gt$. Deduce that it reaches its maximum height when $t = u/g$ and find its mean speed with respect to time in the interval $t = 0$ to $t = u/g$.

(ii) Show also that its speed v at any height s is given by $v^2 = u^2 - 2gs$ (acceleration $= \frac{1}{2} . \mathrm{d}(v^2)/\mathrm{d}s$). Deduce that its maximum height is $u^2/2g$ and find its mean speed with respect to distance s in the interval $s = 0$ to $s = u^2/2g$.

7. An alternating current i_1 is given by

$$i_1 = I_1 \cos (pt + \alpha)$$

Find its root mean square value in the interval $t = 0$ to $t = 2\pi/p$. Deduce the root mean square value of a current i_2, in the interval $t = 0$ to $t = \pi/p$, where

$$i_2 = I_2 \cos (2pt + \alpha)$$

8. Prove that the root mean square value of the sum $i_1 + i_2$ of the two currents given in question 7 is equal to the sum of the root mean square values of i_1 and i_2 separately (use the interval 0 to $2\pi/p$).

9. At any instant a current I passes through an electric fire of resistance R. The power consumed is measured by I^2R. The current I is given by $I = I_0 \sin pt$, where I_0 and p are constants and t is the time. Assuming that R remains constant show that over a period $t = 0$ to $t = 2\pi/p$ the root mean square value of the power is equal to $\sqrt{(3/2)}$ times the mean power over the same period. (Refer to example 19 and note that $\int_0^{2\pi/p} \sin^4 pt \, \mathrm{d}t = \frac{3\pi}{4}$).

10. The planet Mercury is approximately a sphere of radius a and density ρ where

$$\rho = 9{\cdot}45(1 - kr^2/a^2)$$

r being the distance from the centre and k a constant. Obtain an expression for its mean density $\bar{\rho}$ in terms of k. Given that $\bar{\rho} = 5{\cdot}4$ evaluate k and show that the density of its centre is $3\frac{1}{2}$ times the density at its surface.

CHAPTER SIX

METHODS OF INTEGRATION

In this chapter we discuss several methods of integration. They are mainly different ways of manipulating the integral to give a recognisable standard form for which the indefinite integral is known.

6.1 Change of Variable

Consider

$$f(x) = \int e^{x^2} 2x \, dx$$

Part of the integrand is e^{x^2}, which is a function (exponential) of a function (x^2). Let $u = x^2$. Hence $e^{x^2} = e^u$, and noting that $du/dx = 2x$

$$f(x) = \int e^u \frac{du}{dx} \, dx \qquad \text{(i)}$$

By our definition of indefinite integration

$$\frac{d[f(x)]}{dx} = e^u \frac{du}{dx}$$

$$\therefore \qquad \frac{d[f(x)]}{dx} \bigg/ \frac{du}{dx} = e^u$$

or

$$\frac{d[f(x)]}{du} = e^u \qquad \text{(refer to equation 4.25)}$$

and

$$f(x) = \int e^u \, du \qquad \text{(ii)}$$

which is recognisable as a standard form

and

$$f(x) = e^u + C$$

or

$$f(x) = e^{x^2} + C$$

Checking the result by differentiation

$$\frac{d(e^{x^2} + C)}{dx} = \frac{d[e^{(x^2)}]}{d(x^2)} \cdot \frac{d(x^2)}{dx} + 0$$

$$= e^{x^2} 2x$$

which is the original integrand as required.

Consider another example

$$f(x) = \int 4 \cos (4x) \, dx$$

Again part of the integrand is cos (4x), which is a function (cosine) of a function (4x). Let $u = 4x$. Hence $\cos 4x = \cos u$, and noting that $du/dx = 4$

$$f(x) = \int \frac{du}{dx} \cos u \, dx$$

$$= \int \cos u \frac{du}{dx} \, dx \qquad \text{(iii)}$$

$$\therefore \qquad \frac{d[f(x)]}{dx} = \cos u \frac{du}{dx}$$

$$\frac{d[f(x)]}{dx} \Big/ \frac{du}{dx} = \cos u$$

$$\frac{d[f(x)]}{du} = \cos u \qquad \text{(refer to equation 4.25)}$$

and

$$f(x) = \int \cos u \, du \qquad \text{(iv)}$$

$$= \sin u + C$$

or

$$f(x) = \sin 4x + C$$

which can be verified by differentiation. In general, if the integral is of the form $\int \phi(u) \frac{du}{dx} \, dx$, where u is a function of x, then

$$\int \phi(u) \frac{du}{dx} \, dx = \int \phi(u) \, du \qquad (6.1)$$

Because let

$$f(x) = \int \phi(u) \frac{du}{dx} \, dx \qquad \text{(v)}$$

$$\therefore \qquad \frac{d[f(x)]}{dx} = \phi(u) \frac{du}{dx}$$

$$\frac{d[f(x)]}{dx} \Big/ \frac{du}{dx} = \phi(u)$$

$$\frac{d[f(x)]}{du} = \phi(u)$$

$$\therefore \qquad f(x) = \int \phi(u) \, du \qquad \text{(vi)}$$

Example 1. Integrate with respect to x the function $(2x^3 + 1)^{10} 6x^2$.
$(2x^3 + 1)^{10}$ is a function of a function $(2x^3 + 1)$.
Let $u = 2x^3 + 1$; then $du/dx = 6x^2$

$$\therefore \qquad \int (2x^3 + 1)^{10} 6x^2 \, dx = \int u^{10} \frac{du}{dx} \, dx$$

$$= \int u^{10} \, du \qquad \text{(by equation 6.1)}$$

$$= u^{11}/11 + C$$

$$= (2x^3 + 1)^{11}/11 + C$$

which can be verified by differentiation.

Sometimes a **constant** factor has to be introduced.

Example 2. Integrate with respect to x the functions (i) $\sec^2 (3x - 1)$, (ii) $(x + 1) \sin (x^2 + 2x + 2)$ and (iii) $x^2/(x^3 + 1)$.

(i) Let $u = 3x - 1$; then $du/dx = 3$.

$$\therefore \qquad \int \sec^2 (3x - 1) \, dx = \tfrac{1}{3} \int 3 \sec^2 u \, dx$$

$$= \tfrac{1}{3} \int \sec^2 u \frac{du}{dx} \, dx$$

$$= \tfrac{1}{3} \int \sec^2 u \, du$$

$$= \tfrac{1}{3} \tan u + C$$

$$= \tfrac{1}{3} \tan (3x - 1) + C$$

(ii) Let $u = x^2 + 2x + 2$; then $du/dx = 2x + 2$.

$$\therefore \qquad \int (x + 1) \sin (x^2 + 2x + 2) \, dx = \tfrac{1}{2} \int (2x + 2) \sin u \, dx$$

$$= \tfrac{1}{2} \int \sin u \frac{du}{dx} \, dx$$

$$= \tfrac{1}{2} \int \sin u \, du$$

$$= -\tfrac{1}{2} \cos u + C$$

$$= -\tfrac{1}{2} \cos (x^2 + 2x + 2) + C$$

(iii) Let $u = x^3 + 1$; then $du/dx = 3x^2$.

$$\therefore \qquad \int \frac{x^2 \, dx}{(x^3 + 1)} = \tfrac{1}{3} \int \frac{3x^2}{u} \, dx$$

$$= \tfrac{1}{3} \int \frac{1}{u} \frac{du}{dx} \, dx$$

$$= \tfrac{1}{3} \int \frac{du}{u}$$

$$= \tfrac{1}{3} \ln |u| + C$$

$$= \tfrac{1}{3} \ln |x^3 + 1| + C$$

Exercises 6.1

1. Use the substitution $u = x + b$, where b is a constant, to find the indefinite integrals with respect to x of the following functions. Hence verify that there is no essential difference in the form of a standard integral when a constant is added* to x.

(i) $\sin(x + b)$ (ii) $\cos(x + b)$ (iii) e^{x+b}
(iv) $(x + b)^n$ (v) $1/(x + b)$ (vi) $\sec^2(x + b)$

2. Use the substitution $u = ax + b$, where a and b are constants, to find the indefinite integrals with respect to x of the following functions. Hence verify that there is no essential difference in the form of a standard integral when x is multiplied by a constant a but the result is divided by a.

(i) $\sin(ax + b)$ (ii) $\cos(ax + b)$ (iii) e^{ax+b}
(iv) $(ax + b)^n$ (v) $1/(ax + b)$ (vi) $\sec^2(ax + b)$

3. Find the indefinite integrals with respect to x of the following functions:

(i) $\sin(3x + 2)$ (ii) $\cos(4 - 2x)$ (iii) e^{1-2x}
(iv) $\sqrt{(2x + 3)}$ (v) $(5 - 2x)^{14}$ (vi) $1/(3x - 1)$
(vii) $1/(2x + 1)$ (viii) $1/(1 - x)$ (ix) $\operatorname{cosec}^2(1 - 2x)$
(x) $\sec(1 - x)\tan(1 - x)$

Find the indefinite integrals with respect to x of the following functions using the substitutions indicated:

4. $2x \sin(x^2 - 1)$ $\quad u = (x^2 - 1)$

5. $x^2 \sqrt{(x^3 + 1)}$ $\quad u = (x^3 + 1)$

6. $x/(1 - x^2)$ $\quad u = (1 - x^2)$

7. $(\ln x)^3/x$ $\quad u = \ln x$

8. $(x^2 - 1)/\sqrt{(x^3 - 3x + 1)}$ $\quad u = (x^3 - 3x + 1)$

9. $x^2 e^{-x^3}$ $\quad u = -x^3$

10. $(x - 1)\cos(x^2 - 2x + 5)$ $\quad u = x^2 - 2x + 5$

Consider equation 6.1 again: that is

$$\int \phi(u)\frac{du}{dx}\,dx = \int \phi(u)du$$

It appears that writing 'du' instead of '$\frac{du}{dx}\,dx$' gives the correct answer. We know that the complete set of four letters du/dx written in this way means

$$\lim_{\delta x \to 0} (\delta u/\delta x)$$

but what do the combinations 'du' and 'dx' of two of the letters mean?† To

* This includes the addition of a negative constant—that is, subtraction of a constant.

† If our readers regard this as a strange question may we remind them that mathematics has many of the properties of a language and this change of meaning when a set of letters is split up is of everyday occurrence in a language. For example, consider *soup*. We can take pairs of these letters, *so* and *up*, which have other meanings.

explain we return to basic ideas. Consider a particular function, say

$$u(x) = x^3$$

$$\therefore \quad \delta u = (x + \delta x)^3 - x^3$$

$$= 3x^2\delta x + 3x(\delta x)^2 + (\delta x)^3$$

But $du/dx = 3x^2$; therefore in this case

$$\delta u = \frac{du}{dx}\,\delta x + \text{terms in } (\delta x)^2 \text{ and } (\delta x)^3$$

$$\therefore \quad \delta u \simeq \frac{du}{dx}\,\delta x$$

In general, if δx is small then because in the limit as $\delta x \to 0$, $\dfrac{\delta u}{\delta x} \to \dfrac{du}{dx}$

$$\frac{\delta u}{\delta x} \simeq \frac{du}{dx}$$

$$\delta u \simeq \frac{du}{dx}\,\delta x$$

We can look at this in a different way. If du/dx is known take any small value of δx, say dx (because it is a different approach we indicate this by using a different symbol, dx instead of δx), then we define du by the **equality**

$$du = \frac{du}{dx}\,dx \qquad (6.2)$$

The quantities du and dx are called **differentials** and du, dx, du/dx stand for three different quantities but are connected by the equation 6.2. This is illustrated in Fig. 6.1, where PT is the tangent to the graph of the function $u(x)$ and PQ is a small increment δx (or dx).

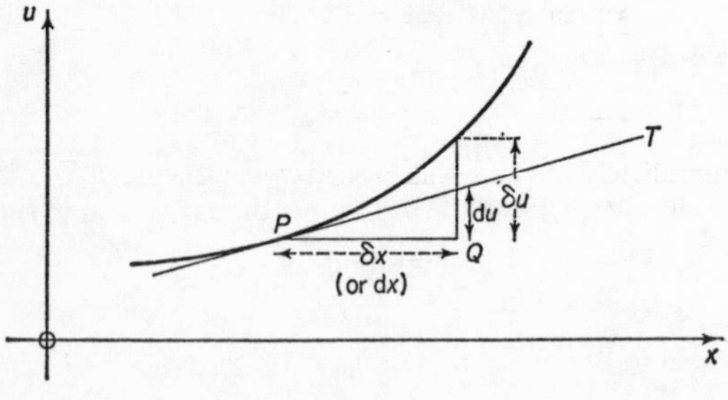

Fig. 6.1

Example 3. Given $u(x) = 1/x^2$, calculate to five significant figures the values of du and δu when $x = 2$ and $dx(= \delta x)$ has the values 0·1, 0·01, 0·001.

$$\frac{du}{dx} = \frac{d(1/x^2)}{dx} = -2/x^3$$

when $x = 2$

$$\frac{du}{dx} = -\frac{2}{(2)^3} = -\frac{1}{4}$$

$$\therefore \qquad du = \frac{du}{dx}\,dx = -\frac{1}{4}\,dx \qquad \text{(i)}$$

$$\delta u = u(x + \delta x) - u(x) = \frac{1}{(x + \delta x)^2} - \frac{1}{x^2}$$

$$= \frac{-2x\delta x - (\delta x)^2}{x^2(x + \delta x)^2}$$

when $x = 2$
$$\delta u = \frac{-4\delta x - (\delta x)^2}{4(2 + \delta x)^2} \qquad \text{(ii)}$$

The values of du and δu corresponding to the given values of dx (δx) are calculated from equations (i) and (ii) and given by

dx (δx)	du	δu
0·1	−0·025	−0·023 24
0·01	−0·002 5	−0·002 48
0·001	−0·000 25	−0·000 25

The relation 6.2 simplifies the work of changing the variable in an integral.

Example 4. Find the indefinite integrals with respect to x of the functions (i) $\sin^3 x \cos x$ and (ii) $1/(x \ln x)$.

(i) In this case $\sin^3 x$ is a 'function of a function', being the 'cube' of $\sin x$. Let $u = \sin x$; then $du = \cos x\, dx$

$$\therefore \qquad \int \sin^3 x \cos x\, dx = \int u^3\, du$$

$$= u^4/4 + C$$

$$= (\sin^4 x)/4 + C$$

(ii) It is not immediately obvious which part of the integrand is a 'function of a function', but

$$\int \frac{1}{x \ln x}\, dx = \int x^{-1} (\ln x)^{-1}\, dx$$

and $(\ln x)^{-1}$ is seen to be a function (raising to the power −1) of a function ($\ln x$).

Let $u = \ln x$; then $du = \frac{1}{x}\,dx$.

$$\therefore \qquad \int \frac{1}{x \ln x}\, dx = \int \frac{1}{u}\, du$$

$$= \ln |u|$$

$$= \ln |\ln (x)| + C$$

When evaluating definite integrals there are two ways of dealing with the limits.

Example 5. Evaluate $\int_0^{\pi/4} \frac{\sec^2 x}{(2 + \tan x)} dx$

Let $u = 2 + \tan x$; then $du = \sec^2 x \, dx$. The limits are values of x and we remind ourselves of this

$$\therefore \quad \int_{x=0}^{x=\pi/4} \frac{\sec^2 x}{(2 + \tan x)} dx = \int_{x=0}^{x=\pi/4} \frac{du}{u}$$

$$= \Big[\ln |u|\Big]_{x=0}^{x=\pi/4}$$

$$= \Big[\ln |2 + \tan x|\Big]_{x=0}^{x=\pi/4}$$

$$= \ln [2 + \tan (\pi/4)] - \ln (2 + 0)$$

$$= \ln (3/2)$$

Alternatively, because $u = 2 + \tan x$: when $x = 0$, $u = 2$ and when $x = \pi/4$ $u = 3$.

$$\therefore \quad \int_{x=0}^{x=\pi/4} \frac{\sec^2 x}{(2 + \tan x)} dx = \int_{u=2}^{u=3} \frac{du}{u}$$

$$= \Big[\ln |u|\Big]_2^3$$

$$= \ln (3/2) \quad \text{(as before)}$$

In the preceding example the two methods are of equal difficulty. In general, the second method is to be preferred.

Example 6. Evaluate $\int_0^{\sqrt{3}} \frac{x^3}{\sqrt{(x^2 + 1)}} dx$

Let $u = x^2 + 1$, then $du = 2x \, dx$, $x \, dx = \frac{1}{2} du$; when $x = 0$, $u = 0^2 + 1 = 1$; when $x = \sqrt{3}$, $u = (\sqrt{3})^2 + 1 = 4$

$$\therefore \quad \int_0^{\sqrt{3}} \frac{x^3 \, dx}{\sqrt{(x^2 + 1)}} = \int_1^4 \frac{x^2}{\sqrt{u}} \frac{1}{2} du$$

A further step is needed to express x^2 in terms of u

$$u = x^2 + 1 \therefore x^2 = u - 1$$

$$\therefore \quad \int_0^{\sqrt{3}} \frac{x^3 \, dx}{\sqrt{(x^2 + 1)}} = \frac{1}{2} \int_1^4 \frac{(u - 1)}{\sqrt{u}} du$$

$$= \frac{1}{2} \int_1^4 (u - 1)u^{-\frac{1}{2}} du$$

$$= \frac{1}{2} \int_1^4 (u^{\frac{1}{2}} - u^{-\frac{1}{2}}) du$$

$$= \frac{1}{2} \left[\frac{2u^{\frac{3}{2}}}{3} - 2u^{\frac{1}{2}}\right]_1^4$$

$$= [4^{\frac{3}{2}}/3 - 4^{\frac{1}{2}}] - [1^{\frac{3}{2}}/3 - 1^{\frac{1}{2}}]$$

$$= (2/3) - (-2/3)$$

$$= 1\tfrac{1}{3}$$

Revision Notes 6.1

Complete the following statements	*Answer*	*Refer to*
1. $\lim_{\delta x \to 0} \dfrac{\delta u}{\delta x} = \ldots$	**1.** $\dfrac{du}{dx}$	Section 1.10
2. $\dfrac{du}{dx}\,dx = \ldots$	**2.** du	Equation 6.2
3. In question 2, 'dx' is known as a . . .	**3.** differential	The discussion after Exercises 6.1
4. When $u = e^{-x}$ then $du = \ldots$	**4.** $-e^{-x}\,dx$	Equation 6.2
5. To find the indefinite integral with respect to x of $\sqrt{(\cos x)} \sin x$, we use the substitution . . .	**5.** $u = \cos x$	Section 6.1
6. Write indefinite integrals with respect to x of (i) $\sin (3x - 1)$ (ii) e^{1-2x} (iii) $\sqrt{(5x + 2)}$ (iv) $1/(3 - 2x)$	**6.** (i) $-\frac{1}{3}\cos (3x - 1)$ (ii) $-e^{(1-2x)}/2$ (iii) $2(5x + 2)^{\frac{3}{2}}/15$ (iv) $-\frac{1}{2}\ln \lvert 3 - 2x \rvert$	Exercises 6.1, No. 2.

Exercises 6.2

Using the given substitutions, find the indefinite integrals with respect to x of the following functions:

1. $3x^2 e^{x^3}$, $u = x^3$
2. $2x/(x^2 + 3)^{14}$, $u = (x^2 + 3)$
3. $3x^2\sqrt{(x^3 + 5)}$, $u = (x^3 + 5)$
4. $x \cos (x^2 - 3)$, $u = (x^2 - 3)$
5. $x^2 \sec^2 (x^3 + 1)$, $u = (x^3 + 1)$
6. $\dfrac{1}{\sqrt{x}} \sin (\sqrt{x})$, $u = \sqrt{x}$
7. $x^3/(x^2 + 4)$, $u = (x^2 + 4)$
8. $x^2/\sqrt{(x + 7)}$, $u = (x + 7)$
9. $1/[x (\ln x)^2]$, $u = \ln x$
10. $1/[x \ln (\sqrt{x})]$, $u = \ln x$
11. $1/[x \ln (x^{-3})]$, $u = \ln x$
12. $\sin^5 x \cos x$, $u = \sin x$
13. $\sin x/\sqrt{\cos x}$, $u = \cos x$
14. $\sin x \cos x$, $u = \cos x$
15. $(x - 1)\sqrt{(x^2 - 2x + 3)}$, $u = (x^2 - 2x + 3)$
16. $\dfrac{(x^2 + 2)}{(x^3 + 6x - 1)}$, $u = (x^3 + 6x - 1)$
17. $\dfrac{\sin 2x}{(1 + \sin^2 x)}$, $u = 1 + \sin^2 x$

Evaluate

18. $\displaystyle\int_0^{\pi/4} \tan^5 x \sec^2 x\,dx$
19. $\displaystyle\int_0^{\pi/4} \tan^5 y \sec^2 y\,dy$

20. $\int_0^{\pi/4} \tan^5 z \sec^2 z \, dz$

21. $\int_1^2 \frac{(\ln x)^4}{x} dx$

22. $\int_0^1 \frac{e^p \, dp}{(3e^p + 1)}$

23. $\int_0^{\pi/4} \frac{\sec y \tan y}{(1 + \sec y)} dy$

24. $\int_0^{\sqrt{5}} x^3\sqrt{(x^2 + 4)} \, dx$

25. $\int_{-1}^0 \frac{y^3}{(y + 2)} dy$

26. $\int_2^5 \frac{w^2}{\sqrt{(w - 1)}} dw$

27. $\int_1^4 \frac{e^{\sqrt{x}}}{\sqrt{x}} dx$

28. $\int_{\ln 2}^{\ln 3} \frac{e^u \, du}{(3e^u - 1)}$

29. $\int_{\frac{1}{2}}^1 \frac{e^{1/y}}{y^2} dy$

6.2 Integration by Parts

Integration of the sum (or difference) of two or more functions has been discussed in section 5.3. **Integration by parts** is the method used to integrate the product of two functions. The formula is derived from the product formula of differentiation. Given two functions of x, say $u(x)$ and $v(x)$, then

$$\frac{d(uv)}{dx} = v\frac{du}{dx} + u\frac{dv}{dx} \qquad \text{(refer to section 4.3)}$$

Integrating with respect to x

$$\int \frac{d(uv)}{dx} dx = \int \left(v\frac{du}{dx}\right) dx + \int \left(u\frac{dv}{dx}\right) dx$$

By the definition of integration as the inverse of differentiation we have

$$uv = \int \left(v\frac{du}{dx}\right) dx + \int \left(u\frac{dv}{dx}\right) dx$$

or

$$\int \left(u\frac{dv}{dx}\right) dx = uv - \int \left(\frac{du}{dx}v\right) dx \qquad (6.3)$$

This is the required formula, and $u(dv/dx)$ is the product to be integrated. The formula is easier to use if a different emphasis is given to it by calling 'u' the '1st' function and 'dv/dx' the '2nd' function. The integral of the '2nd' function is then equal to v and formula 6.3 becomes

$$\int 1\text{st} \times 2\text{nd} = 1\text{st} \int 2\text{nd} - \int \left[\text{derivative of 1st} \times \int 2\text{nd}\right] \qquad (6.4)$$

Example 7. Find the indefinite integral with respect to x of the product $x \cos x$.

$$\int x \cos x \, dx = x \int \cos x \, dx - \int \left(\frac{d(x)}{dx} \int \cos x \, dx\right) dx$$

$$\int 1\text{st } 2\text{nd} = 1\text{st} \int 2\text{nd} - \int (\text{derivative 1st} \times \int 2\text{nd})$$

$$= x \sin x - \int (1 \, . \sin x) \, dx$$

$$= x \sin x - (-\cos x) + C$$

$$= x \sin x + \cos x + C$$

The product which is to be integrated can be written as *ab* or *ba*, and either of the two functions can be taken as the '1st' function, but refer to the remark at the beginning of example 9.

The formula shows that the '1st' function is not integrated, only differentiated. However, the integral of the '2nd' function appears in both terms on the right-hand side. When using the formula, look for a function which can be integrated immediately. If there is only one this must be taken as the '2nd' function.

Example 8. Find the indefinite integral with respect to x of the product $x^2 \ln x$.

x^2 can be integrated immediately, but not $\ln x$. Therefore x^2 is taken as the '2nd' function

$$\begin{aligned}\int \ln x\, x^2\, dx &= \ln x \int x^2\, dx - \int \left(\frac{d(\ln x)}{dx} \int x^2\, dx\right) dx \\ &= \ln x \frac{x^3}{3} - \int \left(\frac{1}{x} \cdot \frac{x^3}{3}\right) dx \\ &= \frac{x^3}{3} \ln x - \int \frac{x^2}{3}\, dx \\ &= \frac{x^3}{3} \ln x - \frac{x^3}{9} + C\end{aligned}$$

If both functions can be integrated immediately and one of them simplifies when differentiated, choose this as the '1st' function.

Example 9. Find the indefinite integral with respect to x of $x\, e^{2x}$.

Both x and e^{2x} can be integrated immediately, but x simplifies when it is differentiated and is therefore taken as the '1st' function

$$\begin{aligned}\int x\, e^{2x}\, dx &= x \int e^{2x}\, dx - \int \left[\frac{d(x)}{dx} \int e^{2x}\, dx\right] dx \\ &= x\, e^{2x}/2 - \int (1 \,.\, e^{2x}/2)\, dx \\ &= x\, e^{2x}/2 - e^{2x}/4 + C\end{aligned}$$

Sometimes repeated applications of the formula are needed.

Example 10. Find the indefinite integral with respect to x of $x^2 \sin x$.

Both x^2 and $\sin x$ can be integrated immediately, but as in example 9 we choose x^2 as the '1st' function

$$\begin{aligned}\int x^2 \sin x\, dx &= x^2 \int \sin x\, dx - \int \left[\frac{d(x^2)}{dx} \int \sin x\, dx\right] dx \\ &= -x^2 \cos x - \int [2x(-\cos x)]\, dx \\ &= -x^2 \cos x + \int 2x \cos x\, dx\end{aligned}$$

The second integral is still a product and we apply the formula again, taking care to preserve the chosen order of the two functions

$$\begin{aligned}\int x^2 \sin x\, dx &= -x^2 \cos x + \left\{2x \int \cos x\, dx - \int \left[\frac{d(2x)}{dx} \int \cos x\, dx\right] dx\right\} \\ &= -x^2 \cos x + 2x \sin x - \int 2 \sin x\, dx \\ &= -x^2 \cos x + 2x \sin x + 2 \cos x + C\end{aligned}$$

If neither function simplifies when differentiated the following method may evaluate the integral.

Example 11. Find the indefinite integral with respect to x of $e^{-x}\cos 2x$.
Indefinite integrals of both functions are known:

$$\int e^{-x}\,dx = -e^{-x} \text{ and } \int \cos 2x\,dx = \tfrac{1}{2}\sin 2x$$

To avoid fractions we take cos 2x as the '1st' function.

$$\int \cos 2x\,e^{-x}\,dx = \cos 2x \int e^{-x}\,dx - \int\left[\frac{d(\cos 2x)}{dx}\int e^{-x}\,dx\right]dx$$

$$= \cos 2x(-e^{-x}) - \int(-2\sin 2x)(-e^{-x})\,dx$$

$$= -e^{-x}\cos 2x - \int 2\sin 2x\,e^{-x}\,dx$$

$$= -e^{-x}\cos 2x - \left\{2\sin 2x\int e^{-x}\,dx - \int\left[\frac{d(2\sin 2x)}{dx}\int e^{-x}\,dx\right]dx\right\}$$

$$= -e^{-x}\cos 2x - \left[-2\sin 2x\,e^{-x} - \int(4\cos 2x)(-e^{-x})\,dx\right]$$

$$= -e^{-x}\cos 2x + 2e^{-x}\sin 2x - 4\int \cos 2x\,e^{-x}\,dx$$

The integral on the right-hand side is the same as the one with which we started. Transfer it to the left-hand side

$$\therefore \quad \int \cos 2x\,e^{-x}\,dx + 4\int \cos 2x\,e^{-x}\,dx = -e^{-x}\cos 2x + 2e^{-x}\sin 2x$$

or

$$5\int \cos 2x\,e^{-x}\,dx = e^{-x}(2\sin 2x - \cos 2x)$$

$$\therefore \quad \int \cos 2x\,e^{-x}\,dx = e^{-x}(2\sin 2x - \cos 2x)/5 + C$$

Another use of the formula is given in the next example.

Example 12. Find the indefinite integral with respect to x of $\ln x$.
We should remember that the *derivative* of $\ln x$ is $1/x$.

$$\int \ln x\,dx = \int \ln x\,.\,1\,dx$$

$$= \ln x\int 1\,dx - \int\left[\frac{d(\ln x)}{dx}\cdot\int 1\,dx\right]dx$$

$$= \ln x\,.\,x - \int\left[\frac{1}{x}\,.\,x\right]dx$$

$$= x\ln x - \int 1\,dx$$

$$\therefore \quad \int \ln x\,dx = x\ln x - x + C \qquad (6.5)$$

Exercises 6.3

Integrate the following functions with respect to x:

1. $x\,e^{3x}$
2. $(2x + 1)\sin x$
3. $(1 - x)\cos x$
4. $(1 + 2x)\ln x$
5. $x^2\cos x$
6. $x^2 e^x$
7. $(x + x^2)\sin x$
8. $x^2\ln x$
9. $x^3(\ln x)^2$
10. $e^{2x}\sin x$
11. $e^{-x}\cos 3x$
12. $\sin 2x\cos x$

13. Integrate by parts $\sin x\sec^2 x$ with respect to x. Prove that the answer is equal to $\sec x + C$.

14. Use the substitution $u = -x^2$ to evaluate $\int_0^1 x^3 e^{-x^2}\,dx$; check your answer by integrating by parts.

15. Evaluate (i) $\int_0^{\pi/4} x\sin x\cos x\,dx$, (ii) $\int (\ln x)^2\,dx$.

16. Show that $\int_1^2 \frac{\ln x}{x^n}\,dx$ $(n > 1)$ is equal to

$$-[(n - 1)\ln 2 + 1 - 2^{n-1}]/(n - 1)^2\,2^{n-1}.$$

17. Evaluate (i) $\int_1^e (\ln w)^3\,dw$, (ii) $\int_1^e (\ln x)^3\,dx$.

18. Evaluate $\int_0^{\pi/4} \cos\sqrt{(\pi y)}\,dy$ (Hint: First let $\pi y = u^2$).

19. Show that $\int \frac{x\,dx}{\sqrt{(x^2 - 4)}} = \sqrt{(x^2 - 4)}$

Hence evaluate $\int_{\sqrt{5}}^{\sqrt{8}} \frac{x\ln(x^2 - 4)}{\sqrt{(x^2 - 4)}}\,dx$.

20. Evaluate $\int_1^2 x\ln(x^2 + 1)\,dx$.

6.3 Integration of Trigonometrical Functions

Of the six elementary trigonometrical functions two have already been integrated (refer to exercises 6.1, No. 2)

$$\int \sin(ax)\,dx = -\frac{1}{a}\cos(ax), \quad \int \cos(ax)\,dx = \frac{1}{a}\sin(ax) \tag{6.6}$$

(where a is a constant)

Example 13. Find the indefinite integrals with respect to x of $\tan ax$, $\cot ax$, $\operatorname{cosec} ax$, $\sec ax$, where a is a positive constant.

$$\int \tan(ax)\,dx = \int \frac{\sin(ax)}{\cos(ax)}\,dx$$

Let $u = \cos(ax)$; then $du = -a \sin(ax)\, dx$

$$\therefore \qquad \int \tan(ax)\, dx = -\frac{1}{a}\int \frac{du}{u}$$

$$= -\frac{1}{a}\ln|u| + C$$

$$= -\frac{1}{a}\ln|\cos(ax)| + C$$

or

$$\frac{1}{a}\ln|\sec(ax)| + C \qquad (6.7)$$

Similarly, using the substitution $u = \sin(ax)$, $du = a\cos(ax)\, dx$

$$\int \cot(ax)\, dx = \int \frac{\cos(ax)}{\sin(ax)}\, dx$$

$$= \frac{1}{a}\int \frac{du}{u}$$

$$= \frac{1}{a}\ln|u| + C$$

$$\therefore \qquad \int \cot(ax)\, dx = \frac{1}{a}\ln|\sin(ax)| + C \qquad (6.8)$$

$$\int \operatorname{cosec}(ax)\, dx = \int \frac{dx}{\sin(ax)}$$

$$= \int \frac{dx}{2\sin(ax/2)\cos(ax/2)}$$

Dividing above and below by $\cos^2(ax/2)$

$$= \int \frac{\sec^2(ax/2)\, dx}{2\tan(ax/2)}$$

Let $u = \tan(ax/2)$; then $du = \frac{a}{2}\sec^2(ax/2)\, dx$

$$= \frac{1}{a}\int \frac{du}{u}$$

$$= \frac{1}{a}\ln|u| + C$$

$$\therefore \qquad \int \operatorname{cosec}(ax)\, dx = \frac{1}{a}\ln|\tan(ax/2)| + C \qquad (6.9)$$

$$\int \sec(ax)\, dx = \int \frac{dx}{\cos ax}$$

$$= \int \frac{dx}{\sin(ax + \pi/2)}$$

$$= \int \operatorname{cosec}(ax + \pi/2)\, dx$$

Using the result 6.9 and referring to exercises 6.1, No. 1

$$= \frac{1}{a} \ln \left| \tan \left(\frac{ax}{2} + \frac{\pi}{4} \right) \right| + C \tag{6.10}$$

Products of sines and/or cosines of multiple angles may be integrated by parts using the method outlined in example 11. It is, however, easier to use the following trigonometrical identities to simplify the integrand before integrating.

$$\left.\begin{aligned} \cos ax \cos bx &= \tfrac{1}{2}[\cos (a+b)x + \cos (a-b)x] \\ \sin ax \cos bx &= \tfrac{1}{2}[\sin (a+b)x + \sin (a-b)x] \\ \sin ax \sin bx &= \tfrac{1}{2}[\cos (a-b)x - \cos (a+b)x] \end{aligned}\right\} \tag{6.11}$$

where a and b are constants.

Example 14. Find the indefinite integrals with respect to x of the following functions: (i) $\cos 6x \cos 2x$, (ii) $\sin 5x \cos 2x$, (iii) $\sin 3x \cos 7x$.

(i)
$$\int \cos 6x \cos 2x \, dx = \tfrac{1}{2} \int (\cos 8x + \cos 4x) \, dx$$
$$= \frac{\sin 8x}{16} + \frac{\sin 4x}{8} + C$$

(ii)
$$\int \sin 5x \cos 2x \, dx = \tfrac{1}{2} \int (\sin 7x + \sin 3x) \, dx$$
$$= -\frac{\cos 7x}{14} - \frac{\cos 3x}{6} + C$$

(iii)
$$\int \sin 3x \cos 7x \, dx = \tfrac{1}{2} \int [\sin 10x + \sin(-4x)] \, dx$$

Note that in this case we have $3x - 7x = -4x$ and that $\sin(-4x) = -\sin 4x$

$$= \tfrac{1}{2} \int (\sin 10x - \sin 4x) \, dx$$
$$= -\frac{\cos 10x}{20} + \frac{\cos 4x}{8} + C$$

When $a = b$ the integrands in equations 6.11 become $\sin(ax)\cos(ax)$; $\sin^2(ax)$; $\cos^2(ax)$. Of these the first can be written as $\tfrac{1}{2}\sin 2ax$ and is immediately integrable. The other two are important and the method of integrating them should be remembered.

Example 15. Find the indefinite integrals with respect to x of the functions (i) $\sin^2 ax$ and (ii) $\cos^2 ax$, where a is a positive constant.

(i)
$$\int \sin^2 ax \, dx = \int \tfrac{1}{2}(1 - \cos 2ax) \, dx$$
$$= \frac{1}{2}\left(x - \frac{\sin 2ax}{2a} \right) + C$$
$$= \frac{x}{2} - \frac{\sin 2ax}{4a} + C$$

(ii)
$$\int \cos^2 ax \, dx = \int \tfrac{1}{2}(1 + \cos 2\,ax)\, dx$$
$$= \frac{1}{2}\left(x + \frac{\sin 2\,ax}{2a}\right) + C$$
$$= \frac{x}{2} + \frac{\sin 2\,ax}{4a} + C$$

The function $\cos^m x \sin^n x$, where m and n are integers and at least one of them is odd, may be integrated by a substitution. If m is odd, use $u = \sin x$; if n is odd, use $u = \cos x$; and if both m and n are odd, use either of these substitutions. The case of m and n both even is considered later (see section 9.5, example 12).

Example 16. Find the indefinite integrals with respect to x of the functions (i) $\sin^5 x \cos^6 x$, (ii) $\cos^3 x \operatorname{cosec}^4 x$, and (iii) $\sin^3 x$.

(i) The power of $\sin x$ is odd; therefore we use the substitution $u = \cos x$, then $du = -\sin x \, dx$.

$$\therefore \qquad \int \sin^5 x \cos^6 x \, dx = -\int \sin^4 x \, u^6 \, du$$
$$= -\int (1 - \cos^2 x)^2 u^6 \, du$$
$$= -\int (1 - u^2)^2 u^6 \, du$$
$$= -\int (u^6 - 2u^8 + u^{10}) \, du$$
$$= -u^7/7 + 2u^9/9 - u^{11}/11 + C$$
$$= -\frac{\cos^7 x}{7} + \frac{2\cos^9 x}{9} - \frac{\cos^{11} x}{11} + C$$

(ii) The power of $\cos x$ is odd; therefore we use the substitution $u = \sin x$, then $du = \cos x \, dx$.

$$\therefore \qquad \int \cos^3 x \operatorname{cosec}^4 x \, dx = \int \cos^3 x \sin^{-4} x \, dx$$
$$= \int \cos^2 x \, u^{-4} \, du$$
$$= \int (1 - \sin^2 x) u^{-4} \, du$$
$$= \int (1 - u^2) u^{-4} \, du$$
$$= \int (u^{-4} - u^{-2}) \, du$$
$$= -\frac{u^{-3}}{3} + u^{-1} + C$$
$$= -\tfrac{1}{3}\operatorname{cosec}^3 x + \operatorname{cosec} x + C$$

(iii) The cosine term is absent but the power of $\sin x$ is odd; therefore let $u = \cos x$, then $du = -\sin x\, dx$.

$$\begin{aligned}\int \sin^3 x\, dx &= -\int \sin^2 x\, du\\ &= -\int (1 - \cos^2 x)\, du\\ &= -\int (1 - u^2)\, du\\ &= -u + u^3/3 + C\\ &= -\cos x + \tfrac{1}{3}\cos^3 x + C\end{aligned}$$

Exercises 6.4

1. Write down the indefinite integrals of

(i) $\operatorname{cosec}(x/2)$ (ii) $\tan(2x/3)$ (iii) $\cot(x/4)$
(iv) $\sec(-3x/5)$ (v) $\tan(x/a)$, where a is a constant

2. Find the indefinite integrals with respect to x of

(i) $\sin x \cos^2 x$ (ii) $\sin^4 x \cos^3 x$ (iii) $\cos^5 x$
(iv) $\cos^3 x \sin^3 x$ (v) $\sin^3 x \sec^4 x$ (vi) $\cos x \operatorname{cosec}^2 x$

3. Evaluate

(i) $\int_{-\pi}^{\pi} \sin 3x \cos 2x\, dx$ (ii) $\int_{-\pi}^{\pi} \sin 6x \sin 7x\, dx$

(iii) $\int_{-\pi}^{\pi} \cos 3x \cos x\, dx$ (iv) $\int_{0}^{\pi} \sin 2x \cos 2x \cos 5x\, dx$

(v) $\int_{-\pi}^{\pi} \sin^2 3x\, dx$ (vi) $\int_{-\pi/2}^{0} \cos^2 (x/5)\, dx$

4. Show that $\tan^3 x = \sec^2 x \tan x - \tan x$. Hence evaluate $\int_0^{\pi/4} \tan^3 x\, dx$.

5. Show that $\cot^3 x = \operatorname{cosec}^2 x \cot x - \cot x$. Hence evaluate $\int_{\pi/4}^{\pi/2} \cot^3 x\, dx$.

6. Show that $\sec^4 x = \sec^2 x + \tan^2 x \sec^2 x$. Hence evaluate $\int_{-\pi/4}^{\pi/4} \sec^4 x\, dx$.

7. Find the indefinite integral with respect to x of the function $\sin 5x \cos 4x$ (i) by parts and (ii) by the method of example 14(ii). Verify that the two answers are equal.

8. Evaluate $\int_0^{\pi/4} \frac{\sin^6 x}{\cos^8 x}\, dx$ by means of the substitution $u = \tan x$.

9. Evaluate $\int_{\pi/4}^{\pi/2} \frac{\cos^4 x}{\sin^8 x}\, dx$ by means of the substitution $u = \cot x$.

10. Evaluate $\int_0^{\pi/6} \sin^2 x \cos^2 x\, dx$. (Hint: $\sin^2 x \cos^2 x = \frac{1}{4}\sin^2 2x$.)

6.4 Trigonometrical Substitutions

Consider the three trigonometrical identities

$$\left.\begin{aligned}\sqrt{(1 - \sin^2 \theta)} &= \cos \theta\\ \sqrt{(1 + \tan^2 \theta)} &= \sec \theta\\ \sqrt{(\sec^2 \theta - 1)} &= \tan \theta\end{aligned}\right\} \qquad (6.12)$$

In each case the square root is equal to a simple trigonometrical function. They suggest the following substitutions, which will simplify the integrand and perhaps lead to a solution of the integral.

If $\sqrt{(a^2 - x^2)}$ occurs in the integrand, try $x = a \sin\theta$ because then

$$\begin{aligned}\sqrt{(a^2 - x^2)} &= \sqrt{(a^2 - a^2\sin^2\theta)}\\ &= \sqrt{a^2(1 - \sin^2\theta)}\\ &= \sqrt{a^2\cos^2\theta}\\ &= a\cos\theta\end{aligned}$$

If $\sqrt{(a^2 + x^2)}$ occurs in the integrand, try $x = a\tan\theta$ because then

$$\begin{aligned}\sqrt{(a^2 + x^2)} &= \sqrt{(a^2 + a^2\tan^2\theta)}\\ &= \sqrt{a^2(1 + \tan^2\theta)}\\ &= \sqrt{a^2\sec^2\theta}\\ &= a\sec\theta\end{aligned}$$

Similarly, for $\sqrt{(x^2 - a^2)}$ use $x = a\sec\theta$ because then

$$\sqrt{(x^2 - a^2)} = \sqrt{(a^2\sec^2\theta - a^2)} = a\tan\theta$$

Example 17. Evaluate (i) $\int_0^{\sqrt{2}} \sqrt{(4 - x^2)}\,dx$, (ii) $\int_{\sqrt{3}}^{3} \frac{dx}{x\sqrt{(9 + x^2)}}$.

(iii) $\int \frac{dx}{x^2\sqrt{(x^2 - 25)}}$

(i) Let $x = 2\sin\theta$; then $dx = 2\cos\theta\,d\theta$, when $x = 0$, $\theta = 0$, and when $x = \sqrt{2}$, $\theta = \pi/4$.

$$\begin{aligned}\therefore\quad \int_0^{\sqrt{2}} \sqrt{(4 - x^2)}\,dx &= \int_0^{\pi/4} \sqrt{(4 - 4\sin^2\theta)}\,.\,2\cos\theta\,d\theta\\ &= \int_0^{\pi/4} \sqrt{4(1 - \sin^2\theta)}\,.\,2\cos\theta\,d\theta\\ &= \int_0^{\pi/4} 2\cos\theta\,.\,2\cos\theta\,d\theta\\ &= 4\int_0^{\pi/4} \cos^2\theta\,d\theta\\ &= 2\int_0^{\pi/4} (1 + \cos 2\theta)\,d\theta\\ &= 2\left[\theta + \frac{\sin 2\theta}{2}\right]_0^{\pi/4}\\ &= 2\left[\frac{\pi}{4} + \frac{1}{2}\right] - 2[0 + 0]\\ &= (\pi + 2)/2\end{aligned}$$

(ii) Let $x = 3\tan\theta$; then $dx = 3\sec^2\theta\,d\theta$, when $x = \sqrt{3}$, $\theta = \pi/6$ and when $x = 3$, $\theta = \pi/4$.

$$\therefore \quad \int_{\sqrt{3}}^{3} \frac{dx}{x\sqrt{(9+x^2)}} = \int_{\pi/6}^{\pi/4} \frac{3\sec^2\theta\, d\theta}{3\tan\theta\sqrt{(9+9\tan^2\theta)}}$$

$$= \int_{\pi/6}^{\pi/4} \frac{\sec^2\theta\, d\theta}{\tan\theta\sqrt{9(1+\tan^2\theta)}}$$

$$= \int_{\pi/6}^{\pi/4} \frac{\sec^2\theta\, d\theta}{\tan\theta\; 3\sec\theta}$$

$$= \frac{1}{3}\int_{\pi/6}^{\pi/4} \frac{\sec\theta\, d\theta}{\tan\theta}$$

$$= \frac{1}{3}\int_{\pi/6}^{\pi/4} \frac{d\theta}{\sin\theta}$$

$$= \frac{1}{3}\Big[\ln|\tan\theta/2|\Big]_{\pi/6}^{\pi/4} \qquad \text{(refer to equation 6.9)}$$

$$= \tfrac{1}{3}\ln\tan(\pi/8) - \tfrac{1}{3}\ln\tan(\pi/12)$$

$$= \tfrac{1}{3}\ln[\tan(\pi/8)/\tan(\pi/12)]$$

(iii) Let $x = 5\sec\theta$; then $dx = 5\sec\theta\tan\theta\, d\theta$.

$$\therefore \quad \int \frac{dx}{x^2\sqrt{(x^2-25)}} = \int \frac{5\sec\theta\tan\theta\, d\theta}{25\sec^2\theta\sqrt{(25\sec^2\theta-25)}}$$

$$= \int \frac{\tan\theta\, d\theta}{5\sec\theta\sqrt{25(\sec^2\theta-1)}}$$

$$= \int \frac{\tan\theta\, d\theta}{5\sec\theta\; 5\tan\theta}$$

$$= \frac{1}{25}\int \cos\theta\, d\theta$$

$$= \frac{1}{25}\sin\theta + C$$

but

$$\sin\theta = \sqrt{(1-\cos^2\theta)} = \sqrt{(1-1/\sec^2\theta)}$$

$$= \sqrt{(1-25/x^2)} = \frac{\sqrt{(x^2-25)}}{x}$$

$$\therefore \quad \int \frac{dx}{x^2\sqrt{(x^2-25)}} = \frac{\sqrt{(x^2-25)}}{25x} + C$$

Two standard integrals can be evaluated by means of trigonometrical substitutions.

Example 18. Find (i) $\int \frac{dx}{\sqrt{(a^2-x^2)}}$ and (ii) $\int \frac{dx}{(a^2+x^2)}$ where a is a positive constant.

(i) Let $x = a \sin \theta$; then $dx = a \cos \theta \, d\theta$

$$\therefore \quad \int \frac{dx}{\sqrt{(a^2 - x^2)}} = \int \frac{a \cos \theta \, d\theta}{\sqrt{(a^2 - a^2 \sin^2 \theta)}}$$

$$= \int \frac{a \cos \theta \, d\theta}{\sqrt{a^2(1 - \sin^2 \theta)}}$$

$$= \int \frac{a \cos \theta \, d\theta}{a \cos \theta}$$

$$= \int d\theta$$

$$= \theta + C$$

$$\therefore \quad \int \frac{dx}{\sqrt{(a^2 - x^2)}} = \theta + C \tag{6.13}$$

where θ is the angle whose sine is x/a, written as $\sin^{-1}(x/a) + C \left(-\frac{\pi}{2} < \theta < \frac{\pi}{2}\right)$ and a is a positive constant.

(ii) Let $x = a \tan \theta$; then $dx = a \sec^2 \theta \, d\theta$

$$\therefore \quad \int \frac{dx}{(a^2 + x^2)} = \int \frac{a \sec^2 \theta \, d\theta}{(a^2 + a^2 \tan^2 \theta)}$$

$$= \int \frac{a \sec^2 \theta \, d\theta}{a^2(1 + \tan^2 \theta)}$$

$$= \int \frac{\sec^2 \theta \, d\theta}{a \sec^2 \theta}$$

$$= \frac{1}{a} \int d\theta$$

$$\therefore \quad \int \frac{dx}{(a^2 + x^2)} = \frac{\theta}{a} + C \tag{6.14}$$

where θ is the angle whose tangent is x/a, written as $\tan^{-1}(x/a) \left(-\frac{\pi}{2} < \theta < \frac{\pi}{2}\right)$ and a is a positive constant.

These results and the reason for the restriction on the range of values of θ will be discussed later (refer to section 8.3).

From equations 6.13 and 6.14 it follows that

$$\frac{d}{dx}\left[\sin^{-1}\left(\frac{x}{a}\right)\right] = \frac{1}{\sqrt{(a^2 - x^2)}}$$

and

$$\frac{d}{dx}\left[\tan^{-1}\left(\frac{x}{a}\right)\right] = \frac{a}{a^2 + x^2}$$

These results will be discussed later (refer to section 8.3).

A rational function of $\sin x$ and $\cos x$ can be integrated by using the substitution $t = \tan (x/2)$

$$dt = \tfrac{1}{2}\sec^2(x/2)\,dx$$

$$\left.\begin{aligned}
\therefore\quad dx &= \frac{2\,dt}{[1+\tan^2(x/2)]} = \frac{2\,dt}{(1+t^2)}\\
\sin x &= \frac{2\tan(x/2)}{[1+\tan^2(x/2)]} = \frac{2t}{(1+t^2)}\\
\cos x &= \frac{[1-\tan^2(x/2)]}{[1+\tan^2(x/2)]} = \frac{(1-t^2)}{(1+t^2)}
\end{aligned}\right\} \qquad (6.15)$$

Example 19. Evaluate (i) $\int_0^{\pi/2} \frac{dx}{(3\cos x + 4\sin x + 5)}$ and (ii) $\int_0^{\pi/3} \frac{dx}{(2+\cos x)}$.

(i) Let $t = \tan(x/2)$; therefore when $x = 0$, $t = 0$ and when $x = \pi/2$, $t = 1$. From equation 6.15

$$\int_0^{\pi/2} \frac{dx}{(3\cos x + 4\sin x + 5)} = \int_0^1 \frac{\dfrac{2\,dt}{(1+t^2)}}{3\left(\dfrac{1-t^2}{1+t^2}\right) + 4\left(\dfrac{2t}{1+t^2}\right) + 5}$$

$$= \int_0^1 \frac{2\,dt}{3(1-t^2) + 4(2t) + 5(1+t^2)}$$

$$= \int_0^1 \frac{2\,dt}{(2t^2 + 8t + 8)}$$

$$= \int_0^1 \frac{dt}{(t+2)^2}$$

$$= \left[-\frac{1}{(t+2)}\right]_0^1$$

$$= (-\tfrac{1}{3}) - (-\tfrac{1}{2})$$

$$= \tfrac{1}{6}$$

(ii) Let $t = \tan(x/2)$; therefore when $x = 0$, $t = 1$ and when $x = \pi/3$, $t = 1/\sqrt{3}$.

$$\therefore \quad \int_0^{\pi/3} \frac{dx}{(2+\cos x)} = \int_0^{1/\sqrt{3}} \frac{\dfrac{2\,dt}{1+t^2}}{2 + \left(\dfrac{1-t^2}{1+t^2}\right)}$$

$$= \int_0^{1/\sqrt{3}} \frac{2\,dt}{2(1+t^2) + (1-t^2)}$$

$$= 2\int_0^{1/\sqrt{3}} \frac{dt}{(3+t^2)}$$

$$= 2\left[\frac{1}{\sqrt{3}}\tan^{-1}(t/\sqrt{3})\right]_0^{1/\sqrt{3}} \qquad \text{(from equation 6.14)}$$

$$= 2\left[\frac{1}{\sqrt{3}}\tan^{-1}(1/3)\right] - 2[0]$$

$$= \frac{2}{\sqrt{3}}\tan^{-1}(1/3)$$

Revision Notes 6.2

Complete the following statements	*Answer*	*Refer to*
1. $\int \frac{dx}{(2 + x^2)} = \ldots$	1. $\frac{1}{\sqrt{2}} \tan^{-1}(x/\sqrt{2}) + C$	Equation 6.14
2. $\int \frac{dx}{\sqrt{(9 - x^2)}} = \ldots$	2. $\sin^{-1}(x/3) + C$	Equation 6.13
3. In the formula for integration by parts the '1st' function is . . .	3. never integrated	Section 6.2
4. $\int \tan 2x\, dx = \ldots$	4. $\frac{1}{2} \ln \lvert\sec(2x)\rvert + C$	Equation 6.7
5. $\int \cot(x/4)\, dx = \ldots$	5. $4 \ln \lvert\sin(x/4)\rvert + C$	Equation 6.8
6. $\frac{d}{dx}[\sin^{-1}(x/a)] = \ldots$	6. $1/\sqrt{(a^2 - x^2)}$	Equation 6.13
7. $\frac{d}{dx}[\tan^{-1}(x/a)] = \ldots$	7. $a/(a^2 + x^2)$	Equation 6.14
8. Given that $\int_0^1 \sqrt{(4 - x^2)}\, dx = (2\pi + 3\sqrt{3})/6$, then $\int_0^1 \sqrt{(4 - y^2)}\, dy = \ldots$	8. $(2\pi + 3\sqrt{3})/6$	
9. Given that $t = \tan\frac{\theta}{2}$	9.	
(i) $\frac{(1 - t^2)}{(1 + t^2)} = \ldots$	(i) $\cos\theta$	Equation 6.15
(ii) $\frac{2t}{(1 + t^2)} = \ldots$	(ii) $\sin\theta$	Equation 6.15
(iii) $\frac{2\, dt}{(1 + t^2)} = \ldots$	(iii) $d\theta$	Equation 6.15
10. The differentials du and dx are connected by the equation . . .	10. $du = \frac{du}{dx} dx$	Equation 6.2

Exercises 6.5

Evaluate the following definite integrals:

1. $\int_0^{\sqrt{3}/2} \frac{x^2\, dx}{\sqrt{(1 - x^2)}}$

2. $\int_0^2 \frac{x\, dx}{\sqrt{(4 + x^2)}}$

3. Verify the answer to question 2 by using the substitution $u^2 = (4 + x^2)$.

4. $\int_{3\sqrt{2}}^{6} \frac{x \, dx}{\sqrt{(x^2 - 9)}}$

5. $\int_{2}^{2\sqrt{2}} \frac{dx}{x^2\sqrt{(16 - x^2)}}$

6. $\int_{0}^{\frac{1}{2}} \sqrt{\frac{(1 + y)}{(1 - y)}} \, dy$ (Hint: use $y = \cos 2\theta$)

7. $\int_{0}^{1 \cdot 5} \sqrt{(9 - x^2)} \, dx$

8. $\int_{0}^{\pi/2} \frac{d\theta}{(1 + \sin \theta)}$

9. $\int_{0}^{\pi/2} \frac{d\theta}{(3 \cos \theta - 4 \sin \theta + 5)}$

10. $\int_{0}^{1} \sqrt{\frac{x}{(2 - x)}} \, dx$ (Hint: use $x = 2 \sin^2 \theta$)

6.5 Partial Fractions

In this section we shall consider integrals of the form $f(x)/g(x)$, where $f(x)$ and $g(x)$ are polynomials in x. When the numerator, $f(x)$, is not of lower degree than the denominator, $g(x)$, we shall first divide out. In some simple cases the answer may then be found.

Example 20. Find the indefinite integrals with respect to x of

(i) $\frac{(4x^2 - 3)}{(2x + 3)}$ and (ii) $\frac{(x^4 - 7)}{(x^2 + 3)}$

(i)
$$\begin{array}{r} 2x + 3\,)\,4x^2 + 0x - 3\,(\,2x - 3 \\ 4x^2 + 6x \\ \hline -6x - 3 \\ -6x - 9 \\ \hline 6 \end{array}$$

$\therefore$
$$\int \frac{(4x^2 - 3)}{(2x + 3)} \, dx = \int \left[2x - 3 + \frac{6}{(2x + 3)} \right] dx$$
$$= x^2 - 3x + 6 \int \frac{dx}{(2x + 3)}$$
$$= x^2 - 3x + 6 \, . \, \tfrac{1}{2} \ln |2x + 3| + C$$
$$= x^2 - 3x + 3 \ln |2x + 3| + C$$

(ii)
$$\begin{array}{r} x^2 + 0x + 3\,)\,x^4 + 0x^3 + 0x^2 + 0x - 7\,(\,x^2 - 3 \\ x^4 + 0x^3 + 3x^2 \\ \hline -3x^2 + 0x - 7 \\ -3x^2 + 0x - 9 \\ \hline 2 \end{array}$$

$\therefore$
$$\int \frac{(x^4 - 7)}{(x^2 + 3)} \, dx = \int \left[x^2 - 3 + \frac{2}{(x^2 + 3)} \right] dx$$
$$= x^3/3 - 3x + 2 \int \frac{dx}{(x^2 + 3)}$$
$$= x^3/3 - 3x + [2 \tan^{-1} (x/\sqrt{3})]/\sqrt{3} + C$$

When $f(x)$ is of lower degree than $g(x)$, then we express $g(x)$ in terms of linear and quadratic factors or powers of these.* The types of partial fractions which arise are

$$\frac{A}{ax+b}, \quad \frac{A}{(ax+b)^r}, \quad \frac{Ax+B}{(ax^2+bx+c)}, \quad \frac{Ax+B}{(ax^2+bx+c)^r},$$

where r is a positive integer. The integration of the fourth of these is beyond the scope of this book and at present we shall consider only examples which give partial fractions of the first two types and of the third case with $b = 0$.

Example 21. Find the indefinite integrals with respect to x of

(i) $\dfrac{(x-25)}{(x+3)^2(2x-1)}$ (ii) $\dfrac{8}{(3x^2+1)(1+3x)}$ (iii) $\dfrac{4x^3-31x+22}{2x^2+5x-3}$

(i) Let $\dfrac{(x-25)}{(x+3)^2(2x-1)} \equiv \dfrac{A}{(x+3)^2} + \dfrac{B}{(x+3)} + \dfrac{C}{(2x-1)}$

$\therefore$ $x - 25 \equiv A(2x-1) + B(x+3)(2x-1) + C(x+3)^2$

Let $x = -3$ $\quad -28 = -7A + 0 + 0$

$\therefore A = 4$

Let $x = \frac{1}{2}$ $\quad -24\frac{1}{2} = 0 + 0 + C(3\frac{1}{2})^2$

$\therefore C = -2$

Equate coefficients of x^2

$0 = 0 + 2B + C$

$\therefore B = 1$

$$\therefore \int \frac{(x-25)}{(x+3)^2(2x-1)}\,dx = \int \frac{4\,dx}{(x+3)^2} + \int \frac{dx}{(x+3)} - \int \frac{2\,dx}{(2x-1)}$$

$$= \frac{-4}{(x+3)} + \ln|x+3| - 2 \,.\, \tfrac{1}{2} \ln|2x-1| + C$$

$$= \frac{-4}{(x+3)} + \ln\left|\frac{x+3}{2x-1}\right| + C$$

(ii) Let $\dfrac{8}{(3x^2+1)(1+3x)} \equiv \dfrac{Ax+B}{(3x^2+1)} + \dfrac{C}{(1+3x)}$

$\therefore$ $8 \equiv (Ax+B)(1+3x) + C(3x^2+1)$

Let $x = -\frac{1}{3}$ $\quad 8 = 0 + C(\frac{1}{3}+1)$

$\therefore C = 6$

Equating coefficient x^2

$0 = 3A + 3C$
$0 = 3A + 18$

$\therefore A = -6$

constants

$8 = B + C$
$8 = B + 6$

$\therefore B = 2$

* This can always be done: see *Theory of Equations*, by H. W. Turnbull, University Mathematical Texts, Oliver and Boyd, 1952.

$$\therefore \quad \int \frac{8}{(3x^2+1)(1+3x)}\,dx = \int \left[\frac{(2-6x)}{(3x^2+1)} + \frac{6}{(1+3x)}\right] dx$$

$$= 2\int \frac{dx}{(3x^2+1)} - \int \frac{6x}{(3x^2+1)}\,dx + 6\int \frac{dx}{(1+3x)}$$

Consider the three integrals separately.

$$2\int \frac{dx}{(3x^2+1)} = \frac{2}{3}\int \frac{dx}{(x^2+\frac{1}{3})} = \frac{2}{3}\cdot\left(1\Big/\frac{1}{\sqrt{3}}\right)\tan^{-1}\left(x\Big/\frac{1}{\sqrt{3}}\right)$$

$$= \frac{2}{\sqrt{3}}\tan^{-1}(\sqrt{3}x) \qquad \text{(i)}$$

In $-\int \frac{6x\,dx}{(3x^2+1)}$, let $u = (3x^2+1)$; then $du = 6x\,dx$, and the integral becomes

$$= -\int \frac{du}{u}$$

$$= -\ln|u|$$

$$= -\ln|3x^2+1| \qquad \text{(ii)}$$

In $\quad +6\int \frac{dx}{(1+3x)} = +6\,.\,\frac{1}{3}\ln|1+3x|$

$$= 2\ln|1+3x| \qquad \text{(iii)}$$

Collecting the results (i), (ii) and (iii) above

$$\int \frac{8\,dx}{(3x^2+1)(1+3x)} = \frac{2}{\sqrt{3}}\tan^{-1}(\sqrt{3}x) - \ln|3x^2+1| + 2\ln|1+3x| + C$$

(iii) The numerator is not of lower order than the denominator; therefore dividing out we have

$$\begin{array}{rl} 2x^2+5x-3) & 4x^3+\ 0x^2-31x+22\ \ (2x-5 \\ & 4x^3+10x^2-6x \\ \hline & \quad -10x^2-25x+22 \\ & \quad -10x^2-25x+15 \\ \hline & \qquad\qquad\qquad 7 \end{array}$$

Also the denominator factorises: $(2x^2+5x-3) = (2x-1)(x+3)$

$$\therefore \quad \int \frac{(4x^3-31x+22)}{(2x^2+5x-3)}\,dx = \int\left[2x-5+\frac{7}{(2x-1)(x+3)}\right] dx$$

$$= x^2-5x+\int \frac{7\,dx}{(2x-1)(x+3)}$$

Consider $\quad \frac{7}{(2x-1)(x+3)} \equiv \frac{A}{(2x-1)} + \frac{B}{(x+3)}$

$$7 \equiv A(x+3) + B(2x-1)$$

Let $x = -3 \quad 7 = \ 0 \ - \ 7B$

$$\therefore B = -1$$

Let $x = \frac{1}{2} \quad 7 = A(3\frac{1}{2}) + 0$

$$\therefore A = 2$$

$$\therefore \quad \int \frac{7}{(2x-1)(x+3)}\,dx = \int \frac{2\,dx}{(2x-1)} - \int \frac{dx}{(x+3)}$$

$$= 2 \cdot \tfrac{1}{2} \ln|2x-1| - \ln|x+3|$$

$$= \ln\left|\frac{2x-1}{x+3}\right|$$

$$\therefore \quad \int \frac{(4x^3 - 31x + 22)}{(2x^2 + 5x - 3)}\,dx = x^2 - 5x + \ln\left|\frac{2x-1}{x+3}\right| + C$$

Exercises 6.6

Find the indefinite integrals with respect to x of the following functions:

1. $x^3/(x^2+1)$
2. $(6x^2 - x + 1)/(2x+1)$
3. $5/(x+2)(x+3)$
4. $3/x(2x-1)(x+1)$
5. $(7x+31)/(x+3)^2(3x-1)$
6. $(2x^3 - 7x^2 - 15x + 10)/(x^2 - 5x)$

Evaluate

7. $\int_{-1}^{1} \frac{x^3}{(9-x^2)}\,dx$
8. $\int_{0}^{1} \frac{(x^2+12)}{(x-2)(x^2-4)}\,dx$
9. $\int_{-2}^{0} \frac{2}{(x-1)(x-2)(x-3)}\,dx$
10. $\int_{2}^{2\sqrt{3}} \frac{5}{(x^2+4)(x-1)}\,dx$
11. $\int_{0}^{2} \frac{3}{(2x^2+1)(2x+1)}\,dx$
12. $\int_{0}^{\sqrt{3}} \frac{4x\,dx}{(x^2+1)(x^2+9)}$.

CHAPTER SEVEN

FURTHER APPLICATIONS OF INTEGRATION

Some applications of integration were discussed earlier in Chapter Five. The definite integral of a function was related to the area under a curve and, when divided by the range of integration, to mean values. Also the integral of the square of a function used, when the result is square-rooted, in electrical engineering was discussed. These two types of integrals will occur again in this chapter when geometrical problems are considered; as will the integral of x times a function

$$\int_a^b xf(x)\,\mathrm{d}x$$

sometimes known as the **first moment**, which occurs when considering centroids, centres of mass and statistical means; and the integral of x^2 times a function

$$\int_a^b x^2f(x)\,\mathrm{d}x$$

the **'second moment'**, which occurs when calculating moments of inertia and statistical variance. The range of the problems considered is wide and our readers must select those which are applicable to their particular area of study.

7.1 The Length of Curves

The length of the perimeter of a rectilinear figure (one bounded by straight lines) is obtained by adding together the lengths of its bounding straight lines. A curve cannot be divided into straight lines and we require a definition of what is meant by 'the length of a curve'. The usual definition is the length to which the perimeter of a polygon inscribed to the curve tends as the number of sides increases indefinitely, the lengths of all sides becoming exceedingly small. We shall assume that the gradient of the curve is continuous and finite at all points: that is, that the difference in the finite values of $\mathrm{d}y/\mathrm{d}x$ at two neighbouring points P and Q on the curve can be made as small as we please by letting $Q \to P$.

Let AB be an arc of the curve $y = f(x)$, the points A and B having abscissae $x = a$ and $x = b$ respectively. Let $P(x,y)$ and $Q(x + \delta x,\ y + \delta y)$ be two neighbouring points on the curve (see Fig. 7.1). By Pythagoras

$$\text{Length of chord } PQ = \sqrt{[(\delta x)^2 + (\delta y)^2]} \tag{7.1}$$

$$= \sqrt{\left[1 + \left(\frac{\delta y}{\delta x}\right)^2\right]}\,\delta x$$

Divide the interval $x = a$ to $x = b$ into n equal portions each of length δx. The length of the portion of the inscribed polygon between A and B is then given by

$$\sum_{x=a}^{x=b} \sqrt{\left[1 + \left(\frac{\delta y}{\delta x}\right)^2\right]}\,\delta x$$

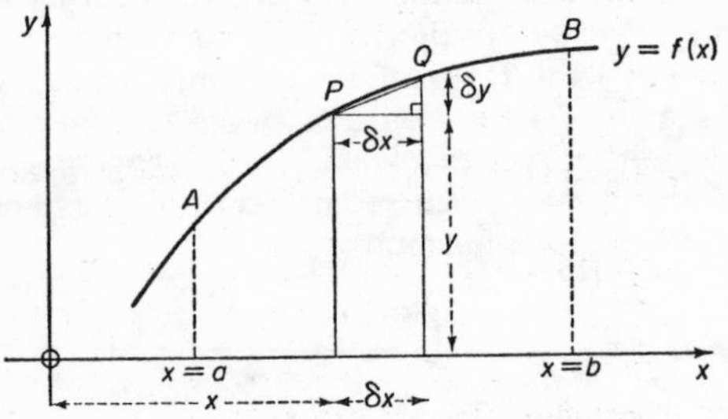

Fig. 7.1

Then by definition the length S of the curve between A and B is given by

$$S = \lim_{\delta x \to 0} \sum_{x=a}^{x=b} \sqrt{\left[1 + \left(\frac{\delta y}{\delta x}\right)^2\right]}\,\delta x$$

Now as $\delta x \to 0$, $\delta y/\delta x \to \mathrm{d}y/\mathrm{d}x$ and by equation 5.18

$$S = \int_a^b \sqrt{\left[1 + \left(\frac{\mathrm{d}y}{\mathrm{d}x}\right)^2\right]}\,\mathrm{d}x \qquad (7.2)$$

Example 1. Find the length of the curve $y = 2x^{\frac{3}{2}}$ between $x = 0$ and $x = 1$.

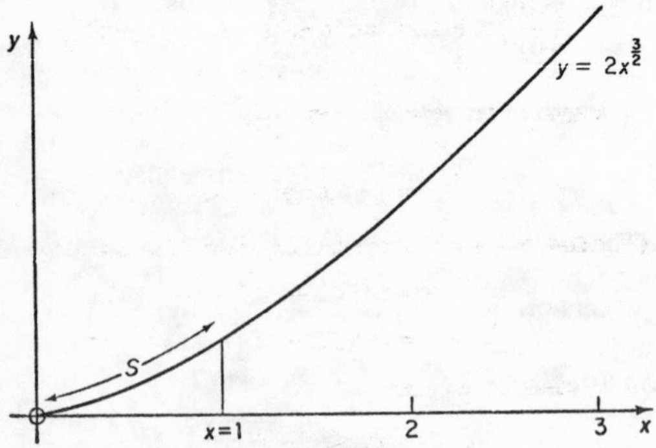

Fig. 7.2

The curve is shown in Fig. 7.2.

$$y = 2x^{\frac{3}{2}}$$

$$\therefore \qquad \frac{dy}{dx} = 3x^{\frac{1}{2}}$$

$$1 + \left(\frac{dy}{dx}\right)^2 = 1 + 9x$$

From equation 7.2 the arc length S is given by

$$S = \int_0^1 \sqrt{(1 + 9x)}\, dx$$

$$= \left[\frac{1}{9} \cdot \frac{2}{3}(1 + 9x)^{\frac{3}{2}}\right]_0^1 \qquad \text{(refer to exercises 6.1, No. 2)}$$

$$= \frac{2}{27}[10^{\frac{3}{2}} - 1]$$

$$\simeq 2{\cdot}27$$

Referring back to equation 7.1, we can write

$$\text{Length of chord } PQ = \sqrt{[(\delta x)^2 + (\delta y)^2]}$$

$$= \sqrt{\left[\left(\frac{\delta x}{\delta y}\right)^2 + 1\right]}\,\delta y$$

and if the equation is given in the form $x = g(y)$, or can be expressed without ambiguity in this form, then

$$\text{Length of curve} = \int_{y_1}^{y_2} \sqrt{\left[\left(\frac{dx}{dy}\right)^2 + 1\right]}\, dy \qquad (7.3)$$

Example 2. Find the length of the curve $x = \ln(\cos y)$ from $y = 0$ to $y = \pi/4$.

$$x = \ln(\cos y)$$

$$\therefore \qquad \frac{dx}{dy} = \frac{1}{\cos y} \cdot (-\sin y) = -\tan y$$

$$\left(\frac{dx}{dy}\right)^2 + 1 = \tan^2 y + 1 \quad = \quad \sec^2 y$$

$$\text{length of curve} = \int_0^{\pi/4} \sec y\, dy$$

$$= \Big[\ln(\sec y + \tan y)\Big]_0^{\pi/4}$$

(The student is recommended to check this result by differentiation.)

$$= \ln(\sqrt{2} + 1) - \ln(1 + 0)$$

$$= \ln(\sqrt{2} + 1)$$

The equation 7.1 can be written

$$\delta s \simeq \sqrt{[(\delta x)^2 + (\delta y)^2]}$$

where s is the length of the curve.

$$\therefore \qquad \frac{\delta s}{\delta x} \simeq \sqrt{\left[1+\left(\frac{\delta y}{\delta x}\right)^2\right]}$$

In the limit as $\delta x \to 0$

$$\frac{ds}{dx} = \sqrt{\left[1+\left(\frac{dy}{dx}\right)^2\right]} \qquad (7.4)$$

If the tangent to the curve $y = f(x)$ makes an angle ψ with Ox, its slope m is equal to $\tan \psi$ and

$$\frac{dy}{dx} = \text{slope of the tangent} = \tan \psi$$

$$\therefore \qquad \frac{dx}{ds} = 1/\sqrt{(1+\tan^2 \psi)} = \frac{1}{\sec \psi}$$

$$= \cos \psi \qquad (7.5)$$

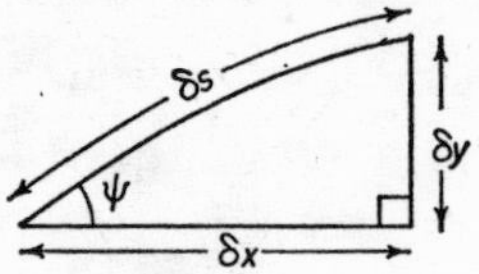

Fig. 7.3

It is left as an exercise for the reader to verify that

$$\frac{ds}{dy} = \sqrt{\left[\left(\frac{dx}{dy}\right)^2 + 1\right]} \qquad (7.6)$$

and
$$\frac{dy}{ds} = \sin \psi \qquad (7.7)$$

It is stressed that in the preceding results 7.3 to 7.7, for example, dx/ds is the derivative of x, where x is a function of s, and there may be more than one such function.

An aid to remembering the results is the 'triangle' shown in Fig. 7.3.

When the equation of the curve is given in parametric form—say, $x = f(\theta)$, $y = g(\theta)$—the equation 7.1 can be written

$$\text{length of chord} = \sqrt{[(\delta x)^2 + (\delta y)^2]}$$

$$= \sqrt{\left[\left(\frac{\delta x}{\delta \theta}\right)^2 + \left(\frac{\delta y}{\delta \theta}\right)^2\right]}\, \delta\theta$$

and in a similar manner to that used in obtaining equation 7.2

$$\text{length of curve} = \lim_{\delta\theta \to 0} \sum_A^B \sqrt{\left[\left(\frac{\delta x}{\delta \theta}\right)^2 + \left(\frac{\delta y}{\delta \theta}\right)^2\right]}\, \delta\theta$$

$$= \int_A^B \sqrt{\left[\left(\frac{dx}{d\theta}\right)^2 + \left(\frac{dy}{d\theta}\right)^2\right]}\, d\theta \qquad (7.8)$$

Alternatively $$\frac{\delta s}{\delta\theta} = \sqrt{\left[\left(\frac{\delta x}{\delta\theta}\right)^2 + \left(\frac{\delta y}{\delta\theta}\right)^2\right]}$$

and hence $$\frac{ds}{d\theta} = \sqrt{\left[\left(\frac{dx}{d\theta}\right)^2 + \left(\frac{dy}{d\theta}\right)^2\right]} \tag{7.9}$$

Example 3. Find the total length of the perimeter of the astroid $x = a\cos^3\theta$, $y = a\sin^3\theta$.

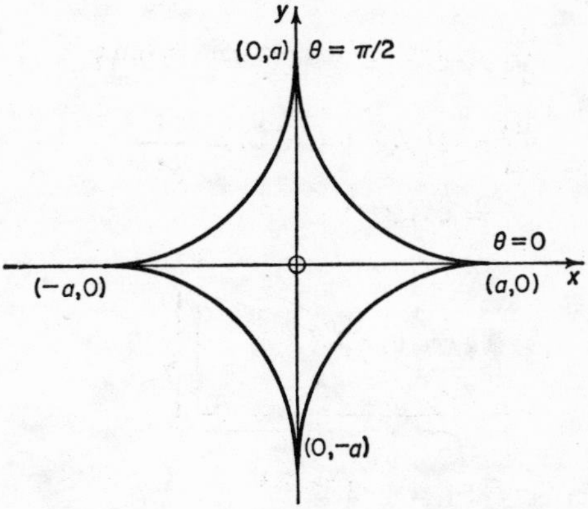

Fig. 7.4

The curve is shown in Fig. 7.4. By symmetry and the result 7.8

$$\text{Perimeter} = 4 \times \int_{\theta=0}^{\theta=\pi/2} \sqrt{\left[\left(\frac{dx}{d\theta}\right)^2 + \left(\frac{dy}{d\theta}\right)^2\right]}\, d\theta$$

$$= 4\int_0^{\pi/2} \sqrt{[(-3a\cos^2\theta\sin\theta)^2 + (3a\sin^2\theta\cos\theta)^2]}\, d\theta$$

$$= 4\int_0^{\pi/2} \sqrt{(9a^2\cos^4\theta\sin^2\theta + 9a^2\sin^4\theta\cos^2\theta)}\, d\theta$$

$$= 4\int_0^{\pi/2} \sqrt{[9a^2\cos^2\theta\sin^2\theta(\cos^2\theta + \sin^2\theta)]}\, d\theta$$

$$= 12a\int_0^{\pi/2} \cos\theta\sin\theta\, d\theta$$

Using the substitution $u = \sin\theta$

$$= 12a\int_0^1 u\, du$$

$$= 12a\left[u^2/2\right]_0^1$$

$$= 6a$$

Exercises 7.1

1. A particle moves along a curve according to the law $x = 5\cos 2t$, $y = 5\sin 2t$ where t is the time. Find its speed ds/dt along the curve.

2. A curve has the equation $y = \frac{1}{2}\ln x - x^2/4$. Show that $1 + (dy/dx)^2 = (1/2x + x/2)^2$. Hence find the length of the curve from $x = 1$ to $x = 4$.

3. Find the length of the curve $y = (e^x + e^{-x})/2$ from $x = 0$ to $x = \ln 4$.

4. Find the length of the curve $y = x^{\frac{3}{2}}$ from $x = 0$ to $x = \frac{1}{4}$.

5. A curve has the equation $8x = -2/y^2 - y^4$. Show that

$$\sqrt{\left[\left(\frac{dx}{dy}\right)^2 + 1\right]} = (1/y^3 + y^3)/2.$$

Hence find the length of the curve from $y = 1$ to $y = 4$.

6. Find the length of the curve $6x = y^3 + 3/y$ from $y = 1$ to $y = 2$.

7. Find the length of the curve $x = 3\cos t$, $y = 3\sin t$ between $t = 0$ and $t = \pi$. Explain the result.

8. Find the length of one arch of the cycloid $x = a(\theta - \sin\theta)$, $y = a(1 - \cos\theta)$ (θ goes from 0 to 2π).

9. Find the length of the curve $x = e^t\cos t$, $y = e^t\sin t$ from $t = 0$ to $t = \ln 3$.

10. Show that the length p of the perpendicular from the origin to the tangent to a curve at the point (x, y) is given by

$$p = x\frac{dy}{ds} - y\frac{dx}{ds}.$$

7.2 Areas of Surfaces of Revolution

To define the areas of curved surfaces in general is beyond our scope. We shall consider only the surface generated when a plane curve rotates about an axis in its plane. The intersection of such a surface by a plane perpendicular to the axis of rotation is a circle.

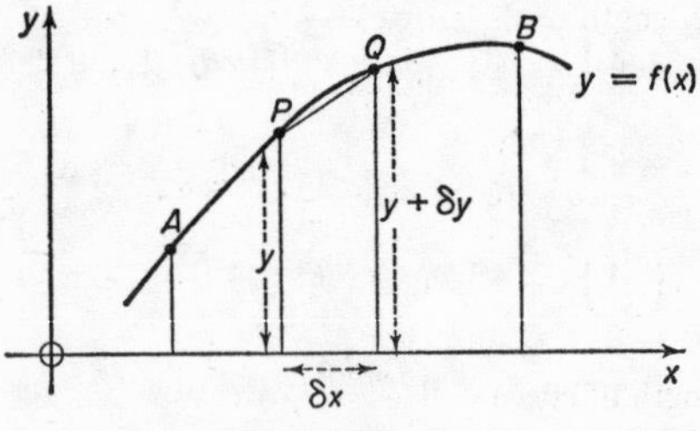

Fig. 7.5

Consider Fig. 7.5, where the arc AB of the curve $y = f(x)$ is to be rotated about the x-axis. Let $P(x,y)$ and $Q(x + \delta x,\ y + \delta y)$ be two neighbouring points on the curve and δs the length of the arc PQ. The area δA swept out by the arc PQ is given by

$$\delta A \simeq 2\pi y\,\delta s$$

Divide the curve AB into n parts each of length δs. The area swept out by the whole curve from A to B is the sum of all such elemental areas like δA

$$\therefore \qquad \text{Area} \simeq \sum_A^B 2\pi y\, \delta s$$

The limiting value of this summation as $\delta s \to 0$ is taken as the area of the surface.

$$\therefore \qquad \text{Area} = \lim_{\delta s \to 0} \sum_A^B 2\pi y\, \delta s$$

$$= \int_A^B 2\pi y\, ds \qquad (7.10)$$

Example 4. Find the area of the surface swept out when the curve $y^2 = 4x$ between $x = 0$ and $x = 3$, rotates about the x-axis.

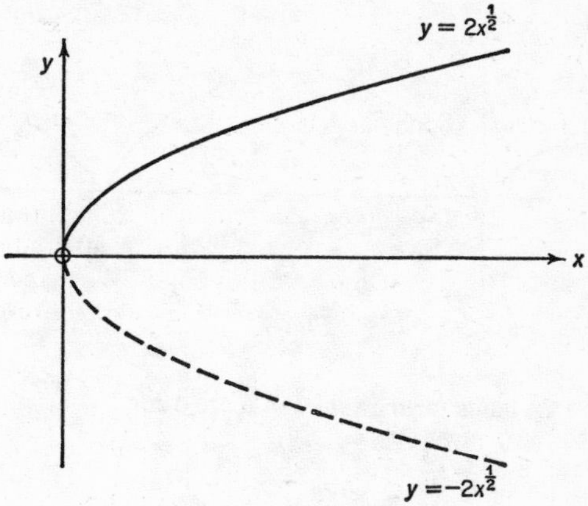

Fig. 7.6

Referring to Fig. 7.6, by symmetry, both parts of the curve sweep out the same surface. Consider the portion

$$y = 2x^{\frac{1}{2}}$$

$$\therefore \qquad \frac{dy}{dx} = x^{-\frac{1}{2}} = 1/\sqrt{x}$$

$$ds = \frac{ds}{dx}\,dx = \sqrt{\left[1 + \left(\frac{dy}{dx}\right)^2\right]}\,dx \qquad \text{(from equation 7.4)}$$

$$\therefore \qquad \text{Area} = \int_0^3 2\pi y\, ds$$

$$= 2\pi \int_0^3 y\left[1 + \left(\frac{dy}{dx}\right)^2\right]^{\frac{1}{2}} dx$$

$$= 2\pi \int_0^3 2x^{\frac{1}{2}} \sqrt{[1 + (1/\sqrt{x})^2]}\, dx$$

$$= 4\pi \int_0^3 x^{\frac{1}{2}}\sqrt{(1 + 1/x)}\, dx$$

$$= 4\pi \int_0^3 (1 + x)^{\frac{1}{2}}\, dx$$

$$= 4\pi \left[2/3(1 + x)^{\frac{3}{2}}\right]_0^3$$

$$= 4\pi[16/3 - 2/3]$$

$$= 56\pi/3$$

Example 5. Find the area of the surface swept out when one arch of the cycloid $x = a(\theta - \sin \theta)$, $y = a(1 - \cos \theta)$ rotates about the x-axis.

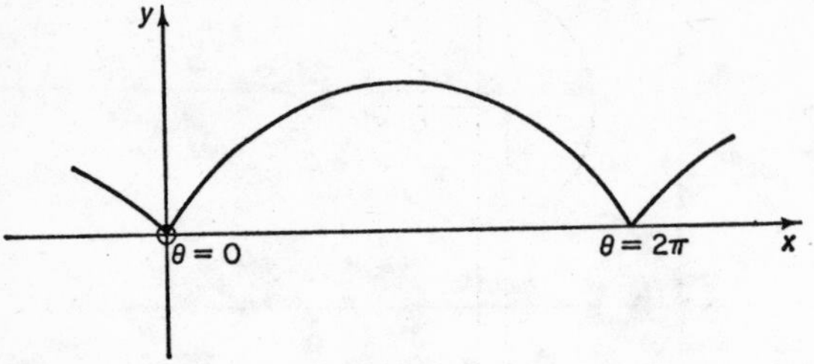

Fig. 7.7

From Fig. 7.7 the limits for the values of θ are 0 and 2π.

and $$ds = \frac{ds}{d\theta}\, d\theta$$

$$= \sqrt{\left[\left(\frac{dx}{d\theta}\right)^2 + \left(\frac{dy}{d\theta}\right)^2\right]}\, d\theta \quad \text{(from equation 7.9)}$$

$$= \sqrt{[a^2(1 - \cos \theta)^2 + a^2 \sin^2 \theta]}\, d\theta$$

$$= a\sqrt{(1 - 2 \cos \theta + \cos^2 \theta + \sin^2 \theta)}\, d\theta$$

$$= a\sqrt{2(1 - \cos \theta)}\, d\theta$$

$$= a\sqrt{[2 \,.\, 2 \sin^2 (\theta/2)]}\, d\theta$$

$$= 2a \sin (\theta/2)\, d\theta$$

$\therefore$ $$\text{Surface area} = \int_A^B 2\pi y\, ds$$

$$= \int_0^{2\pi} 2\pi a(1 - \cos \theta)\, 2a \sin (\theta/2)\, d\theta$$

$$= 4\pi a^2 \int_0^{2\pi} 2 \sin^2 (\theta/2) \sin (\theta/2)\, d\theta$$

Let $u = \cos (\theta/2)$; then $du = -\frac{1}{2} \sin (\theta/2)\, d\theta$ and when $\theta = 0$ $u = 1$, $\theta = 2\pi$ $u = -1$.

$$\therefore \qquad \text{Surface area} = 8\pi a^2 \int_1^{-1} \sin^2(\theta/2)(-2\,du)$$
$$= -16\pi a^2 \int_1^{-1} [1 - \cos^2(\theta/2)]\,du$$
$$= -16\pi a^2 \int_1^{-1} (1 - u^2)\,du$$
$$= -16\pi a^2 \Big[u - u^3/3\Big]_1^{-1}$$
$$= -16\pi a^2[(-1 + \tfrac{1}{3}) - (1 - \tfrac{1}{3})]$$
$$= 64\pi a^2/3$$

Example 6. Find the area of the surface swept out when a circle of radius *a* rotates about a line in its plane at a distance *b* from its centre ($b > a$) (Anchor Ring).

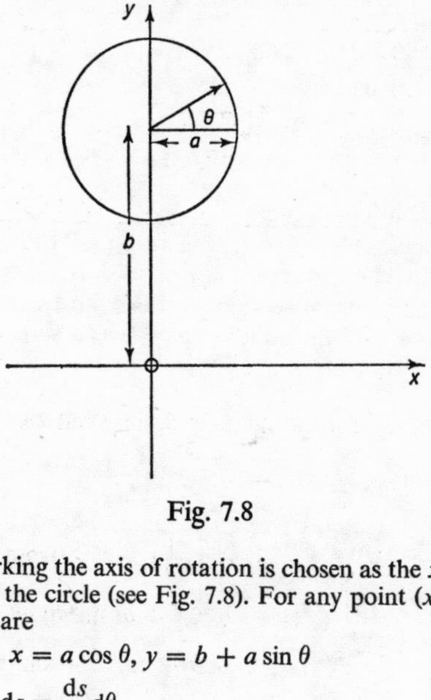

Fig. 7.8

To simplify the working the axis of rotation is chosen as the *x*-axis with the *y*-axis through the centre of the circle (see Fig. 7.8). For any point (x, y) on the circle the parametric equations are

$$x = a\cos\theta,\ y = b + a\sin\theta$$

$$\therefore \qquad ds = \frac{ds}{d\theta}\,d\theta$$
$$= \sqrt{\left[\left(\frac{dx}{d\theta}\right)^2 + \left(\frac{dy}{d\theta}\right)^2\right]}\,d\theta \qquad \text{(from equation 7.9)}$$
$$= \sqrt{[(-a\sin\theta)^2 + (a\cos\theta)^2]}\,d\theta$$
$$= a\,d\theta$$

$$\therefore \qquad \text{Surface area} = \int_0^{2\pi} 2\pi y\,ds$$
$$= 2\pi \int_0^{2\pi} (b + a\sin\theta)\,a\,d\theta$$
$$= 2\pi a\Big[b\theta - a\cos\theta\Big]_0^{2\pi}$$
$$= 2\pi a[(2\pi b - a) - (0 - a)]$$
$$= 4\pi^2 ab$$

Exercises 7.2

1. Verify that the area of the curved surface of a cone of height h and semi-vertical angle α is $\pi h^2 \tan \alpha \sec \alpha$. (Hint: consider the surface swept out by the line $y = x \tan \alpha$ when it rotates about the x-axis.)

2. Verify that the area of the surface of a sphere of radius a is $4\pi a^2$.

3. Find the area A of the portion of the surface of a sphere cut off by two parallel planes distance d apart. A cylinder circumscribes the sphere with its axis perpendicular to the two planes. Verify that the area of the surface of the cylinder cut off by the two parallel planes is also A.

4. Find the area of the surface swept out when the curve $y = (e^x + e^{-x})/2$ between $x = 0$ and $x = \ln 2$ rotates about the x-axis.

5. Find the area of the surface swept out when the curve $12y^2 = x(x - 4)^2$ rotates about the x-axis.

6. Find the area of the surface swept out when the portion of the astroid $x = a \cos^3 \theta$, $y = a \sin^3 \theta$ between $\theta = 0$ and $\theta = \pi$ rotates about the x-axis.

7. Find the area of the surface swept out when the portion of the semi-cubical parabola $y = t^2/2$, $x = t^3/3$ from $t = 0$ to $t = 1$ rotates about the x-axis.

7.3 Volumes of Revolution

When the area enclosed between the graph of the continuous function $f(x)$, the x-axis and the ordinates $x = a$, $x = b$ is rotated about the x-axis a solid is generated. The cross section of this solid by a plane perpendicular to the x-axis is a circle and the solid is known as a **solid of revolution.**

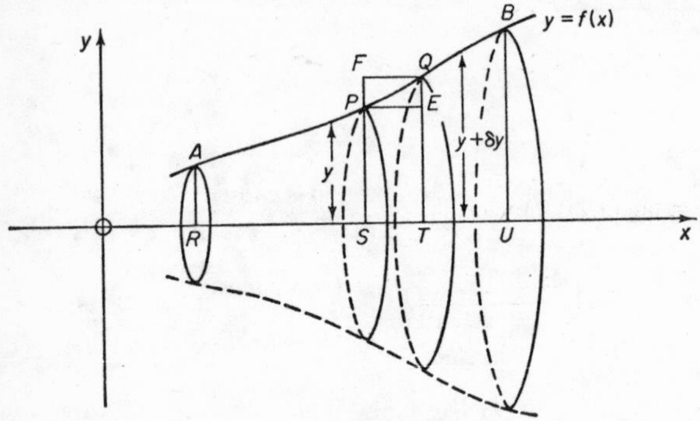

Fig. 7.9

Refer to Fig. 7.9, where $f(x)$ is shown increasing as x increases. Let AR, BU be the ordinates at the points $x = a$ and $x = b$ respectively. Divide RU into n equal parts by points such as $S(x, 0)$, $T(x + \delta x, 0)$. Let PS, QT be the ordinates at the points, S, T meeting the curve $y = f(x)$ at points P and Q, whose coordinates are (x, y) and $(x + \delta x, y + \delta y)$ respectively. As the area $ARUB$ rotates about the x-axis, the small area $PQTS$ will sweep out a portion δV of the total volume in the form of a cylinder of thickness δx. The lines PE and QF are drawn parallel to the x-axis as shown, and

Circular disc swept out by *PETS* $< \delta V <$ Circular disc swept out by *FQTS**

$$\therefore \qquad \pi y^2 \delta x < \delta V < \pi(y + \delta y)^2\, \delta x \tag{7.11}$$

Summing for all such sections

$$\sum_{x=a}^{x=b} \pi y^2\, \delta x < V < \sum_{x=a}^{x=b} \pi(y + \delta y)^2\, \delta x$$

In the limit as n becomes very large $\delta x \to 0$ and $\delta y \to 0$

$$\therefore \qquad V = \lim_{\delta x \to 0} \sum_{x=a}^{x=b} \pi y^2\, \delta x$$

$$\therefore \qquad V = \int_a^b \pi y^2\, dx \tag{7.12}$$

Example 7. Find the volume of (i) a sphere of radius r and (ii) the portion of a sphere radius r cut off by two parallel planes, and deduce the volume of a spherical cap of height h.

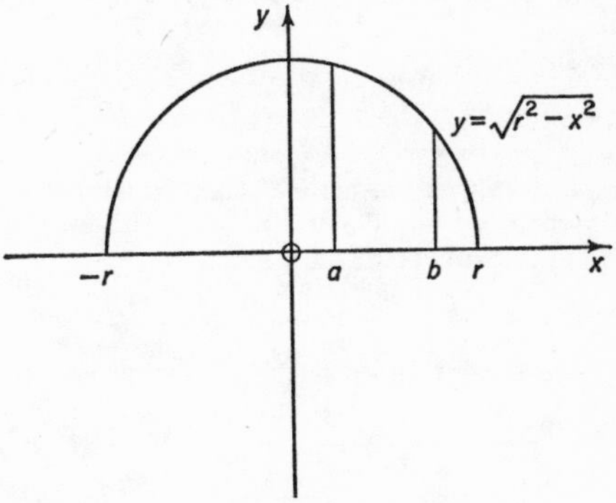

Fig. 7.10

(i) A sphere is swept out when a semi-circular area rotates about its bounding diameter. Refer to Fig. 7.10, where the origin and the axes have been chosen as conveniently as possible.

$$\begin{aligned} \text{Volume} &= \int_{-r}^{r} \pi y^2\, dx \\ &= \pi \int_{-r}^{r} (r^2 - x^2)\, dx \\ &= \pi \Big[r^2 x - x^3/3 \Big]_{-r}^{r} \\ &= \pi[r^3 - r^3/3] - \pi[-r^3 + r^3/3] \\ &= 4\pi r^3/3 \end{aligned}$$

* If $f(x)$ decreases as x increases the inequalities are reversed.

(ii) Consider the portion of the semi-circle enclosed between the ordinates $x = a$ and $x = b$. This will be the required volume V'.

$$V' = \int_a^b \pi y^2 \, dx$$

$$= \pi \int_a^b (r^2 - x^2) \, dx$$

$$= \pi \left[r^2x - x^3/3 \right]_a^b$$

$$= \pi[r^2b - b^3/3] - \pi[r^2a - a^3/3]$$

$$= \pi[r^2(b - a) - (b^3 - a^3)/3]$$

$$= \pi(b - a)[3r^2 - (b^2 + ab + a^2)]/3$$

If we now let $b = r$ and $a = r - h$, the volume of a spherical cap of height h is obtained

$$\pi[r - (r - h)]\{3r^2 - [r^2 + r(r - h) + (r - h)^2]\}/3$$

$$= \pi h(3r^2 - r^2 - r^2 + rh - r^2 + 2rh - h^2)/3$$

$$= \pi h(3rh - h^2)/3$$

$$= \pi h^2(r - h/3)$$

Example 8. The shape of a thrust washer is formed by the rotation about the y-axis of the area enclosed between the curve $10y = x^2$, the x-axis and the ordinates $x = 1$ and $x = 3$. Find the volume of the washer.

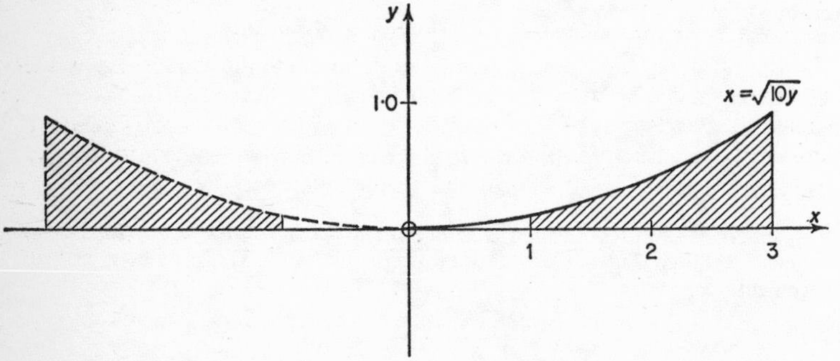

Fig. 7.11

We note that rotation about the y-axis is now to be considered. By means of a similar argument to that used in obtaining the formula 7.12

$$\text{Required volume} = \int_{y_1}^{y_2} \pi x^2 \, dy \qquad (7.13)$$

In this case with $x^2 = 10y$ when $x = 1$ $y = 0{\cdot}1$, and when $x = 3$, $y = 0{\cdot}9$. Referring to Fig. 7.11

$$\text{Volume} = \int_{0\cdot 1}^{0\cdot 9} \pi\, 10y\, dy$$

$$= 10\pi \int_{0\cdot 1}^{0\cdot 9} y\, dy$$

$$= 10\pi \Big[y^2/2 \Big]_{0\cdot 1}^{0\cdot 9}$$

$$= 5\pi[(0\cdot 9)^2 - (0\cdot 1)^2]$$

$$= 4\pi \text{ cubic units}$$

Exercises 7.3

1. Find the volume of a right circular cone of height h and semi-vertical angle α. (Consider the volume swept out when the area enclosed by the line $y = x \tan \alpha$, the x-axis and the ordinate $x = h$ rotates about the x-axis.)

2. Find the volume swept out when the area enclosed between the curve $y = \sin x$ and the portion of the x-axis from $x = 0$ to $x = \pi$ rotates about the x-axis.

3. Find the volume swept out when the area enclosed between the curve $y = \sqrt{(6x)}$, the x-axis and the ordinate $x = 6$ rotates about the x-axis.

4. The shape of an ornamental vase is formed by rotating about the y-axis the area enclosed between the curve $y = \sqrt{(12x)}$, the y-axis and the line $y = 6$. Find the volume of the vase.

5. An oblate spheroid is swept out when an ellipse rotates about its minor axis. Show that the volume of an oblate spheroid is $4\pi a^2 b/3$, where a and b are, respectively, the semi-major and semi-minor axes of the ellipse ($a > b$). The Earth is an oblate spheroid, being slightly flattened at the poles. Its equatorial and polar radii are 6399·6 km and 6378·2 km respectively. Find the volume of the Earth correct to *four* significant figures.

7.4 Centres of Mass, Centres of Gravity and Centroids

In the study of mechanics one of the fundamental quantities is mass. Forces, in particular the force of gravity, can be measured by the product of mass and acceleration. The position of the centre of mass $(\bar{x}, \bar{y}, \bar{z})$ of a number of particles of masses $m_1, m_2, \ldots m_n$ situated at the points (x_1, y_1, z_1) $(x_2, y_2, z_2), \ldots (x_n, y_n, z_n)$ is defined by the equations

$$\left.\begin{aligned} \bar{x} &= \frac{m_1x_1 + m_2x_2 + \ldots + m_nx_n}{m_1 + m_2 + \ldots + m_n} = \frac{\Sigma mx}{\Sigma m} \\ \bar{y} &= \frac{m_1y_1 + m_2y_2 + \ldots + m_ny_n}{m_1 + m_2 + \ldots + m_n} = \frac{\Sigma my}{\Sigma m} \\ \bar{z} &= \frac{m_1z_1 + m_2z_2 + \ldots + m_nz_n}{m_1 + m_2 + \ldots + m_n} = \frac{\Sigma mz}{\Sigma m} \end{aligned}\right\} \tag{7.14}$$

To define the centre of gravity of the masses $m_1, m_2, \ldots m_n$ we use the forces $m_1g, m_2g, \ldots m_ng$, where g is the acceleration due to gravity, in place of $m_1, m_2, \ldots m_n$, and obtain

$$\bar{x} = \frac{\Sigma mg\, x}{\Sigma mg} \qquad \bar{y} = \frac{\Sigma mg\, y}{\Sigma mg} \qquad \bar{z} = \frac{\Sigma mg\, z}{\Sigma mg} \tag{7.15}$$

In terrestrial calculations, when the distance between any two particles is small compared to the radius of the earth, g can be considered constant and cancelled throughout equations 7.15, which become identical with equations 7.14—that is, the centre of mass and the centre of gravity coincide. We shall assume this is so unless otherwise stated.

In order to define the centre of mass (or centre of gravity) of a solid body the concept of a **triple integral** is required. The problem is simplified by using two principles, which can be proved by triple integration.

1 The centre of mass of a body lies on any axis (or plane) of symmetry.

2 When a solid body is divided into a number of smaller parts (which have no common interior points) of masses $\delta m_1, \delta m_2, \ldots \delta m_n$ and centres of mass $(\bar{x}_1, \bar{y}_1, \bar{z}_1), (\bar{x}_2, \bar{y}_2, \bar{z}_2), \ldots (\bar{x}_n, \bar{y}_n, \bar{z}_n)$, the centre of mass of the whole body is given by

$$\bar{x} = \frac{\bar{x}_1\delta m_1 + \bar{x}_2\delta m_2 + \ldots + \bar{x}_n\delta m_n}{\delta m_1 + \delta m_2 + \ldots + \delta m_n} = \frac{\Sigma \bar{x}_r \delta m_r}{\Sigma \delta m_r} \qquad (7.16)$$

and two similar expressions for $\bar{y}$ and $\bar{z}$

$$\bar{y} = \frac{\Sigma \bar{y}_r \delta m_r}{\Sigma \delta m_r} \qquad \bar{z} = \frac{\Sigma \bar{z}_r \delta m_r}{\Sigma \delta m_r}$$

When the smaller parts are thin and regular, such as thin plates or thin shells, the number of them can be considered as increasing indefinitely as the thickness tends to zero. In the limiting case the summations become integrals and are written

$$\bar{x} = \frac{\int x\, dm}{\int dm} \qquad \bar{y} = \frac{\int y\, dm}{\int dm} \qquad \bar{z} = \frac{\int z\, dm}{\int dm} \qquad (7.17)$$

where the range of integration covers the whole body. It must be remembered that the x, y, z of the formulae 7.17 refer to the position of the centre of mass of the elemental piece. Also considerations of symmetry will often enable one or more of $\bar{x}$, $\bar{y}$, and $\bar{z}$ to be found immediately.

Example 9. Find the position of the centre of mass of a uniform solid hemisphere of radius a and uniform density ρ.

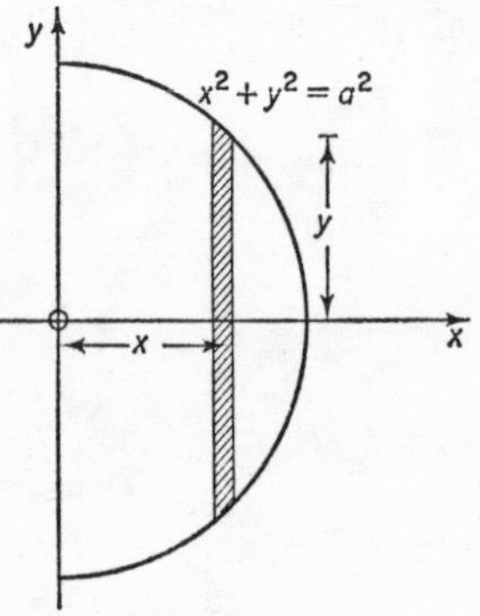

Fig. 7.12

By definition

$$\text{density} = \text{mass/volume}$$

or

$$\text{mass} = \text{volume} \times \text{density}$$

Refer to Fig. 7.12, where the centre of the plane face of the hemisphere is the origin and the x-axis perpendicular to the plane face. By symmetry, the centre of mass lies on the x-axis—that is, $\bar{y} = 0 = \bar{z}$. To find $\bar{x}$ consider an elemental portion of the hemisphere in the shape of a disc of thickness δx, with its plane face perpendicular to the x-axis and distance x from the origin. Let its radius be y.

The volume δV of the disc is given by

$$\delta V \simeq \pi y^2 \, \delta x$$

and its mass δm by

$$\delta m \simeq \pi y^2 \, \delta x \rho$$

and the x coordinate of the centre of mass of the elemental disc *is* x.

$$\therefore \qquad \bar{x} \simeq \frac{\sum_{x=0}^{x=a} x \,.\, \pi y^2 \rho \, \delta x}{\Sigma \delta m}$$

$$\simeq \sum_{x=0}^{x=a} x \pi y^2 \rho \, \delta x/\text{Total mass}$$

In the limit as $\delta x \to 0$

$$\text{Total mass} \times \bar{x} = \int_0^a x \,.\, \pi y^2 \rho \, \mathrm{d}x$$

or

$$\bar{x} \,.\, 2\pi a^3 \rho/3 = \pi \rho \int_0^a x y^2 \, \mathrm{d}x \quad (\rho \text{ is constant})$$

$$\therefore \qquad \bar{x} \,.\, 2a^3/3 = \int_0^a x(a^2 - x^2) \, \mathrm{d}x$$

$$= \int_0^a (a^2 x - x^3) \, \mathrm{d}x$$

$$= \Big[a^2 x^2/2 - x^4/4 \Big]_0^a$$

$$= [(a^4/2 - a^4/4) - 0]$$

$$= a^4/4$$

$$\therefore \qquad \bar{x} = \frac{a^4}{4} \times \frac{3}{2a^3}$$

$$= 3a/8$$

Example 10. Find the position of the centre of mass of a uniform thin hemispherical shell of radius a and thickness t.

Take the centre of the circular end of the hemisphere as the origin and the x-axis perpendicular to the circular end. By symmetry, the centre of mass lies on the x-axis. Refer to Fig. 7.13 and consider an elemental circular ring cut off by two planes perpendicular to Ox and distance δx apart.

$$\therefore \qquad \delta V = 2\pi y \, \delta s \, t$$

$$\delta m = 2\pi y \, \delta s \, t \rho$$

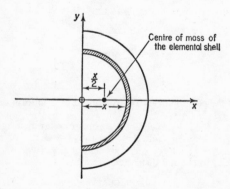

The x coordinate of the centre of mass of δm is x

$$\therefore \qquad \bar{x} = \frac{\int_0^a x \,.\, 2\pi y \, ds \, t\rho}{\text{Total mass}} \qquad \text{(from formulae 7.17)}$$

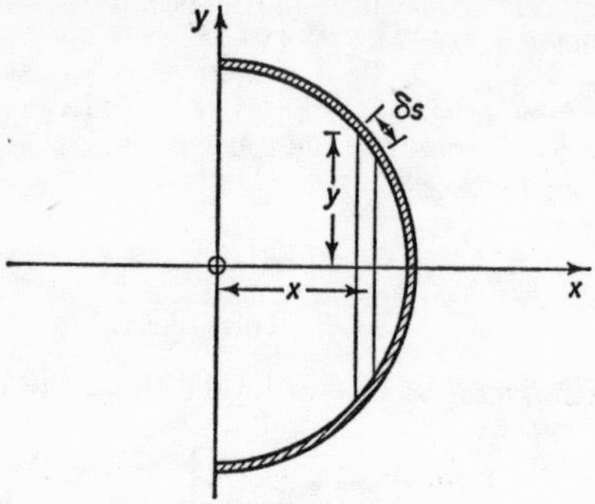

Fig. 7.13

Let the equation of the bounding curve be $x = a \cos \theta$, $y = a \sin \theta$

$$\therefore \qquad ds = \frac{ds}{d\theta} d\theta$$

$$= \sqrt{[(-a \sin \theta)^2 + (a \cos \theta)^2]} \, d\theta \quad \text{(from equation 7.9)}$$

$$= a \, d\theta$$

$$\therefore \quad \text{Total mass} \times \bar{x} = t\rho \int_0^{\pi/2} a \cos \theta \, 2\pi \, a \sin \theta \, a \, d\theta$$

t and ρ are constants because the hemisphere is uniform.

$$\therefore \qquad 2\pi a^2 t\rho \bar{x} = t\rho 2\pi a^3 \int_0^{\pi/2} \sin \theta \cos \theta \, d\theta$$

$$\bar{x} = a \left[\frac{\sin^2 \theta}{2}\right]_0^{\pi/2}$$

$$= a/2$$

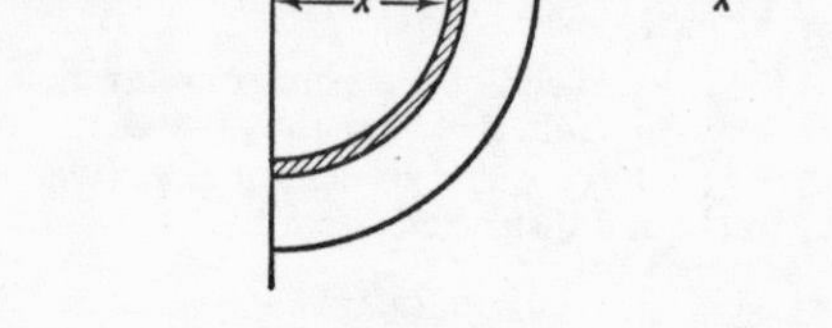

Fig. 7.14

In the two previous examples the x coordinate of the centre of the elemental mass has been simply x, but now consider the following example.

Example 11. Find the position of the centre of mass of a uniform solid hemisphere of radius a by using concentric hemispherical shells.

Divide the uniform solid hemisphere into concentric (centre O) hemispherical shells of thickness δx as shown in Fig. 7.14.

$$\delta V = 2\pi x^2\, \delta x$$
$$\delta m = 2\pi x^2\, \delta x \rho$$

The centre of mass of the hemispherical shell radius x is at a distance $x/2$; therefore

$$\bar{x} = \frac{\int_0^a x/2 \,.\, 2\pi x^2 \rho \, dx}{\text{Total mass}} \qquad \text{(from formulae 7.17)}$$

$$\text{Total mass} \times \bar{x} = \pi\rho \int_0^a x^3 \, dx$$

$$2\pi a^3 \rho \bar{x}/3 = \pi\rho \Big[x^4/4 \Big]_0^a$$

$$2a^3\bar{x}/3 = a^4/4$$

$$\bar{x} = 3a/8 \text{ (as in example 9)}$$

Example 12. A straight thin rod PQ of length $2a$ and constant cross-sectional area A is of variable density ρ. Given that $\rho = \rho_0(1 + 2x^2/a^2)$, where x is the distance along the rod from the end P and ρ_0 is a constant, find the position of its centre of mass.

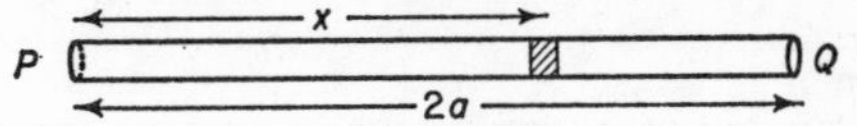

Fig. 7.15

Consider a portion of the rod of length δx and distance x from P (see Fig. 7.15)

$$\delta V = A\, \delta x$$
$$\delta m = A\, \delta x \rho$$
$$= A\, \delta x \rho_0(1 + 2x^2/a^2)$$

The x coordinate of the centre of mass of δm is x

$$\therefore \qquad \bar{x} = \frac{\int_0^{2a} x \,.\, A\, dx \rho_0(1 + 2x^2/a^2)}{\int_0^{2a} A\, dx \rho_0 (1 + 2x^2/a^2)} \qquad \text{(from formulae 7.17)}$$

$$= \frac{A\rho_0 \int_0^{2a} (x + 2x^3/a^2)\, dx}{A\rho_0 \int_0^{2a} (1 + 2x^2/a^2)\, dx}$$

$$= \frac{\Big[x^2/2 + 2x^4/4a^2 \Big]_0^{2a}}{\Big[x + 2x^3/3a^2 \Big]_0^{2a}}$$

$$= (2a^2 + 8a^2)/(2a + 16a/3)$$

$$= 15a/11 \quad \text{from the end } P$$

If in the formulae 7.17 we had used elements of volume $\mathrm{d}V$ or of area $\mathrm{d}A$ the points so defined would have been called centroids of volume or of area. Centroids are related to the geometrical shape of the body. In the case of a homogeneous body, which has a constant density (say ρ) throughout, equations 7.17 for the position of the centre of mass become

$$\bar{x} = \frac{\int x\,\mathrm{d}m}{\int \mathrm{d}m} = \frac{\int x\rho\,\mathrm{d}V}{\int \rho\,\mathrm{d}V} = \frac{\rho \int x\,\mathrm{d}V}{\rho \int \mathrm{d}V}$$

$$= \frac{\int x\,\mathrm{d}V}{\int \mathrm{d}V}$$

and similarly for $\bar{y}$ and $\bar{z}$: that is, for a homogeneous body the centroid coincides with the centre of mass. The coordinates of centres of gravity can often be found without use of the Calculus and our readers are referred to standard textbooks.

Exercises 7.4

Find the positions of the centres of mass of the following:

1. A uniform solid right circular cone. (Consider rotation about the x-axis of the area between the line $y = x \tan \alpha$, the x-axis and $x = 0$ and $x = h$.)

2. A hollow thin right circular cone of uniform thickness and density.

3. A homogeneous piece of steel plate of constant thickness in the form of a quadrant of a circle. (Hint: take its bounding radii as axes and parametric equations $x = a \cos \theta$, $y = a \sin \theta$.)

4. Find the position of the centroid of the volume swept out when the area enclosed between the parabola $y^2 = 4ax$, the ordinate $x = a$ and the x-axis rotates about the x-axis.

5. A straight thin rod PQ of length $2a$ and constant cross section A is of variable density ρ. Given that $\rho = \rho_0[1 + x^3/a^3]$, where x is the distance along the rod from the end P and ρ_0 is a constant, find the position of its centre of mass.

6. A solid hemisphere of radius a has a variable density $\rho = \rho_0(1 + 2x/a)$, where x is the distance from the centre of its plane face and ρ_0 is a constant. Find the position of its centre of mass.

7. A piece of homogeneous steel plate of constant thickness is in the form of a trapezium whose parallel sides are of lengths a and b. Show that its centre of mass divides the line joining the mid-points of the parallel sides in the ratio $(2a + b) : (a + 2b)$.

8. A portion of a thin uniform homogeneous spherical shell is cut off by two parallel planes distance d apart. Show that its centre of mass is on the axis of symmetry halfway between the two planes.

7.5 Moments of Inertia

In the study of Mechanics, the moment of inertia of a particle mass m about an axis is defined as mr^2, where r is the perpendicular distance of the particle from the axis. This is a scalar quantity and necessarily positive. The moment of inertia I of a system of particles masses $m_1, m_2, \ldots m_n$ at perpendicular distances $r_1, r_2, \ldots r_n$ from the axis is defined by

$$I = m_1 r_1^2 + m_2 r_2^2 + \ldots + m_n r_n^2 \qquad (7.18)$$

In order to define the moment of inertia of a solid body, like the case of centre of mass (section 7.4), the concept of triple integration is required. The problem can be simplified by using the following two principles which can be proved by triple integration.

1 If a solid body is divided into a number of smaller parts (which have no common interior parts) the moment of inertia of the whole body is equal to the sum of the moments of inertia of its separate parts

$$I = I_1 + I_2 + \ldots + I_n \tag{7.19}$$

2 The moment of inertia I of a body of mass M is expressed in the form

$$I = Mk^2$$

where k is a positive constant known as the radius of gyration. Note that the radius of gyration of a particle is equal to its distance from the axis.

The second proposition is easily verified: because I and M are positive constants I/M is a positive constant

let $$+\sqrt{(I/M)} = k$$

$\therefore$ $$I/M = k^2$$

$$I = Mk^2$$

In the relation 7.19, let $I_1 = k_1{}^2\,\delta m_1$, $I_2 = k_2{}^2\,\delta m_2, \ldots I_n = k_n{}^2\,\delta m_n$

$\therefore$ $$I = k_1{}^2\,\delta m_1 + k_2{}^2\,\delta m_2 + \ldots + k_n{}^2\,\delta m_n = \Sigma k^2\,\delta m \tag{7.20}$$

Like in equation 7.16 in section 7.4, when the smaller parts are thin and regular such as plates or shells, the number n can be considered as increasing indefinitely as the thickness diminishes and in the limiting case

$$I = \lim_{\delta m \to 0} \Sigma k^2\,\delta m = \int k^2\,dm \tag{7.21}$$

where k is the radius of gyration of the elemental piece and the integration is taken throughout the body.

Example 13. Find the moment of inertia and the radius of gyration of a thin circular ring of radius a.

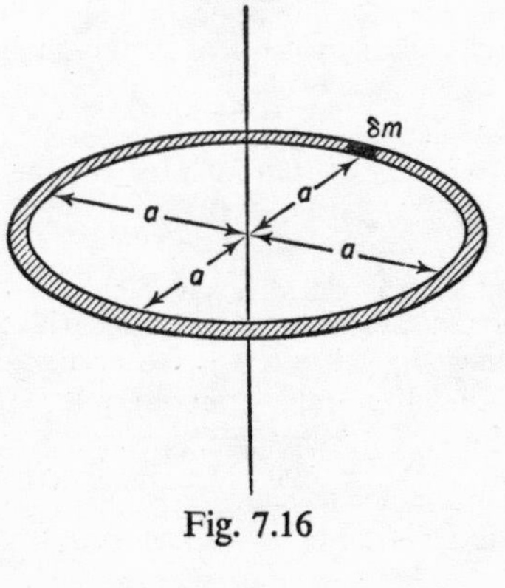

Fig. 7.16

Refer to Fig. 7.16: because the ring is thin all parts of the ring can be taken to be the same distance from the axis. The moment of inertia of a small piece of mass δm is $a^2\,\delta m$

$$\therefore \qquad \text{Total moment of inertia} = \Sigma a^2\,\delta m = a^2\Sigma\,\delta m$$
$$= Ma^2 \qquad (7.22)$$

and the radius of gyration is a.

Example 14. A thin uniform rod has length $2a$ and mass per unit length k. Find its moment of inertia and radius of gyration about an axis through its centre of mass perpendicular to its length.

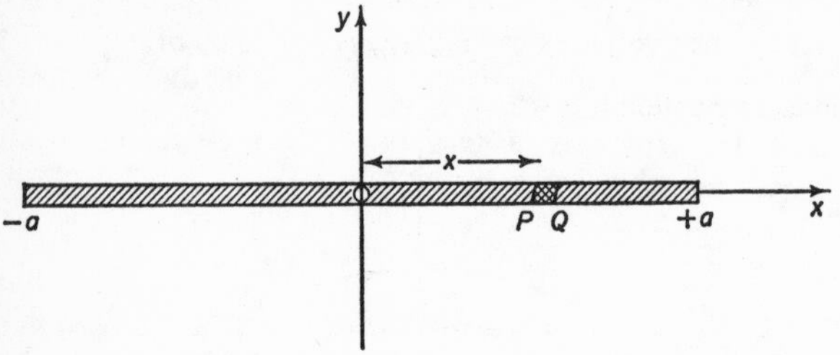

Fig. 7.17

Refer to Fig. 7.17, where the centre of the rod has been taken as the origin of co-ordinates and the x-axis is along the rod. Consider the rod to be made up of a large number of segments such as PQ of length δx. The mass of PQ is $k\,\delta x$ and its radius of gyration about Oy is x. Therefore by equation 7.21

$$I = \int k^2\,\mathrm{d}m$$
$$= \int_{-a}^{a} x^2k\,\mathrm{d}x$$
$$= k\left[x^3/3\right]_{-a}^{+a}$$
$$= 2ka^3/3$$

The mass M of the rod is given by

$$M = k\,.\,2a$$
$$\therefore \qquad I = Ma^2/3 \qquad (7.23)$$

and the radius of gyration is $a/\sqrt{3}$.

Example 15. A uniform thin circular disc has radius a and mass per unit area k. Find its moment of inertia and radius of gyration about an axis through its centre O perpendicular to its plane.

Refer to Fig. 7.18, where the centre of the disc has been taken as the origin of coordinates and its axis as the y-axis. Consider the disc to be made up of a large number of circular rings. A typical one of radius x and thickness δx is shown in the diagram. Its mass is $2\pi x\,\delta x\,k$, and its radius of gyration about Oy is x. Therefore by equation 7.21

$$I = \int k^2 \, dm$$

$$= \int_0^a x^2 2\pi x \, dx \, k$$

$$= 2\pi k \int_0^a x^3 \, dx$$

$$= 2\pi k \left[x^4/4 \right]_0^a$$

$$= \pi k a^4/2$$

The mass M of the circular disc is given by

$$M = \pi a^2 k$$

$$\therefore \qquad I = Ma^2/2 \qquad (7.24)$$

and the radius of gyration is $a/\sqrt{2}$.

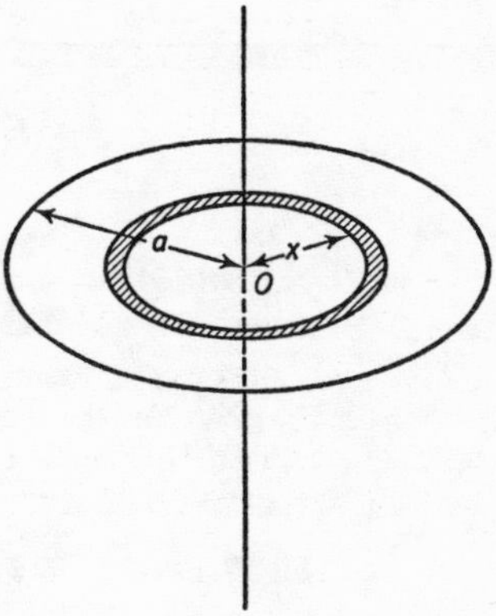

Fig. 7.18

In the two previous examples the radius of gyration of the elemental mass has been simply x, but consider the following example.

Example 16. Find the moment of inertia of a homogeneous sphere of radius a about a diameter AB.

In Fig. 7.19 the origin of coordinates is the centre of the sphere and the x-axis is the diameter AB. Consider the sphere to be made up of a large number of thin circular discs whose planes are perpendicular to Ox. A typical one of radius y, thickness δx and distance x from O is shown in the diagram. Let ρ be the density of the sphere. The typical disc has a mass of $\pi y^2 \, \delta x \rho$ and its radius of gyration about the x-axis is, by the result of example 15, $y/\sqrt{2}$. Therefore by equation 7.21

$$I = \int k^2 \, dm$$

$$= \int_{-a}^{a} (y/\sqrt{2})^2 \pi y^2 \, dx \rho$$

$$= \frac{\pi\rho}{2} \int_{-a}^{a} y^4 \, dx$$

By Pythagoras (see Fig. 7.19), $x^2 + y^2 = a^2$

$$\therefore \quad I = \frac{\pi\rho}{2}\int_{-a}^{a} (a^2 - x^2)^2\,dx$$

$$= \frac{\pi\rho}{2}\int_{-a}^{a} (a^4 - 2a^2x^2 + x^4)\,dx$$

$$= \frac{\pi\rho}{2}\Big[a^4x - 2a^2x^3/3 + x^5/5\Big]_{-a}^{a}$$

$$= \frac{\pi\rho}{2}[(a^5 - 2a^5/3 + a^5/5) - (-a^5 + 2a^5/3 - a^5/5)]$$

$$= \frac{\pi\rho a^5}{2}[(1 - 2/3 + 1/5) - (-1 + 2/3 - 1/5)]$$

$$= 8\pi\rho a^5/15$$

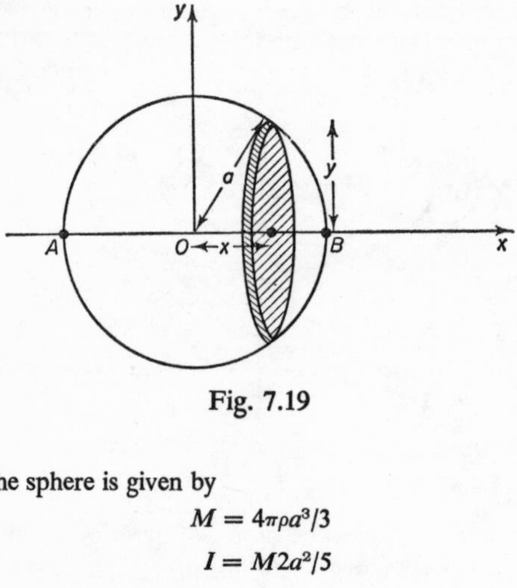

Fig. 7.19

The mass M of the sphere is given by

$$M = 4\pi\rho a^3/3$$

$$\therefore \quad I = M2a^2/5 \tag{7.25}$$

The radius of gyration is $a\sqrt{2}/\sqrt{5}$.

Exercises 7.5

Find the moments of inertia and radii of gyration of the following:

1. A uniform rectangular lamina, of sides $2a$ and $2b$ ($a > b$), about an axis through its centre perpendicular to its larger side.

2. A uniformly thin spherical shell of radius a about a diameter.

3. A homogeneous sphere of radius a by considering thin concentric shells and using the result of exercise 2.

4. A uniform rectangular parallelepiped, of dimensions $2a \times 2b \times 2c$, about an axis through its centre of mass parallel to the edges of length $2a$.

5. A uniform thin straight rod of length $2a$ about an axis through one end perpendicular to its length.

6. A uniform thin shell in the form of a right circular cone, the radius of whose base is r, about its axis.

7. A uniform solid cone, the radius of whose base is r, about its axis.

8. (i) A uniform hollow right circular cylinder of radius a about its axis; (ii) a uniform solid right circular cylinder of radius a about its axis.

9. A uniform lamina in the shape of an isosceles triangle of height h and base $2a$ about its axis of symmetry.

10. Use the result of question 5 to verify that the moment of inertia of a uniform rectangle of length $2a$ and breadth $2b$ about an edge of length $2b$ is also $4Ma^2/3$.

The standard results obtained in exercises 7.5 and the previous examples can be used to deduce moments of inertia about other axes by using two theorems which we shall prove.

1 *The Parallel Axis Theorem*

This theorem applies to all bodies and relates the moment of inertia about any axis to the moment of inertia about a parallel axis through the centre of mass of the body.

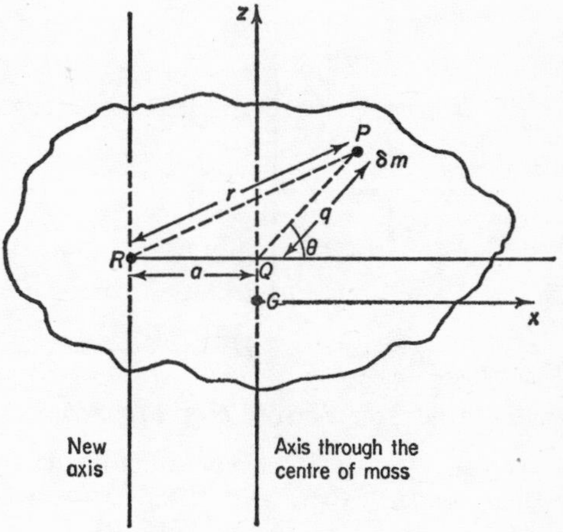

Fig. 7.20

Theorem. Given that the moment of inertia of a body of mass M about an axis through its centre of mass is Mk^2, then its moment of inertia about a parallel axis distance a away is $M(k^2 + a^2)$.

Let the centre of mass G be the origin of coordinates, the axis through G the axis of z and the common perpendicular through G to the two parallel axes be the x-axis. Refer to Fig. 7.20, where δm is a typical element of the body at a point P. The perpendiculars from P to the two axes are PQ and PR, of lengths q and r respectively. Then

$$r^2 = a^2 + q^2 + 2aq \cos \theta$$

The moment of inertia I about the new axis is

$$I = \int_M r^2 \, dm$$

where $\int_M$ indicates that the integration is to be taken throughout the body

$$\therefore \qquad I = \int_M (a^2 + q^2 + 2aq \cos \theta) \, dm$$

$$= \int_M a^2 \, dm + \int_M q^2 \, dm + \int_M 2aq \cos \theta \, dm$$

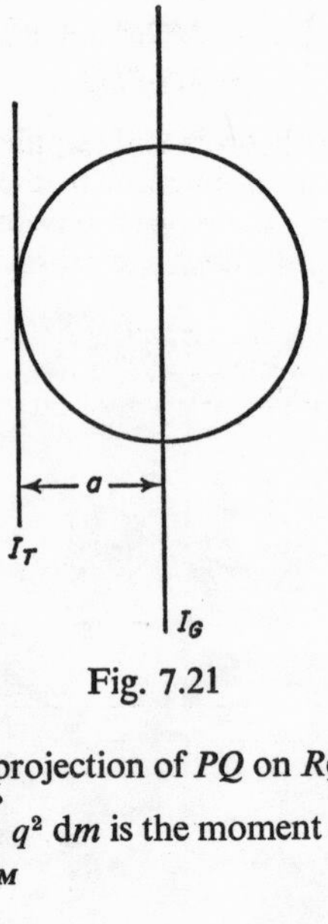

Fig. 7.21

a^2 is constant, $q \cos \theta$ is the projection of PQ on RQ and hence on the x-axis—that is, $q \cos \theta = x$—and $\int_M q^2 \, dm$ is the moment of inertia of the body about the axis through G.

$$\therefore \qquad I = a^2 \int_M dm + \int_M q^2 \, dm - 2a \int_M x \, dm$$

$$= Ma^2 + Mk^2 - 2a \int_M x \, dm$$

Now

$$\int_M x \, dm \Big/ \int_M dm$$

gives the x coordinate of the centre of mass G, and since G has been chosen as origin $\bar{x} = 0$ and

$$\int_M x\,dm \Big/ \int_M dm = 0 \qquad \text{or} \qquad \int_M x\,dm = 0$$

$$\therefore \qquad I = Ma^2 + Mk^2$$
$$= M(a^2 + k^2) \qquad (7.26)$$

Example 17. Find the moment of inertia of a solid homogeneous sphere of radius a about a tangent.

From equation 7.26 and Fig. 7.21

$$I_T = M(a^2 + k^2)$$

where Mk^2 is the moment of inertia about the diameter of the sphere, which is parallel to the tangent. From equation 7.25

$$Mk^2 = M2a^2/5$$
$$\therefore \qquad I_T = M(2a^2/5 + a^2)$$
$$= M7a^2/5$$

It is emphasised that the theorem only applies when one of the parallel axes passes through the centre of mass. If neither of the parallel axes passes through the centre of mass two applications of the theorem are required, using a parallel axis through the centre of mass as a half-way stage.

Example 18. The moment of inertia of a uniform right circular cone of height h and radius of base a about an axis through the vertex perpendicular to the axis of the cone is $M(3h^2/5 + 3a^2/20)$. Find its moment of inertia about a diameter of its base.

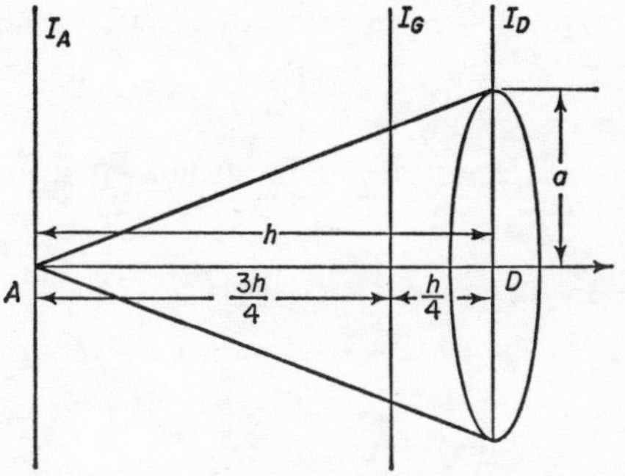

Fig. 7.22

By symmetry the moments of inertia about all diameters of the base are the same. Consider the diameter which is parallel to the given axis and also a parallel axis through the centre of mass G (see Fig. 7.22). The centre of mass of a solid cone divides the axis AD in the ratio 3 : 1; therefore $AG = 3h/4$ (refer to exercises 7.4, question 1). Applying the parallel axis theorem to the axes through G and A

$$I_G + M(3h/4)^2 = I_A$$
$$I_G + M9h^2/16 = M(3h^2/5 + 3a^2/20)$$
$$\therefore \qquad I_G = M(3h^2/5 + 3a^2/20 - 9h^2/16)$$
$$= M(3h^2/80 + 3a^2/20)$$

Again applying the parallel axis theorem to the axes through G and D

$$I_D = I_G + M(h/4)^2$$
$$= M(3h^2/80 + 3a^2/20) + Mh^2/16$$
$$= M(h^2/10 + 3a^2/20)$$

2 *Perpendicular Axis Theorem for a Lamina**

It is emphasised that this theorem applies to laminas, *not* to solid bodies.

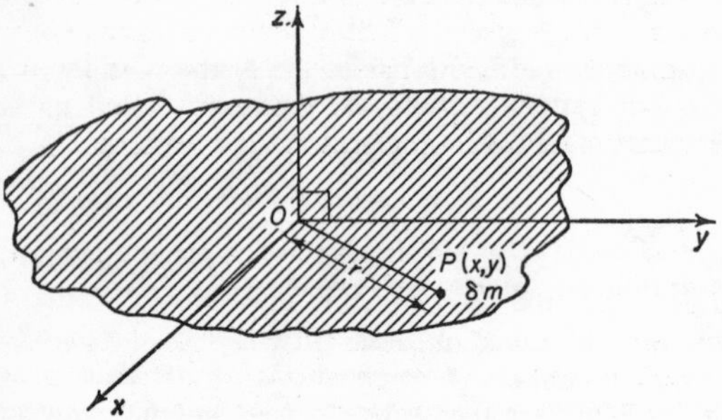

Fig. 7.23

Theorem. Given that the moments of inertia of a lamina about two perpendicular axes Ox, Oy in its plane are I_x I_y respectively, then the moment of inertia I_z of the lamina about an axis Oz through O perpendicular to the plane of the lamina is given by

$$I_z = I_x + I_y$$

Consider a typical element δm of the lamina at a point $P(x,y)$ where $OP = r$ (see Fig. 7.23)

$$I_z = \int OP^2 \, dm$$
$$= \int r^2 \, dm$$
$$= \int (x^2 + y^2) \, dm$$
$$= \int x^2 \, dm + \int y^2 \, dm$$
$$= I_x + I_y \qquad (7.27)$$

Example 19. Find the moment of inertia of a uniform circular lamina about a diameter.

By symmetry, the moments of inertia about all diameters are the same—say, Mk^2

$$\therefore \qquad I_x = I_y = Mk^2$$

* A lamina is a thin flat plate.

The moment of inertia I_z about Oz, which is perpendicular to the plane of the circular lamina, is $Ma^2/2$ (refer to equation 7.24)

but $$I_z = I_x + I_y$$

$$\therefore \quad Ma^2/2 = Mk^2 + Mk^2$$

$$Ma^2/2 = 2Mk^2$$

$$\therefore \quad Ma^2/4 = Mk^2 \tag{7.28}$$

When moments of inertia are required about axes other than those through the centre of mass, it is best first to find the moment of inertia about a parallel axis through the centre of mass and *then* to apply the parallel axis theorem. Only occasionally is it better to apply the theorem to find the moment of inertia of the elemental mass before integrating (see exercise 7.6, No. 5).

Exercises 7.6

1. Find the moment of inertia of a thin circular lamina about a tangent, given that its moment of inertia about a diameter is $Ma^2/4$.

2. The moment of inertia of a uniform rectangular lamina of dimensions $2a \times 2b$ about an axis through its centre of mass perpendicular to the side of length $2a$ is $Ma^2/3$. Deduce its moment of inertia about axes through its centre of mass (i) perpendicular to the side of length $2b$ and (ii) perpendicular to the plane of the lamina.

3. Using the result 7.22 and the perpendicular axis theorem, deduce the moment of inertia of a uniform thin circular ring of radius a about a diameter. Also deduce its moment of inertia about a tangent.

4. The moment of inertia of a uniform right circular cylinder of height h and radius of base a about a diameter of one of its circular ends is $M(a^2/4 + h^2/3)$. Deduce its moment of inertia about a parallel axis through its centre of mass.

5. Verify that the moment of inertia of a circular disc of mass δm and radius y about an axis parallel to one of its diameters and distance x away from the disc is $(y^2/4 + x^2)\,\delta m$. (Use the result 7.28 and the parallel axis theorem.) Show that the moment of inertia of a solid uniform right circular cone of height h and radius of base a about a line through its vertex and perpendicular to its axis is $M(3a^2/20 + 3h^2/5)$. (Consider the cone as a collection of thin circular discs each parallel to the base and use the result of the first part of the question.)

6. Using the result of the previous question, deduce the moment of inertia of a solid right circular cone about a line through its centre of mass perpendicular to its axis.

7. A governor consists of three solid metal spheres whose centres rotate in the same horizontal plane in a circle of radius 0·12 m about a vertical axis. The spheres are each of mass 1·5 kg and radius 0·035 m. Find the moment of inertia of the system about the vertical axis.

A large number of the results which have been calculated can be obtained immediately from **Routh's Rule,** which is that the moment of inertia of a lamina or a solid body which is symmetrical about three mutually perpendicular axes through its centre of mass about one of these axes is given by

$$M \times \frac{\text{sum of the squares of the } \textit{other} \text{ two semi-axes}}{3,\ 4 \text{ or } 5}$$

the divisor to be 3 for a thin rod, rectangular lamina or cuboid, 4 for a circular or elliptical disc, 5 for a sphere or ellipsoid. Occasionally, for bodies which do not fall into any of the above categories, the other two semi-axes can be considered separately with different divisors.

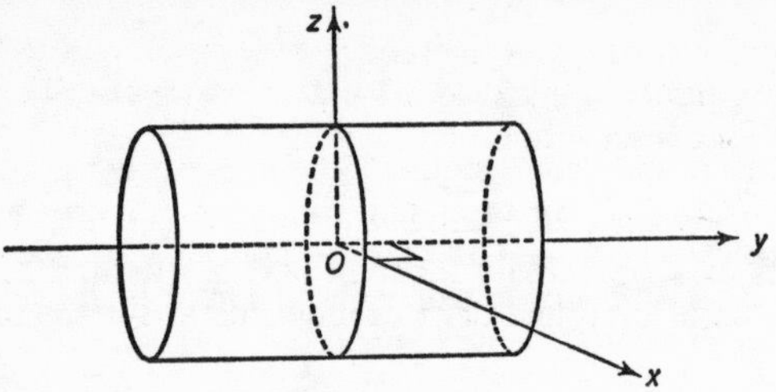

Fig. 7.24

Consider the case of the moment of inertia of a right circular cylinder height h and radius of base a about a line through its centre of mass perpendicular to its axis (see Fig. 7.24). The moment of inertia about Oz is required. The other semi-axes are

(i) Along Ox of length a associated with a circular section
(ii) Along Oy of length $h/2$ associated with a rectangular section

$$\therefore \qquad I_z = M\left[a^2/4 + \left(\frac{h}{2}\right)^2 \Big/ 3\right]$$

$$= M(a^2/4 + h^2/12)$$

7.6 Statistics

Probability Functions

When two unbiased coins are tossed simultaneously there are four possible outcomes: namely, (T, T), (T, H), (H, T), (H, H), where T and H are tails and heads respectively. The number of heads x is either $x = 0$, 1 or 2. The probabilities of these three values are respectively $\frac{1}{4}(T, T)$, $\frac{1}{2}[(H, T)$ and $(T, H)]$, and $\frac{1}{4}(H, H)$. Although x has only three discrete values, with each of these is associated one and only one probability value and we can say that the probability is a function of x (refer to section 1.5) and write $p(x)$. It is stressed that in the above case the function $p(x)$ consists of only three pairs of values $(0, \frac{1}{4})$, $(1, \frac{1}{2})$, and $(2, \frac{1}{4})$ but it *is* a function.

Consider another example. An unbiased six-sided die is thrown; if x is the number of spots shown uppermost, $x = 1, 2, 3, 4, 5$ or 6 with probabilities $\frac{1}{6}, \frac{1}{6}, \frac{1}{6}, \frac{1}{6}, \frac{1}{6}$ and $\frac{1}{6}$. The probability is again a function of x because for each value of x there is one and only one value of the probability. In this case the function $p(x)$ consists of the six pairs $(1, \frac{1}{6})$, $(2, \frac{1}{6})$, $(3, \frac{1}{6})$, $(4, \frac{1}{6})$, $(5, \frac{1}{6})$, and $(6, \frac{1}{6})$. Note that in both examples $\Sigma p(x) = 1$, which is a property of $p(x)$.

When the values of x are continuous—for example, the life of an electric light bulb—the probability $\mathrm{d}p$ that x lies in the range $(x - \mathrm{d}x/2, x + \mathrm{d}x/2)$ is written $\mathrm{d}p = p(x)\,\mathrm{d}x$, where $\mathrm{d}p$ and $\mathrm{d}x$ are differentials (refer to section

6.1), and $p(x)$ is known as the **probability density function** or **probability function** and has the property that

$$\int_R p(x)\,dx = 1 \tag{7.29}$$

where the integral is taken over the range of values of x. A variable x which has a probability function is called a **variate.** We shall only consider cases when x and $p(x)$ are both continuous.

Moments and Mathematical Expectation

The moments of a probability function $p(x)$ are written as μ_1', μ_2', . . . μ_n', where the 'dash' or prime denotes moments about the origin, and are defined by

$$\text{First moment } \mu_1' = \int_R xp(x)\,dx \tag{7.30}$$

$$\text{Second moment } \mu_2' = \int_R x^2p(x)\,dx \tag{7.31}$$

and generally

$$n\text{th moment } \mu_n' = \int_R x^np(x)\,dx \tag{7.32}$$

where the integrals are taken over the whole range of x. Moments are special cases of mathematical expectation of any function $f(x)$, which is written as $\mathscr{E}[f(x)]$ and is defined by

$$\mathscr{E}[f(x)] = \int_R f(x)p(x)\,dx \tag{7.33}$$

When $f(x)$ is simply a power of x, $f(x) = x$ or $f(x) = x^2$, . . . the expectation is the same as the corresponding moment.

Arithmetic Mean and Variance for Continuous Variates

The main features of probability and frequency distributions can be described by the values of various parameters; two of these are the **arithmetic mean** and the **variance.** The arithmetic mean $\bar{x}$ is the most widely used 'measure of position', and for a probability distribution is equal to the first moment (or expectation of x)

$$\bar{x} = \mu_1' = \int_R xp(x)\,dx \tag{7.34}$$

The variance, written as σ^2, is a widely used measure of the 'spread of distribution' and for a probability distribution is given by

$$\sigma^2 = \mu_2' - (\mu_1')^2 \tag{7.35}$$

The square root of this is known as the **standard deviation** σ

$$\sigma = \sqrt{[\mu_2' - (\mu_1')^2]} \tag{7.36}$$

Example 20. Find the mean and variance of the variate x which has the probability function $p(x) = (4x - x^3)/4$ $(0 \leqslant x \leqslant 2)$.

$$\text{Mean} = \mu_1' = \int_0^2 xp(x)\,\mathrm{d}x$$

$$= \int_0^2 x(4x - x^3)/4\,\mathrm{d}x$$

$$= \left[x^3/3 - x^5/20\right]_0^2$$

$$= (8/3 - 8/5) - (0)$$

$$= 16/15$$

$$\mu_2' = \int_0^2 x^2p(x)\,\mathrm{d}x$$

$$= \int_0^2 x^2(4x - x^3)/4\,\mathrm{d}x$$

$$= \left[x^4/4 - x^6/24\right]_0^2$$

$$= (4 - 8/3) - (0)$$
$$= 4/3$$

$$\therefore \quad \text{Variance} = \mu_2' - (\mu_1')^2$$
$$= 4/3 - (16/15)^2$$
$$= 44/225$$

$$\text{Standard Deviation} = 2\sqrt{11}/15$$

Exercises 7.7

1. A variate x has the probability function $p(x) = k\,\mathrm{e}^{-3x}$ $(0 \leqslant x \leqslant 1)$. Find the mean of the distribution. Use the property that $\int_0^1 p(x)\,\mathrm{d}x = 1$ to evaluate k.

2. A variate x has the probability function $2/[\pi(1 + x^2)]$ $(-1 \leqslant x \leqslant 1)$. Find the $\mathscr{E}(x)$ and $\mathscr{E}(x^2)$ and deduce the value of the variance.

3. A variate x has a probability function $A\,\mathrm{e}^{-2x}$ $(0 \leqslant x \leqslant 1)$, where A is a constant. Find $\mathscr{E}(x)$ and $\mathscr{E}(x^2)$ in terms of A.

4. A radio valve has a life of x hours. The probability function of x is $192x^2(500 - x)10^{-12}$ $(0 \leqslant x \leqslant 500)$. Find the mean and standard deviation of x.

5. A plane is bombing a target. The distance r metres of the bomb bursts from the target has a probability function $f(r) = A\,\mathrm{e}^{-r/\theta}$ $(0 \leqslant r \leqslant \theta)$. Given that $\int_0^\theta f(r)\,\mathrm{d}r = 1$ show that $A = \mathrm{e}/[\theta(\mathrm{e} - 1)]$. Hence find the mean distance of the bombs from the target in terms of θ.

6. Find μ_1' and μ_2', the first and second moments of the probability function $p(r) = A\,\mathrm{e}^{-r}$ $(0 \leqslant r \leqslant 1)$, where $A = \mathrm{e}/(\mathrm{e} - 1)$. Prove that the value of $M(a) = \int_0^1 p(x)\,\mathrm{e}^{ax}\,\mathrm{d}x$ is $(\mathrm{e}^a - \mathrm{e})/[(1 - \mathrm{e})(1 - a)]$. Expand $M(a)$ in ascending powers of a and verify that the coefficients of a and $a^2/2!$ give the values of μ_1' and μ_2'. $M(a)$ is known as the **moment generating function.**

7. In the theory of quantum mechanics the wave function ψ for a particle constrained to move within a short distance a in the x direction only is

$$\psi = A \sin (n\pi x/a)$$

where n is the quantum number and A is a constant (see section 4.11, Problems). The probability function for the particle is

$$p(x) = \psi^2 = A^2 \sin^2 (n\pi x/a) \quad (0 \leqslant x \leqslant a)^*$$

Using equation 7.29 prove that $A = \sqrt{(2/a)}$. Hence show that the mean position μ_1' and the mean square position μ_2' are given by

$$\mu_1' = a/2, \quad \mu_2' = \frac{a^2}{3}\left(1 - \frac{3}{2n^2\pi^2}\right)$$

8. In classical mechanics the probability density $p(x)$ for the particle in question 7 is given by

$$p(x) = 1/a$$

Show that in classical theory the value of μ_1' is also $a/2$ but the value of μ_2' is $a^2/3$.

* Generally $p(x) = \psi \,.\, \bar{\psi}$, where $\bar{\psi}$ is the complex conjugate. When ψ is real $\bar{\psi} = \psi$ and hence $\psi \,.\, \bar{\psi} = \psi^2$.

CHAPTER EIGHT

FURTHER DIFFERENTIATION

In this chapter we shall find the derivatives of hyperbolic functions and inverse trigonometrical and hyperbolic functions and consider some of their applications, which are mainly in the study of engineering and physics. We shall also discuss a further application of the calculus to centres and radii of curvature and consider the uses of Maclaurin's Theorem and Taylor's Theorem.

8.1 Hyperbolic Functions

Hyperbolic functions are combinations of the exponential function e^{ax}, which we encountered in section 2.2. Several particular combinations of e^{ax} occur so often in engineering and in physics that it has been found convenient to consider them as separate entities and give them their own names. Their derivatives and identities are similar to those for trigonometric functions and they are known as hyperbolic sine, hyperbolic cosine, hyperbolic tangent, etc., or more shortly as $\sinh x$, $\cosh x$, $\tanh x$, etc. They are not, however, periodic for real values of x. Sinh x and $\cosh x$ are defined by

$$\sinh x = (e^x - e^{-x})/2 \qquad (8.1)$$

$$\cosh x = (e^x + e^{-x})/2 \qquad (8.2)$$

Their graphs, together with those of e^x and e^{-x}, are shown in Fig. 8.1.

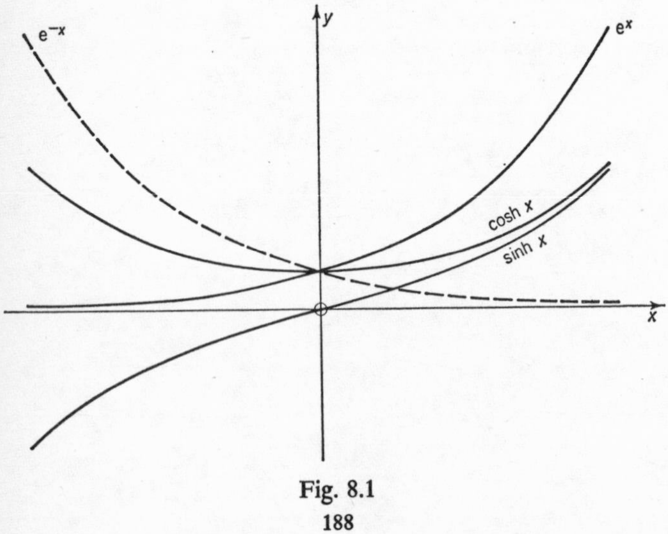

Fig. 8.1

Tanh x is defined as $\dfrac{\sinh x}{\cosh x}$

$$\therefore \qquad \tanh x = \frac{e^x - e^{-x}}{e^x + e^{-x}} = \frac{e^{2x} - 1}{e^{2x} + 1} = \frac{1 - e^{-2x}}{1 + e^{-2x}}$$

When x is positive consider

$$\tanh x = \frac{1 - e^{-2x}}{1 + e^{-2x}} = 1 - \frac{2e^{-2x}}{1 + e^{-2x}} < 1 \qquad (8.3)$$

and because

$$\lim_{x \to \infty} e^{-2x} = 0$$

therefore

$$\lim_{x \to \infty} \tanh x = 1$$

and as $x \to +\infty$, $\tanh x \to 1-$ (i.e. through a series of values which are always less than 1).

When x is negative consider

$$\tanh x = \frac{e^{2x} - 1}{e^{2x} + 1} = -1 + \frac{2e^{2x}}{e^{2x} + 1} > -1$$

and because

$$\lim_{x \to -\infty} e^{2x} = 0$$

therefore

$$\lim_{x \to -\infty} \tanh x = -1$$

and as $x \to -\infty$, $\tanh x \to -1+$ (i.e. through a series of values which are always greater than -1).

Both $\sinh x$ and $\cosh x$ are continuous for all values of x and $\cosh x$ is never zero; therefore $\tanh x$ is continuous for all values of x. Its graph is shown in Fig. 8.2.

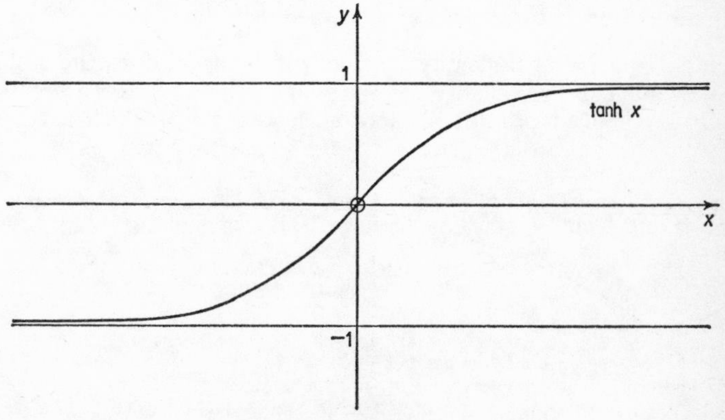

Fig. 8.2

By analogy with the trigonometrical functions, three further hyperbolic functions are defined

$$\operatorname{cosech} x = 1/\sinh x = 2/(e^x - e^{-x}) \tag{8.4}$$

$$\operatorname{sech} x = 1/\cosh x = 2/(e^x + e^{-x}) \tag{8.5}$$

$$\coth x = \cosh x/\sinh x = (e^x + e^{-x})/(e^x - e^{-x}) \tag{8.6}$$

Example 1. Prove that (i) $\cosh^2 x - \sinh^2 x = 1$, (ii) $\sinh 2x = 2 \sinh x \cosh x$; evaluate (iii) $\sinh 1{\cdot}5$, (iv) $\cosh (\ln 3)$.

(i) By definition

$$\begin{aligned}\cosh^2 x - \sinh^2 x &= [(e^x + e^{-x})/2]^2 - [(e^x - e^{-x})/2]^2 \\ &= [(e^{2x} + 2 + e^{-2x}) - (e^{2x} - 2 + e^{-2x})]/4 \\ &= 4/4 \\ &= 1 \end{aligned} \tag{8.7}$$

(ii) By definition

$$\begin{aligned} 2 \sinh x \cosh x &= 2\left(\frac{e^x - e^{-x}}{2}\right)\left(\frac{e^x + e^{-x}}{2}\right) \\ &= (e^{2x} - 1 + 1 - e^{-2x})/2 \\ &= (e^{2x} - e^{-2x})/2 \\ &= \sinh 2x \end{aligned} \tag{8.8}$$

(iii)

$$\begin{aligned}\sinh 1{\cdot}5 &= (e^{1\cdot5} - e^{-1\cdot5})/2 \\ &\simeq (4{\cdot}482 - 0{\cdot}223)/2 \\ &\simeq 2{\cdot}129\end{aligned}$$

(iv)

$$\begin{aligned}\cosh (\ln 3) &= (e^{\ln 3} + e^{-\ln 3})/2 \\ &= (3 + e^{\ln \frac{1}{3}})/2 \\ &= (3 + \tfrac{1}{3})/2 \\ &= 5/3\end{aligned}$$

or direct from tables.

Any trigonometrical identity which does not depend on the periodicity of the trigonometrical functions, gives a similar hyperbolic identity by means of the following rule, known as **Osborne's Rule.**

In any trigonometrical identity for sine write sinh, for cos write cosh, for tan write tanh, etc. Then change the *sign* of any term containing a product of *sinhs* or any implied product of sinhs such as $\tanh^2 x$ which is equal to $\sinh^2 x/\cosh^2 x$, or $\operatorname{cosech}^2 x$, etc.

Example 2. Given (i) $\cos^2 A - \sin^2 A = \cos 2A$, (ii) $\sin 3A = 3 \sin A - 4 \sin^3 A$, (iii) $\sec^2 A = 1 + \tan^2 A$, obtain similar hyperbolic identities.

(i) $\quad \cos^2 A - \sin^2 A = \cos 2A$

becomes $\quad \cosh^2 A - (-\sinh^2 A) = \cosh 2A$

that is $\quad \cosh^2 A + \sinh^2 A = \cosh 2A \qquad (8.9)$

(ii) $\quad \sin 3A = 3 \sin A - 4 \sin^3 A$

can be written $\quad \sin 3A = 3 \sin A - 4 \sin^2 A \sin A$

and becomes $\quad \sinh 3A = 3 \sinh A - 4(-\sinh^2 A) \sinh A$

that is $\quad \sinh 3A = 3 \sinh A + 4 \sinh^3 A \qquad (8.10)$

(iii)	$\sec^2 A = 1 + \tan^2 A$
can be written	$1/\cos^2 A = 1 + (\sin^2 A/\cos^2 A)$
and becomes	$1/\cosh^2 A = 1 + (-\sinh^2 A/\cosh^2 A)$
that is	$\text{sech}^2 A = 1 - \tanh^2 A \quad (8.11)$

These results can be verified by using the definitions of the hyperbolic functions as in example 1.

Exercises 8.1

1. Evaluate cosh (ln 2), sinh (ln 3), tanh (ln 1·5).

2. Write down a hyperbolic identity which is similar to the trigonometrical identity $\cos (A + B) = \cos A \cos B - \sin A \sin B$.

3. Using the definitions of the hyperbolic sine and cosine prove that $\sinh (A + B) = \sinh A \cosh B + \cosh A \sinh B$.

4. Prove that $1/(\cosh x + \sinh x) = \cosh x - \sinh x$.

5. Prove that (i) $\sinh(-x) = -\sinh x$, (ii) $\cosh(-x) = +\cosh x$, (iii) $\tanh(-x) = -\tanh x$.

6. Prove that (i) $\cosh A \cosh B - \sinh A \sinh B = \cosh (A - B)$, (ii) $\tanh (A + B) = (\tanh A + \tanh B)/(1 + \tanh A \tanh B)$.

7. By considering the series for e^x and e^{-x} (refer to equation 2.16), show that

$$\text{(i) } \sinh x = x + x^3/3! + x^5/5! + \ldots$$
$$\text{(ii) } \cosh x = 1 + x^2/2! + x^4/4! + \ldots$$

8. Given that $\sec \theta = \cosh x$ show that

$$\text{(i) } \sin \theta = \tanh x \qquad \text{(ii) } x = \ln (\sec \theta + \tan \theta)$$

9. In the study of Relativity the equations for the restricted Lorentz's Transformation are given by

$$x' = px + qct$$
$$y' = y$$
$$z' = z$$
$$ct' = rx + sct$$

where c is the speed of light and p, q, r, s are constants such that

$$p^2 - r^2 = 1 \quad \text{(i)}$$
$$s^2 - q^2 = 1 \quad \text{(ii)}$$
$$pq - rs = 0 \quad \text{(iii)}$$

Verify that $p = \cosh A$, $r = \sinh A$, $s = \cosh B$, $q = \sinh B$ satisfy equations (i) and (ii) and by substituting in equation (iii) prove that $A = B$, and therefore that $p = s$ and $q = r$. Given also that $\tanh A = -V/c$, verify that $\cosh A = 1/\sqrt{(1 - V^2/c^2)}$ and hence that

$$x' = \frac{x - Vt}{\sqrt{(1 - V^2/c^2)}}$$

$$t' = \frac{t - xV/c^2}{\sqrt{(1 - V^2/c^2)}}$$

10. In the study of Relativity S_1, S_2, S_3 are three inertial frames in standard configuration. V_1 is the velocity of S_2 relative to S_1, V_2 is the velocity of S_3 relative to S_2, and V_3 is the velocity of S_3 relative to S_1, where $V_1 = -c \tanh A$, $V_2 = -c \tanh B$

and $V_3 = -c \tanh(A + B)$. Using the result of question 6(ii) obtain an expression for V_3 in terms of V_1 and V_2 and verify that as V_1 and V_2 tend to c, V_3 also tends to c (where c is the speed of light).

8.2 Derivatives of the Hyperbolic Functions

The derivatives of the hyperbolic sine and cosine are easily obtained from their definitions

$$\begin{aligned}\frac{d(\sinh x)}{dx} &= \frac{d[(e^x - e^{-x})/2]}{dx} \\ &= (e^x + e^{-x})/2 \\ &= \cosh x \qquad (8.12)\end{aligned}$$

$$\begin{aligned}\frac{d(\cosh x)}{dx} &= \frac{d[(e^x + e^{-x})/2]}{dx} \\ &= (e^x - e^{-x})/2 \\ &= \sinh x \qquad (8.13)\end{aligned}$$

Using the rule for the differentiation of a quotient

$$\begin{aligned}\frac{d(\tanh x)}{dx} &= \frac{d(\sinh x/\cosh x)}{dx} \\ &= \frac{\cosh x \cosh x - \sinh x \sinh x}{\cosh^2 x} \\ &= \frac{1}{\cosh^2 x} \\ &= \operatorname{sech}^2 x \qquad (8.14)\end{aligned}$$

$$\begin{aligned}\frac{d(\operatorname{sech} x)}{dx} &= \frac{d(1/\cosh x)}{dx} \\ &= \frac{\cosh x \,.\, 0 - 1 \,.\, \sinh x}{\cosh^2 x} \\ &= \frac{-\sinh x}{\cosh^2 x} \\ &= -\operatorname{sech} x \tanh x \qquad (8.15)\end{aligned}$$

It is left as an exercise for the reader to prove that

$$\frac{d(\operatorname{cosech} x)}{dx} = -\operatorname{cosech} x \coth x \qquad (8.16)$$

$$\frac{d(\coth x)}{dx} = -\operatorname{cosech}^2 x \qquad (8.17)$$

These results are very similar to those obtained from the corresponding trigonometrical functions. The differences in the signs can be confusing, but note that for the trigonometrical functions the negative sign occurs when differentiating *co*-sine, *co*-secant, *co*-tangent. For the hyperbolic functions the negative signs occur when differentiating the three less used functions sech, cosech and coth.

Example 3. Find the derivatives with respect to t of (i) $\sinh(2t^2 + 1)$, (ii) $\cosh^3 t$, (iii) $t^2 \tanh t$.

(i)
$$\frac{d\sinh(2t^2+1)}{dt} = \frac{d\sinh(2t^2+1)}{d(2t^2+1)} \cdot \frac{d(2t^2+1)}{dt}$$
$$= \cosh(2t^2+1) \,.\, 4t$$
$$= 4t\cosh(2t^2+1)$$

(ii)
$$\frac{d(\cosh^3 t)}{dt} = \frac{d(\cosh t)^3}{d(\cosh t)} \cdot \frac{d\cosh t}{dt}$$
$$= 3\cosh^2 t \sinh t$$

(iii)
$$\frac{d(t^2\tanh t)}{dt} = 2t\tanh t + t^2 \operatorname{sech}^2 t$$

Revision Questions 8.1

Complete the following statements	*Answer*	*Refer to*
1. $\frac{d\cosh x}{dx} = \ldots$	**1.** $\sinh x$	Equation 8.13
2. $\frac{d\sinh x}{dx} = \ldots$	**2.** $\cosh x$	Equation 8.12
3. $\cosh^2 3A + \sinh^2 3A = \ldots$	**3.** $\cosh 6A$	Equation 8.9
4. $\sqrt{(1 + \sinh^2 A)} = \ldots$	**4.** $\cosh A$	Equation 8.7
5. By definition	**5.**	
(i) $\sinh 2\theta = \ldots$	(i) $(e^{2\theta} - e^{-2\theta})/2$	Equation 8.1
(ii) $\cosh 3\theta = \ldots$	(ii) $(e^{3\theta} + e^{-3\theta})/2$	Equation 8.2

Exercises 8.2

1. Given that $t = \tanh \theta/2$, verify that $d\theta = 2dt/(1 - t^2)$.

2. Given that $f(t) = (1 + \tanh t)/(1 - \tanh t)$, verify that $\frac{df(t)}{dt} = 2f(t)$

3. Differentiate with respect to x:

(i) $\sinh^2 x$ (ii) $\cosh(3x - 1)$ (iii) $\tanh^3 x$
(iv) $x\sinh x$ (v) $(1 - \sinh x)/(1 + \sinh x)$
(vi) $\ln(\sinh x)$ (vii) $e^{\cosh x}$
(viii) $\ln(\sinh x + \cosh x)$

4. A body is falling freely in a medium whose resistance is proportional to the square of the speed v. At any time t, $dv/dt = g - kv^2$, where k and g are constants. Verify that $v = a\tanh akt$ is a solution of the equation where $a = \sqrt{(g/k)}$.

5. In a tie with lateral loading the bending moment M at a point distance x from one end is given by $d^2M/dx^2 - \alpha^2 M = -w$, where α and w are constants. Verify that $M = A\sinh\alpha x + B\cosh\alpha x + w/\alpha^2$, where A and B are arbitrary constants, is a solution of the equation. Given that $M = 0$ when $x = 0$ and $dM/dx = 0$ when $x = L/2$, find the values of A and B in terms of w, α, L. Also show that at the centre of the tie ($x = L/2$) the value of M is given by $M = (w/\alpha^2)[1 - \operatorname{sech}(\alpha L/2)]$.

6. The displacement x of a particle at any time t, measured from a fixed point, is given by the equation $dx/dt = a(c^2 - x^2)$ where a and c are constants. Verify that $x = c \tanh(act)$ is a solution such that $x = 0$ when $t = 0$. Given that $a = \ln 2$ and $c = 3$, express $\tanh(act)$ in powers of e and show that $x = 189/65$ when $t = 1$.

7. A uniform flexible chain hangs in equilibrium in a curve whose equation is $y = c \cosh(x/c)$, where c is a constant (a catenary). Its arc length s is measured from the point $x = 0$. Prove that $s = c \sinh(x/c)$ and deduce that $x = c \ln[(y + s)/c]$.

8.3 Inverse Trigonometrical Functions

An example of an inverse function has already been given in section 2.3—that is, $\ln x$ is the inverse of e^x.

1 Consider $x = \sin \theta$. This can be written $\theta = \sin^{-1} x$* (or arc sin x), where $\sin^{-1} x$ means *the angle*, in radians, *whose sine is x*. (8.18)

For example $\theta = \sin^{-1}(0{\cdot}5)$ means that $\sin \theta = 0{\cdot}5$ and there are many possible values of θ because

$$\theta = \sin^{-1}(0{\cdot}5) = \pi/6, \quad 5\pi/6, \ldots \text{ or } -7\pi/6, \quad -11\pi/6, \ldots \tag{8.19}$$

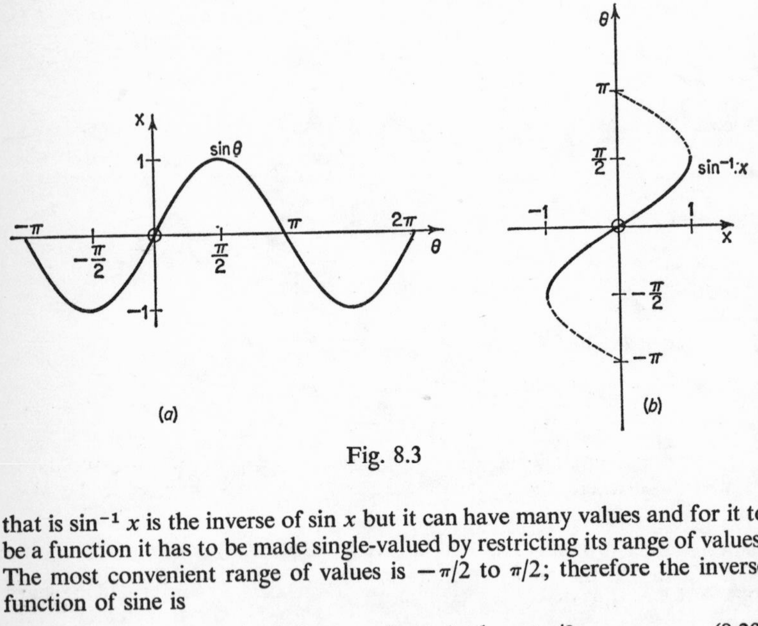

Fig. 8.3

that is $\sin^{-1} x$ is the inverse of $\sin x$ but it can have many values and for it to be a function it has to be made single-valued by restricting its range of values. The most convenient range of values is $-\pi/2$ to $\pi/2$; therefore the inverse function of sine is

$$\sin^{-1} x, \text{ where } -\pi/2 \leqslant \sin^{-1} x \leqslant \pi/2 \tag{8.20}$$

This is shown in Fig. 8.3, and we also note that for real values of $\sin^{-1} x$ the domain of $\sin^{-1} x$ is $-1 \leqslant x \leqslant 1$ (refer back to Chapter Six, example 18).

* Note that this is not the usual use of the index '−1', which generally denotes the reciprocal: thus $x^{-1} = 1/x$. Because of this $1/\sin x$ has to be written with brackets $(\sin x)^{-1}$.

Example 4. Evaluate (i) $\sin^{-1}(-1/2)$ and (ii) $\sin^{-1}(1/\sqrt{2})$.
Referring to Fig. 8.3

(i) $$\sin^{-1}(-1/2) = -\pi/6$$
(ii) $$\sin^{-1}(1/\sqrt{2}) = \pi/4$$

To find the derivative of an inverse function it is sufficient to note that

$$\frac{\delta\theta}{\delta x} = 1\bigg/\frac{\delta x}{\delta\theta}$$

where $x = f(\theta)$ and $\theta = f^{-1}(x)$, the range of f^{-1} being restricted as necessary to make it a function. In the limit $\delta x \to 0$ and $\delta\theta \to 0$

$$\frac{d\theta}{dx} = 1\bigg/\frac{dx}{d\theta} \quad \left(\frac{dx}{d\theta} \neq 0\right) \tag{8.21}$$

To find the derivative of $\sin^{-1}(x/a)$, where a is a positive constant

let $$\theta = \sin^{-1}(x/a) \qquad (-\pi/2 \leqslant \theta \leqslant \pi/2)$$

$$\therefore \quad a\sin\theta = x$$

Differentiating with respect to θ

$$a\cos\theta = \frac{dx}{d\theta}$$

therefore by equation 8.21

$$\frac{d\theta}{dx} = \frac{1}{a\cos\theta}$$

because $-\pi/2 \leqslant \theta \leqslant \pi/2$ $\cos\theta$ is positive

$$\therefore \quad \frac{d\theta}{dx} = \frac{1}{+a\sqrt{(1-\sin^2\theta)}}$$

$$= \frac{1}{\sqrt{(a^2 - a^2\sin^2\theta)}}$$

$$\therefore \quad \frac{d[\sin^{-1}(x/a)]}{dx} = \frac{1}{\sqrt{(a^2 - x^2)}} \qquad (-a \leqslant x \leqslant a) \tag{8.22}$$

The positive root agrees with the restricted range of the inverse sine (see Fig. 8.3(*b*), where the slope of the restricted curve is seen to be always positive).

2 Consider $x = \cos\theta$. This can be written $\theta = \cos^{-1} x$ (or arc cos x), where $\cos^{-1} x$ means the angle, in radians, whose cosine is x. For example, $\theta = \cos^{-1} 0{\cdot}5$ means that $\cos\theta = 0{\cdot}5$ and there are many possible values of θ because

$$\theta = \cos^{-1}(0{\cdot}5) = \pm\pi/3, \pm 7\pi/3, \ldots$$

$\cos^{-1}$ is the inverse of cosine but it is many-valued and for it to be a function we have to make it single-valued by restricting its range of values. The range of values chosen is 0 to π; therefore the inverse function to cosine is

$$\cos^{-1} x, \text{ where } 0 \leqslant \cos^{-1} x \leqslant \pi \tag{8.23}$$

This is shown in Fig. 8.4 and we also note that the domain of $\cos^{-1} x$ is $-1 \leqslant x \leqslant 1$.

Example 5. Evaluate (i) $\cos^{-1}(\sqrt{3}/2)$ and (ii) $\cos^{-1}(-1/2)$.
Referring to Fig. 8.4

(i) $$\cos^{-1}(\sqrt{3}/2) = \pi/6$$
(ii) $$\cos^{-1}(-1/2) = 2\pi/3$$

To find the derivative of $\cos^{-1}(x/a)$, where a is a positive constant

let $$\theta = \cos^{-1}(x/a) \qquad (0 \leqslant \theta \leqslant \pi)$$

$$\therefore \quad a \cos \theta = x$$

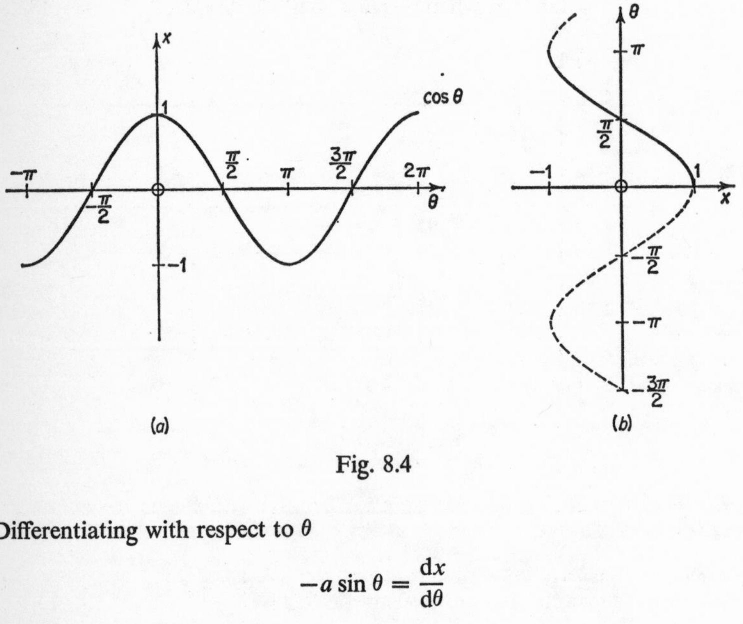

Fig. 8.4

Differentiating with respect to θ

$$-a \sin \theta = \frac{dx}{d\theta}$$

Therefore by equation 8.21

$$\frac{d\theta}{dx} = \frac{-1}{a \sin \theta}$$

because $0 \leqslant \theta \leqslant \pi$, $\sin \theta$ is positive

$$\therefore \quad \frac{d\theta}{dx} = \frac{-1}{+a\sqrt{(1 - \cos^2 \theta)}}$$

$$= \frac{-1}{\sqrt{(a^2 - a^2 \cos^2 \theta)}}$$

$$\therefore \quad \frac{d[\cos^{-1}(x/a)]}{dx} = \frac{-1}{\sqrt{(a^2 - x^2)}} \qquad (-a \leqslant x \leqslant a) \qquad (8.24)$$

Taking the positive root gives a negative value of the derivative which agrees with the restricted range of $\cos^{-1} x$ (see Fig. 8.4(*b*) where the slope of the restricted curve is seen to be always negative).

3 Consider $x = \tan \theta$. This can be written $\theta = \tan^{-1} x$ (or arc tan x), where $\tan^{-1} x$ means the angle whose tangent is x. For example, $\theta = \tan^{-1} 1$ means that $\tan \theta = 1$ and there are many possible values of θ because

$$\theta = \tan^{-1} 1 = \pi/4,\ 5\pi/4, \ldots \text{ or } -3\pi/4,\ -7\pi/4, \ldots$$

$\tan^{-1}$ is the inverse of tangent but it is many-valued, and we restrict it to the range $-\pi/2$ to $\pi/2$. Therefore the inverse function to tangent is

$$\tan^{-1} x, \text{ where } -\pi/2 \leqslant \tan^{-1} x \leqslant \pi/2 \tag{8.25}$$

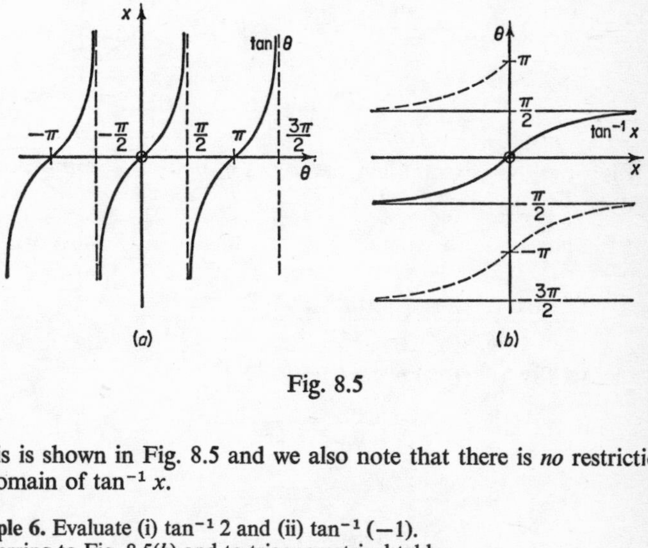

Fig. 8.5

This is shown in Fig. 8.5 and we also note that there is *no* restriction on the domain of $\tan^{-1} x$.

Example 6. Evaluate (i) $\tan^{-1} 2$ and (ii) $\tan^{-1}(-1)$.
Referring to Fig. 8.5(*b*) and to trigonometrical tables

(i) $\tan^{-1} 2 = 1{\cdot}107^c$ (to four significant figures)
(ii) $\tan^{-1}(-1) = -\pi/4$

To find the derivative of $\tan^{-1}(x/a)$, where a is a positive constant

let $$\theta = \tan^{-1}(x/a) \qquad \left(-\frac{\pi}{2} \leqslant \theta \leqslant \frac{\pi}{2}\right)$$

$\therefore$ $$a \tan \theta = x$$

Differentiating with respect to θ

$$a \sec^2 \theta = \frac{dx}{d\theta}$$

$$\therefore \qquad \frac{d\theta}{dx} = \frac{1}{a \sec^2 \theta}$$

$$= \frac{1}{a(1 + \tan^2 \theta)}$$

$$= \frac{a}{(a^2 + a^2 \tan^2 \theta)}$$

$$\therefore \qquad \frac{d[\tan^{-1}(x/a)]}{dx} = \frac{a}{(a^2 + x^2)} \qquad (8.26)$$

There is no choice of sign required (see Fig. 8.5(*b*), where for all ranges of values $\tan^{-1}(x/a)$ is seen to be increasing).

The results 8.22 and 8.26 give rise to the standard results which we first met in Chapter Six (equations 6.13 and 6.14)

$$\left.\begin{aligned} \int \frac{dx}{\sqrt{(a^2 - x^2)}} &= \sin^{-1}(x/a) + C \\ \int \frac{dx}{(a^2 + x^2)} &= \frac{1}{a}\tan^{-1}(x/a) + C \end{aligned}\right\} \qquad (8.27)$$

where a is a positive constant and the values of both inverse functions are restricted to the range $[-\pi/2, \pi/2]$.

Example 7. Differentiate (i) $\tan^{-1}(x^2 + 1)$ and (ii) $\sin^{-1}[(1 - x)/(1 + x)]$ with respect to x.

(i) $$\frac{d \tan^{-1}(x^2 + 1)}{dx} = \frac{d[\tan^{-1}(x^2 + 1)]}{d(x^2 + 1)} \cdot \frac{d(x^2 + 1)}{dx}$$

Using equation 8.26 with $a = 1$ and x replaced by $x^2 + 1$

$$= \frac{1}{1 + (x^2 + 1)^2} \cdot 2x$$

$$= \frac{2x}{x^4 + 2x^2 + 2}$$

(ii) $$\frac{d \sin^{-1}[(1 - x)/(1 + x)]}{dx} = \frac{d \sin^{-1}[(1 - x)/(1 + x)]}{d[(1 - x)/(1 + x)]} \cdot \frac{d[(1 - x)/(1 + x)]}{dx}$$

Using equation 8.22 with $a = 1$ and x replaced by $(1 - x)/(1 + x)$ and the quotient rule for differentiation

$$= \frac{1}{\sqrt{\left[1 - \left(\frac{1 - x}{1 + x}\right)^2\right]}} \cdot \frac{(1 + x)(-1) - (1 - x) \cdot 1}{(1 + x)^2}$$

$$= \frac{1}{\sqrt{[(1 + x)^2 - (1 - x)^2]}} \cdot \frac{-2}{(1 + x)}$$

$$= \frac{-2}{(1 + x)\sqrt{(4x)}}$$

$$= \frac{-1}{(1 + x)\sqrt{x}}$$

8.4 Inverse Hyperbolic Functions

1 Consider $x = \sinh \theta$. This can be written $\theta = \sinh^{-1} x$ (or arc sinh x), where $\sinh^{-1} x$ means the quantity whose sinh is x. For example, $\theta = \sinh^{-1} 1{\cdot}8$ means that $\sinh \theta = 1{\cdot}8$ and from tables the value of θ is 1·35 (to three significant figures). The inverse of sinh is $\sinh^{-1}$ and, referring to Fig. 8.6, it is seen to be single-valued and to need no restriction. Therefore the inverse function of $\sinh x$ is

$$\sinh^{-1} x \quad \text{(for all values of } x) \tag{8.28}$$

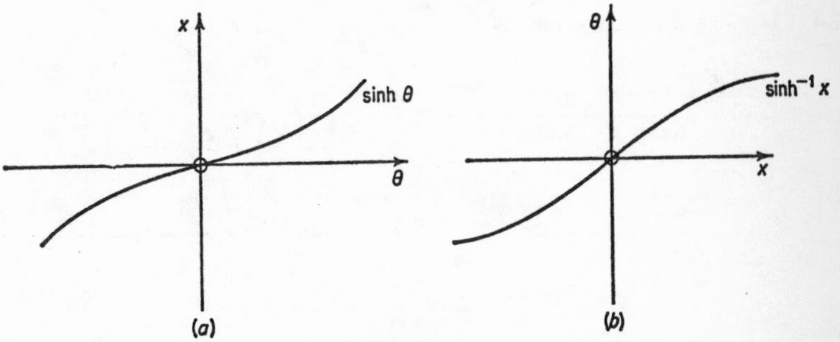

Fig. 8.6

To find the derivative of $\sinh^{-1}(x/a)$, where a is a positive constant

$$\text{let } \theta = \sinh^{-1}(x/a)$$

$$\therefore \quad a \sinh \theta = x$$

Differentiating with respect to θ

$$a \cosh \theta = \frac{dx}{d\theta}$$

$$\therefore \quad \frac{d\theta}{dx} = \frac{1}{a \cosh \theta}$$

$$= \frac{1}{a\sqrt{(1 + \sinh^2 \theta)}}$$

The positive root is chosen because $\cosh \theta$ is always positive

$$= \frac{1}{\sqrt{(a^2 + a^2 \sinh^2 \theta)}}$$

$$\therefore \quad \frac{d[\sinh^{-1}(x/a)]}{dx} = \frac{1}{\sqrt{(a^2 + x^2)}} \tag{8.29}$$

2 Consider $x = \cosh \theta$. This can be written $\theta = \cosh^{-1} x$ (or arc cosh x), where $\cosh^{-1} x$ means the quantity whose hyperbolic cosine is x. For example, if $\theta = \cosh^{-1} 2{\cdot}6$ then $\cosh \theta = 2{\cdot}6$ and from tables

$$\theta = \cosh^{-1} 2{\cdot}6 = \pm 1{\cdot}61 \text{ (to three significant figures)}$$

There are two possible values equal in magnitude but opposite in sign and we restrict $\cosh^{-1}$ to the positive values. This is shown in Fig. 8.7.

The inverse function of $\cosh x$ is

$$\cosh^{-1} x, \text{ where } \cosh^{-1} x \geqslant 0 \tag{8.30}$$

We also note that $x \geqslant 1$.

To find the derivative of $\cosh^{-1}(x/a)$, where a is a positive constant

$$\text{let } \theta = \cosh^{-1}(x/a) \qquad (\theta \geqslant 0)$$

$$\therefore \quad a \cosh \theta = x$$

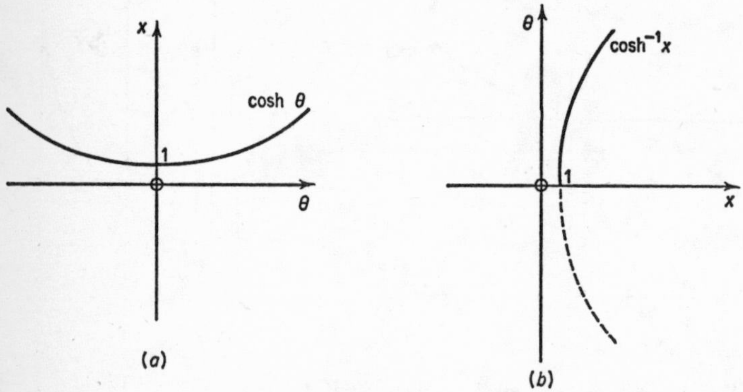

Fig. 8.7

Differentiating with respect to θ

$$a \sinh \theta = \frac{dx}{d\theta}$$

$$\therefore \quad \frac{d\theta}{dx} = \frac{1}{a \sinh \theta}$$

$$= \frac{1}{+a\sqrt{(\cosh^2 \theta - 1)}}$$

Taking the positive square root in order to agree with the restriction on the value of $\cosh^{-1}$

$$= \frac{1}{\sqrt{(a^2 \cosh^2 \theta - a^2)}}$$

$$\therefore \quad \frac{d[\cosh^{-1}(x/a)]}{dx} = \frac{1}{\sqrt{(x^2 - a^2)}} \tag{8.31}$$

3 Consider $x = \tanh \theta$. This can be written $\theta = \tanh^{-1} x$ (or arc tanh x), where $\tanh^{-1} x$ means the quantity whose tanh is x. For example, if $\theta = \tanh^{-1} 0{\cdot}6$, then $\tanh \theta = 0{\cdot}6$ and from tables

$$\theta = \tanh^{-1} 0{\cdot}6 = 0{\cdot}54 \text{ (to two significant figures)}$$

Tanh^{-1} is single valued and we need not impose any extra restriction on its range of values (refer to Fig. 8.8: it can be seen that $-1 < \tanh^{-1} < 1$).

The inverse function of tanh x is

$$\tanh^{-1} x \text{ for all values of } x \tag{8.32}$$

To find the derivative of $\tanh^{-1}(x/a)$, where a is a positive constant

$$\text{let } \theta = \tanh^{-1}(x/a)$$

$$\therefore \quad a \tanh \theta = x$$

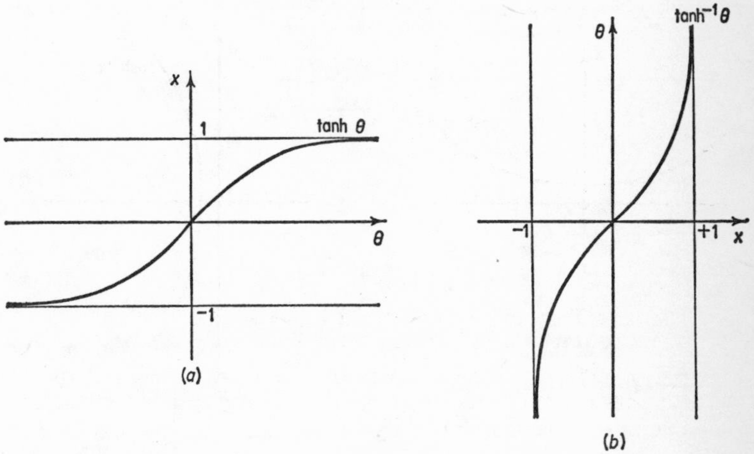

Fig. 8.8

Differentiating with respect to θ

$$a \operatorname{sech}^2 \theta = \frac{dx}{d\theta}$$

$$\therefore \quad \frac{d\theta}{dx} = \frac{1}{a \operatorname{sech}^2 \theta}$$

$$= \frac{1}{a(1 - \tanh^2 \theta)}$$

$$= \frac{a}{(a^2 - a^2 \tanh^2 \theta)}$$

$$\therefore \quad \frac{d[\tanh^{-1}(x/a)]}{dx} = \frac{a}{(a^2 - x^2)} \tag{8.33}$$

Example 8. Differentiate with respect to x (i) $\sinh^{-1}(x/5)$, (ii) $\sinh^{-1}(-x/5)$, and (iii) $\sinh^{-1}(5/x)$.

(i) $$\frac{d \sinh^{-1}(x/5)}{dx} = \frac{1}{\sqrt{(25 + x^2)}} \quad \text{(from equation 8.29)}$$

(ii) In the formula 8.29, '*a*' is positive; therefore

$$\frac{\mathrm{d}\sinh^{-1}(-x/5)}{\mathrm{d}x} = \frac{\mathrm{d}\sinh^{-1}[(-x)/+5]}{\mathrm{d}(-x)} \cdot \frac{\mathrm{d}(-x)}{\mathrm{d}x}$$

$$= \frac{1}{\sqrt{(25 + x^2)}} \cdot (-1)$$

$$= \frac{-1}{\sqrt{(25 + x^2)}}$$

(iii) In the formula 8.29, '*a*' is a *constant*; therefore we can only regard $(5/x)$ as $(5/x)/1$.

$$\therefore \qquad \frac{\mathrm{d}\sinh^{-1}(5/x)}{\mathrm{d}x} = \frac{\mathrm{d}\sinh^{-1}\left(\frac{5/x}{1}\right)}{\mathrm{d}(5/x)} \cdot \frac{\mathrm{d}(5/x)}{\mathrm{d}x}$$

$$= \frac{1}{\sqrt{[1 + (5/x)^2]}} \cdot \frac{-5}{x^2}$$

$$= \frac{-5}{x\sqrt{(x^2 + 25)}}$$

8.5 Logarithmic Form of Inverse Hyperbolic Functions

We remarked at the beginning of section 8.1 that hyperbolic functions are combinations of the exponential function e^{ax}. It is not, therefore, surprising that the inverse hyperbolic functions can be expressed in a logarithmic form because 'ln' is the inverse of 'e'.

1 Let $\theta = \sinh^{-1}(x/a)$, where a is a positive constant

$$\therefore \qquad a \sinh \theta = x$$

or

$$a(\mathrm{e}^{\theta} - \mathrm{e}^{-\theta})/2 = x$$

Multiply throughout by $2\mathrm{e}^{\theta}$

$$a\mathrm{e}^{2\theta} - a = 2x\mathrm{e}^{\theta}$$

$$a\mathrm{e}^{2\theta} - 2x\mathrm{e}^{\theta} - a = 0$$

This is a quadratic equation in e^{θ}

and

$$\mathrm{e}^{\theta} = \frac{2x \pm \sqrt{(4x^2 + 4a^2)}}{2a}$$

$$= [x \pm \sqrt{(x^2 + a^2)}]/a$$

However, e^{θ} is always positive and we therefore have to take the positive square root ($\sqrt{(x^2 + a^2)} > x$: therefore $x - \sqrt{(x^2 + a^2)}$ is negative).

$$\therefore \qquad \theta = \sinh^{-1}(x/a) = \ln\{[(x + \sqrt{(x^2 + a^2)}]/a\} \qquad (8.34)$$

2 Let $\theta = \cosh^{-1}(x/a)$, where a is a positive constant

$$\therefore \qquad a \cosh \theta = x$$

$$a(\mathrm{e}^{\theta} + \mathrm{e}^{-\theta})/2 = x$$

Multiply throughout by $2e^{\theta}$

$$ae^{2\theta} + a = 2xe^{\theta}$$
$$ae^{2\theta} - 2xe^{\theta} + a = 0$$

As before, this is a quadratic in e^{θ}

and $$e^{\theta} = \frac{2x \pm \sqrt{(4x^2 - 4a^2)}}{2a}$$

$$= [x \pm \sqrt{(x^2 - a^2)}]/a$$

$\therefore$ $$\theta = \ln \{[x + \sqrt{(x^2 - a^2)}]/a\}$$

The two values of θ are equal in magnitude but opposite in sign because

$$\begin{aligned}\theta_1 + \theta_2 &= \ln \{[x + \sqrt{(x^2 - a^2)}]/a\} + \ln \{[x - \sqrt{(x^2 - a^2)}]/a\} \\ &= \ln \{[x + \sqrt{(x^2 - a^2)}][x - \sqrt{(x^2 - a^2)}]/a^2\} \\ &= \ln \{[x^2 - (x^2 - a^2)]/a^2\} \\ &= \ln 1 \\ &= 0\end{aligned}$$

Thus $\theta_1 = -\theta_2$, as can be seen geometrically in Fig. 8.7(*b*). The positive square root is chosen and

$$\cosh^{-1}(x/a) = \ln \{[x + \sqrt{(x^2 - a^2)}]/a\} \tag{8.35}$$

3 Let $\theta = \tanh^{-1}(x/a)$, where a is a positive constant

$\therefore$ $$a \tanh \theta = x$$

$$\frac{a(e^{2\theta} - 1)}{(e^{2\theta} + 1)} = x$$

Cross-multiplying

$$ae^{2\theta} - a = xe^{2\theta} + x$$

$\therefore$ $$e^{2\theta} = (a + x)/(a - x)$$

$\therefore$ $$\theta = \tanh^{-1}(x/a) = \tfrac{1}{2} \ln [(a + x)/(a - x)] \tag{8.36}$$

Note that for all the inverse trigonometrical and hyperbolic functions where there was a choice between the positive and negative square root it was always the positive square root which had to be taken to conform with any restriction on the values.

Revision Questions 8.2

Complete the following statements	*Answer*	*Refer to*
1. (i) $\dfrac{d[\sin^{-1}(x/2)]}{dx} = \ldots$	**1.** (i) $1/\sqrt{(4 - x^2)}$	Equation 8.22
(ii) $\dfrac{d[\tan^{-1}(x/3)]}{dx} = \ldots$	(ii) $3/(9 + x^2)$	Equation 8.26
2. $\text{Sin}^{-1} x$, $\cos^{-1} x$ and $\tan^{-1} x$ are . . .	**2.** angles in radians	Section 8.3

Complete the following statements	*Answer*	*Refer to*
3. $\sin^{-1} x$ and $\tan^{-1} x$ only have values in the range . . .	**3.** $-\pi/2$, $\pi/2$	Equations 8.20, 8.25
4. No extra restrictions have to be imposed on the values of the inverse hyperbolic functions . . .	**4.** $\sinh^{-1}$ and $\tanh^{-1}$	Equations 8.28, 8.32
5. A restriction has to be imposed on the inverse hyperbolic . . .: it is that . . .	**5.** cosine, $\cosh^{-1} \geqslant 0$	Equation 8.30
6. (i) $\dfrac{d[\sinh^{-1}(x/3)]}{dx} = \ldots$	**6.** (i) $1/\sqrt{(x^2 + 9)}$	Equation 8.29
(ii) $\dfrac{d[\tanh^{-1}(x/4)]}{dx} = \ldots$	(ii) $4/(16 - x^2)$	Equation 8.33
(iii) $\dfrac{d[\cosh^{-1}(x/2)]}{dx} = \ldots$	(iii) $1/\sqrt{(x^2 - 4)}$	Equation 8.31
7. $\cosh^{-1}(x/2) = \ln\{\ldots\}$	**7.** $\{[x + \sqrt{(x^2 - 4)}]/2\}$	Equation 8.35
8. Inverse hyperbolic functions can be expressed in terms of . . . functions	**8.** ln	Section 8.5
9. $\sin[\sin^{-1}(0{\cdot}5)] = \ldots$	**9.** 0·5	Equation 8.20
10. $\sin^{-1}[\sin(3\pi/2)] = \ldots$	**10.** $-\pi/2$	Equation 8.20

Exercises 8.3

1. Express as logarithms to the base e (i) $\sinh^{-1}(4/3)$, (ii) $\cosh^{-1}(2{\cdot}6)$, and (iii) $\tanh^{-1}(0{\cdot}5)$.

2. Express $\operatorname{cosech}^{-1} x$ as a logarithm to the base e.

3. Differentiate with respect to x:

(i) $\sinh^{-1}(3x)$ (ii) $\cosh^{-1}(5x + 1)$ (iii) $\tanh^{-1}(2x - 3)$
(iv) $\sinh^{-1}(1/x)$ (v) $\cosh^{-1}(\sqrt{x})$ (vi) $\tanh^{-1}[1/(1 - x)]$

4. Given that $\theta = \tanh^{-1}(\sin x)$, prove that $d\theta/dx = \sec x$.

5. Prove that $\tanh^{-1}(\cos 2\theta) = \ln(\cot \theta)$.

6. A balloon is rising vertically at a rate of 2·5 m/s from a point 200 m from an observer whose eye level is 2 m above the ground. At any time t seconds the height of the balloon is h metres ($h > 2$). Show that the angle of elevation θ of the balloon is given by

$$\theta = \tan^{-1}[(h - 2)/200]$$

Find the rate of increase of θ with respect to (i) the height, (ii) the time, when $h = 102$ metres.

7. A picture 1·25 m high is hanging vertically on the wall of an art gallery. Its base is 1 m above the level of an observer's eye. Show that the angle θ subtended by the picture at his eye is given by

$$\theta = \tan^{-1} [1{\cdot}25x/(x^2 + 2{\cdot}25)]$$

where x is the distance of the observer from the wall. Prove that θ is a maximum when $x = 1{\cdot}5$ m.

8. To find the time of transit of a star a meridian circle is used to measure the declination δ. There are three possible instrumental errors: the azimuth error t_1, the level error t_2 and the collimation error t_3. The three errors are given by $t_1 = a \sin (\phi - \delta) \sec \delta$, $t_2 = b \cos (\phi - \delta) \sec \delta$ and $t_3 = c \sec \delta$, where ϕ is the observer's latitude and a, b and c are constants. Prove that the total error $T = t_1 + t_2 + t_3$ has a limiting value for a star whose declination δ is given by $\delta = \sin^{-1} [(a \cos \phi - b \sin \phi)/c]$.

9. In the theory of relativity the 'rapidities' u_1, u_2, u_3 associated with the relative velocities V_1, V_2, V_3 are given by $u_1 = \tanh^{-1} (V_1/c)$, $u_2 = \tanh^{-1} (V_2/c)$, $u_3 = \tanh^{-1} (V_3/c)$. Also $V_3 = \dfrac{(V_1 + V_2)}{(1 + V_1V_2/c^2)}$. Show that the relative rapidities are additive by proving that $u_1 + u_2 = u_3$.

8.6 Curvature, Evolutes and Involutes

In section 3.3 we considered the direction of a tangent to the curve $y = f(x)$ and found that the angle of inclination ψ of the tangent to the axis of x is given by $\tan \psi = \mathrm{d}y/\mathrm{d}x$. We shall now consider how ψ varies as we move along the curve and define the **curvature** of the curve as $\mathrm{d}\psi/\mathrm{d}s$, the rate of change of ψ with respect to s, the arc length. Curvature and its reciprocal, known as the **radius of curvature**, are used in numerous applications in physics and engineering, including the banking of railway tracks to avoid side thrust on the rails, involute teeth of gear wheels, approximation to the bending moment in loaded beams and motion in a plane curve.

Consider two neighbouring points P and Q on the curve $y = f(x)$. Let the tangents PT and QU at P and Q make angles of ψ and $\psi + \delta\psi$ respectively with the axis of x and let the length of the arc PQ be δs (see Fig. 8.9).

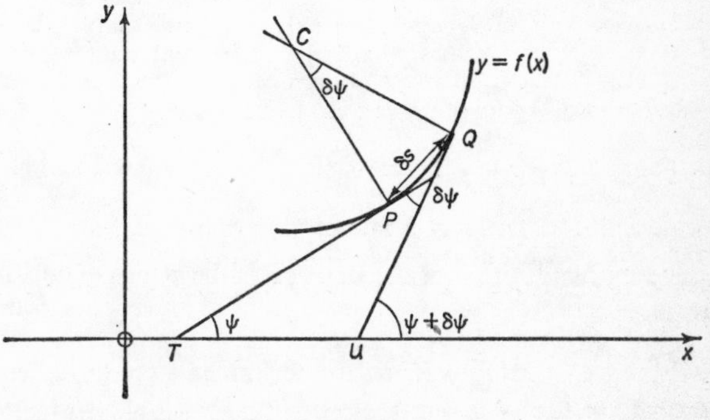

Fig. 8.9

Definition: the curvature at P is defined as

$$\kappa = \lim_{Q \to P} \frac{\delta\psi}{\delta s} = \frac{d\psi}{ds} \tag{8.37}$$

In the case of a circle of radius ρ the angle $\delta\psi$ between the tangents at P and Q is equal to the angle subtended by the arc PQ at the centre of the circle.

For a circle $\qquad \delta s = \rho\delta\psi$

$$\therefore \qquad \frac{\delta\psi}{\delta s} = \frac{1}{\rho} \qquad \text{a constant}$$

$$\therefore \qquad \frac{d\psi}{ds} = \frac{1}{\rho}$$

That is, the curvature of a circle is constant and equal to the reciprocal of its radius ρ.

Definition: a circle drawn touching the curve at P, with its concavity in the same direction and having the same curvature as the curve at P is called the **circle of curvature** at P. Its radius ρ is called the **radius of curvature** at P and its centre is called the **centre of curvature** at P.

$$\rho = \frac{ds}{d\psi} = \frac{1}{\kappa} \tag{8.38}$$

The centre of curvature is the limiting position of the point of intersection of the normals at P and Q, as Q tends to P. Referring to Fig. 8.9, in triangle PCQ

$$\frac{PC}{\text{chord } PQ} = \frac{\sin PQC}{\sin \delta\psi} \qquad \text{(from the sine rule)}$$

$$\therefore \qquad PC = \frac{\text{chord } PQ}{\sin \delta\psi} \sin PQC$$

$$= \frac{\text{chord } PQ}{\delta s} \cdot \frac{\delta s}{\delta\psi} \cdot \frac{\delta\psi}{\sin \delta\psi} \cdot \sin PQC$$

as $\quad Q \to P, \ \delta\psi \to 0, \ \dfrac{\delta\psi}{\sin \delta\psi} \to 1, \ \dfrac{\text{chord } PQ}{\delta s} \to 1, \ $ and $\angle PQC \to 90°$

$$\therefore \qquad \lim_{Q \to P} PC = 1 \, . \frac{ds}{d\psi} \, . \, 1 \, . \, 1$$

$$= \frac{ds}{d\psi}$$

$$= \rho$$

Therefore the limiting position of C as $Q \to P$ is the centre of curvature at P.

There are a number of curves whose equations have been found in the form $s = f(\psi)$—for example, the catenary $s = c \tan \psi$ and the cycloid $s = 4a \sin \psi$—and $\rho(= ds/d\psi)$ can be found immediately by differentiation. In practice such 'intrinsic equations' are seldom used and we proceed to find a formula for ρ in terms of x and y.

We know that

$$\tan \psi = \frac{dy}{dx}$$

Differentiating with respect to s

$$\frac{d(\tan \psi)}{ds} = \frac{d}{ds}\left(\frac{dy}{dx}\right)$$

or

$$\frac{d(\tan \psi)}{d\psi} \cdot \frac{d\psi}{ds} = \frac{d}{dx}\left(\frac{dy}{dx}\right) \cdot \frac{dx}{ds}$$

$$\sec^2 \psi \frac{d\psi}{ds} = \frac{d^2y}{dx^2} . \cos \psi \text{ (refer to equation 7.5)}$$

$$\therefore \quad \frac{1}{\rho} = \frac{d\psi}{ds} = \frac{d^2y}{dx^2} \Big/ \sec^3 \psi$$

$$\therefore \quad \rho = \sec^3 \psi \Big/ \frac{d^2y}{dx^2}$$

$$= (\sec^2 \psi)^{\frac{3}{2}} \Big/ \frac{d^2y}{dx^2}$$

$$= (1 + \tan^2 \psi)^{\frac{3}{2}} \Big/ \frac{d^2y}{dx^2}$$

$$\therefore \quad \rho = \frac{\left[1 + \left(\frac{dy}{dx}\right)^2\right]^{\frac{3}{2}}}{\frac{d^2y}{dx^2}} \tag{8.39}$$

The usual convention is to take the positive square root for the numerator and the sign for ρ is the same as the sign for d^2y/dx^2 or $d(dy/dx)/dx$, the rate of change of the slope of the tangent. If the curve is concave upwards, as in Fig. 8.9, dy/dx increases as x increases and the slope of the tangent is increasing—that is, d^2y/dx^2 and ρ are both positive. Conversely, if the curve is concave downwards, d^2y/dx^2 and ρ are both negative.

Note that in general, for a point of inflexion (where the curve crosses its tangent), $d^2y/dx^2 = 0$. This condition is necessary but not sufficient; d^2y/dx^2 must change sign as x increases through the value in question.

Example 9. Find the radius of curvature ρ of the catenary $y = c \cosh (x/c)$ at the point (x, y).

$$y = c \cosh (x/c)$$

$$\therefore \quad \frac{dy}{dx} = \sinh (x/c)$$

$$1 + \left(\frac{dy}{dx}\right)^2 = 1 + \sinh^2 (x/c) = \cosh^2 (x/c)$$

$$\frac{d^2y}{dx^2} = \frac{1}{c} \cosh (x/c)$$

$$\therefore \qquad \rho = \left[1 + \left(\frac{dy}{dx}\right)^2\right]^{\frac{3}{2}} \bigg/ \frac{d^2y}{dx^2}$$

$$= [\cosh^2 (x/c)]^{\frac{3}{2}} \bigg/ \frac{1}{c} \cosh (x/c)$$

$$= c \cosh^3 (x/c)/\cosh (x/c)$$
$$= c \cosh^2 (x/c)$$

The equation 8.39 can be modified to suit the case when the equation of the curve is given in parametric form. It is not, however, necessary; we can proceed as follows.

Example 10. Find the radius of curvature ρ of the cycloid $x = a(\theta - \sin \theta)$, $y = a(1 - \cos \theta)$ at any point θ.

$$\frac{dx}{d\theta} = a(1 - \cos \theta), \frac{dy}{d\theta} = a \sin \theta$$

$$\therefore \qquad \frac{dy}{dx} = \frac{a \sin \theta}{a(1 - \cos \theta)} = \frac{2 \sin (\theta/2) \cos (\theta/2)}{2 \sin^2 (\theta/2)}$$

$$= \cot (\theta/2)$$

$$\therefore \qquad \frac{d^2y}{dx^2} = \frac{d \cot (\theta/2)}{d\theta} \cdot \frac{d\theta}{dx}$$

$$= -\tfrac{1}{2} \operatorname{cosec}^2 (\theta/2)/a(1 - \cos \theta)$$
$$= -\operatorname{cosec}^2 (\theta/2)/4a \sin^2 (\theta/2)$$

$$= -\frac{1}{4a} \operatorname{cosec}^4 (\theta/2)$$

$$\therefore \qquad \rho = \left[1 + \left(\frac{dy}{dx}\right)^2\right]^{\frac{3}{2}} \bigg/ \frac{d^2y}{dx^2}$$

$$= [1 + \cot^2 (\theta/2)]^{\frac{3}{2}} \bigg/ -\frac{1}{4a} \operatorname{cosec}^4 (\theta/2)$$

$$= -4a[\operatorname{cosec}^2 (\theta/2)]^{\frac{3}{2}}/\operatorname{cosec}^4 (\theta/2)$$
$$= -4a \sin (\theta/2)$$

Exercises 8.4

For each of the following four curves verify that the given value of ρ, the radius of curvature, is correct.

1. $y = \ln (\sin x)$, $\rho = -\operatorname{cosec} x$
2. Parabola $y^2 = 16x$, $\rho = -(x + 4)^{\frac{3}{2}}$
3. Astroid $x = a \cos^3 \theta$, $y = a \sin^3 \theta$, $\rho = 3a \sin \theta \cos \theta$
4. Rectangular hyperbola $x = a \cosh \theta$, $y = a \sinh \theta$, $\rho = -a(\cosh^2\theta + \sinh^2 \theta)^{\frac{3}{2}}$
5. Given that $x = a \sin 2\theta(1 + \cos 2\theta)$, $y = a \cos 2\theta(1 - \cos 2\theta)$, prove that $dy/dx = \tan \theta$. Hence prove that $\rho = 4a \cos 3\theta$.
6. Given that $x = a(2 \cos \theta + \cos 2\theta)$, $y = a(2 \sin \theta - \sin 2\theta)$, prove that $dy/dx = -\tan (\theta/2)$. Hence prove that $\rho = 8a \sin (3\theta/2)$.

7. Find the radius of curvature for any point on the curve $y = (2 \ln x - x^2)/4$. Hence show that with the usual notation ρ is always negative and therefore the curve is always concave downwards. (Note: ln [negative values] does not exist.)

The centre of curvature at any point P on a curve is the centre C of the circle of curvature. To find its coordinates (X, Y) refer to Fig. 8.10.

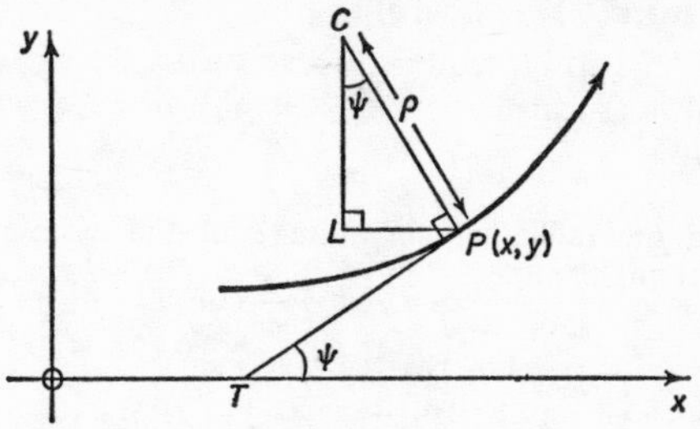

Fig. 8.10

$P(x,y)$ is any point on the curve, PT is the tangent to the curve, PL and CL are parallel to Ox and Oy respectively and the radius of the circle of curvature CP is perpendicular to the tangent PT. Then

$$\left.\begin{aligned} X &= x - PL = x - \rho \sin \psi \\ Y &= y + CL = y + \rho \cos \psi \end{aligned}\right\} \tag{8.40}$$

Using dashes to denote differentiation with respect to x, that is

$$y' = \frac{dy}{dx}, \quad y'' = \frac{d^2y}{dx^2}$$

we have that $y' = \tan \psi$, $\sin \psi = y'/\sqrt{[1 + (y')^2]}$, $\cos \psi = 1/\sqrt{[1 + (y')^2]}$ and $\rho = [1 + (y')^2]^{\frac{3}{2}}/y''$.

Substituting in equations 8.40

$$X = x - \frac{[1 + (y')^2]^{\frac{3}{2}}}{y''} \cdot \frac{y'}{[1 + (y')^2]^{\frac{1}{2}}}$$

$$= x - y'[1 + (y')^2]/y'' \tag{8.41}$$

$$Y = y + \frac{[1 + (y')^2]^{\frac{3}{2}}}{y''} \cdot \frac{1}{[1 + (y')^2]^{\frac{1}{2}}}$$

$$= y + [1 + (y')^2]/y'' \tag{8.42}$$

Example 11. Find the coordinates (X, Y) of the centre of curvature for any point P on the ellipse $x = a \cos \theta$, $y = b \sin \theta$, where a and b are constants.

$$y' = \frac{dy}{d\theta}\Big/\frac{dx}{d\theta} = \frac{b \cos \theta}{-a \sin \theta}$$

$$= -\frac{b}{a} \cot \theta$$

$$y'' = \frac{d^2y}{dx^2} = \frac{d\left[-\frac{b}{a}\cot\theta\right]}{d\theta}\cdot\frac{d\theta}{dx}$$

$$= \left(+\frac{b}{a}\operatorname{cosec}^2\theta\right)\Big/\frac{dx}{d\theta}$$

$$= \left(\frac{b}{a}\operatorname{cosec}^2\theta\right)\Big/(-a\sin\theta)$$

$$= -\frac{b}{a^2}\operatorname{cosec}^3\theta$$

$$\therefore \qquad X = x - y'[1 + (y')^2]/y''$$

$$= a\cos\theta - \left[\left(-\frac{b}{a}\cot\theta\right)\left(1 + \frac{b^2}{a^2}\cot^2\theta\right)\right]\Big/\left(-\frac{b}{a^2}\operatorname{cosec}^3\theta\right)$$

$$= a\cos\theta - \frac{b}{a}\cot\theta\left(1 + \frac{b^2}{a^2}\cot^2\theta\right)\left(\frac{a^2}{b}\sin^3\theta\right)$$

$$= a\cos\theta - [a\cos\theta(a^2\sin^2\theta + b^2\cos^2\theta)]/a^2$$

$$= \cos\theta[a^2 - a^2(1 - \cos^2\theta) - b^2\cos^2\theta]/a$$

$$= \cos\theta[a^2\cos^2\theta - b^2\cos^2\theta]/a$$

$$= \cos^3\theta\left[\frac{a^2 - b^2}{a}\right]$$

$$Y = y + [1 + (y')^2]/y''$$

$$= b\sin\theta + \left(1 + \frac{b^2}{a^2}\cot^2\theta\right)\Big/\left(-\frac{b}{a^2}\operatorname{cosec}^3\theta\right)$$

$$= b\sin\theta - \left(1 + \frac{b^2}{a^2}\cot^2\theta\right)\frac{a^2}{b}\sin^3\theta$$

$$= (b^2\sin\theta - a^2\sin^3\theta - b^2\cos^2\theta\sin\theta)/b$$

$$= \sin\theta[b^2 - a^2\sin^2\theta - b^2(1 - \sin^2\theta)]/b$$

$$= -\sin^3\theta\left[\frac{a^2 - b^2}{b}\right]$$

The two equations for X and Y in example 11, as θ varies, are parametric equations for the locus of the centre of curvature as the point P moves around the ellipse. Eliminating θ gives the cartesian equation of the locus of the centre of curvature (known as the **evolute**).

$$X = \frac{(a^2 - b^2)}{a}\cos^3\theta$$

$$Y = -\frac{(a^2 - b^2)}{b}\sin^3\theta$$

$$\therefore \qquad (aX)^{\frac{2}{3}} + (bY)^{\frac{2}{3}} = (a^2 - b^2)^{\frac{2}{3}}\cos^2\theta + (a^2 - b^2)^{\frac{2}{3}}\sin^2\theta$$

$$\therefore \qquad (aX)^{\frac{2}{3}} + (bY)^{\frac{2}{3}} = (a^2 - b^2)^{\frac{2}{3}}$$

which is an astroid. The two curves are shown in Fig. 8.11. The astroid is not always contained within the ellipse: it may intersect it.

The astroid is the **evolute** of the ellipse and the ellipse is known as an **involute** of the astroid.

Evolutes have an important characteristic: the length of any arc of the evolute is equal to the difference between the radii of curvature of the corresponding points on the involute. For example, in Fig. 8.11 the length of the arc AB of the astroid is given by

$$AB = BQ - AP \tag{8.43}$$

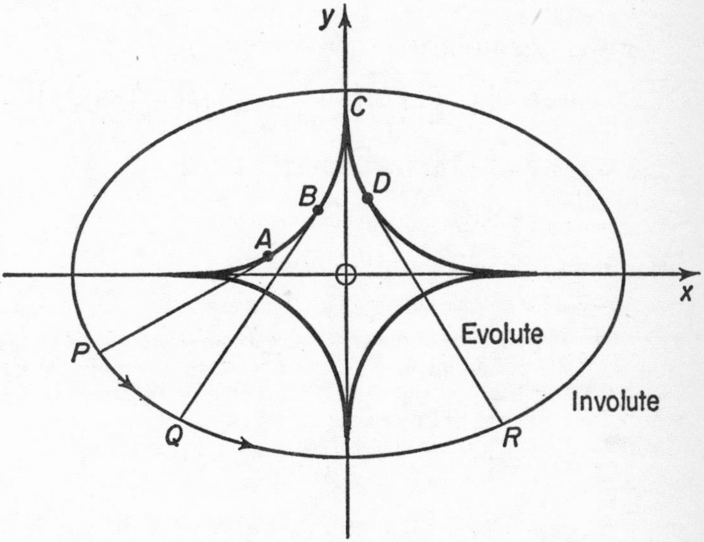

Fig. 8.11

To prove this, consider the coordinates of the centre of curvature (that is coordinates of points such as A and B); from equation 8.40

$$X = x - \rho \sin \psi$$

Differentiating with respect to ρ

$$\begin{aligned}\frac{dX}{d\rho} &= \frac{dx}{d\rho} - \sin\psi - \rho\frac{d(\sin\psi)}{d\psi}\frac{d\psi}{d\rho} \\ &= \frac{dx}{d\rho} - \sin\psi - \rho\cos\psi\frac{d\psi}{d\rho} \\ &= \frac{dx}{d\rho} - \sin\psi - \frac{ds}{d\psi}\cdot\frac{dx}{ds}\cdot\frac{d\psi}{d\rho} \\ &= \frac{dx}{d\rho} - \sin\psi - \frac{dx}{d\rho} \\ &= -\sin\psi \end{aligned} \tag{i}$$

Similarly

$$Y = y + \rho \cos \psi$$

$$\frac{dY}{d\rho} = \frac{dy}{d\rho} + \cos \psi - \rho \sin \psi \frac{d\psi}{d\rho}$$

$$= \frac{dy}{d\rho} + \cos \psi - \frac{ds}{d\psi} \cdot \frac{dy}{ds} \cdot \frac{d\psi}{d\rho}$$

$$= \frac{dy}{d\rho} + \cos \psi - \frac{dy}{d\rho}$$

$$= \cos \psi$$

From equation 7.8 the arc length s of the evolute is given by

$$s = \int_A^B \sqrt{\left[\left(\frac{dX}{d\rho}\right)^2 + \left(\frac{dY}{d\rho}\right)^2\right]}\, d\rho$$

$$= \int_A^B \sqrt{(\sin^2 \psi + \cos^2 \psi)}\, d\rho$$

$$= \int_A^B d\rho$$

$$s = \rho_B - \rho_A \qquad (8.44)$$

This property of the length of the arc of an evolute enables us to visualise a physical description of an involute. Consider a length of string fastened at C and wrapped round the evolute curve CBA. If the string is kept taut and gradually unwound its end will sweep out the lower half of an involute curve.

The involute of a circle is used to give the profile of gear wheels.

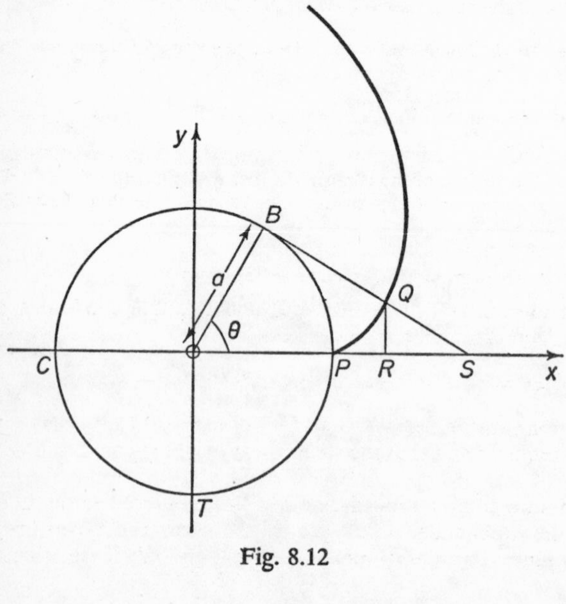

Fig. 8.12

Example 12. Find the parametric equations of the involute of the circle $x = a \cos \theta$, $y = a \sin \theta$.

Refer to Fig. 8.12; the string to be unwound is supposed to be attached at C and wrapped round to P. Let $Q(x, y)$ be any point on the involute when a length BQ of the string has been unwound and let $\angle BOx = \theta$. Produce BQ to meet Ox at S and draw QR perpendicular to Ox.

$$\begin{aligned}
BQ &= \text{arc } BP = a\theta \\
y = QR &= QS \sin QSR \\
&= (BS - BQ) \sin (90 - \theta) \\
&= (a \tan \theta - a\theta) \cos \theta \\
&= a(\sin \theta - \theta \cos \theta) \\
x = RO &= OS - SR \\
&= a \sec \theta - QS \cos QSR \\
&= a \sec \theta - (BS - BQ) \cos (90 - \theta) \\
&= a \sec \theta - (a \tan \theta - a\theta) \sin \theta \\
&= a(\sec \theta - \sin^2 \theta \sec \theta + \theta \sin \theta) \\
&= a[\sec \theta(1 - \sin^2 \theta) + \theta \sin \theta] \\
&= a(\sec \theta \cos^2 \theta + \theta \sin \theta) \\
&= a(\cos \theta + \theta \sin \theta) \quad (0 \leqslant \theta \leqslant \pi)
\end{aligned}$$

Note: To obtain the other half of the involute the string is wound round the lower half of the circle CTP.

Exercises 8.5

1. Show that the coordinates (X, Y) of the centre of curvature of any point on the parabola $x = at^2$, $y = 2at$, are given by $X = 3at^2 + 2a$, $Y = -2at^3$. Eliminate t and find the cartesian equation of the evolute of the parabola.

2. The parametric equations of a curve are $x = c(t - \tanh t)$, $y = c \operatorname{sech} t$. Prove that $dy/dx = -1/\sinh t$ and find ρ the radius of curvature. Show that the equation of the evolute of the curve is $y = c \cosh (x/c)$.

3. Show that for the involute of a circle (refer to example 12) radius a, the radius of curvature, is $\sqrt{(2as)}$, where s is the arc length.

4. Prove that the evolute of the rectangular hyperbola $x = a \cosh \theta$, $y = a \sinh \theta$ is $x^{\frac{2}{3}} - y^{\frac{2}{3}} = (2a)^{\frac{2}{3}}$.

5. Verify that the evolute of the curve $x = a(\cos \theta + \theta \sin \theta)$, $y = a(\sin \theta - \theta \cos \theta)$ is the circle $x^2 + y^2 = a^2$ (refer to example 12 and note that the evolute of the evolute of a circle is a circle).

8.7 Taylor's Theorem and Maclaurin's Theorem

Using one or other of these theorems, under certain conditions, a function $f(x)$ may be represented by a power series

$$f(x) = a_0 + a_1x + a_2x^2 + a_3x^3 + \ldots + a_nx^n + \ldots$$

The conditions are that $f(x)$ and all its derivatives of all orders exist in the range of x required and that the series on the right is convergent to the value of $f(x)$.

The technique is not a difficult one and has been used earlier in section 2.2 to obtain the exponential series. We should stress that when the technique produces a power series, the function is equal to it only if the given conditions are satisfied. For example, for the function $(1 + x)^n$ the technique produces the power series

$$1 + nx + \frac{n(n-1)}{1.2}x^2 + \frac{n(n-1)(n-2)}{1.2.3}x^3 + \ldots$$

If, however, we let $x = -2$ and $n = -1$ then

$$(1 + x)^n = (1 - 2)^{-1} = 1/-1 = -1$$

and $1 + nx + \dfrac{n(n-1)}{1.2}x^2 + \ldots$

$$= 1 + (-1)(-2) + \frac{(-1)(-2)}{1.2}(-2)^2 + \ldots$$

$$= 1 + 2 + 4 + 8 + \ldots$$

and to say that

$$(1 + x)^n = 1 + nx + \frac{n(n-1)}{1.2}x^2 + \ldots$$

for these values of x and n is absurd.

Our readers will recognise the binomial series and know that for n fractional or negative the expansion is only valid for $-1 < x < 1$. However, the point is made that although the technique may produce a power series it only represents the function when the conditions stated earlier are satisfied.

A complete and rigorous proof of these theorems is beyond the scope of this book. If our readers wish to use them for functions other than those mentioned in this section they should consult more advanced textbooks. Here the technique will be used to obtain the power series in the general case of $f(x)$; the result will then be used in particular cases.

Suppose the function $f(x)$ satisfies the necessary and sufficient conditions and let

$$f(x) = a_0 + a_1x + a_2x^2 + \ldots + a_nx^n + \ldots \qquad (8.45)$$

By repeatedly differentiating the series term by term* with respect to x we obtain

$$f'(x) = a_1 + 2a_2x + 3a_3x^2 + \ldots + na_nx^{n-1} + \ldots$$

$$f''(x) = \quad 1.2a_2 + 2.3a_3x + \ldots + n(n-1)a_nx^{n-2} + \ldots$$

$$\cdot \quad \cdot \quad \cdot \quad \cdot \quad \cdot \quad \cdot \quad \cdot \quad \cdot \quad \cdot \quad \cdot \quad \cdot \quad \cdot \quad \cdot \quad \cdot \quad \cdot \quad \cdot \quad \cdot \quad \cdot$$

$$f^{(n)}(x) = \qquad\qquad n(n-1)\ldots 2.1a_n + \ldots$$

$$\cdot \quad \cdot \quad \cdot \quad \cdot \quad \cdot \quad \cdot \quad \cdot \quad \cdot \quad \cdot \quad \cdot \quad \cdot \quad \cdot \quad \cdot \quad \cdot \quad \cdot \quad \cdot \quad \cdot \quad \cdot$$

* A power series may be differentiated term by term within its interval of convergence.

Putting $x = 0$ in these equations we obtain

$$\begin{aligned} f(0) &= a_0 \\ f'(0) &= a_1 \\ f''(0) &= 2!a_2 \\ f'''(0) &= 3!a_3 \\ &\cdots \\ f^{(n)}(0) &= n!a_n \\ &\cdots \end{aligned}$$

Substituting for $a_0, a_1, a_2, \ldots a_n \ldots$ in equation 8.45

$$f(x) = f(0) + \frac{f'(0)}{1!}x + \frac{f''(0)}{2!}x^2 + \ldots + \frac{f^{(n)}(0)}{n!}x^n + \ldots \quad (8.46)$$

where $f^{(n)}(0)$ means the value of the nth derivative of $f(x)$ when $x = 0$.

This is **Maclaurin's Series**, and, if x is small, taking the first one, two, three . . . terms of the series gives successive approximations to the value of $f(x)$. For example, neglecting x^2 and higher powers of x

$$\begin{aligned} f(x) &\simeq f(0) + xf'(0) \\ &\simeq f(0) + x \tan \psi \end{aligned}$$

which is illustrated in Fig. 8.13.

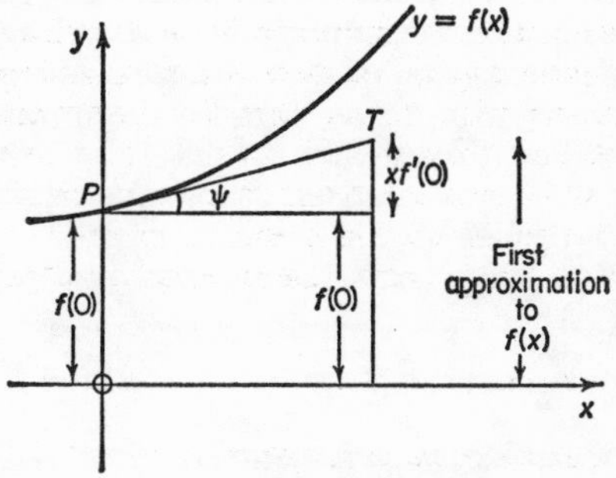

Fig. 8.13

Including the next term $f''(0)/2!$ improves the approximation by making some allowance for the changing slope of the tangent as we move away from $x = 0$, with similar improvements as more terms are added.

Example 13. Obtain a power series in x for the functions (i) $\sin x$ and (ii) $\sinh x$, using Maclaurin's Theorem.

(i) $f(x) = \sin x$, $f'(x) = \cos x$, $f''(x) = -\sin x$, $f'''(x) = -\cos x$, $f^{iv}(x) = \sin x$, $f^{v}(x) = \cos x \ldots$

$\therefore$ $f(0) = 0$, $f'(0) = 1$, $f''(0) = 0$, $f'''(0) = -1$, $f^{iv}(0) = 0$, $f^{v}(0) = 1 \ldots$

From equation 8.46

$$f(x) = \sin x = x - x^3/3! + x^5/5! - \ldots + (-)^n \frac{x^{2n+1}}{(2n+1)!} + \ldots \qquad (8.47)$$

(ii) $f(x) = \sinh x, f'(x) = \cosh x, f''(x) = \sinh x, f'''(x) = \cosh x, f^{iv}(x) = \sinh x$
$f^{v}(x) = \cosh x \ldots$

$\therefore \quad f(0) = 0, f'(0) = 1, f''(0) = 0, f'''(0) = 1, f^{iv}(0) = 0, f^{v}(0) = 1, \ldots$

From equation 8.46

$$f(x) = \sinh x = x + x^3/3! + x^5/5! + \ldots + \frac{x^{2n+1}}{(2n+1)!} + \ldots \qquad (8.48)$$

Note the similarity between these two series for sine and hyperbolic sine.

Exercises 8.6

1. Obtain a power series in x for the following functions using Maclaurin's Theorem.

(i) $\ln (1 + x)$ $\quad (-1 < x \leqslant 1)$
(ii) $\cos x$ $\quad$ (all x)
(iii) $\ln (a - x)$ $\quad (-a \leqslant x < a$, where a is a constant)

2. Obtain a power series in x for the function $\cosh x$ (true all x). Deduce a power series for $c \cosh (x/c)$, where c is a constant, and find the approximate shape of the catenary $y = c \cosh (x/c)$ when x/c is so small that $(x/c)^4$ and higher powers can be neglected.

3. Obtain a power series in x for the function e^{ax} where a is a constant. Hence, using the identity $\sinh x = (e^x - e^{-x})/2$, verify the result of example 13(ii).

4. Obtain the first *two* non-zero terms of the Maclaurin's Series for the following functions: (i) $\tan x$, (ii) $\tan^{-1} x$, (iii) $\sec x$.

5. Given that $f(x) = \sin x \sinh x$ verify that $f^{4n+2}(0) = (-)^n 2^{2n+1}$. Hence obtain a power series in x for $f(x)$.

6. Use the power series for $\sin x$ (example 13(i)) and $\cos x$ (question 1(ii)) to show that

$$\frac{(x - \sin x)}{x(1 - \cos x)} = \tfrac{1}{3} + \text{terms in } x \text{ or higher powers of } x$$

Hence find the value of

$$\lim_{x \to 0} \frac{(x - \sin x)}{x(1 - \cos x)}$$

7. Use the power series for $\sin x$ and $\cos x$ to find the value of

$$\lim_{x \to 0} \frac{x(2 + \cos x) - 3 \sin x}{x^5}$$

8. Obtain the Maclaurin's Series for the function $\ln (1 + x)$ $(-1 < x \leqslant 1)$. Deduce the series for $\ln [(1 + x)/(1 - x)]$, and state the range of values of x for which it is valid.

9. Using the appropriate power series, find the limiting value as x approaches 0 of the following functions:

(i) $[\ln (1 + x)]/x$ $\quad$ (ii) $[e^x - (1 + x)]/x^2$
(iii) $[\ln (1 - x^2)]/\sin x^2$ $\quad$ (iv) $[\ln (1 + x^2)]/(1 - \cos x)$

10. Show that

$$\sin^3\theta - \theta^3\cos\theta = k\theta^7 + \text{terms in higher powers of } \theta$$

and find the value of k.

Maclaurin's Theorem (equation 8.46) gives the value of a function $f(x)$ at a point x in terms of its value and those of its derivatives when $x = 0$; that is, in terms of $f(0), f'(0), f''(0) \ldots$

Taylor's Theorem is a slightly different form of the same basic result. The value of $f(x + h)$ is given in terms of $f(x)$ and the value of its derivatives at the point x—that is, in terms of $f(x)$, $f'(x)$, $f''(x)$, ... Assuming that $f(x + h)$ can be represented by a series of ascending powers of h and that $f(x + h)$ and all its derivatives exist in the range of values of x required and that the series converges to the value $f(x + h)$, let

$$f(x + h) = a_0 + a_1h + a_2h^2 + a_3h^3 + \ldots + a_nh^n + \ldots \quad (8.49)$$

We now wish to use the method by which Maclaurin's Series was obtained and differentiate both sides* with respect to h. However, the 'dash notation' for indicating derivatives of a function $f(u)$ denotes differentiation with respect to u. In this case, if we let $u = x + h$

$$f'(x + h) = \frac{\mathrm{d}f(x + h)}{\mathrm{d}(x + h)}$$

that is, differentiation with respect to $x + h$. However

$$\frac{\mathrm{d}f(x + h)}{\mathrm{d}h} = \frac{\mathrm{d}f(x + h)}{\mathrm{d}(x + h)} \cdot \frac{\mathrm{d}(x + h)}{\mathrm{d}h}$$

$$= f'(x + h) \,.\, 1$$

so that *in this case*

$$f'(x + h) = \frac{\mathrm{d}f(x + h)}{\mathrm{d}h}$$

Similarly

$$f''(x + h) = \frac{\mathrm{d}^2f(x + h)}{\mathrm{d}h^2}$$

Therefore, differentiating equation 8.49 successively with respect to h

$$f'(x + h) = a_1 + 2a_2h + 3a_3h^2 + \ldots + na_nh^{n-1} + \ldots$$

$$f''(x + h) = 1 \,.\, 2a_2 + 2 \,.\, 3a_3h + \ldots + n(n - 1)a_nh^{n-2} + \ldots$$

. . . .

$$f^{(n)}(x + h) = n(n - 1) \ldots 2 \,.\, 1a_n + \ldots$$

. . . .

* See footnote concerning the equation 8.45.

Putting $h = 0$ in these equations

$$
\begin{aligned}
f(x) &= a_0 \\
f'(x) &= a_1 \\
f''(x) &= 2!a_2 \\
f'''(x) &= 3!a_3 \\
&\dots \\
f^{(n)}(x) &= n!a_n \\
&\dots
\end{aligned}
$$

Substituting for $a_0, a_1, a_2 \dots$ in equation 8.49

$$f(x+h) = f(x) + \frac{f'(x)}{1!}h + \frac{f''(x)}{2!}h^2 + \dots \tag{8.50}$$

This is **Taylor's Series.** If we put $x = 0$ it has the same form as equation 8.46 and Maclaurin's Series is a special case of Taylor's Series.

If $f(x)$ is known and h is small, considering only the first one, two, three . . . terms of the series gives successive approximations to the value of $f(x + h)$. We usually use the δ notation to denote small changes; let $h = \delta x$ and equation 8.50 can be written

$$f(x+\delta x) = f(x) + f'(x)\,\delta x + \frac{f''(x)}{2!}(\delta x)^2 + \dots$$

or

$$f(x+\delta x) - f(x) = f'(x)\,\delta x + \frac{f''(x)}{2!}(\delta x)^2 + \dots$$

The left-hand side is the change in $f(x)$ due to a small change in x and can be written $\delta[f(x)]$; therefore

$$\delta[f(x)] = f'(x)\,\delta x + \frac{f''(x)}{2!}(\delta x)^2 + \dots \tag{8.51}$$

and this is the exact expression for the change in $f(x)$ when x changes by an amount δx.

If δx is small we have, ignoring $(\delta x)^2$ and higher powers,

$$\delta[f(x)] \simeq f'(x)\,\delta x$$

or

$$\delta f = \frac{df}{dx}\delta x$$

which is the same as the equation 3.2 already used in section 3.5 for the calculation of approximations and errors. We can now improve the accuracy of the approximation by considering more than one term of the equation 8.51. Practically, when calculating errors in $f(x)$ due to small errors in x, the term in $(\delta x)^2$ is seldom significant.

Example 14. The linear radius R of the moon is calculated from the formula $R = a \sin S/\sin P$, where a is the earth's equatorial radius, S is the mean semi-diameter of the moon and P is the mean equatorial horizontal parallax of the moon. Using the values $a = 6400$ kilometres, $P = 60'\ 55{\cdot}2''$, $S = 16'\ 32{\cdot}5''$, it is found that

$R = 1734$ kilometres. Assuming that a and P are exact but that the error in S is $\delta S = \pm 2{\cdot}5''$, calculate the possible error δR in the calculated value of R.

$$R = a \sin S/\sin P$$

$$\therefore \qquad \frac{dR}{dS} = a \cos S/\sin P$$

$$\frac{d^2R}{dS^2} = -a \sin S/\sin P$$

From equation 8.51

$$\delta R = \frac{a \cos S}{\sin P}\delta S - \frac{a \sin S}{\sin P}(\delta S)^2$$

$$\delta S = 2{\cdot}5'' = 0{\cdot}000\,012\,12 \text{ radians}$$

$$\text{1st term } \frac{a \cos S}{\sin P}\delta S = \frac{6400 \cos (16'\ 32{\cdot}5'')}{\sin (60'\ 55{\cdot}2'')}\delta S$$

$$= 4{\cdot}37$$

$$\text{2nd term } -\frac{a \sin S}{\sin P}(\delta S)^2 = -\frac{aS}{P}(\delta S)^2$$

$$= -\frac{6400 \,.\, 16{\cdot}54}{60{\cdot}92}(\delta S)^2$$

$$= -\,0{\cdot}000\,000\,61$$

which is negligible compared to the first term. Because δS can be positive or negative

$$\delta R = \pm 4{\cdot}37 \text{ kilometres}$$

In section 3.4 we discussed methods of finding values of x for which a differentiable function $f(x)$ had a maximum or minimum value. The necessary and sufficient conditions were

$$f'(a) = 0 \text{ and } f''(a) > 0 \text{ then } f(a) \text{ is a minimum value of } f(x)$$

$$f'(a) = 0 \text{ and } f''(a) < 0 \text{ then } f(a) \text{ is a maximum value of } f(x)$$

We shall examine these conditions again, as well as the case of $f'(x) = 0$ *and* $f''(x) = 0$, using Taylor's Theorem.

If $f(x)$ is a minimum value it is smaller than any other value in its immediate neighbourhood: that is, both $f(x + \varepsilon)$ and $f(x - \varepsilon)$ are larger than $f(x)$ for small values of ε, and $f(x + h) > f(x)$ for small positive *or* negative values of h. By equation 8.50

$$f(x + h) = f(x) + hf'(x) + \frac{h^2}{2!}f''(x) + \ldots$$

$$\therefore \qquad f(x + h) - f(x) = hf'(x) + \frac{h^2}{2!}f''(x) + \ldots$$

For sufficiently small values of h the terms containing h^2 and h^3 will be negligible compared to the terms containing h. The sign of $f(x + h) - f(x)$, which must always be positive for a minimum, will depend on the sign of

$hf'(x)$, but $f'(x)$ is fixed and h can vary from positive to negative values. Therefore

$$f(x+h)-f(x) \text{ can be positive; } f(x+h) > f(x)$$

or

$$f(x+h)-f(x) \text{ can be negative; } f(x+h) < f(x)$$

and $f(x)$ cannot be a minimum. For a minimum value the term $hf'(x) = 0$; now $h \neq 0$ and therefore a necessary condition is that $f'(x) = 0$.

It follows that

$$f(x+h)-f(x) = \frac{h^2}{2!}f''(x) + \frac{h^3}{3!}f'''(x) + \ldots$$

and for sufficiently small values of h the values of h^3, h^4, . . . are negligible compared with h^2. The sign of $f(x+h)-f(x)$ will depend on $h^2f''(x)/2!$; h^2 is always positive and therefore if $f''(x)$ is positive

$f(x+h)-f(x)$ is positive for positive *and* negative values of h

$\therefore$ $f(x+h) > f(x)$ for positive *and* negative values of h

$\therefore$ $f(x)$ is a minimum if $f'(x) = 0$ and $f''(x) > 0$

This agrees with section 3.4.

However, consider the case when $f''(x)$ is also zero: then the sign of $f(x+h)-f(x)$ depends on the next term $h^3f'''(x)/3!$ Therefore h^3 can be positive or negative as the sign of h changes;

$$f(x+h)-f(x) \text{ can be positive } f(x+h) > f(x)$$

or

$$f(x+h)-f(x) \text{ can be negative } f(x+h) < f(x)$$

There is no minimum. However, because $f'(x) = 0$ there is a horizontal tangent and we have a horizontal point of inflexion, as shown in Fig. 8.14.

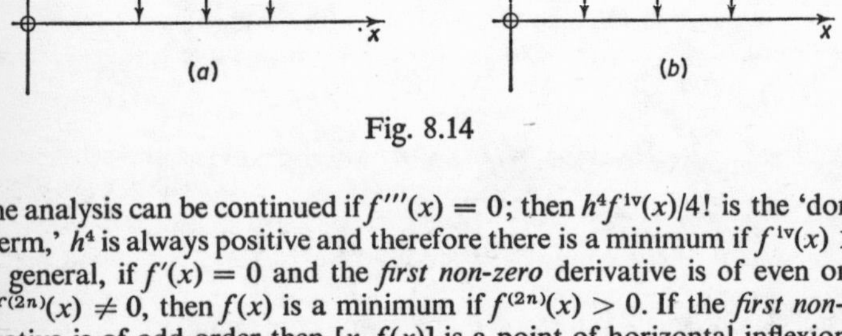

Fig. 8.14

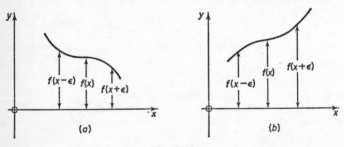

The analysis can be continued if $f'''(x) = 0$; then $h^4f^{iv}(x)/4!$ is the 'dominant term,' h^4 is always positive and therefore there is a minimum if $f^{iv}(x) > 0$.

In general, if $f'(x) = 0$ and the *first non-zero* derivative is of even order, say $f^{(2n)}(x) \neq 0$, then $f(x)$ is a minimum if $f^{(2n)}(x) > 0$. If the *first non-zero* derivative is of odd order then $[x, f(x)]$ is a point of horizontal inflexion.

A similar argument shows that if $f'(x) = 0$ and the first non-zero derivative is of even order then $f(x)$ is a maximum if $f^{(2n)}(x) < 0$. If the first non-zero derivative is a derivative of odd order then $[x, f(x)]$ is a point of horizontal inflexion. In general, if $f''(x) = 0$ it is better to consider the sign of $f'(x)$ around the turning point, as in section 3.4. However, we give an example of the method.

Example 15. Find the stationary points on the curve $y = x^4 - 12x^3 + 54x^2 - 108x$ and distinguish between them.

$$y = x^4 - 12x^3 + 54x^2 - 108x$$

$$\therefore \quad \begin{aligned} y' &= 4x^3 - 36x^2 + 108x - 108 \\ &= 4(x^3 - 9x^2 + 27x - 27) \\ &= 4(x - 3)^3 \end{aligned}$$

The only turning point is $x = 3$.

$$\begin{aligned} y'' &= 12(x - 3)^2 \\ y''' &= 24(x - 3) \\ y^{iv} &= 24 \end{aligned}$$

The first non-zero derivative (when $x = 3$) is y^{iv}, which is even and positive; therefore $x = 3$ gives a minimum value.

In general most equations have no exact analytical solution and are solved by methods of approximation. One way is to find a first approximation by graphical methods and improve it by Newton's Formula.

If x_1 is an approximation to the root of an equation $f(x) = 0$ then x_2 is, in general, a closer approximation where

$$x_2 = x_1 - f(x_1)/f'(x_1) \tag{8.52}$$

It can be obtained from Taylor's Theorem. Any equation $f(x) = 0$ is a particular case of the function $f(x)$ when $f(x)$ has the value zero. Suppose that x_1 is a first approximation to the required root of $f(x) = 0$: then its exact value will be $x_1 + h$, where h can be positive or negative, and $f(x_1 + h) = 0$. By Taylor's Theorem

$$f(x_1 + h) = 0 = f(x_1) + hf'(x_1) + \frac{h^2}{2!}f''(x) + \ldots \tag{8.53}$$

If h is small then

$$f(x_1) + hf'(x_1) \simeq 0$$

$$\therefore \quad h \simeq -f(x_1)/f'(x_1)$$

In general

$$\begin{aligned} x_2 &= x_1 + h \\ &= x_1 - f(x_1)/f'(x_1) \end{aligned}$$

is a better approximation to the required root. The method is illustrated in Fig. 8.15. The curve $y = f(x)$ crosses the x-axis at A. The required root is the value of OA. The ordinate of the first approximation $OS = x_1$ meets the curve at P. If the tangent at P meets the Ox at T, the value of OT is, in general, a better approximation to the root

$$\begin{aligned} OT &= OS - ST \\ &= x_1 - PS/\tan\psi \\ &= x_1 - f(x_1)/f'(x_1) \end{aligned}$$

Successive applications of the formula are continued until two successive approximations give the required accuracy.

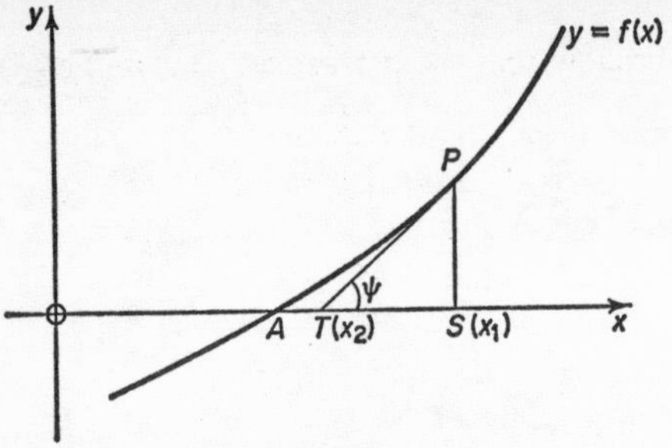

Fig. 8.15

Example 16. Find the root of the equation $x \sin x - 1 = 0$, which is near to $x = 1{\cdot}11$, correct to four significant figures.

$$x_1 = 1{\cdot}11$$

$$f(x) = x \sin x - 1 \qquad f'(x) = \sin x + x \cos x$$

$$f(1{\cdot}11) = 1{\cdot}11 \sin (1{\cdot}11) - 1 = -0{\cdot}005\,77 \qquad f'(1{\cdot}11) = \sin (1{\cdot}11) + 1{\cdot}11 \cos (1{\cdot}11) = 1{\cdot}389\,27$$

$$\therefore \quad x_2 = 1{\cdot}11 - (-0{\cdot}005\,77)/1{\cdot}389\,27 = 1{\cdot}11 + 0{\cdot}004\,15 = 1{\cdot}114\,15$$

$$f(x_2) = 1{\cdot}114\,15 \sin (1{\cdot}114\,15) - 1 = -0{\cdot}000\,00$$

$$f'(x_2) = \sin (1{\cdot}114\,15) + 1{\cdot}114\,15 \cos (1{\cdot}114\,15) = 1{\cdot}388\,81$$

The correction is negligible; therefore the root is

$$1{\cdot}114 \text{ (correct to four significant figures)}$$

The calculations are tedious and are best done on a calculating machine or a computer.

From equation 8.53 it can be seen that the method will fail to give a better approximation if the term $h^2 f''(x_1)/2!$ is not negligible compared with $hf'(x_1)$. This will be so if $f''(x_1)$ is numerically large—that is, the rate of change of $f'(x)$ at the point $x = x_1$ is numerically large. The method can be self regulating, and if x_2 is such that $f''(x_2)$ is small successive applications will give better and better approximations (see Fig. 8.16).

In some cases successive applications of the method do not give better approximations (see Fig. 8.17). The remedy is to obtain a better first approximation x_1, thus making the value of h smaller.

8.8 L'Hôpital's Rule

A very useful rule for finding the limiting value of a quotient $f(x)/g(x)$ as $x \to a$, where

$$\lim_{x \to a} f(x) = 0 \quad \text{and} \quad \lim_{x \to a} g(x) = 0$$

is **L'Hôpital's Rule,*** which states that

$$\underset{x\to a+}{\text{limit}}\frac{f(x)}{g(x)} = \underset{x\to a+}{\text{limit}}\frac{f'(x)}{g'(x)} \tag{8.54}$$

The conditions are broadly that the derivatives $f'(x)$ and $g'(x)$ and

$$\underset{x\to a+}{\text{limit}}\frac{f'(x)}{g'(x)}$$

exist in a domain $(a < x < a + h)$.

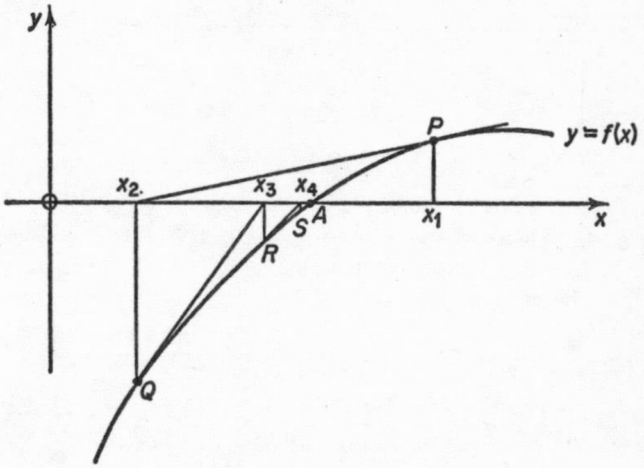

Fig. 8.16

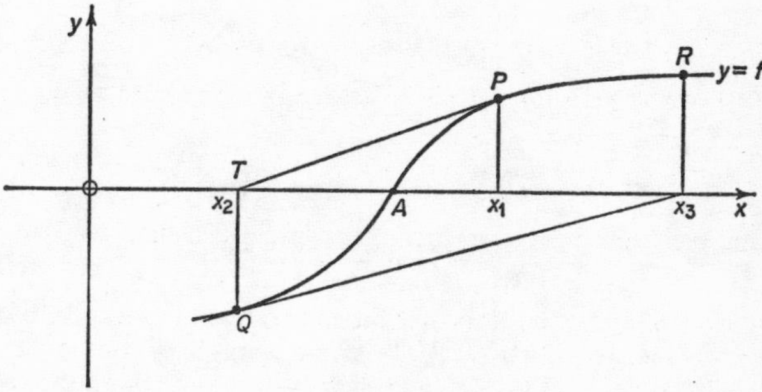

Fig. 8.17

Example 17. Find the values of (i) $\underset{x\to 3}{\text{limit}}\frac{(x^2 - x - 6)}{(2x^2 - 5x - 3)}$, (ii) $\underset{x\to 0}{\text{limit}}\frac{\tan(3x)}{\sin(2x)}$,

(iii) $\underset{x\to 0}{\text{limit}}\ x \coth x$.

(i) $f(x) = x^2 - x - 6$ and $f(3) = 9 - 3 - 6 = 0$
$g(x) = 2x^2 - 5x - 3$ and $g(3) = 18 - 15 - 3 = 0$

$$\therefore \quad \underset{x\to 3}{\text{limit}}\frac{(x^2 - x - 6)}{(2x^2 - 5x - 3)} = \underset{x\to 3}{\text{limit}}\frac{(2x - 1)}{(4x - 5)} = 5/7$$

* For a discussion of the proof of this rule our readers are referred to *Calculus*, by T. M. Apostol, Vol. 1, Blaisdell, 1961.

(ii)
$$f(x) = \tan 3x \quad \text{and} \quad f(0) = 0$$
$$g(x) = \sin 2x \quad \text{and} \quad g(0) = 0$$

$$\therefore \qquad \lim_{x\to 0} \frac{\tan(3x)}{\sin(2x)} = \lim_{x\to 0} \frac{3\sec^2(3x)}{2\cos(2x)} = 3/2$$

(iii) $x \coth x$ is not a quotient; therefore write it as $\dfrac{x\cosh x}{\sinh x}$

$$f(x) = x\cosh x \quad \text{and} \quad f(0) = 0$$
$$g(x) = \sinh x \quad \text{and} \quad g(0) = 0$$

$$\therefore \qquad \lim_{x\to 0} (x\coth x) = \lim_{x\to 0} \frac{x\cosh x}{\sinh x}$$
$$= \lim_{x\to 0} \frac{(\cosh x + x\sinh x)}{\cosh x}$$
$$= 1$$

The rule may have to be used again if both $f'(x)$ and $g'(x)$ are zero at $x = a$ as well as $f(x)$ and $g(x)$.

Example 18. Find the values of

(i) $\displaystyle\lim_{x\to 2} \frac{(x^3 - 4x^2 + 4x)}{(2x^3 - 9x^2 + 12x - 4)}$ (ii) $\displaystyle\lim_{x\to 0} \frac{(x - \sin x)}{x^3}$

(i) $f(2) = 8 - 16 + 8 = 0, \quad g(2) = 16 - 36 + 24 - 4 = 0$

$$\lim_{x\to 2} \frac{(x^3 - 4x^2 + 4x)}{(2x^3 - 9x^2 + 12x - 4)} = \lim_{x\to 2} \frac{(3x^2 - 8x + 4)}{(6x^2 - 18x + 12)} \left(= \frac{0}{0}\right)$$

Applying the rule again

$$= \lim_{x\to 2} \frac{(6x - 8)}{(12x - 18)} = \tfrac{4}{6} = \tfrac{2}{3}$$

(ii) $f(0) = 0 - 0 = 0, \quad g(0) = 0^3 = 0$

$$\therefore \qquad \lim_{x\to 0} \frac{(x - \sin x)}{x^3} = \lim_{x\to 0} \frac{1 - \cos x}{3x^2} \left(= \frac{0}{0}\right)$$
$$= \lim_{x\to 0} \frac{\sin x}{6x} \left(= \frac{0}{0}\right)$$
$$= \lim_{x\to 0} \frac{\cos x}{6}$$
$$= \tfrac{1}{6}$$

Revision Questions 8.3

Complete the following statements	*Answers*	*Refer to*
1. If κ is the curvature and ρ the radius of curvature at a point on a curve then $\rho = \ldots$	**1.** $1/\kappa$	Equation 8.38
2. If a curve is concave upwards then d^2y/dx^2 has a . . . value.	**2.** positive value	Equation 8.39 and the discussion after it

Complete the following statements	*Answers*	*Refer to*
3. The circle of curvature at a point P on a curve touches the curve at P and has . . .	**3.** the same curvature as the curve at P.	Section 8.6
4. The evolute of a curve is . . .	**4.** The locus of its centre of curvature.	The note after example 11
5. Maclaurin's Theorem is a special case of . . .	**5.** Taylor's Theorem.	Section 8.7
6. The first three terms of Taylor's Series are $f(x + h) = f(x) + \ldots + \ldots$	**6.** $hf'(x) + \frac{h^2}{2!}f''(x)$	Equation 8.50
7. Given that $f'(x_1) = f''(x_1) = f'''(x_1) = 0$ and $f^{iv}(x_1)$ is positive, then $f(x_1)$ has a . . . value.	**7.** minimum	The discussion after example 14
8. If the results of successive applications of Newton's Formula fail to converge then the remedy is . . .	**8.** to obtain a better first approximation.	The Note near the end of page 222
9. The involute of a circle is used as . . .	**9.** the profile of a gear tooth.	

Exercises 8.7

Evaluate the following limits using L'Hôpital's rule:

1. $\lim\limits_{x \to -3} \dfrac{(2x^2 + 7x + 3)}{(x^2 - 9)}$

2. $\lim\limits_{x \to 0} \dfrac{\sin x}{6x}$

3. $\lim\limits_{x \to \pi/2} \dfrac{\ln (\sin x)}{(1 - \sin x)}$

4. $\lim\limits_{x \to \pi/2} \dfrac{\cos x}{(1 - \sin^2 x)}$

5. $\lim\limits_{x \to a} \dfrac{(x^n - a^n)}{(x^{n-2} - a^{n-2})}$

6. $\lim\limits_{x \to 0} [\ln (1 + x)^{1/x}]$

7. $\lim\limits_{x \to 0} (x^2 \coth^2 x)$

8. The length L of a belt passing directly around two pulleys of radii a and b $(a > b)$ whose centres are at a distance x apart is given by

$$L = 2\sqrt{(x^2 - s^2)} + \pi(a + b) + 2s\theta$$

where $s = b - a$ and $\sin \theta = s/x$. Prove that to a first approximation

$$\delta L = 2 \cos \theta \, \delta x$$

9. Show that the stationary values of the function $x^7 - 3x^6 + 3x^5 - x^4$ are given by $x = 0$, $x = 1$, $x = 4/7$, and find if they are maxima, minima, or points of horizontal inflexion.

10. Find the maxima, minima and horizontal points of inflexion of the function $\sin^3 x$ in the range $-\pi \leqslant x \leqslant \pi$.

11. In a simple alloy system the free energy per atom e is given in terms of the concentration c by the equation

$$ke = 4c(1 - c) + c \ln c + (1 - c) \ln (1 - c)$$

where k is a constant. Show that for stationary values $4(2c - 1) = \ln [c/(1 - c)]$. On the same graph paper draw graphs of the two functions $4(2c - 1)$ and $\ln [c/(1 - c)]$ and find the approximate values of c for which e has a stationary value. Using Newton's Formula find these values of c correct to three decimal places. Determine which of them are maxima or minima.

12. In Kepler's equation $E = M + e \sin E$ find, correct to three significant figures, the eccentric anomaly E given that $e = 0{\cdot}08$ and $M = 0{\cdot}05$.

CHAPTER NINE

FURTHER INTEGRATION

The last three sections of this chapter, on Infinite and Improper Integrals and Simpson's Rule, are of general interest. The earlier sections are of interest mainly to engineers, physicists and mathematicians.

9.1 Hyperbolic Functions

In section 8.1 hyperbolic functions were defined and their derivatives were found. From these results we have immediately that

$$\int \sinh(ax)\,dx = \frac{1}{a}\cosh(ax) + C \qquad \int \cosh(ax)\,dx = \frac{1}{a}\sinh(ax) + C \quad (9.1)^*$$

Both tanh (ax) and coth (ax) can be integrated by writing them in terms of sinh (ax) and cosh (ax)

$$\int \tanh(ax)\,dx = \int \frac{\sinh(ax)}{\cosh(ax)}\,dx$$

Let $u = \cosh(ax)$; then $du = a\sinh(ax)dx$

$$= \frac{1}{a}\int \frac{du}{u}$$

$$\therefore \qquad \int \tanh(ax)\,dx = \frac{1}{a}\ln[\cosh(ax)] + C \qquad (9.2)$$

Note that cosh (ax) is always positive: therefore $\ln|\cosh(ax)| = \ln[\cosh(ax)]$.

Similarly

$$\int \coth(ax)\,dx = \frac{1}{a}\ln|\sinh(ax)| + C \qquad (9.3)$$

The integrals of sech (ax) and cosech (ax) are not normally used in practice but can be obtained as follows

$$\int \operatorname{sech}(ax)\,dx = \int \frac{2}{(e^{ax} + e^{-ax})}\,dx$$

$$= \int \frac{2e^{ax}}{(e^{2ax} + 1)}\,dx$$

* Throughout this section a will be taken as a constant.

Let $u = e^{ax}$; then $du = a\,e^{ax}\,dx$

$$= \frac{2}{a}\int \frac{du}{(u^2 + 1)}$$

$$\therefore \qquad \int \text{sech}\,(ax)\,dx = \frac{2}{a}\tan^{-1}(e^{ax}) + C \qquad (9.4)$$

It is left as an exercise for the reader to prove that

$$\int \text{cosech}\,(ax)\,dx = \frac{1}{a}\ln\left[\frac{(e^{ax} - 1)}{(e^{ax} + 1)}\right] \quad (e^{ax} > 1) \qquad (9.5)$$

9.2 Hyperbolic Substitutions

In section 6.4 three trigonometrical substitutions were suggested to simplify integrands containing $\sqrt{(a^2 - x^2)}$, $(x = a\sin\theta)$, $\sqrt{(x^2 - a^2)}$, $(x = a\sec\theta)$, $\sqrt{(x^2 + a^2)}$, $(x = a\tan\theta)$. Hyperbolic substitutions can be used in the last two cases.

Consider the hyperbolic identity

$$\cosh^2\theta - \sinh^2\theta = 1$$

This can be written as

$$\sqrt{(\cosh^2\theta - 1)} = \sinh\theta$$

or

$$\sqrt{(\sinh^2\theta + 1)} = \cosh\theta$$

and in each case the square root is equal to a simple hyperbolic function. Thus

$$\left.\begin{array}{ll}\text{if} & \sqrt{(x^2 - a^2)} \text{ occurs in the integrand use } x = a\cosh\theta \\ \text{if} & \sqrt{(x^2 + a^2)} \text{ occurs in the integrand use } x = a\sinh\theta\end{array}\right\} \qquad (9.6)$$

Example 1. Evaluate (i) $\int_5^{10} \frac{\sqrt{(x^2 - 25)}}{x^2}\,dx$ and (ii) $\int \sqrt{(x^2 + 16)}\,dx$.

(i) Let $x = 5\cosh\theta$; then $dx = 5\sinh\theta\,d\theta$; when $x = 5$, $\theta = 0$; and when $x = 10$ $\theta = 1{\cdot}32$ (from tables).

$$\therefore \qquad \int_5^{10} \frac{\sqrt{(x^2 - 25)}}{x^2}\,dx = \int_0^{1\cdot32} \frac{\sqrt{(25\cosh^2\theta - 25)}}{25\cosh^2\theta}\,.\,5\sinh\theta\,d\theta$$

$$= \int_0^{1\cdot32} \frac{5\sqrt{(\cosh^2\theta - 1)}\,.\,5\sinh\theta}{25\cosh^2\theta}\,d\theta$$

$$= \int_0^{1\cdot32} \frac{\sinh^2\theta}{\cosh^2\theta}\,d\theta$$

$$= \int_0^{1\cdot32} \tanh^2\theta\,d\theta$$

$$= \int_0^{1\cdot32} (1 - \text{sech}^2\theta)\,d\theta \quad \text{(from 8.11)}$$

$$= \Big[\theta - \tanh\theta\Big]_0^{1\cdot32}$$

$$= (1{\cdot}32 - 0{\cdot}87) - (0 - 0)$$
$$= 0{\cdot}45$$

(ii) Let $x = 4 \sinh \theta$, $dx = 4 \cosh \theta \, d\theta$

$$\therefore \quad \int \sqrt{(x^2 + 16)}\, dx = \int \sqrt{(16 \sinh^2 \theta + 16)}\, 4 \cosh \theta \, d\theta$$

$$= \int 4\sqrt{(\sinh^2 \theta + 1)}\, 4 \cosh \theta \, d\theta$$

$$= 16 \int \cosh^2 \theta \, d\theta$$

From equation 8.9 $\cosh^2 \theta + \sinh^2 \theta = \cosh 2\theta$, and $\cosh^2 \theta - \sinh^2 \theta = 1$ Therefore, by addition $2 \cosh^2 \theta = 1 + \cosh 2\theta$

$$= 8 \int (1 + \cosh 2\theta)\, d\theta$$

$$= 8(\theta + \tfrac{1}{2} \sinh 2\theta) + C$$

$$= 8(\theta + \sinh \theta \cosh \theta) + C$$

$$= 8 \left[\sinh^{-1} \frac{x}{4} + \frac{x}{4}\sqrt{\left(1 + \frac{x^2}{16}\right)}\right] + C$$

$$= 8 \sinh^{-1} \frac{x}{4} + \frac{x}{2}\sqrt{(16 + x^2)} + C$$

Integrals of the type

$$\int \frac{dx}{(a \cosh x + b \sinh x + c)},$$

where a, b, c are constants, can be integrated by using the substitution $t = \tanh x/2$.

Then $\quad dt = \tfrac{1}{2} \operatorname{sech}^2 \dfrac{x}{2}\, dx$

$$\therefore \quad dx = \frac{2\, dt}{(1 - \tanh^2 x/2)} = \frac{2\, dt}{(1 - t^2)} \tag{9.7}$$

$$\sinh x = \frac{2 \sinh \frac{x}{2} \cosh \frac{x}{2}}{1} = \frac{2 \sinh \frac{x}{2} \cosh \frac{x}{2}}{\left(\cosh^2 \frac{x}{2} - \sinh^2 \frac{x}{2}\right)}$$

$$= \frac{2 \tanh \frac{x}{2}}{\left(1 - \tanh^2 \frac{x}{2}\right)} = \frac{2t}{(1 - t^2)} \tag{9.8}$$

Similarly
$$\cosh x = \frac{(1 + t^2)}{(1 - t^2)} \tag{9.9}$$

Example 2. Evaluate (i) $\displaystyle\int_0^{\ln 2} \frac{dx}{(\cosh x + 3 \sinh x + 1)}$ and

(ii) $\displaystyle\int \frac{8\,dx}{(\cosh x + 7\sinh x + 4)}$

(i) Let $t = \tanh\dfrac{x}{2}\left(= \dfrac{e^x - 1}{e^x + 1}\right)$

When $x = 0$, $t = 0$.

When $x = \ln 2$, $t = \dfrac{e^{\ln 2} - 1}{e^{\ln 2} + 1} = \dfrac{1}{3}$

From equations 9.7, 9.8 and 9.9

$$\int_0^{\ln 2} \frac{dx}{(\cosh x + 3\sinh x + 1)} = \int_0^{1/3} \frac{\dfrac{2\,dt}{(1 - t^2)}}{\left(\dfrac{1 + t^2}{1 - t^2}\right) + 3\left(\dfrac{2t}{1 - t^2}\right) + 1}$$

$$= \int_0^{1/3} \frac{2\,dt}{(1 + t^2) + 3(2t) + (1 - t^2)}$$

$$= \int_0^{1/3} \frac{2\,dt}{(2 + 6t)}$$

$$= \int_0^{1/3} \frac{dt}{(1 + 3t)}$$

$$= \left[\frac{1}{3}\ln(1 + 3t)\right]_0^{1/3}$$

$$= \tfrac{1}{3}\ln 2 - 0$$
$$= \tfrac{1}{3}\ln 2$$

(ii) Let $t = \tanh\dfrac{x}{2}$.

From equations 9.7, 9.8 and 9.9

$$\int \frac{8\,dx}{(\cosh x + 7\sinh x + 4)} = \int \frac{8\left(\dfrac{2\,dt}{1 - t^2}\right)}{\left(\dfrac{1 + t^2}{1 - t^2}\right) + 7\left(\dfrac{2t}{1 - t^2}\right) + 4}$$

$$= \int \frac{16\,dt}{(1 + t^2) + 14t + 4(1 - t^2)}$$

$$= \int \frac{16\,dt}{(-3t^2 + 14t + 5)}$$

$$= \int \frac{16\,dt}{(3t + 1)(5 - t)}$$

$$= \int \left[\frac{3}{(3t + 1)} + \frac{1}{(5 - t)}\right] dt$$

$$= 3 \,.\, \tfrac{1}{3}\ln|3t + 1| - \ln|5 - t| + C$$
$$= \ln|(3t + 1)/(5 - t)| + C$$

9.3 Inverse Hyperbolic and Trigonometrical Functions

The integrals of inverse hyperbolic and trigonometrical functions are not often required. They can, if necessary, be obtained by integrating by parts in a similar way to that used in section 6.2, example 12.

Example 3. Find the indefinite integrals with respect to x of (i) $\sin^{-1} x/2$ and (ii) $\tanh^{-1} x/3$.

(i) $$\int \sin^{-1}\frac{x}{2}\,\mathrm{d}x = \int \sin^{-1}\frac{x}{2}\,.\,1\,\mathrm{d}x$$

Integrating by parts

$$= \left(\sin^{-1}\frac{x}{2}\right) x - \int \frac{1}{\sqrt{(4-x^2)}}\,x\,\mathrm{d}x$$

To evaluate the second integral, let $u^2 = 4 - x^2$; then $2u\,\mathrm{d}u = -2x\,\mathrm{d}x$

$$\therefore \quad \int \sin^{-1}\frac{x}{2}\,\mathrm{d}x = x\sin^{-1}\frac{x}{2} + \int \frac{u\,\mathrm{d}u}{u}$$

$$= x\sin^{-1}\frac{x}{2} + \int \mathrm{d}u$$

$$= x\sin^{-1}\frac{x}{2} + u + C$$

$$= x\sin^{-1}\frac{x}{2} + \sqrt{(4-x^2)} + C$$

(ii) $$\int \tanh^{-1}\frac{x}{3}\,\mathrm{d}x = \int \tanh^{-1}\frac{x}{3}\,.\,1\,\mathrm{d}x$$

$$= \left(\tanh^{-1}\frac{x}{3}\right) x - \int \frac{3}{(9-x^2)}\,x\,\mathrm{d}x$$

To evaluate the second integral, let $u = 9 - x^2$; then $\mathrm{d}u = -2x\,\mathrm{d}x$

$$\therefore \quad \int \tanh^{-1}\frac{x}{3}\,\mathrm{d}x = x\tanh^{-1}\frac{x}{3} + \frac{3}{2}\int \frac{\mathrm{d}u}{u}$$

$$= x\tanh^{-1}\frac{x}{3} + \frac{3}{2}\ln|9-x^2| + C$$

Example 4. Evaluate $\int_0^{\frac{3}{4}} 4\theta \sinh^{-1}\theta\,\mathrm{d}\theta$.

$$\int_0^{\frac{3}{4}} 4\theta\sinh^{-1}\theta\,\mathrm{d}\theta = \int_0^{\frac{3}{4}} (\sinh^{-1}\theta)4\theta\,\mathrm{d}\theta$$

Integrating by parts

$$= \left[(\sinh^{-1}\theta)\,2\theta^2 - \int \frac{1}{\sqrt{(1+\theta^2)}}\,2\theta^2\,\mathrm{d}\theta\right]_0^{\frac{3}{4}}$$

In the second integral, let $\theta = \sinh u$; then $d\theta = \cosh u\, du$; when $\theta = 0$, $u = 0$ and when $\theta = \frac{3}{4}$, $u = 0{\cdot}69$ (to two significant figures)

$$= \frac{9}{8}\sinh^{-1}\frac{3}{4} - \int_0^{0\cdot69} \frac{2\sinh^2 u \cosh u\, du}{\sqrt{(1 + \sinh^2 u)}}$$

$$= \frac{9}{8} \times 0{\cdot}69 - \int_0^{0\cdot69} 2\sinh^2 u\, du$$

$$= 0{\cdot}78 - \int_0^{0\cdot69} (\cosh 2u - 1)\, du$$

$$= 0{\cdot}78 - \left[\frac{1}{2}\sinh 2u - u\right]_0^{0\cdot69}$$

$$= 0{\cdot}78 - [\tfrac{1}{2}\sinh 1{\cdot}38 - 0{\cdot}69] + [0 - 0]$$
$$= 0{\cdot}78 - 0{\cdot}93 + 0{\cdot}69$$
$$= 0{\cdot}54$$

Exercises 9.1

1. Find the indefinite integrals with respect to x of the following functions:

(i) $\dfrac{1}{5 + 4\cosh x}$ (ii) $\dfrac{\sinh x}{5 + 4\cosh x}$

(iii) $\dfrac{1}{x^2\sqrt{(x^2 + 4)}}$ (iv) $\dfrac{x}{\sqrt{(x^2 + 4)}}$

(v) $\dfrac{1}{\cosh 2\theta + \sinh 2\theta + 1}$ (let $t = \tanh \theta$)

(vi) $\sqrt{(9 + x^2)}$ (vii) $x\sqrt{(x^2 - 4)}$

(viii) $\dfrac{2\sinh^{-1} x}{\sqrt{(1 - x^2)}}$ (ix) $\dfrac{1}{3\sinh x + 3\cosh x + 1}$

2. Verify that the following results are correct:

(i) $$\int \tan^{-1} x\, dx = x\tan^{-1} x - \tfrac{1}{2}\ln(1 + x^2) + C$$

(ii) $$\int \sinh^{-1} x\, dx = x\sinh^{-1} x - \sqrt{(1 + x^2)} + C$$

(iii) $$\int \cosh^{-1} x\, dx = x\cosh^{-1} x - \sqrt{(x^2 - 1)} + C$$

3. Find to three significant figures the length of the curve $y = \ln\left(\tanh\dfrac{x}{2}\right)$ from $x = 1$ to $x = 2$.

4. A catenary has the equation $y = c\cosh x/c$, where c is a positive constant. Find an expression for the arc length s from the point (O, c) to the point (x, y) and verify that $s^2 = y^2 - c^2$.

5. Evaluate $\displaystyle\int \frac{x\, dx}{\sqrt{(x^2 - 9)}}$ by using the substitution $u^2 = (x^2 - 9)$. Verify your result by using the substitution $x = 3\cosh\theta$.

6. Evaluate, correct to two significant figures, $\displaystyle\int_1^3 \frac{dx}{x^2\sqrt{(1 + x^2)}}$.

7. The area contained between the axis of x and the portion of the catenary $y = \cosh x$ between $x = 0$ and $x = \ln 2$ rotates about the axis of x. Find the volume swept out and the area of its curved surface.

8. Evaluate $\int_0^1 2x \tan^{-1} x \, dx$.

9.4 Integrals of the Type $\int \frac{\text{linear}}{\sqrt{\text{quadratic}}}$

The results 8.27, 8.29 and 8.31 for the derivatives of $\sin^{-1} x/a$, $\sinh^{-1} x/a$, and $\cosh^{-1} x/a$ give the three standard forms.

$$\left.\begin{aligned} &\int \frac{dx}{\sqrt{(a^2 - x^2)}} = \sin^{-1}\frac{x}{a} + C \quad \int \frac{dx}{\sqrt{(x^2 - a^2)}} = \cosh^{-1}\frac{x}{a} + C \\ &\int \frac{dx}{\sqrt{(x^2 + a^2)}} = \sinh^{-1}\frac{x}{a} + C \end{aligned}\right\} \tag{9.10}$$

where a is a positive constant. This can be extended to

$$\left.\begin{aligned} \int \frac{dx}{\sqrt{[a^2 - (x+k)^2]}} &= \sin^{-1}\left(\frac{x+k}{a}\right) + C \\ \int \frac{dx}{\sqrt{[(x+k)^2 - a^2]}} &= \cosh^{-1}\left(\frac{x+k}{a}\right) + C \\ \int \frac{dx}{\sqrt{[(x+k)^2 + a^2]}} &= \sinh^{-1}\left(\frac{x+k}{a}\right) + C \end{aligned}\right\} \tag{9.11}$$

where k is any constant.

Example 5. Integrate the following functions with respect to x:

(i) $\dfrac{5}{\sqrt{(2x^2 + 2x + 5)}}$ (ii) $\dfrac{6}{\sqrt{(7 + 6x - 9x^2)}}$

(i)
$$\begin{aligned} \int \frac{5\,dx}{\sqrt{(2x^2 + 2x + 5)}} &= \frac{5}{\sqrt{2}} \int \frac{dx}{\sqrt{(x^2 + x + 5/2)}} \\ &= \frac{5}{\sqrt{2}} \int \frac{dx}{\sqrt{\left[\left(x + \frac{1}{2}\right)^2 + \left(\frac{3}{2}\right)^2\right]}} \\ &= \frac{5}{\sqrt{2}} \sinh^{-1}\left[\left(x + \frac{1}{2}\right)\Big/\frac{3}{2}\right] + C \\ &= \frac{5}{\sqrt{2}} \sinh^{-1}\frac{(2x+1)}{3} + C \end{aligned}$$

(ii)
$$\int \frac{6\,dx}{\sqrt{(7 + 6x - 9x^2)}} = \frac{6}{3} \int \frac{dx}{\sqrt{\left(\frac{7}{9} + \frac{2}{3}x - x^2\right)}}$$

Note that the coefficient of x^2 is -1 and we cannot immediately 'complete the square'. We proceed as follows

$$= 2\int \frac{dx}{\sqrt{\left[\frac{7}{9} - \left(x^2 - \frac{2}{3}x\right)\right]}}$$

$$= 2\int \frac{dx}{\sqrt{\left[\frac{8}{9} - \left(x - \frac{1}{3}\right)^2\right]}}$$

$$= 2\int \frac{dx}{\sqrt{\left[\left(\frac{2\sqrt{2}}{3}\right)^2 - \left(x - \frac{1}{3}\right)^2\right]}}$$

$$= 2 \sin^{-1} \frac{\left(x - \frac{1}{3}\right)}{\left(\frac{2\sqrt{2}}{3}\right)} + C$$

$$= 2 \sin^{-1} \frac{(3x - 1)}{2\sqrt{2}} + C$$

If the numerator is a linear function of x it is expressed as a multiple of the derivative of the quadratic in the denominator plus a constant.

Example 6. Integrate the following functions with respect to x:

(i) $\dfrac{(12x + 11)}{\sqrt{(2x^2 + 2x + 5)}}$ (ii) $\dfrac{(3x - 7)}{\sqrt{(4x^2 - 24x + 11)}}$

(i) The derivative of $2x^2 + 2x + 5$ is $4x + 2$

$$\therefore \quad \int \frac{(12x + 11)\,dx}{\sqrt{(2x^2 + 2x + 5)}} = \int \frac{3(4x + 2) + 5}{\sqrt{(2x^2 + 2x + 5)}}\,dx$$

$$= 3\int \frac{(4x + 2)\,dx}{\sqrt{(2x^2 + 2x + 5)}} + \int \frac{5\,dx}{\sqrt{(2x^2 + 2x + 5)}}$$

In the first integral let $u = 2x^2 + 2x + 5$; then $du = (4x + 2)\,du$, which is the denominator as we arranged

$$= 3\int \frac{du}{\sqrt{u}} + \int \frac{5\,dx}{\sqrt{(2x^2 + 2x + 5)}}$$

$$= 6\sqrt{u} + \int \frac{5\,dx}{\sqrt{(2x^2 + 2x + 5)}}$$

The second integral has already been evaluated in example 5(i)

$$= 6\sqrt{(2x^2 + 2x + 5)} + \frac{5}{\sqrt{2}} \sinh^{-1} \frac{(2x + 1)}{3} + C$$

(ii) The derivative of $4x^2 - 24x + 11$ is $8x - 24$

$$\therefore \quad \int \frac{(3x - 7)\,dx}{\sqrt{(4x^2 - 24x + 11)}} = \int \frac{\frac{3}{8}(8x - 24) + 2}{\sqrt{(4x^2 - 24x + 11)}}\,dx$$

$$= \frac{3}{8}\int \frac{(8x - 24)\,dx}{\sqrt{(4x^2 - 24x + 11)}} + 2\int \frac{dx}{\sqrt{(4x^2 - 24x + 11)}}$$

In the first integral let $u = 4x^2 - 24x + 11$; then $du = (8x - 24)\,dx$, the second integral, is manipulated like those in example 5

$$= \frac{3}{8}\int \frac{du}{\sqrt{u}} + \frac{2}{2}\int \frac{dx}{\sqrt{(x^2 - 6x + 2\frac{3}{4})}}$$

$$= \tfrac{3}{4}\sqrt{u} + \int \frac{dx}{\sqrt{\left[(x-3)^2 - \left(\frac{5}{2}\right)^2\right]}}$$

$$= \tfrac{3}{4}\sqrt{(4x^2 - 24x + 11)} + \cosh^{-1}\left[(x-3)\Big/\frac{5}{2}\right] + C$$

$$= \tfrac{3}{4}\sqrt{(4x^2 - 24x + 11)} + \cosh^{-1}\left(\frac{2x-6}{5}\right) + C$$

If the integral is of the form

$$\int \frac{dx}{(px+q)\sqrt{\text{quadratic}}}\,\cdot$$

the substitution $(px + q) = 1/t$ reduces it to one of the type already considered in examples 5 and 6.

Example 7. Find the indefinite integral with respect to x of the function

$$\frac{1}{(3x-1)\sqrt{(34x^2 - 26x + 5)}}\,\cdot$$

Let $(3x - 1) = \dfrac{1}{t}$. Therefore $x = \dfrac{1}{3t} + \dfrac{1}{3}$, and $dx = -\dfrac{1}{3t^2}\,dt$

and
$$34x^2 - 26x + 5 = 34\left(\frac{1}{3t} + \frac{1}{3}\right)^2 - 26\left(\frac{1}{3t} + \frac{1}{3}\right) + 5$$

$$= \frac{34}{9t^2} + \frac{68}{9t} + \frac{34}{9} - \frac{26}{3t} - \frac{26}{3} + 5$$

$$= \frac{34}{9t^2} - \frac{10}{9t} + \frac{1}{9}$$

$$= [34 - 10t + t^2]/9t^2$$

$$\therefore \quad \int \frac{dx}{(3x-1)\sqrt{(34x^2 - 26x + 5)}} = \int \frac{-\dfrac{dt}{3t^2}}{\dfrac{1}{t}\sqrt{[(34 - 10t + t^2)/9t^2]}}$$

$$= -\int \frac{dt}{\sqrt{(34 - 10t + t^2)}}$$

$$= -\int \frac{dt}{\sqrt{[(t-5)^2 + 9]}}$$

$$= -\sinh^{-1}\frac{(t-5)}{3} + C$$

$$= -\sinh^{-1}\left\{\left[\frac{1}{(3x-1)} - 5\right]\Big/3\right\} + C$$

$$= -\sinh^{-1}\frac{(2-5x)}{(3x-1)} + C$$

Revision Questions 9.1

State the substitutions required when integrating the following functions	*Answers*	*Refer to*
1. $\sqrt{(x^2 - 16)}$	**1.** $x = 4 \cosh \theta$ or $4 \sec \theta$	Sections 9.2 and 6.4
2. $\dfrac{x^2}{\sqrt{(x^2 + 25)}}$	**2.** $x = 5 \sinh \theta$ or $5 \tan \theta$	Sections 9.2 and 6.4
3. $\sqrt{(9 - x^2)}$	**3.** $x = 3 \sin \theta$	Section 6.4
4. $\dfrac{1}{(3 + 4 \cosh x)}$	**4.** $t = \tanh \dfrac{x}{2}$	Section 9.2
5. $\dfrac{1}{x\sqrt{(x^2 + 9)}}$	**5.** $x = \dfrac{1}{t}$	Example 7
Complete the following statements		
6. $\displaystyle\int \frac{dx}{\sqrt{(9 - x^2)}} = \ldots$	**6.** $\sin^{-1}\dfrac{x}{3} + C$	Standard forms 9.10
7. $\displaystyle\int \frac{dx}{\sqrt{(36 + x^2)}} = \ldots$	**7.** $\sinh^{-1}\dfrac{x}{6} + C$	
8. $\displaystyle\int \frac{dx}{\sqrt{(x^2 - 16)}} = \ldots$	**8.** $\cosh^{-1}\dfrac{x}{4} + C$	

Exercises 9.2

Write down the indefinite integrals with respect to x of the following functions

1. $\dfrac{1}{\sqrt{[(x + 2)^2 - 9]}}$
2. $\dfrac{1}{\sqrt{[(x - 3)^2 + 4]}}$
3. $\dfrac{1}{\sqrt{[25 + (x - 1)^2]}}$
4. $\dfrac{1}{\sqrt{[9 - (x - 5)^2]}}$

Find the indefinite integrals with respect to x of the following functions

5. $\dfrac{1}{\sqrt{(9x^2 - 6x + 5)}}$
6. $\dfrac{1}{\sqrt{(16x^2 + 24x)}}$
7. $\dfrac{1}{\sqrt{(16 - 9x - 4x^2)}}$
8. $\dfrac{(4 - 3x)}{\sqrt{(3 + 2x - x^2)}}$
9. $\dfrac{(3x + 2)}{\sqrt{(9x^2 - 6x - 3)}}$
10. $\dfrac{(6x + 11)}{\sqrt{(4x^2 + 20x + 34)}}$

9.5 Reduction Formulae

The results of this section are obtained by use of the formula for integration by parts. To revise the formula we start with the following important example which has applications in mechanical and electrical engineering.

Example 8. Find the indefinite integrals with respect to x of (i) $e^{ax} \cos bx$ and (ii) $e^{ax} \sin bx$, where a and b are constants.

Let $C = \int e^{ax} \cos bx \, dx$ and $S = \int e^{ax} \sin bx \, dx$

From equation 6.4

$$\int e^{ax} \cos bx \, dx = e^{ax} \int \cos bx \, dx - \int \left[\frac{de^{ax}}{dx} \int \cos bx \, dx \right] dx$$

$$\therefore \qquad C = \frac{e^{ax} \sin bx}{b} - \int \frac{ae^{ax} \sin bx}{b} dx$$

$$C = \frac{e^{ax} \sin bx}{b} - \frac{a}{b} S \qquad \text{(i)}$$

Similarly

$$\int e^{ax} \sin bx \, dx = e^{ax} \int \sin bx \, dx - \int \left[\frac{de^{ax}}{dx} \int \sin bx \, dx \right] dx$$

$$\therefore \qquad S = -\frac{e^{ax} \cos bx}{b} + \int \frac{ae^{ax} \cos bx}{b} dx$$

$$S = -\frac{e^{ax} \cos bx}{b} + \frac{a}{b} C \qquad \text{(ii)}$$

Substituting from equation (i) in equation (ii)

$$S = -\frac{e^{ax} \cos bx}{b} + \frac{a}{b} \left[\frac{e^{ax} \sin bx}{b} - \frac{a}{b} S \right]$$

$$\therefore \qquad S\left(1 + \frac{a^2}{b^2}\right) = -\frac{e^{ax} \cos bx}{b} + \frac{ae^{ax} \sin bx}{b^2}$$

$$S(b^2 + a^2) = -be^{ax} \cos bx + ae^{ax} \sin bx$$

$$\therefore \qquad S = \int e^{ax} \sin bx \, dx = \frac{e^{ax}(a \sin bx - b \cos bx)}{(a^2 + b^2)} \qquad (9.12)$$

Similarly

$$C = \int e^{ax} \cos bx \, dx = \frac{e^{ax}(a \cos bx + b \sin bx)}{(a^2 + b^2)} \qquad (9.13)$$

If we let $r = +\sqrt{(a^2 + b^2)}$ and $\alpha = \tan^{-1}(b/a)$

$$\int e^{ax} \cos bx \, dx = \frac{e^{ax} \cos (bx - \alpha)}{r} \qquad (9.14)$$

$$\int e^{ax} \sin bx \, dx = \frac{e^{ax} \sin (bx - \alpha)}{r} \qquad (9.15)$$

which are easier to remember. The derivatives of these two functions are

$$\frac{d(e^{ax} \cos bx)}{dx} = re^{ax} \cos (bx + \alpha)$$

$$\frac{d(e^{ax} \sin bx)}{dx} = re^{ax} \sin (bx + \alpha)$$

the verification of which is left as an exercise for our readers.

To return to our main theme of Reduction Formulae, consider $\int x^4 e^x \, dx$. We could write

$$I = \int x^4 \, e^x \, dx$$

This notation could be improved by the addition of a suffix to denote the power of the x: thus

$$I_4 = \int x^4 \, e^x \, dx$$

Then $\int x^{12} \, e^x \, dx$ could be denoted by I_{12}

and $$I_{23} = \int x^{23} \, e^x \, dx$$

Generally $$I_n = \int x^n \, e^x \, dx$$

The notation can include two suffices: thus

$$I_{2,4} = \int \sin^2 x \cos^4 x \, dx$$

and $$I_{12,33} = \int \sin^{12} x \cos^{33} x \, dx$$

Generally $$I_{m,n} = \int \sin^m x \cos^n x \, dx$$

It is not necessarily confined to indefinite integration; we can write

$$I_n = \int_0^{\pi/4} \tan^n x \, dx$$

Exercises 9.3

1. Given that $I_n = \int x^n \sin x \, dx$, write down I_4, I_{23}, I_0.

2. Given that $I_{m,n} = \int_0^{\pi/2} x^m \cos nx \, dx$, write down $I_{2,3}$, $I_{4,2}$, $I_{0,4}$, $I_{3,0}$, $I_{0,0}$.

3. Given that $I_{m,n} = \int_0^1 (1 - x)^m x^n \, dx$, write down $I_{1,1}$, $I_{3,4}$, $I_{0,12}$, $I_{23,0}$, $I_{0,0}$.

4. Given that $\int \cos^m x \cos nx \, dx$ is denoted by the symbol $I_{m,n}$, write down the symbols for

(i) $\int \cos^3 x \cos x \, dx$ (ii) $\int \cos^4 x \cos 7x \, dx$

(iii) $\int \cos^{12} x \, dx$ (iv) $\int \cos 9x \, dx$

5. Let the symbol I_n denote $\int \operatorname{cosec}^n x \, dx$. Hence rewrite the following relation, as far as possible, in symbolic form

$$(n-1)\int \operatorname{cosec}^n x \, dx = (n-2)\int \operatorname{cosec}^{n-2} x \, dx - \cos x \operatorname{cosec}^{n-1} x$$

(refer to example 11)

Returning to our initial example

$$I_n = \int x^n \, e^x \, dx$$

integrating by parts

$$I_n = x^n \, e^x - \int nx^{n-1} \, e^x \, dx$$

$$I_n = x^n \, e^x - n\int x^{n-1} \, e^x \, dx$$

$$I_n = x^n \, e^x - nI_{n-1} \ (n \text{ a positive integer}) \tag{9.16}$$

This is an example of a **reduction formula.** The integral I_n has been found in terms of I_{n-1}. The power of x has been reduced. The formula is true for all $n > 0$ and can be applied successively.

Example 9. Evaluate $\int x^3 e^x \, dx$ using the reduction formula 9.16.

$$\int x^3 e^x \, dx = I_3$$

from equation 9.16

$$I_n = x^n e^x - nI_{n-1} \qquad (n > 0)$$

Let $n = 3$; then

$$I_3 = x^3 e^x - 3I_2 \tag{i}$$

Let $n = 2$; then

$$I_2 = x^2 e^x - 2I_1 \tag{ii}$$

From equations (i) and (ii) above

$$\begin{aligned} I_3 &= x^3 e^x - 3[x^2 e^x - 2I_1] \\ &= x^3 e^x - 3x^2 e^x + 6I_1 \end{aligned}$$

Let $n = 1$ in equation 9.16. Then

$$\begin{aligned} I_3 &= x^3 e^x - 3x^2 e^x + 6[xe^x - I_0] \\ &= e^x(x^3 - 3x^2 + 6x) - 6\int e^x \, dx \\ &= e^x(x^3 - 3x^2 + 6x) - 6e^x + C \\ &= e^x(x^3 - 3x^2 + 6x - 6) + C \end{aligned}$$

Sometimes more than one application of the integration by parts formula is needed to obtain the reduction formula.

Example 10. Obtain a reduction formula for $I_n = \int_0^{\pi/2} x^n \cos x \, dx$ and hence evaluate $\int_0^{\pi/2} x^4 \cos x \, dx$.

$$I_n = \int_0^{\pi/2} x^n \cos x \, dx$$

$$= \Big[x^n \sin x\Big]_0^{\pi/2} - \int_0^{\pi/2} nx^{n-1} \sin x \, dx$$

$$= (\pi/2)^n - n\int_0^{\pi/2} x^{n-1} \sin x \, dx$$

Although the power of x has been reduced, the new integral cannot be expressed in terms of I because the integrand involves $\sin x$ instead of $\cos x$. Integrating by parts again

$$I_n = (\pi/2)^n - n\Big[-x^{n-1}\cos x + \int (n-1)x^{n-2}\cos x \, dx\Big]_0^{\pi/2}$$

$$= (\pi/2)^n + \Big[nx^{n-1}\cos x\Big]_0^{\pi/2} - n(n-1)\int_0^{\pi/2} x^{n-2}\cos x \, dx$$

$$= (\pi/2)^n + 0 - n(n-1)\, I_{n-2}$$

$$\therefore \quad I_n = (\pi/2)^n - n(n-1)\, I_{n-2} \qquad (n \geqslant 2) \qquad (9.17)$$

To evaluate $I_4 = \int_0^{\pi/2} x^4 \cos x \, dx$, let $n = 4$ in the reduction formula 9.17

$$\therefore \quad I_4 = (\pi/2)^4 - 4{\cdot}3 \,.\, I_2$$

Using the reduction formula again, with $n = 2$

$$I_4 = (\pi/2)^4 - 12[(\pi/2)^2 - 2.1 \,.\, I_0]$$

$$= (\pi/2)^4 - 3\pi^2 + 24\int_0^{\pi/2} \cos x \, dx$$

$$I_4 = \frac{\pi^4}{16} - 3\pi^2 + 24$$

Manipulation of the integrand is sometimes necessary to obtain the reduction formula.

Example 11. Obtain a reduction formula for $I_n = \int \operatorname{cosec}^n x \, dx$.

To integrate $\operatorname{cosec}^n x$ by parts we note that $\int \operatorname{cosec}^2 x \, dx = -\cot x$ and write

$$I_n = \int \operatorname{cosec}^{n-2} x \operatorname{cosec}^2 x \, dx$$

$$= \operatorname{cosec}^{n-2} x(-\cot x) - \int (n-2)\operatorname{cosec}^{n-3} x(-\operatorname{cosec} x \cot x)(-\cot x)\, dx$$

$$= -\operatorname{cosec}^{n-2} x \cos x/\sin x - (n-2)\int \operatorname{cosec}^{n-2} x \cot^2 x \, dx$$

$$= -\operatorname{cosec}^{n-1} x \cos x - (n-2)\int \operatorname{cosec}^{n-2} x(\operatorname{cosec}^2 x - 1)\, dx$$

$$= -\operatorname{cosec}^{n-1} x \cos x - (n-2)\int \operatorname{cosec}^n x \, dx + (n-2)\int \operatorname{cosec}^{n-2} x \, dx$$

$\therefore \quad I_n = -\operatorname{cosec}^{n-1} x \cos x - (n-2)I_n + (n-2)I_{n-2}$

$$\therefore \quad [1 + (n-2)]I_n = -\operatorname{cosec}^{n-1} x \cos x + (n-2)I_{n-2}$$

$$(n-1)I_n = -\operatorname{cosec}^{n-1} x \cos x + (n-2)I_{n-2} \quad (n \geqslant 2) \qquad (9.18)$$

One of the important uses of reduction formulae is to evaluate the integral

$$I_{m,n} = \int_{p\pi/2}^{q\pi/2} \cos^m x \sin^n x \, dx \qquad (9.19)^*$$

where m, n, p, q are integers.

We note that

$$I_{m,0} = \int_{p\pi/2}^{q\pi/2} \cos^m x \, dx \quad \text{and} \quad I_{0,n} = \int_{p\pi/2}^{q\pi/2} \sin^n x \, dx$$

are special cases of the more general form 9.19.

This integral has already been discussed in section 6.3 (example 16) for the cases when m and/or n are odd.

The indefinite integral will be considered first and denoted by a 'dash'.

Example 12. Obtain a reduction formula for $I'_{m,n} = \int \cos^m x \sin^n x \, dx$.

Neither part of the integrand can be integrated immediately but we note that using the substitution $u = \sin x$

$$\int \cos x \sin^n x \, dx = \frac{\sin^{n+1} x}{(n+1)}$$

and write

$$I'_{m,n} = \int (\cos^{m-1} x)(\cos x \sin^n x) \, dx$$

$$= \frac{\cos^{m-1} x \sin^{n+1} x}{(n+1)} - \int (m-1) \cos^{m-2} x(-\sin x) \frac{\sin^{n+1} x}{(n+1)} \, dx$$

$$= \frac{\cos^{m-1} x \sin^{n+1} x}{(n+1)} + \frac{(m-1)}{(n+1)} \int \cos^{m-2} x \sin^{n+2} x \, dx$$

The power of $\cos x$ has been reduced but the power of $\sin x$ has been increased. However, $\sin^2 x = 1 - \cos^2 x$ and

$$I'_{m,n} = \frac{\cos^{m-1} x \sin^{n+1} x}{(n+1)} + \frac{(m-1)}{(n+1)} \int \cos^{m-2} x \sin^n x(1 - \cos^2 x) \, dx$$

$$= \frac{\cos^{m-1} x \sin^{n+1} x}{(n+1)} + \frac{(m-1)}{(n+1)} \int (\cos^{m-2} x \sin^n x - \cos^m x \sin^n x) \, dx$$

$$= \frac{\cos^{m-1} x \sin^{n+1} x}{(n+1)} + \frac{(m-1)}{(n+1)} I'_{m-2,n} - \frac{(m-1)}{(n+1)} I'_{m,n}$$

Multiplying throughout by $(n+1)$

$$(n+1)I'_{m,n} = \cos^{m-1} x \sin^{n+1} x + (m-1)I'_{m-2,n} - (m-1)I'_{m,n}$$

$$\therefore \quad (m+n)I'_{m,n} = \cos^{m-1} x \sin^{n+1} x + (m-1)I'_{m-2,n}$$

* This integral is generally quoted with 0 and $\pi/2$ as the limits. The use of the more general $p\pi/2$ and $q\pi/2$ extends the usefulness of the reduction formula.

or $$I'_{m,n} = \frac{\cos^{m-1} x \sin^{n+1} x}{(m+n)} + \frac{(m-1)}{(m+n)} I'_{m-2,n} \quad (m \geqslant 2) \qquad (9.20)^*$$

The reduction formula for the definite integral

$$I_{m,n} = \int_{p\pi/2}^{q\pi/2} \cos^m x \sin^n x \, dx$$

is $$I_{m,n} = \left[\frac{\cos^{m-1} x \sin^{n+1} x}{(m+n)}\right]_{p\pi/2}^{q\pi/2} + \frac{(m-1)}{(m+n)} I_{m-2,n}$$

Because both p and q are integers this reduces to

$$I_{m,n} = \frac{(m-1)}{(m+n)} I_{m-2,n} \, (m \geqslant 2) \qquad (9.21)^*$$

A similar formula to reduce the value of n can be obtained by writing the integrand $\cos^m x \sin^n x$ as $(\cos^m x \sin x)(\sin^{n-1} x)$, and it is left as an exercise for the reader to show that

$$I'_{m,n} = \frac{-\cos^{m+1} x \sin^{n-1} x}{(m+n)} + \frac{(n-1)}{(m+n)} I'_{m,n-2} \, (n \geqslant 2) \qquad (9.22)^*$$

and $$I_{m,n} = \frac{(n-1)}{(m+n)} I_{m,n-2} \quad (n \geqslant 2) \qquad (9.23)^*$$

Example 13. Evaluate (i) $\int_{\pi/2}^{3\pi/2} \cos^4 x \sin^2 x \, dx$, (ii) $\int_0^{\pi/2} \sin^7 x \, dx$,

(iii) $\int_{\pi}^{7\pi/2} \cos^4 x \, dx$.

(i) From formula 9.21, with $m = 4$, $n = 2$, $p = 1$, and $q = 3$

$$I_{4,2} = \frac{3}{4+2} I_{2,2}$$
$$= \frac{1}{2} I_{2,2}$$

Using formula 9.21 again with $m = 2$, $n = 2$

$$= \frac{1}{2} \cdot \frac{1}{(2+2)} I_{0,2}$$
$$= \frac{1}{2} \cdot \frac{1}{4} I_{0,2}$$

From formula 9.23 with $m = 0$, $n = 2$, $p = 1$ and $q = 3$

$$I_{4,2} = \frac{1}{8} \cdot \frac{1}{2} I_{0,0}$$
$$= \frac{1}{16} \int_{\pi/2}^{3\pi/2} dx$$
$$= \pi/16$$

* If m is a negative integer $|m-2| > |m|$ and formulae 9.20 and 9.21 can be rearranged to give $I_{m-2,n}$ in terms of $I_{m,n}$ (similarly for formulae 9.22 and 9.23).

(ii) $I_{0,7} = \int_0^{\pi/2} \sin^7 x \, dx$

From formula 9.23, with $m = 0, n = 7, p = 0, q = 1$

$$I_{0,7} = \frac{6}{7} I_{0,5}$$

Repeating the use of formula 9.23 with appropriate values of n

$$I_{0,7} = \frac{6}{7} \cdot \frac{4}{5} I_{0,3}$$

$$= \frac{6}{7} \cdot \frac{4}{5} \cdot \frac{2}{3} I_{0,1}$$

$$= \frac{16}{35} \int_0^{\pi/2} \sin x \, dx$$

$$= 16/35$$

(iii) $I_{4,0} = \int_{\pi}^{7\pi/2} \cos^4 x \, dx$

From formula 9.21

$$I_{4,0} = \frac{3}{4} I_{2,0}$$

$$= \frac{3}{4} \cdot \frac{1}{2} I_{0,0}$$

$$= \frac{3}{8} \int_{\pi}^{7\pi/2} dx$$

$$= 15\pi/16$$

Exercises 9.4

1. Evaluate the following integrals using formulae 9.21 and 9.23:

(i) $\int_0^{3\pi/2} \sin^6 x \cos^8 x \, dx$ (ii) $\int_{\pi/2}^{\pi} \sin^7 x \cos^6 x \, dx$

(iii) $\int_0^{5\pi/2} \sin^4 x \cos^9 x \, dx$ (iv) $\int_0^{\pi/2} \sin^7 x \cos^5 x \, dx$

(v) $\int_0^{\pi/2} \sin^{10} x \, dx$ (vi) $\int_{\pi}^{2\pi} \cos^8 x \, dx$

(vii) $\int_0^{\pi/2} \cos^9 x \, dx$ (viii) $\int_0^{\pi/2} \sin^5 x \, dx$

2. Using the reduction formula 9.18, evaluate $\int \operatorname{cosec}^4 x \, dx$.

3. Show that $\tan^n x = \tan^{n-2} x(\sec^2 x - 1)$. Hence if $I_n = \int_0^{\pi/4} \tan^n x \, dx$, prove that

$$I_n = \frac{1}{(n-1)} - I_{n-2} \quad (n \geqslant 2)$$

and evaluate I_5.

4. Show that $\cot^n x = \cot^{n-2} x(\operatorname{cosec}^2 x - 1)$. Hence if $I_n = \int_{\pi/4}^{\pi/2} \cot^n x \, dx$, prove that

$$I_n = \frac{1}{(n-1)} - I_{n-2} \quad (n \geqslant 2)$$

and evaluate I_6.

5. Given that $I_{m,n} = \int_0^1 x^m(1-x)^n \, dx$, prove that

$$I_{m,n} = \frac{n}{(m+n+1)} I_{m,n-1} \qquad (n \geqslant 1)$$

and evaluate $I_{4,4}$.

6. Given that $I_n = \int (\ln x)^n \, dx$, prove that

$$I_n = x(\ln x)^n - nI_{n-1} \qquad (n \geqslant 1)$$

and evaluate I_3.

7. Given that $I = \int_0^a e^x \cos x \, dx$ and $J = \int_0^a e^x \sin x \, dx$, show that

$$I = e^a \sin a - J \qquad \text{and} \qquad J = 1 - e^a \cos a + I$$

Hence evaluate $\int_0^{\pi/2} e^x \cos x \, dx$.

8. By integrating by parts twice, verify the value for $\int e^{ax} \sin bx \, dx$ given in formula 9.12. Similarly verify the result 9.13 for $\int e^{ax} \cos bx \, dx$.

9.6 Some Properties of Definite Integrals

We recall that when evaluating $\int f(x)dx$, we assumed that both a and b are finite and that $f(x)$ is continuous and finite throughout the range a to b. The cases when a and/or b are infinite, or $f(x)$ is undefined in the range a to b, will be considered in the next two sections.

Theorem I

$$\int_a^b f(x)dx = -\int_b^a f(x)dx \qquad (9.24)$$

That is, the interchange of the limits changes the sign of the definite integral.

It follows that $\int_a^a f(x)dx = 0$.

If $F(x)$ is the appropriate indefinite integral of $f(x)$

$$\int_a^b f(x)dx = F(b) - F(a)$$

and

$$\begin{aligned}\int_b^a f(x)dx &= F(a) - F(b)\\ &= -[F(b) - F(a)]\\ &= -\int_a^b f(x)dx\end{aligned}$$

Theorem II $$\int_a^b f(x)\mathrm{d}x = \int_a^c f(x)\mathrm{d}x + \int_c^b f(x)\mathrm{d}x \qquad (9.25)$$

$$\begin{aligned}\int_a^c f(x)\mathrm{d}x + \int_c^b f(x)\mathrm{d}x &= [F(c) - F(a)] + [F(b) - F(c)] \\ &= F(c) - F(a) + F(b) - F(c) \\ &= F(b) - F(a) \\ &= \int_a^b f(x)\mathrm{d}x\end{aligned}$$

The value of c can lie within the range a to b or outside it. This can be illustrated by representing the definite integral as an area under the curve $y = f(x)$: see Fig. 9.1(*a*) and (*b*), where the particular case of $f(x) > 0$

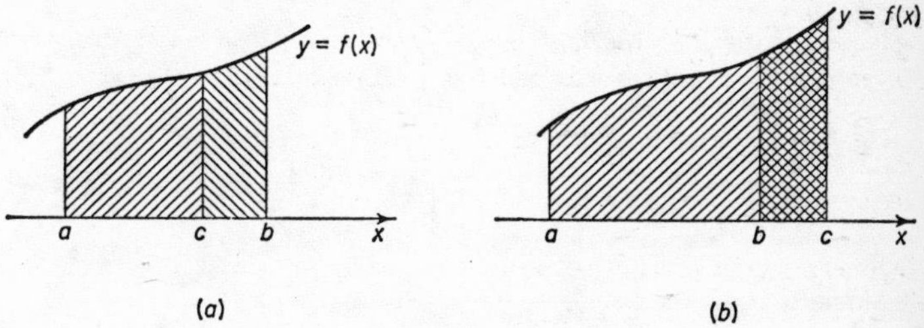

Fig. 9.1

throughout the range is illustrated. In the first case the two part areas are added. In the second case

$$\int_c^b f(x)\mathrm{d}x = -\int_b^c f(x)\mathrm{d}x$$

and the second part area is subtracted from the first. In both cases we obtain the area under the curve from $x = a$ to $x = b$ which represents

$$\int_a^b f(x)\mathrm{d}x$$

Theorem III $$\int_a^b f(x)\mathrm{d}x = \int_a^b f(z)\mathrm{d}z = \int_a^b f(w)\mathrm{d}w = \ldots \qquad (9.26)$$

That is, the definite integral is a function of its limits and $x, z, w, \ldots$ are pseudo-variables. For example

$$\int_a^b 3x^2\,\mathrm{d}x = [x^3]_a^b = b^3 - a^3$$

$$\int_a^b 3z^2\,\mathrm{d}z = [z^3]_a^b = b^3 - a^3$$

This is illustrated in Fig. 9.2. The algebraic sum of the areas between the curve and the axis is not altered when the axis is relabelled.

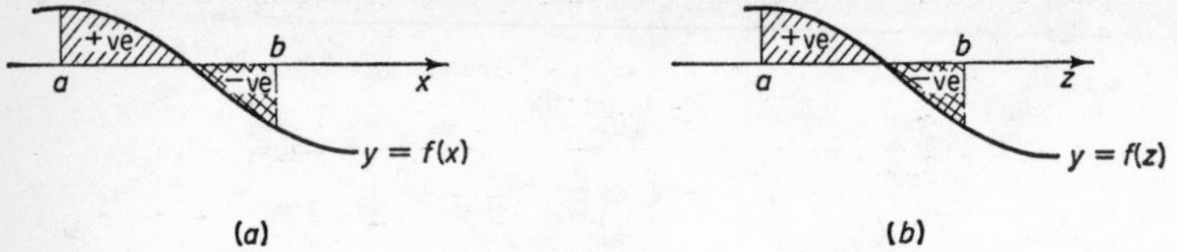

Fig. 9.2

Example 14. Prove that $\int_{1/a}^{a} \frac{\ln z}{(z^2+1)} dz = 0 \qquad (a > 0)$

Let $$I = \int_{1/a}^{a} \frac{\ln z}{(z^2+1)} dz$$

Using the substitution $z = 1/u$, $dz = -(1/u^2)\,du$, when $z = a$, $u = 1/a$, when $z = 1/a$, $u = a$.

$$\therefore \qquad I = \int_{a}^{1/a} \frac{\ln\left(\frac{1}{u}\right)}{\left[\left(\frac{1}{u}\right)^2 + 1\right]} \left(-\frac{1}{u^2} du\right)$$

$$= \int_{a}^{1/a} \frac{-\ln u}{(1+u^2)} (-\,du)$$

$$= \int_{a}^{1/a} \frac{\ln u}{(u^2+1)} du$$

$$= -\int_{1/a}^{a} \frac{\ln u}{(u^2+1)} du \qquad \text{(by Theorem I)}$$

$$= -\int_{1/a}^{a} \frac{\ln z}{z^2+1} dz \qquad \text{(by Theorem III)}$$

$$\therefore \qquad I = -I$$

$$2I = 0$$

$$I = 0$$

What appears to be a triviality, but is nevertheless often overlooked, is

Theorem IV $$\int_a^b f(x)dx + \int_a^b g(x)dx = \int_a^b [f(x) + g(x)]dx$$

It is important that the limits are identical and that the separate integrals exist.

Example 15. Prove that

$$\int_0^{\pi/2} \frac{\cos^3 x}{(\cos^3 x + \sin^3 x)} dx = \int_0^{\pi/2} \frac{\sin^3 x}{(\cos^3 x + \sin^3 x)} dx$$

Hence evaluate the integrals.

Let
$$I = \int_0^{\pi/2} \frac{\cos^3 x}{(\cos^3 x + \sin^3 x)}\,dx$$

and let $x = \pi/2 - u$; then $dx = -du$, and when $x = 0$, $u = \pi/2$, when $x = \pi/2$ $u = 0$.

$$\therefore \quad I = \int_{\pi/2}^{0} \frac{\cos^3\left(\frac{\pi}{2} - u\right)}{\left[\cos^3\left(\frac{\pi}{2} - u\right) + \sin^3\left(\frac{\pi}{2} - u\right)\right]}(-du)$$

$$= -\int_{\pi/2}^{0} \frac{\sin^3 u}{(\sin^3 u + \cos^3 u)}\,du$$

$$= \int_0^{\pi/2} \frac{\sin^3 u}{(\sin^3 u + \cos^3 u)}\,du \qquad \text{(from Theorem I)}$$

$$= \int_0^{\pi/2} \frac{\sin^3 x}{(\sin^3 x + \cos^3 x)}\,dx \qquad \text{(from Theorem III)}$$

as was required.

To evaluate the integrals

$$2I = \int_0^{\pi/2} \frac{\sin^3 x}{(\sin^3 x + \cos^3 x)}\,dx + \int_0^{\pi/2} \frac{\cos^3 x}{(\sin^3 x + \cos^3 x)}\,dx$$

$$= \int_0^{\pi/2} \left[\frac{\sin^3 x}{(\sin^3 x + \cos^3 x)} + \frac{\cos^3 x}{(\sin^3 x + \cos^3 x)}\right] dx \qquad \text{(by Theorem IV)}$$

$$= \int_0^{\pi/2} \frac{(\sin^3 x + \cos^3 x)}{(\sin^3 x + \cos^3 x)}\,dx$$

$$= \int_0^{\pi/2} 1 \,.\, dx$$

$$= \pi/2$$

$$\therefore \quad I = \pi/4$$

Theorem IV can also be of value when proving a given reduction formula.

Example 16. Given that $I_n = \int_0^{\pi/2} \frac{\cos(2n + 1)\theta}{\cos\theta}\,d\theta$, prove that $I_n = -I_{n-1}$ $(n > 0)$.

Hence show that $I_n = (-1)^n\,\pi/2$ for all positive integral values of n.

$$I_n + I_{n-1} = \int_0^{\pi/2} \frac{\cos(2n + 1)\theta}{\cos\theta}\,d\theta + \int_0^{\pi/2} \frac{\cos(2n - 1)\theta}{\cos\theta}\,d\theta$$

$$= \int_0^{\pi/2} \frac{[\cos(2n + 1)\theta + \cos(2n - 1)\theta]}{\cos\theta}\,d\theta \qquad \text{(by Theorem IV)}$$

$$= \int_0^{\pi/2} \frac{2\cos 2n\theta\cos\theta}{\cos\theta}\,d\theta$$

$$= \int_0^{\pi/2} 2\cos 2n\theta\,d\theta$$

$$= \left[\frac{\sin 2n\theta}{n}\right]_0^{\pi/2}$$

$$= \frac{1}{n}[\sin n\pi - \sin 0]$$

$\therefore \quad I_n + I_{n-1} = 0$

and $\qquad I_n = -I_{n-1}$

Repeated applications of this result when n is a positive integer give

$$\begin{aligned} I_n &= -I_{n-1} = (-1)^2 I_{n-2} = (-1)^3 I_{n-3} = \ldots \\ &= (-1)^n I_0 \\ &= (-1)^n \int_0^{\pi/2} \frac{\cos\theta}{\cos\theta}\, d\theta \\ &= (-1)^n \pi/2 \end{aligned}$$

Theorem V depends on $f(x)$ having special properties. It is concerned with odd and even functions.

Definition. A function $f(x)$ is said to be *even* if its domain contains $-x$ whenever it contains x and $f(-x) = f(x)$ for all x in its domain.

For example, $f(x) = x^2 + 6/x^4 + 4$ $(x \neq 0)$ is an even function because

$$f(-x) = (-x)^2 + \frac{6}{(-x)^4} + 4 = x^2 + \frac{6}{x^4} + 4 = f(x) \quad (x \neq 0)$$

The functions $\cos x$, $\cosh ax$, $\operatorname{sech} ax$ and $\sec x$ $[x \neq (2n+1)\pi/2]$ are other examples and their expansions in series (refer to exercises 8.6) contain only a constant and even powers of x.

The graphs of such functions are symmetrical about the axis of y, as shown in Fig. 9.3.

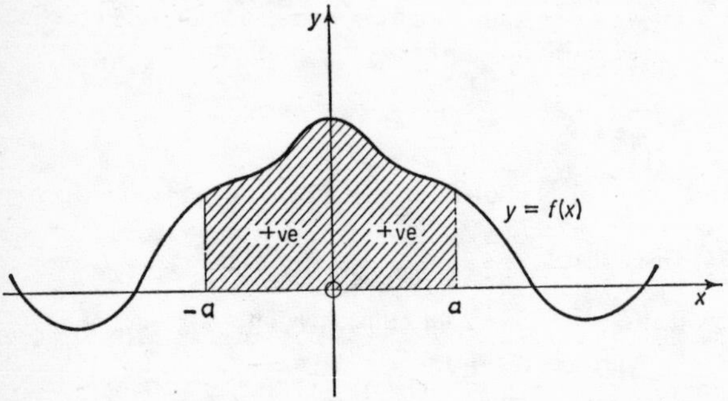

Fig. 9.3

Definition. A function $f(x)$ is said to be *odd* if its domain contains $-x$ whenever it contains x and $f(-x) = -f(x)$ for all x in its domain.

For example, $f(x) = 4x^3 - 7/x$ $(x \neq 0)$ is an odd function because

$$f(-x) = 4(-x)^3 - \frac{7}{(-x)} = -4x^3 + \frac{7}{x} = -f(x) \quad (x \neq 0)$$

The functions $\tan x$ $[x \neq (2n+1)\pi/2]$, $\sin x$, and $\sinh x$ are other examples and their expansions in series (refer to exercises 8.6) contain only odd powers of x. If $f(x)$ is an odd function and its domain includes the value $x = 0$, then $f(0) = 0$ because by definition

$$f(-x) = -f(x)$$

$$\therefore \qquad f(-0) = -f(0)$$

or $$f(0) = -f(0)$$

and therefore $$f(0) = 0$$

The graphs of such functions have symmetry about the origin (see Fig. 9.4).

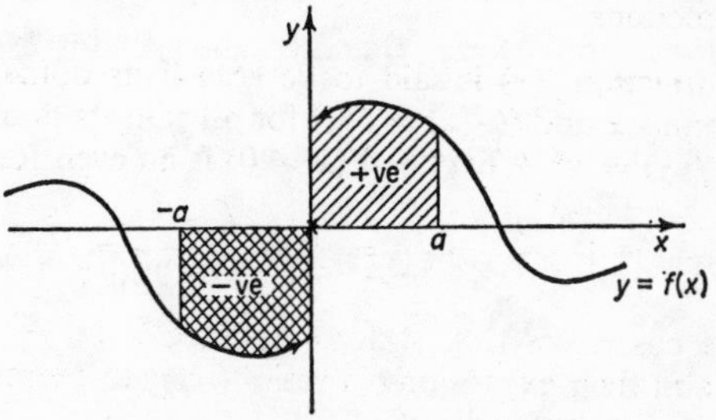

Fig. 9.4

Most functions are neither odd nor even but if their domain includes all values of x they can be split into two parts, one of which defines an even function and the other an odd function. For example

$$e^x = \tfrac{1}{2}e^x + \tfrac{1}{2}e^x \qquad \text{(all } x\text{)}$$

Adding and subtracting $\frac{1}{2}e^{-x}$

$$= \tfrac{1}{2}e^x + \tfrac{1}{2}e^{-x} + \tfrac{1}{2}e^x - \tfrac{1}{2}e^{-x}$$
$$= \cosh x + \sinh x \qquad \text{(all } x\text{)}$$

Now $\cosh(-x) = \cosh x$ (all x) and $\cosh x$ is an even function

and $\sinh(-x) = -\sinh x$ (all x) and $\sinh x$ is an odd function

Theorem V $\displaystyle\int_{-a}^{a} f(x)dx = 0$ if $f(x)$ is an odd function

$$= 2\int_0^a f(x)dx \text{ if } f(x) \text{ is an even function}$$

Let $$I = \int_{-a}^{a} f(x)dx = \int_{-a}^{0} f(x)dx + \int_0^a f(x)dx \quad \text{(Theorem II)}$$

In the first integral on the right-hand side, let $x = -y$: then $dx = -dy$ and when $x = -a$, $y = a$ and when $x = 0$, $y = 0$.

$$\therefore \quad \int_{-a}^{a} f(x)dx = \int_{a}^{0} f(-y)(-dy) + \int_{0}^{a} f(x)dx$$

$$= \int_{0}^{a} f(-y)dy + \int_{0}^{a} f(x)dx \quad \text{(Theorem I)}$$

$$= \int_{0}^{a} f(-x)dx + \int_{0}^{a} f(x)dx \quad \text{(Theorem III)}$$

$$= \int_{0}^{a} [f(-x) + f(x)]dx \quad \text{(Theorem IV)}$$

If $f(x)$ is odd $f(-x) = -f(x)$ and the integrand is zero

If $f(x)$ is even $f(-x) = f(x)$ and the integrand is $2f(x)$

The results follow.

From the definitions it follows that the product of an even function and an odd function is an odd function.

Let $F(x) = f(x)\,g(x)$

where $f(x)$ is odd $\therefore \; f(-x) = -f(x)$

and $g(x)$ is even $\therefore \; g(-x) = g(x)$

(all defined within a common domain).

Then $F(-x) = f(-x)g(-x) = -f(x)g(x) = -F(x)$

The rules for such products follow those for the products of + and − signs and their proofs are left as an exercise for the reader.

$$\left.\begin{array}{rl} \text{Odd} \times \text{Odd} = \text{Even} & (-) \times (-) = (+) \\ \text{Even} \times \text{Odd} = \text{Odd} \times \text{Even} = \text{Odd} & (-) \times (+) = (-) \\ \text{Even} \times \text{Even} = \text{Even} & (+) \times (+) = (+) \end{array}\right\} \quad (9.27)$$

Example 17

$$\int_{-\pi}^{\pi} \sin^3 x \cosh x \, dx = \int_{-\pi}^{\pi} \text{Odd function } dx \quad [(-)^3(+) = (-)]$$

$$= 0$$

$$\int_{-1}^{+1} x^2 \sinh x \, dx = \int_{-1}^{+1} \text{Odd function } dx \quad [(+)(-) = (-)]$$

$$= 0$$

$$\int_{-2}^{+2} (3x^3 + 5x^7)\, dx = \int_{-2}^{2} 3x^3 \, dx + \int_{-2}^{2} 5x^7 \, dx$$

$$= \int_{-2}^{2} \text{Odd function } dx + \int_{-2}^{2} \text{Odd function } dx$$

$$= 0 + 0$$

$$= 0$$

A result similar to Theorem V is obtained when $f(2a - x) = f(x)$ or $-f(x)$ $(0 \leqslant x \leqslant 2a)$, but it is not of such practical importance

Theorem VI $$\int_0^{2a} f(x)dx = 0 \text{ if } f(2a - x) = -f(x)$$

$$= 2\int_0^{a} f(x)dx \text{ if } f(2a - x) = f(x)$$

This can be proved by writing

$$\int_0^{2a} = \int_0^{a} + \int_a^{2a}$$

and substituting $x = (2a - y)$ in the second integral. The result is interpreted geometrically in terms of areas in Fig. 9.5.

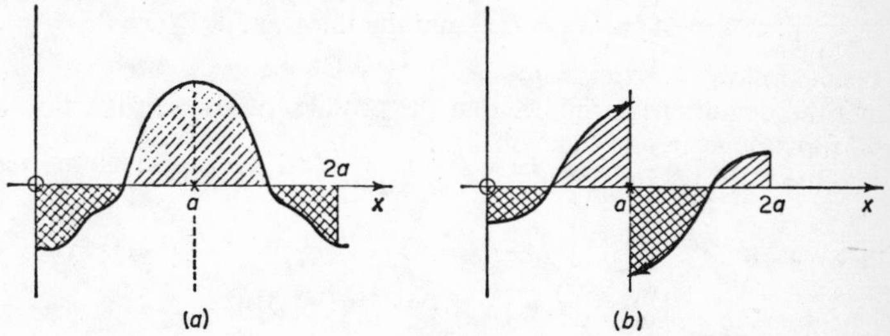

Fig. 9.5

Another result sometimes quoted as a theorem is

$$\int_0^{a} f(x)dx = \int_0^{a} f(a - x)dx$$

which is proved by the substitution $x = a - y$ and shows that it is only a particular substitution dignified by the name of a theorem. We have already used it in example 15.

Revision Questions 9.2

Complete the following statements	*Answers*	*Refer to*
1. A definite integral is a function of . . .	**1.** its limits.	Section 9.6, Theorem III
2. In $\int_a^b f(x)\,dx$, x is known as a . . .	**2.** pseudo-variable.	Section 9.6, Theorem III
3. (Odd function)^3 × (Even function) = . . .	**3.** Odd function.	Notes after Section 9.6, Theorem V
4. (Odd function)^2 × (Even function)^3 = . . .	**4.** Even function.	Notes after Section 9.6, Theorem V
5. $\int_{-a}^{a}$ (Odd function) dx = . . .	**5.** Zero.	Theorem V

Exercises 9.5

1. Use the substitution $x = \pi/2 - y$ to prove that

$$\int_0^{\pi/2} \frac{(2\cos x + \sin x)}{(\cos x + \sin x)}\,dx = \int_0^{\pi/2} \frac{(\cos x + 2\sin x)}{(\cos x + \sin x)}\,dx$$

Hence, by considering the sum of the two integrals, prove that each has the value $3\pi/4$.

2. Use the substitution $y = -u$ to prove that

$$\int_{-2}^{2} \frac{y^4\,dy}{(e^y + 1)} = \int_{-2}^{2} \frac{y^4 e^y\,dy}{(e^y + 1)}$$

Hence, by considering the sum of the two integrals, prove that each has a value of 32/5.

3. Given that

$$I_n = \int_0^{\pi/2} \frac{\sin (2n + 1)x}{\sin x}\,dx$$

prove that $I_n - I_{n-1} = 0$. Hence show that $I_n = \pi/2$ for all positive integral values of n.

4. Prove that

$$\int_0^a f(x)\,dx = \int_0^{a/2} [f(x) + f(a - x)]\,dx$$

Hence prove that

$$\int_0^{\pi} x \sin^6 x\,dx = \pi \int_0^{\pi/2} \sin^6 x\,dx$$

and evaluate this integral by means of the reduction formula 9.23.

5. Define an odd function. From your definition prove that the integrands of all the following integrals are odd functions and that therefore the value of each integral is zero:

(i) $\displaystyle\int_{-\pi}^{\pi} x^3 \sin^4 x \cos^5 x\,dx$ (ii) $\displaystyle\int_{-\pi/4}^{\pi/4} \frac{x^3}{\cos^4 x}\,dx$

(iii) $\displaystyle\int_{-\pi/2}^{\pi/2} \sin^5 x \cos^3 x\,dx$

6. Given that

$$\int_{1/\sqrt{3}}^{\sqrt{3}} \frac{\ln x}{(x^2 + 1)}\,dx = 0$$

use the substitution $x = \sqrt{3}/z$ to prove that

$$\int_1^3 \frac{\ln x}{(x^2 + 3)}\,dx = \frac{\pi\sqrt{3}\ln 3}{36}$$

(Hint: $\ln (\sqrt{3}/z) = \frac{1}{2}\ln 3 - \ln z$.)

7. Prove that

$$\int_0^{\pi/2} \frac{(4\cos x - 3\sin x)}{(\cos x + \sin x)}\,dx = \int_0^{\pi/2} \frac{(4\sin x - 3\cos x)}{(\cos x + \sin x)}\,dx = \pi/4$$

(refer to questions 1 and 2).

8. Prove that

$$\int_0^{\pi} (x - \pi/2)^6 \cos^3 x \, dx = -\int_{-\pi/2}^{\pi/2} x^6 \sin^3 x \, dx = 0$$

9. The function $f(x)$ is defined by

$$\begin{aligned} f(x) &= -2 && x \leqslant -2 \\ f(x) &= x && -2 < x < 2 \\ f(x) &= 2 && x \geqslant 2 \end{aligned}$$

(Note: All the above define *one* function.) Verify that $f(x)$ is an odd function and hence that $\int_{-a}^{a} f(x) \, dx = 0$ for all values of a. Sketch its graph.

10. The function $f(x)$ is defined by

$$\begin{aligned} f(x) &= 0 && x < -\pi \\ f(x) &= -x - \pi && -\pi \leqslant x < -\pi/2 \\ f(x) &= x && -\pi/2 \leqslant x \leqslant \pi/2 \\ f(x) &= \pi - x && \pi/2 < x \leqslant \pi \\ f(x) &= 0 && x > \pi \end{aligned}$$

(Note: All the above define *one* function.) Verify that $f(x)$ is an odd function and hence that $\int_{-a}^{a} f(x) \, dx = 0$ for all values of a. Sketch its graph.

9.7 Infinite Integrals

An infinite integral is one in which either one or both of the limits of integration are infinite and we define

$$\int_a^{\infty} f(x)dx = \lim_{X \to \infty} \int_a^X f(x)dx \tag{9.28}$$

if this limit exists

$$\int_{-\infty}^{a} f(x)dx = \lim_{X \to -\infty} \int_X^a f(x)dx \tag{9.29}$$

if this limit exists.

If both these limits exist *independently* then

$$\int_{-\infty}^{\infty} f(x)dx = \int_{-\infty}^{a} f(x)dx + \int_a^{\infty} f(x)dx \tag{9.30}$$

Example 18. Find, where possible, the values of the following integrals:

(i) $\int_1^{\infty} x^{-2} \, dx$, (ii) $\int_1^{\infty} x^{-1} \, dx$, (iii) $\int_{-\infty}^{0} e^{-x} \, dx$, (iv) $\int_{-\infty}^{\infty} \frac{dx}{(x^2 + 4)}$

(i)
$$\int_1^X x^{-2} \, dx = \Big[-x^{-1}\Big]_1^X = 1 - \frac{1}{X}$$

as $X \to \infty$, $\quad \frac{1}{X} \to 0$

$$\therefore \qquad \int_1^{\infty} x^{-2} \, dx = \lim_{X \to \infty} \left(1 - \frac{1}{X}\right) = 1$$

(ii)
$$\int_1^X x^{-1}\,dx = \Big[\ln x\Big]_1^X = \ln X$$

$$\therefore \quad \int_1^\infty x^{-1}\,dx = \underset{X\to\infty}{\text{limit}}\,(\ln X)$$

There is no limit to $\ln X$ as X increases indefinitely; therefore $\int_1^\infty x^{-1}\,dx$ does not exist.

(iii)
$$\int_X^0 e^x\,dx = \Big[e^x\Big]_X^0 = (1 - e^X)$$

$$\therefore \quad \int_{-\infty}^0 e^x\,dx = \underset{X\to-\infty}{\text{limit}}\,(1 - e^X)$$

Let $X = -N$; therefore $N \to +\infty$ as $X \to -\infty$

and
$$\int_{-\infty}^0 e^x\,dx = \underset{N\to\infty}{\text{limit}}\,(1 - e^{-N})$$
$$= \underset{N\to\infty}{\text{limit}}\left(1 - \frac{1}{e^N}\right)$$
$$= 1$$

(iv)
$$\int_{-\infty}^\infty \frac{dx}{(x^2+4)} = \int_{-\infty}^a \frac{dx}{(x^2+4)} + \int_a^\infty \frac{dx}{(x^2+4)}$$

where a is any convenient value, say 0.

$$\int_{+X}^0 \frac{dx}{(x^2+4)} = \left[\frac{1}{2}\tan^{-1}x\right]_X^0 = \left(-\frac{1}{2}\tan^{-1}X\right)$$

$$\therefore \quad \int_{-\infty}^0 \frac{dx}{(x^2+4)} = \underset{X\to-\infty}{\text{limit}}\left(-\frac{1}{2}\tan^{-1}X\right) = -\frac{1}{2}(-\pi/2) = \pi/4$$

$$\int_0^X \frac{dx}{(x^2+4)} = \left[\frac{1}{2}\tan^{-1}\frac{x}{2}\right]_0^X = \left(\frac{1}{2}\tan^{-1}\frac{X}{2}\right)$$

$$\therefore \quad \int_0^\infty \frac{dx}{(x^2+4)} = \underset{X\to\infty}{\text{limit}}\left(\frac{1}{2}\tan^{-1}\frac{X}{2}\right) = \pi/4$$

$$\therefore \quad \int_{-\infty}^\infty \frac{dx}{(x^2+4)} = \pi/4 + \pi/4 = \pi/2$$

Exercises 9.6

Find, where possible, the values of the following integrals:

1. $\int_1^\infty 1/\sqrt{x^3}\,dx$

2. $\int_1^\infty \ln x\,dx$

3. $\int_0^\infty xe^{-x^2}\,dx$

4. $\int_{-\infty}^{-\sqrt{2}} \frac{dx}{x\sqrt{(x^2-1)}}$

5. $\int_{-\infty}^\infty \frac{dx}{(a^2+x^2)}$ (where a is a positive integer).

6. Given that $u_n = \int_0^\infty x^n e^{-x}\,dx$, prove that $u_n = nu_{n-1}$. If n is a positive integer deduce that $u_n = n!$.

7. Prove that

$$\int_0^{\infty} e^{-ax} \cos b\,x\,dx = \frac{a}{(a^2 + b^2)}$$

where a and b are constants (refer to formula 9.13), given that

$$\lim_{X \to \infty} \left\{ e^{-ax} \left[\frac{-a \cos bx + b \sin bx}{(a^2 + b^2)} \right] \right\} = 0$$

8. In the theory of servomechanisms the amplitude spectrum F of a signal is given by

$$F = \int_0^{\infty} Ee^{-kt}\,dt$$

where E and k are constants. Verify that the integral exists and has the value E/k.

9. In Bohr's theory of the atom the potential energy U of an orbital electron is given by

$$U = -\int_r^{\infty} \frac{Ze^2}{x^2}\,dx$$

where Z and e are the charges on the nucleus and the electron respectively. Show that the integral exists and that $U = -Ze^2/r$.

10. From the kinetic theory of matter the arithmetic mean speed $\bar{v}$ of the molecules is given by

$$\bar{v} = 4\pi \left(\frac{m}{2\pi kT}\right)^{\frac{3}{2}} \int_0^{\infty} e^{-mv^2/2kT}\,v^3\,dv$$

where k is the Boltzmann Constant, T the absolute temperature, m the mass of each molecule and v the speed of any particular molecule. Using the substitution $x = mv^2/2kT$, show that

$$\bar{v} = \left(\frac{8kT}{\pi m}\right)^{\frac{1}{2}} \int_0^{\infty} e^{-x}\,x\,dx$$

Verify that the integral exists and has the value unity, and therefore that

$$\bar{v} = \left(\frac{8kT}{\pi m}\right)^{\frac{1}{2}}$$

9.8 Improper Integrals

When defining the definite integral

$$\int_a^b f(x)\,dx$$

it was assumed that the integrand $f(x)$ was finite and continuous for all values in the range of integration $a \leqslant x \leqslant b$. We shall now extend the definition to include cases when the integrand becomes infinite when $x = a$, or $x = b$, or at a point within the range of integration.

Definition. Given that $x = a$ is a point where $f(x)$ becomes infinite, we define

$$\int_a^b f(x)\,dx = \lim_{h \to 0} \int_{a+h}^b f(x)\,dx \qquad (h \text{ positive}) \qquad (9.31)$$

where this limit exists.

Similarly, if $f(x)$ is infinite when $x = b$

$$\int_a^b f(x)\mathrm{d}x = \underset{h'\to 0}{\text{limit}} \int_a^{b-h'} f(x)\mathrm{d}x \qquad (h' \text{ positive}) \tag{9.32}$$

If $f(x)$ is infinite when $x = c$, where $a < c < b$, we define

$$\int_a^b f(x)\mathrm{d}x = \underset{h\to 0}{\text{limit}} \int_a^{c-h} f(x)\mathrm{d}x + \underset{h'\to 0}{\text{limit}} \int_{c+h'}^{b} f(x)\mathrm{d}x \tag{9.33}$$

where both h and h' are positive and both limits exist as h and h' tend to zero *independently*.

Example 19. Find, where possible, the values of the integrals

(i) $\displaystyle\int_0^{\pi/2} \sec^2 x \,\mathrm{d}x$, (ii) $\displaystyle\int_{-2}^{7} \frac{\mathrm{d}x}{\sqrt{(x+2)}}$, (iii) $\displaystyle\int_{-8}^{1} x^{-\frac{2}{3}}\,\mathrm{d}x$

(i) When $x = \pi/2$, $\sec^2 x$ is infinite. Therefore by formula 9.31 consider

$$\int_0^{(\pi/2-h)} \sec^2 x \,\mathrm{d}x = \Big[\tan x\Big]_0^{(\pi/2-h)} = \tan\left(\frac{\pi}{2} - h\right)$$

There is no limit to the value of $\tan\left(\frac{\pi}{2} - h\right)$ as $h \to 0$; therefore $\int_0^{\pi/2} \sec^2 x \,\mathrm{d}x$ does not exist.

(ii) When $x = -2$, $1/\sqrt{(x+2)}$ is infinite; therefore consider

$$\int_{-2+h}^{7} \frac{1}{\sqrt{(x+2)}}\,\mathrm{d}x = \Big[2\sqrt{(x+2)}\Big]_{-2+h}^{7}$$
$$= (6 - 2\sqrt{h})$$

as $h \to 0$, $(6 - 2\sqrt{h}) \to 6$

$$\therefore \qquad \int_{-2}^{7} \frac{\mathrm{d}x}{\sqrt{(x+2)}} = 6$$

(iii) When $x = 0$, $x^{-\frac{2}{3}}$ is infinite; therefore consider

$$\int_{-8}^{0-h} x^{-\frac{2}{3}}\,\mathrm{d}x + \int_{0+h}^{1} x^{-\frac{2}{3}}\,\mathrm{d}x$$

(a) $$\int_{-8}^{0-h} x^{-\frac{2}{3}}\,\mathrm{d}x = \Big[3x^{\frac{1}{3}}\Big]_{-8}^{0-h} = (-3h^{\frac{1}{3}} + 6)$$

as $h \to 0$, $(-3h^{\frac{1}{3}} + 6) \to 6$

(b) $$\int_{0+h'}^{1} x^{-\frac{2}{3}}\,\mathrm{d}x = \Big[3x^{\frac{1}{3}}\Big]_{0+h'}^{1} = [3 - 3(h')^{\frac{1}{3}}]$$

as $h' \to 0$, $[3 - 3(h')^{\frac{1}{3}}] \to 3$

$$\therefore \qquad \int_{-8}^{1} x^{-\frac{2}{3}}\,\mathrm{d}x = 6 + 3 = 9$$

Exercises 9.7

Find, where possible, the values of the following integrals:

1. $\displaystyle\int_{-1}^{3} \frac{1}{\sqrt{(3-x)}}\,\mathrm{d}x$

2. $\displaystyle\int_{-1}^{7} (x+1)^{-\frac{2}{3}}\,\mathrm{d}x$

3. $\int_0^1 \ln x\, dx$

4. $\int_{\pi/2}^{3\pi/2} \operatorname{cosec}^2 x\, dx$

5. $\int_0^8 \frac{dx}{\sqrt{x(8-x)}}$

6. $\int_{-\pi/4}^{\pi/4} \frac{\sec^2 x\, dx}{\sqrt{(\tan x)}}$

7. $\int_0^2 \frac{(3+x)}{\sqrt{(6x+x^2)}}\, dx$

8. $\int_2^4 \frac{dx}{\sqrt{(x^2-4)}}$

9. $\int_0^{\ln 2} \coth x\, dx$

10. $\int_0^1 \frac{\ln x}{x}\, dx$

9.9 Numerical Integration—Simpson's Rule

Sometimes the indefinite integral of a function $f(x)$ cannot be found or $f(x)$ is given as a table of values or a digital computer is being used to solve a problem. In these cases a good method of approximating to the value of the definite integral

$$\int_{x_1}^{x_2} f(x)dx$$

is to use **Simpson's Rule.**

Suppose that the range of integration x_1 to x_2 is of length $2h$ and that a is the midpoint. Then

$$x_1 = a - h \quad \text{and} \quad x_2 = a + h$$

and the integral can be written in the form

$$\int_{a-h}^{a+h} f(x)dx$$

Simpson's Rule states that

$$\int_{a-h}^{a+h} f(x)dx \simeq \frac{h}{3}(y_1 + 4y_2 + y_3) \tag{9.34*}$$

where $\quad y_1 = f(a-h), \quad y_2 = f(a), \quad y_3 = f(a+h)\ldots \qquad$ (i)

To prove it we use Taylor's Theorem (see section 8.7). Use the substitution $x = a + z$; then $dx = dz$ and when $x = a - h$, $z = -h$, when $x = a + h$, $z = h$.

$$\therefore \quad \int_{a-h}^{a+h} f(x)dx = \int_{-h}^{h} f(a+z)dz$$

$$= \int_{-h}^{h}\left[f(a) + zf'(a) + \frac{z^2}{2!}f''(a) + \frac{z^3}{3!}f'''(a) + \ldots\right]dz$$

(by Taylor's Theorem)

$$= \left[zf(a) + \frac{z^2}{2!}f'(a) + \frac{z^3}{3!}f''(a) + \frac{z^4}{4!}f'''(a) + \ldots\right]_{-h}^{h}$$

$$\simeq 2h\left[f(a) + \frac{h^2}{3!}f''(a) + \frac{h^4}{5!}f^{\text{iv}}(a)\ldots\right] \tag{ii}$$

* The rule is exact if (x) is a quadratic or a cubic function.

From equation (i) above,

$$y_1 + y_3 = f(a - h) + f(a + h)$$

$$= \left[f(a) - hf'(a) + \frac{h^2}{2!}f''(a) \ldots\right]$$

$$+ \left[f(a) + hf'(a) + \frac{h^2}{2!}f''(a) + \ldots\right]$$

(by Taylor's Theorem)

$$= 2f(a) + \frac{2h^2}{2!}f''(a) + \frac{2h^4}{4!}f^{\text{iv}}(a) + \ldots$$

$$\therefore \quad \frac{1}{3}h(y_1 + 4y_2 + y_3)$$

$$= \frac{1}{3}h\left[2f(a) + \frac{2h^2}{2!}f''(a) + \frac{2h^4}{4!}f^{\text{iv}}(a) + \ldots + 4f(a)\right]$$

$$= 2h\left[f(a) + \frac{h^2 f''(a)}{3!} + \frac{h^4 f^{\text{iv}}(a)}{3 \times 4!} \ldots\right] \qquad \text{(iii)}$$

Comparing equations (ii) and (iii)

$$\int_{a-h}^{a+h} f(x)\mathrm{d}x \simeq 2h\left[f(a) + \frac{h^2 f''(a)}{3!}\right] = \frac{1}{3}h[y_1 + 4y_2 + y_3]$$

as required. The error is approximately the difference between the third terms in equations (ii) and (iii)—namely

$$\frac{2h^5 f^{\text{iv}}(a)}{3 \times 4!} - \frac{2h^5 f^{\text{iv}}(a)}{5!} = \frac{h^5 f^{\text{iv}}(a)}{90} \qquad (9.35)$$

To obtain a good approximation, h is kept small by dividing the range of integration into an *even* number $2n$ of small parts each of width h, and applying Simpson's Rule to successive ranges of width $2h$.

$$\int_a^b f(x)\mathrm{d}x \simeq \frac{1}{3}h[(y_1 + 4y_2 + y_3)$$

$$+ (y_3 + 4y_4 + y_5)$$

$$+ (y_5 + 4y_6 + y_7)$$

$$\cdots\cdots$$

$$+ (y_{2n-1} + 4y_{2n} + y_{2n+1})]$$

$$\simeq \tfrac{1}{3}h(y_1 + 4y_2 + 2y_3 + 4y_4 + 2y_5 + \ldots + 4y_{2n} + y_{2n+1})$$

$\simeq \tfrac{1}{3}h$[First + Last ordinate + 4 × Sum of the even ordinates + 2 × Sum of the remaining odd ordinates]

(9.36)

The error term (refer to equation 9.35) is of the order of h^5 and decreases very rapidly with decreasing h.

To illustrate the method, the definite integral

$$\int_0^1 \frac{dx}{\sqrt{(x^2+1)}} \; (= \sinh^{-1} 1)$$

will be evaluated.

Example 20. Find an approximate value of $\int_0^1 \frac{dx}{\sqrt{(x^2+1)}}$ using Simpson's Rule with ten strips.

The range is 0 to 1 and each strip is of width 0·1; thus $h = 0{\cdot}1$. Using the formula 9.36, the work can be set out as follows:

x	*First and last ordinates*	*Even ordinates*	*Odd ordinates*
0	1		
0·1		0·9951	
0·2			0·9806
0·3		0·9578	
0·4			0·9285
0·5		0·8944	
0·6			0·8575
0·7		0·8192	
0·8			0·7809
0·9		0·7433	
1·0	0·7071		
Totals	1·7071	4·4098	3·5475
		4	2
		17·6392	7·0950

$$\therefore \quad \int_0^1 \frac{dx}{\sqrt{(x^2+1)}} \simeq \frac{0{\cdot}1}{3}[1{\cdot}7071 + 17{\cdot}6392 + 7{\cdot}0950]$$

$$\simeq 0{\cdot}8814$$

The result analytically to four places is also 0·8814.

The formula can also be used when the function is given as a table of values, such as a computer print-out or a set of measurements.

Example 21. A river is 24 m wide. The depth of the river is found at nine equidistant points on a line PQ, perpendicular to the direction of flow, joining points P and Q at the water's edge on opposite sides of the river. The results were as follows.

Distance from P in metres	0	3	6	9	12	15	18	21	24
Depth in metres	0	0·5	2·3	3·0	3·3	3·2	2·8	0·9	0

The water is flowing at 1·2 m/s. Find approximately the flow of the river in cubic metres per second.

	First and last ordinates	*Even ordinates*	*Odd ordinates*
	0		
		0·5	
			2·3
		3·0	
			3·3
		3·2	
			2·8
		0·9	
	0		
Totals	0	7·6	8·4
		4	2
		30·4	16·8

Cross-sectional area $\simeq \frac{3}{3}[0 + 30{\cdot}4 + 16{\cdot}8]$

$\simeq 47{\cdot}2\ \text{m}^2$

Flow per second $\simeq 47{\cdot}2 \times 1{\cdot}2$

$\simeq 56{\cdot}6\ \text{m}^3/\text{s}$

Exercises 9.8

1. Find an approximate value for π by evaluating $4\int_0^1 \frac{dx}{(1+x^2)}$ (use ten strips).

2. Find an approximation to the arc length s of an ellipse where

$$s = \int_0^{\pi/2} \sqrt{(1 - 0{\cdot}9 \sin^2\theta)}\, d\theta$$

Use four strips with $h = \pi/8$.

3. Verify that Simpson's Rule gives the exact value of $\int_{-1}^{+1} (x^3 + px^2 + r)\, dx$.

4. Find, to four significant figures, the approximate value of $\int_0^2 e^{-x^2/2}\, dx$.

5. The vertical depth of water a short distance behind a straight dam was measured at seven equidistant points on a line AB, parallel to the dam face, with the following results:

Distance from A in metres	0	45	90	135	180	225	270
Depth in metres	0	64	92	100	98	68	0

AB is 270 m long and the dam face slopes uniformly into the water at an angle of 10° to the downward vertical. Calculate to the nearest 100 m² the wetted area of the dam's face.

6. An inertial device for monitoring the vertical acceleration of a rocket gave the following values during the first ten seconds of powered ascent:

Time in seconds	0	1	2	3	4	5	6	7	8	9	10
Acceleration in m/s^2	5	15	24	32	33	32	30	29	28	27	26

Using Simpson's Rule, show that the rocket's vertical speed relative to the earth at the end of 10 seconds is 267 m/s.

CHAPTER TEN

DIFFERENTIAL EQUATIONS

10.1 Introduction

In section 2.1 we translated several laws of growth into mathematical symbols and found that the mathematical model was

$$\frac{\mathrm{d}[f(x)]}{\mathrm{d}x} = af(x)$$

where a is a constant. This equation involves an unknown function $f(x)$ and its first derivative. Such equations involving one or more derivatives of a function are known as **differential equations.** They are more generally written as

$$\frac{\mathrm{d}y}{\mathrm{d}x} = ay \tag{10.1}$$

and we recall that the solution is

$$y = C\mathrm{e}^{ax} \tag{10.2}$$

where C is an arbitrary constant.

Example 1. In simple harmonic motion a particle P moves in a straight line so that its acceleration is proportional to its distance s from a fixed point O in the straight line and directed towards O. Express this statement in mathematical symbols.

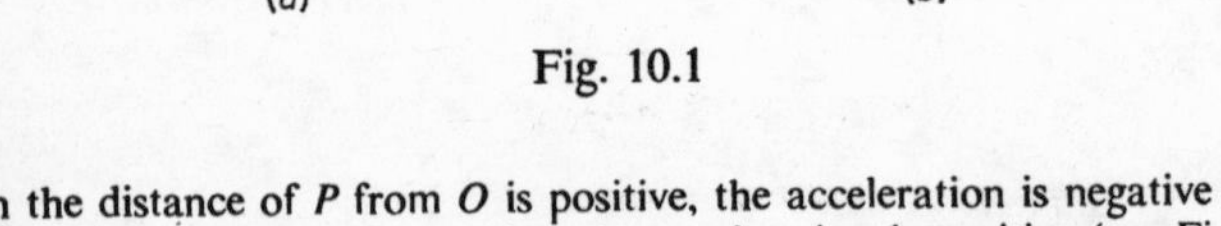

Fig. 10.1

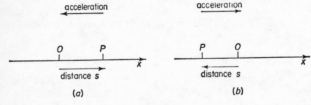

When the distance of P from O is positive, the acceleration is negative (see Fig. 10.1*a*). When the distance is negative, the acceleration is positive (see Fig. 10.1*b*). Thus

$$\text{acceleration} \propto -s$$

This can be written as either

$$\text{acceleration} = -ks \text{ (where } k \text{ is a positive constant)}$$

or $$\text{acceleration} = -w^2 s$$

From section 1.14 acceleration is the second derivative of the distance s with respect to the time t; therefore

$$\frac{d^2s}{dt^2} = -w^2 s \tag{10.3}$$

In this example, the equation involves the second derivative of s with respect to time t and s must be a function of t. We shall see later (see example 8) that the general expression for $s(t)$ is

$$s(t) = A \cos wt + B \sin wt \tag{10.4}$$

where A and B are two arbitrary constants. Other physical phenomena give rise to equations involving more than one derivative. The equation

$$\frac{d^2y}{dx^2} + a\frac{dy}{dx} + by = f(x) \tag{10.5}$$

where a and b are constants, like the growth equation, is the mathematical model of many different physical situations—for example, some electrical circuits, vibration of bodies in a resisting medium and servomechanisms.

Differential equations have been extensively studied and many books have been written about them. All that we can do here is to consider some of the simpler types which occur in practice. They have solutions which can be found relatively simply by various devices and are of value to our readers. We shall consider only *ordinary* as distinct from *partial* differential equations —that is, those which contain partial derivatives (see Chapter Eleven).

They are classified according to the *order* of the highest derivative which appears. For example, equation 10.1 is a *first*-order equation and equations 10.3 and 10.5 are *second*-order equations. Whatever the order of the equation, it is also *linear* if it includes y and its derivatives in the first degree only. Equation 10.5 is a linear equation of the second order but, for example

$$x\left(\frac{dy}{dx}\right)^2 - y\left(\frac{dy}{dx}\right) + 1 = 0 \tag{10.6}$$

is of the first order but *non-linear* because of $(dy/dx)^2$ and $y(dy/dx)$. Its general solution is

$$y = Cx + \frac{1}{C} \tag{10.7}$$

where C is an arbitrary constant. As C varies it is represented by a family of straight lines. The general solutions of the *first*-order equations 10.1 and 10.6 each contained *one* arbitrary constant. The general solution of the *second*-order equation 10.3 contained *two* arbitrary constants. The general solution of an nth order equation involves n arbitrary constants. The proof of this important theorem is beyond the scope of this book. However, in most of the cases we shall deal with the necessary constants will be seen to occur as the equations are integrated.

The general solution of a differential equation does not necessarily give rise to all possible solutions: so-called *singular solutions* can exist. For example, the equation 10.6 has the solution

$$y^2 = 4x \tag{10.8}$$

which cannot be obtained from the general solution 10.7. There is a connection between the family of lines of equation 10.7 and the singular solution. By referring to Fig. 10.2, it can be seen that when a number of the lines $y = Cx + 1/C$ are drawn for varying values of C they outline the singular solution $y^2 = 4x$.

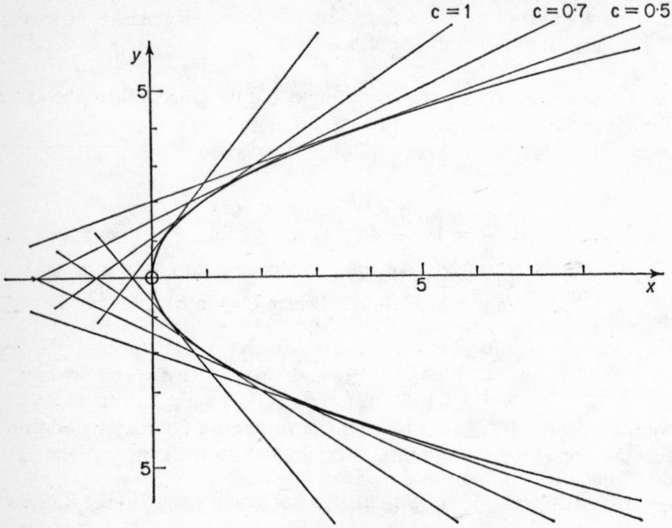

Fig. 10.2

The equations which we shall consider do not contain any singular solutions.

10.2 First-Order Equations with Variables Separable

The equations considered in this section contain only the first derivative $\mathrm{d}y/\mathrm{d}x$ (or $\mathrm{d}x/\mathrm{d}t$ . . .) and can be put into the form

$$\frac{\mathrm{d}y}{\mathrm{d}x} = f(x) \, . \, g(y) \tag{10.9}$$

That is, $\mathrm{d}y/\mathrm{d}x$ can be expressed as the product of a function of x and a function of y.

Equation 10.9 can be rewritten

$$\frac{1}{g(y)} \frac{\mathrm{d}y}{\mathrm{d}x} = f(x) \qquad [g(y) \neq 0]$$

Integrating with respect to x gives

$$\int \frac{1}{g(y)} \frac{\mathrm{d}y}{\mathrm{d}x} \mathrm{d}x = \int f(x) \mathrm{d}x$$

or

$$\int \frac{\mathrm{d}y}{g(y)} = \int f(x) \mathrm{d}x \qquad \text{(from equation 6.1)}$$

The variables have been separated; hence the name given to this type of equation. Many physical problems can be expressed as separable differential equations.

Example 2. A suspension bridge carries a uniform horizontal load. The chain is in the shape of the curve $y = f(x)$, where

$$\frac{dy}{dx} = \frac{2y}{x}$$

the origin of coordinates being the lowest point and the tangent there the axis of x. Find the equation of the curve.

$$\frac{dy}{dx} = \frac{2y}{x}$$

$$\therefore \quad \int \frac{dy}{y} = \int \frac{2\,dx}{x}$$

$$\ln y = 2 \ln x + C$$

$$\ln y = \ln x^2 + \ln E \text{ (where } C = \ln E)$$

$$= \ln Ex^2$$

$$\therefore \quad y = Ex^2$$

That is, a parabola with its axis vertical.

In simple cases the function of y or the function of x may be absent. The equation 2.6 (repeated as equation 10.1) is of this type.

Example 3. The current i flowing in an electrical circuit at any time t is given by

$$L\frac{di}{dt} + Ri = E$$

where E, the external electromotive force, L, the self-inductance, and R, the resistance of the circuit, are all constant. Initially the current is zero. Find its limiting value as t becomes very large.

$$L\frac{di}{dt} = E - Ri$$

$$\therefore \quad \int \frac{L\,di}{(E - Ri)} = \int dt$$

$$-\frac{L}{R} \ln (E - Ri) = t + C$$

$$\therefore \quad \ln (E - Ri) = -\frac{Rt}{L} + D \left(\text{where } D = -\frac{RC}{L}\right)$$

$$E - Ri = e^{-Rt/L + D}$$

$$= e^D e^{-Rt/L}$$

$$E - Ri = K e^{-Rt/L}$$

$$Ri = E - Ke^{-Rt/L}$$

When $t = 0$, $i = 0$; therefore $K = E$

$$\therefore \quad Ri = E(1 - e^{-Rt/L})$$

$$i = \frac{E}{R}(1 - e^{-Rt/L})$$

As $t \to \infty$, $e^{-Rt/L} \to 0$ because $R > 0$ and $L > 0$, and in the limit $i = E/R$.

Exercises 10.1

1. A particle moves in a straight line so that its speed v at any time is given by $v = 4 \sin 2t$. Initially it is at a point P. Find its distance x from P at any time t.

2. Two concentric spherical conductors radii a and b are at potentials V_1 and 0 respectively. The potential V at a distance x from their common centre is given by

$$\frac{d\left[x^2 \frac{dV}{dx}\right]}{dx} = 0$$

Find V in terms of x, a, b, and V_1. (Note $V = V_1$ when $x = a$ and $V = 0$ when $x = b$.)

3. The rate of growth of a colony of bacteria is proportional to the number x present at any time t. Initially $x = N$ and at time $t = 1$ h, $x = 2N$. What will be the value of x when $t = 2$ h? Assume that sufficient food is available and that treating x as continuous and differentiable will give meaningful results.

4. The rate of decay of a radioactive substance is proportional to the amount remaining at any time t, the constant of proportionality being k. Initially the amount of the substance is 10 g. Obtain an expression for its half-life (the time which elapses until the amount of radioactive substance is 5 g).

5. A body is falling in the earth's atmosphere. The forces on it are the earth's gravitational attraction and the air resistance, which is proportional to its speed v. Its acceleration a is given by $a = g - kv$. Expressing a in the form dv/dt, obtain an expression for v. Show that whatever its initial speed, as t becomes very large the final speed of the body tends to g/k.

6. At any height in a compressible atmosphere of constant temperature the rate of fall of the pressure p with respect to the height z is proportional to the pressure, the constant of proportionality being g/RT, where g is the acceleration due to gravity, R the specific gas constant for dry air and T the absolute temperature. The pressure at sea level is p_0. Show that

$$p = p_0 e^{-gz/RT} \text{ (see section 2.1, example 3)}$$

The tropopause is at a height of 10 000 m and $g = 9{\cdot}8$, $R = 287$, $T = 250$ in compatible units. Deduce that the atmospheric pressure at the tropopause is approximately $p_0/4$.

7. A calorimeter containing hot water is standing in a room which has a constant temperature of 20°C. The rate of fall of temperature of the water and calorimeter at any time t is proportional to the difference in temperature between the calorimeter and its surroundings (Newton's law of cooling—see section 2.1, example 4). Initially the temperature was 80°C and after 5 minutes it had dropped to 60°C. What will its temperature be after 10 minutes?

8. In question 5, if the body were initially at rest, show that $v = g(1 - e^{-kt})/k$. Express v in the form ds/dt and hence find an expression for s, the distance fallen, in terms of t, g and k.

9. A mixture of two liquids, X and Y, is boiling. At any time t there is present in the mixture a quantity x of one and y of the other liquid. The ratio of the amounts of X and Y passing off at any one time is proportional to the ratio of the quantities still in the liquid state. Prove that $y = Cx^k$, where C and k are constant.

10. The rate of growth of the population x of a country is proportional to the product of x and $(M - x)$, where M is a constant. Assume that x can be regarded as a

continuous function of the time t with a continuous derivative at all times and show that if $x = M/2$ when $t = 50$, then

$$x = \frac{M}{[1 + e^{-Mk(t-50)}]}$$

where k is a constant.

11. In a bimolecular chemical reaction the speed of reaction is given by

$$\frac{dx}{dt} = k(10 - x)(5 - x)$$

where x is the amount combined at any time t and k is a constant. Initially $x = 0$. Express x in terms of k and t.

12. Two oppositely charged particles in space, each of mass m, attract each other with a force inversely proportional to s^2, where s is their distance apart. One particle is fixed and the acceleration a of the other particle P is given by $a = -\mu/s^2$. Given that the speed v is zero when $s = 2k$, show that v is given by

$$v = -\sqrt{\left[\frac{\mu(2k - s)}{ks}\right]}$$

Write v in the form ds/dt and find the value of t when $s = k$. (Hint: use the substitution $s = 2k \cos^2 \theta$.)

13. A rocket moves vertically upwards by expelling material vertically downwards with a constant speed u relative to itself. Neglecting air resistance at any time t, while still firing, its acceleration a is given by

$$a = \frac{ku}{(1 - kt)} - g$$

where k is a constant. Assuming that g is constant and that initially the rocket was at rest, find its speed and height reached after firing for a time t.

14. A body falling in the earth's atmosphere experiences an air resistance which is proportional to the square of its speed v. Its acceleration a at any time t is given by $a = g - kv^2$, where g and k are constants. It starts from rest; show that $v^2 = g(1 - e^{-2ks})/k$, where s is the distance fallen at any time t. Also show that

$$v = \frac{n}{k} \tanh nt$$

where $n^2 = gk$.

10.3 First-Order Linear Equations

Consider the equation

$$\frac{dy}{dx} - \frac{y}{x} = 3x^3 \qquad (10.10)$$

The variables are not separable, as may easily be seen by rewriting the equation in the form

$$\frac{dy}{dx} = \frac{3x^4 + y}{x}$$

However, if we multiply throughout by $1/x$ $(x \neq 0)$, equation 10.10 becomes

$$\frac{1}{x}\cdot\frac{dy}{dx} - \frac{y}{x^2} = 3x^2 \qquad (x \neq 0)$$

The two parts of the left-hand side of this equation can be written as the derivative of a product, thus

$$\frac{d(y/x)}{dx} = 3x^2$$

and the equation is now easily solved

$$\frac{y}{x} = \int 3x^2 dx$$

$$= x^3 + C$$

$$\therefore \qquad y = x^4 + Cx$$

The multiplying factor $1/x$ enabled us to express the two terms in dy/dx and y as the derivative of a product of y and the multiplying factor and hence to solve the equation. The multiplying factor is known as an **integrating factor.**

Consider the general case of

$$\frac{dy}{dx} + P(x)y = Q(x) \tag{10.11}$$

(Note that the coefficient of dy/dx is unity and that the terms in dy/dx and y are on the left-hand side of the equation.) Suppose an integrating factor $I(x)$ exists. Multiplying throughout by $I(x)$

$$I(x)\frac{dy}{dx} + I(x)P(x)y = I(x)Q(x)$$

The left-hand side of this equation is now the derivative of the product $y \,.\, I(x)$.

$$\therefore \qquad I(x)\frac{dy}{dx} + I(x)P(x)y = \frac{d[yI(x)]}{dx}$$

$$= I(x)\frac{dy}{dx} + y\frac{d[(I(x)]}{dx}$$

or

$$I(x)P(x)y = y\frac{d[I(x)]}{dx}$$

$$I(x)P(x) = \frac{d[I(x)]}{dx}$$

This is a differential equation whose variables are separable

$$\therefore \qquad \int \frac{d[I(x)]}{I(x)} = \int P(x)dx$$

$$\ln [I(x)] = \int P(x)dx$$

$$I(x) = e^{\int P(x)dx} \tag{10.12}$$

The constant of integration is ignored to obtain the simplest possible integrating factor.

Reconsider equation 10.10, comparing it with the standard case of equation 10.11

$$P(x) = -\frac{1}{x}$$

and from 10.12

$$I(x) = e^{\int -dx/x} = e^{-\ln x} = e^{\ln 1/x} = \frac{1}{x}$$

which was the integrating factor we used.

Example 4. Solve the equation $\cos x \frac{dy}{dx} + 2y \sin x = \sin 2x$, given that $y = 3$ when $x = 0$.

The coefficient of dy/dx is not unity; therefore we first divide by $\cos x$ and, remembering that $\sin 2x = 2 \sin x \cos x$, we have

$$\frac{dy}{dx} + 2y \tan x = 2 \sin x$$

Comparing with equation 10.11, $P(x) = 2 \tan x$, and from equation 10.12

$$I(x) = e^{\int 2 \tan x\, dx} = e^{2 \ln(\sec x)} = e^{\ln(\sec^2 x)} = \sec^2 x$$

Multiplying throughout by $\sec^2 x$

$$\sec^2 x \frac{dy}{dx} + 2y \sec^2 x \tan x = 2 \sin x \sec^2 x$$

$$\frac{d[y \sec^2 x]}{dx} = 2 \sec x \tan x$$

$$\therefore \quad y \sec^2 x = 2 \int \sec x \tan x\, dx$$

$$= 2 \sec x + C$$

$$\therefore \quad y = 2 \cos x + C \cos^2 x$$

when $x = 0$, $y = 3$; therefore $C = 1$.

Hence $$y = 2 \cos x + \cos^2 x$$

Revision Questions 10.1

In each of the following one and only one answer is correct. State which it is.	*Answers*	*Refer to*
1. $e^{2 \ln x} = \ldots$ (a) $2x$, (b) x^2, (c) $1/x^2$, (d) $x^{\frac{1}{2}}$	**1.** (b) x^2	Formula 2.20 and Revision Questions 2.2, No. 6
2. $e^{-3 \ln x} = \ldots$ (a) $x^{\frac{1}{3}}$, (b) $-3x$, (c) $1/x^3$, (d) x^3	**2.** (c) $1/x^3$	
3. $e^{-\ln \cos x + \ln \sin x} = \ldots$ (a) $\sin x/\cos x$, (b) $\sin x - \cos x$, (c) $-\cos x/\sin x$, (d) $\frac{1}{\cos x - \sin x}$	**3.** (a) $\sin x/\cos x = \tan x$	

Complete the following statement:		
4. The integrating factor for the equation $\frac{dy}{dx} - \frac{3y}{x} = x^5$ is $e^{\int \cdots\cdots}$	**4.** $e^{\int -(3/x)\,dx}$	Equation 10.12
In the following indicate which alternative is correct:		
5. The integrating factor for the equation $(x+2)\frac{dy}{dx} - 2y = (x+2)^3$ is/is not $e^{\int -2\,dx}$	**5.** 'Is not'; the coefficient of dy/dx has to be unity before finding the integrating factor.	Example 4
6. The variables in the following equations are/are not separable.	**6.**	Equation 10.9
(a) $(x^2-1)\frac{dy}{dx} + y^2x^5 = x^3y^2$	(a) are separable	
(b) $xy\frac{dy}{dx} = x^2y^2 - 2y^2$	(b) are separable	
(c) $x(x-1)\frac{dy}{dx} + xy = x^3$	(c) are not separable	

Exercises 10.2

Solve the following equations:

1. $\frac{dy}{dx} + 2y = e^{-2x}$
2. $x\frac{dy}{dx} + y = 5x^4$
3. $\frac{dy}{dx} - y\tan x = \sec^3 x$
4. $x\ln x\frac{dy}{dx} + y = 2\ln x$
5. $\frac{dy}{dx} = 3x^2y + 2x\,e^{x^3}$

10.4 Second-Order Linear Equations with Constant Coefficients

The type of equation considered here is

$$\frac{d^2y}{dx^2} + a\frac{dy}{dx} + by = f(x) \qquad (10.13)$$

where a and b are constants and $f(x)$ is of the form x^n or $e^{px}\cos qx$ or $e^{px}\sin qx$. It occurs when studying electrical circuits and vibratory mechanical systems with damping. The level of the work is suitable for Advanced Level students, but for a wider treatment, using Laplace Transforms or Operator Theory, the reader is referred to more specialist textbooks.

We first discuss the case when $f(x) = 0$. Consider for example the equation

$$\frac{d^2y}{dx^2} + 5\frac{dy}{dx} + 6y = 0$$

This can be rewritten in the form

$$\frac{d^2y}{dx^2} + 3\frac{dy}{dx} = -2\frac{dy}{dx} - 6y$$

or

$$\frac{d}{dx}\left[\frac{dy}{dx} + 3y\right] = -2\left[\frac{dy}{dx} + 3y\right]$$

Let $z = \dfrac{dy}{dx} + 3y$

$$\therefore \qquad \frac{dz}{dx} = -2z$$

or

$$\int\frac{dz}{z} = -2\int dx$$

$$\ln z = -2x + B$$

$$z = Ce^{-2x}$$

that is

$$\frac{dy}{dx} + 3y = Ce^{-2x}$$

Multiply by the integrating factor e^{3x}

$$e^{3x}\frac{dy}{dx} + 3ye^{3x} = Ce^{x}$$

$$\frac{d(ye^{3x})}{dx} = Ce^{x}$$

$$ye^{3x} = Ce^{x} + D$$

$$\therefore \qquad y = Ce^{-2x} + De^{-3x}$$

This has two arbitrary constants and is the general solution of the equation.

If in the original equation we replace d^2y/dx^2 by m^2 and dy/dx by m, we obtain

$$m^2 + 5m + 6 = 0$$

which is known as the **auxiliary equation.** It is a quadratic whose solution is

$$(m + 2)(m + 3) = 0$$

or

$$m = -2 \text{ or } -3$$

These values of m lead to the indices, $-2x$ and $-3x$, of the exponential functions in the general solution.

In general, the auxiliary equation for

$$\frac{d^2y}{dx^2} + a\frac{dy}{dx} + by = 0 \qquad (10.14)$$

is

$$m^2 + am + b = 0$$

When the quadratic has two real and distinct roots α and β it can be written

$$m^2 - (\alpha + \beta)m + \alpha\beta = 0$$

and the original differential equation can be written

$$\frac{d^2y}{dx^2} - (\alpha + \beta)\frac{dy}{dx} + \alpha\beta y = 0 \tag{10.15}$$

or

$$\frac{d^2y}{dx^2} - \alpha\frac{dy}{dx} = \beta\frac{dy}{dx} - \alpha\beta y$$

that is

$$\frac{d}{dx}\left[\frac{dy}{dx} - \alpha y\right] = \beta\left[\frac{dy}{dx} - \alpha y\right]$$

Let $z = \dfrac{dy}{dx} - \alpha y$

$$\therefore \quad \frac{dz}{dx} = \beta z$$

$$\int\frac{dz}{z} = \beta\int dx$$

$$\ln z = \beta x + A$$

$$z = B\,e^{\beta x}$$

or

$$\frac{dy}{dx} - \alpha y = B\,e^{\beta x}$$

Multiply throughout by the integrating factor $e^{-\alpha x}$

$$e^{-\alpha x}\frac{dy}{dx} - \alpha y\,e^{-\alpha x} = B\,e^{(\beta-\alpha)x}$$

$$\frac{d(y\,e^{-\alpha x})}{dx} = B\,e^{(\beta-\alpha)x}$$

$$y\,e^{-\alpha x} = \frac{B}{(\beta-\alpha)}\,e^{(\beta-\alpha)x} + D$$

$$y = \frac{B}{(\beta-\alpha)}\,e^{\beta x} + D\,e^{\alpha x}$$

Because α and β are constants this can be written

$$y = C\,e^{\beta x} + D\,e^{\alpha x} \tag{10.16}$$

where C and D are arbitrary constants.

Thus the general solution can be written down immediately if the roots of the auxiliary equation are real and distinct.

Example 5. Find the general solution of the equation

$$\frac{d^2y}{dx^2} - \frac{dy}{dx} - 6y = 0$$

The auxiliary equation is

$$m^2 - m - 6 = 0$$

or

$$(m-3)(m+2) = 0$$

$$m = 3 \text{ or } -2$$

The general solution is, from equation 10.16

$$y = C\,e^{3x} + D\,e^{-2x}$$

When the differential equation is of the form

$$\frac{d^2y}{dx^2} + 2a\frac{dy}{dx} + a^2y = 0 \qquad (10.17)$$

the auxiliary equation $m^2 + 2am + a^2 = 0$ has two equal roots and only gives one value of m and hence one arbitrary constant in the equation 10.16. The general solution requires two arbitrary constants so we have to reconsider the case of equation 10.17. It can be written

$$\frac{d^2y}{dx^2} + a\frac{dy}{dx} = -a\frac{dy}{dx} - a^2y$$

or

$$\frac{d}{dx}\left[\frac{dy}{dx} + ay\right] = -a\left[\frac{dy}{dx} + ay\right]$$

Let $z = \dfrac{dy}{dx} + ay$

$$\frac{dz}{dx} = -az$$

$$\therefore \qquad \int\frac{dz}{z} = -a\int dx$$

or

$$\ln z = -ax + C$$

$$z = C\,e^{-ax}$$

that is

$$\frac{dy}{dx} + ay = C\,e^{-ax}$$

Multiply throughout by the integrating factor e^{ax}

$$e^{ax}\frac{dy}{dx} + ay\,e^{ax} = C$$

$$\frac{d(y\,e^{ax})}{dx} = C$$

$$y\,e^{ax} = Cx + D$$

$$\therefore \qquad y = (Cx + D)\,e^{-ax} \qquad (10.18)$$

which contains two arbitrary constants and is the general solution of equation 10.17.

Example 6. Find the general solution of the equation

$$\frac{d^2y}{dx^2} - 6\frac{dy}{dx} + 9y = 0$$

The auxiliary equation is

$$m^2 - 6m + 9 = 0$$

or

$$(m - 3)^2 = 0$$

$$m = 3$$

The general solution is, from equation 10.18

$$y = (Cx + D)e^{3x}$$

In the case when the roots of the auxiliary equation are imaginary, for example

$$\frac{d^2y}{dx^2} + 2p\frac{dy}{dx} + (p^2 + q^2)y = 0 \qquad (10.19)$$

whose auxiliary equation is $m^2 + 2pm + (p^2 + q^2) = 0$

that is $$m = \frac{-2p \pm \sqrt{[4p^2 - 4(p^2 + q^2)]}}{2}$$

$$= -p \pm q\sqrt{(-1)}$$

it can be shown that the general solution is

$$y = e^{-px}[C \cos qx + D \sin qx] \qquad (10.20)$$

The proof of this is beyond the scope of this book but the solution can be verified by differentiation and substitution in the original equation.

Example 7. Find the general solution of the equation

$$\frac{d^2y}{dx^2} + 6\frac{dy}{dx} + 25y = 0$$

The auxiliary equation is $m^2 + 6m + 25 = 0$

$$m = \frac{-6 \pm \sqrt{(36 - 100)}}{2}$$

$$= \frac{-6 \pm 8\sqrt{(-1)}}{2}$$

$$= -3 \pm 4\sqrt{(-1)}$$

The general solution is, from equation 10.20

$$y = e^{-3x}[C \cos 4x + D \sin 4x]$$

When $a = 0$ the equation simplifies to one of the two forms

$$\frac{d^2y}{dx^2} \pm w^2x = 0$$

but can still be solved by using the auxiliary equation.

Example 8. Find the general solution of

(i) $\dfrac{d^2y}{dx^2} + w^2y = 0$ (where w is a constant)

(ii) $\dfrac{d^2y}{dx^2} - 9y = 0$

(i) This is the case of simple harmonic motion referred to at the beginning of the chapter (see equations 10.3 and 10.4). The auxiliary equation is $m^2 + w^2 = 0$

$$\therefore \qquad m^2 = -w^2$$

$$m = \pm w\sqrt{-1} = 0 \pm w\sqrt{-1}$$

Therefore the general solution is, from equation 10.20

$$y = e^0(C\cos wx + D\sin wx)$$

or

$$y = C\cos wx + D\sin wx$$

(ii) $\dfrac{d^2y}{dx^2} - 9y = 0$

The auxiliary equation is $m^2 - 9 = 0$

or

$$(m-3)(m+3) = 0$$
$$m = 3 \text{ or } -3$$

$\therefore$

$$y = A\,e^{3x} + B\,e^{-3x}$$

this can be written

$$y = (A+B)\cosh 3x + (A-B)\sinh 3x$$

or

$$y = C\cosh 3x + D\sinh 3x$$

(Compare this with the general solution to part (i).)

Exercises 10.3

Find the general solutions of the equations:

1. $\dfrac{d^2y}{dx^2} + 7\dfrac{dy}{dx} + 12y = 0$

2. $\dfrac{d^2y}{dx^2} + 16y = 0$

3. $\dfrac{d^2y}{dx^2} + 8\dfrac{dy}{dx} + 16y = 0$

4. $2\dfrac{d^2y}{dt^2} - 5\dfrac{dy}{dt} - 3y = 0$

5. $\dfrac{d^2y}{dx^2} + 2\dfrac{dy}{dx} + 10y = 0$

6. $\dfrac{d^2y}{dt^2} - 25y = 0$

7. $\dfrac{d^2\theta}{dt^2} - 6\dfrac{d\theta}{dt} + 34\theta = 0$

8. $\dfrac{d^2y}{dx^2} + 4\dfrac{dy}{dx} = 0$

9. Find the general solution of the equation $\dfrac{d^2y}{dt^2} + 2\dfrac{dy}{dt} + 10y = 0$ given that when $t = 0$, $y = 0$ and $\dfrac{dy}{dt} = -3$.

10. Show that $y = f(x)$ is the solution of the equation $\dfrac{d^2y}{dx^2} + 6\dfrac{dy}{dx} + 25y = 0$ such that when $x = 0$, $y = -1$ and $\dfrac{dy}{dx} = 7$, where $f(x) = e^{-3x}(\sin 4x - \cos 4x)$.

Express $f(x)$ in the form $R\,e^{-3x}\sin(4x - \varepsilon)$.

11. A long thin rod is clamped vertically at its lower end and a mass M is attached to its upper end. The coordinates (x, y) of any point on it satisfy the equation

$$EI\frac{d^2x}{dy^2} = Mg(a - x)$$

where E, I and a are constants. Given that $x = 0$ when $y = 0$ and $x = a$ when $y = L$, show that

$$x = a\left[1 - \frac{\sin n(L - y)}{\sin nL}\right]$$

where $n^2 = Mg/EI$. (Hint: let $z = (a - x)$.)

12. An electromotive force E is applied to a circuit of self-inductance L, resistance R and containing a condenser of capacitance C, where L, R, C and E are constants. At any time t the charge q on the plates of the condenser is given by

$$L\frac{d^2q}{dt^2} + R\frac{dq}{dt} + q/C = E$$

The values of L, R, C and E are, in compatible units, 0·01, 200, 5×10^{-7} and 200 respectively. Verify that $q = 0{\cdot}0001 + Ke^{-10^4t}\sin(10^4t + \varepsilon)$, where K and ε are arbitrary constants.

Consider now a more general case

$$\frac{d^2y}{dx^2} + 5\frac{dy}{dx} + 6y = 6x + 5 \qquad (10.21)$$

A solution of this equation is $y = x$, as may be verified by differentiation and substitution. It does not involve any arbitrary constants and is not therefore the general solution (note that $y = Cx$, where C is an arbitrary constant, is not a solution). If we now suppose that $y = x + u(x)$ is a solution of the equation, then

$$\frac{dy}{dx} = 1 + \frac{du}{dx} \quad \text{and} \quad \frac{d^2y}{dx^2} = \frac{d^2u}{dx^2}$$

Substituting in the equation 10.21

$$\frac{d^2u}{dx^2} + 5\left(1 + \frac{du}{dx}\right) + 6(x + u) = 6x + 5$$

$$\frac{d^2u}{dx^2} + 5 + 5\frac{du}{dx} + 6x + 6u = 6x + 5$$

that is

$$\frac{d^2u}{dx^2} + 5\frac{du}{dx} + 6u = 0$$

The solution of this equation can be obtained from its auxiliary equation

$$m^2 + 5m + 6 = 0$$
$$(m + 2)(m + 3) = 0$$
$$m = -2 \text{ or } -3$$

and is

$$u(x) = Ce^{-2x} + De^{-3x}$$

$\therefore$

$$y = x + u(x) = x + Ce^{-2x} + De^{-3x}$$

is the general solution of equation 10.21 because it contains two arbitrary constants.

The solution of the equation was found in two parts. First a particular solution $y = x$, generally known as the **particular integral,** was found. To this was added the function $u(x)$, which was obtained by equating the sum of the terms in d^2y/dx^2, dy/dx and y to zero. This second part of the solution is known as the **complementary function.**

In general, the solution of the equation

$$\frac{d^2y}{dx^2} + a\frac{dy}{dx} + by = f(x)$$

can be found in two parts, viz.

First find the complementary function $u(x)$ by letting $f(x) = 0$. *Then* find a particular integral $v(x)$ which satisfies the whole equation. The complete general solution is then $y = u(x) + v(x)$.

The difficulty is to find the particular integral; for the simple cases of $f(x)$ which we shall consider it is convenient to do this by inspection.

I. $f(x) = e^{ax}$ where a is a constant

The derivatives of e^{ax} always involve e^{ax} and we consider a particular integral $A\,e^{ax}$ where the value of A is found by differentiation and substitution in the equation.

Example 9. Find the general solution of the equation

$$\frac{d^2y}{dx^2} - 7\frac{dy}{dx} + 12y = 6\,e^{2x}$$

The complementary function (C.F.) is given by

$$\frac{d^2u}{dx^2} - 7\frac{du}{dx} + 12u = 0$$

The auxiliary equation is

$$m^2 - 7m + 12 = 0$$
$$(m - 3)(m - 4) = 0$$

$$\therefore \qquad \text{C.F. is } C\,e^{3x} + D\,e^{4x} \qquad \text{(i)}$$

To find the particular integral (P.I.), let $y = A\,e^{2x}$

$$\therefore \qquad \frac{dy}{dx} = 2A\,e^{2x}, \qquad \frac{d^2y}{dx^2} = 4A\,e^{2x}$$

Substituting in the equation

$$4A\,e^{2x} - 7(2A\,e^{2x}) + 12A\,e^{2x} = 6\,e^{2x}$$

$$\therefore \qquad 2A\,e^{2x} = 6\,e^{2x} \qquad \text{and} \qquad A = 3$$

$$\therefore \qquad \text{P.I. is } 3\,e^{2x} \qquad \text{(ii)}$$

Combining (i) and (ii)

$$y = C\,e^{3x} + D\,e^{4x} + 3\,e^{2x}$$

This method can be used when $f(x)$ is of the form sinh ax and/or cosh ax.

Example 10. Find the general solution of the equation

$$4\frac{d^2y}{dx^2} + 4\frac{dy}{dx} + y = 3\cosh x + 5\sinh x$$

Rewriting sinh x and cosh x in terms of 'e'

$$4\frac{d^2y}{dx^2} + 4\frac{dy}{dx} + y = \frac{3}{2}(e^x + e^{-x}) + \frac{5}{2}(e^x - e^{-x}) = 4e^x - e^{-x}$$

The complementary function is given by

$$4\frac{d^2u}{dx^2} + 4\frac{du}{dx} + u = 0$$

The auxiliary equation is

$$4m^2 + 4m + 1 = 0$$
$$(2m + 1)^2 = 0$$

$\therefore$ C.F. is $(Cx + D)e^{-\frac{1}{2}x}$ (i)

To find the particular integral we note that both e^x and e^{-x} are on the right-hand side of the equation and therefore to find the particular integral, let $y = Ae^x + Be^{-x}$,

$\dfrac{dy}{dx} = Ae^x - Be^{-x}$ and $\dfrac{d^2y}{dx^2} = Ae^x + Be^{-x}$.

Substituting in the equation

$$4(Ae^x + Be^{-x}) + 4(Ae^x - Be^{-x}) + Ae^x + Be^{-x} = 4e^x - e^{-x}$$

$$\therefore \qquad 9Ae^x + Be^{-x} = 4e^x - e^{-x}$$

which is true for all values of x.

$\therefore$ $9A = 4$ and $B = -1$

the P.I. is $\frac{4}{9}e^x - e^{-x}$ (ii)

Combining (i) and (ii)

$$y = (Cx + D)e^{-\frac{1}{2}x} + \tfrac{4}{9}e^x - e^{-x}$$

II. $f(x) = \sin ax$ or $\cos ax$ where a is a constant

The derivatives of either sin ax or cos ax involve *both* sin ax *and* cos ax and we consider a composite particular integral $A \sin ax + B \cos ax$ in each case.

Example 11. Find the general solution of the equation

$$\frac{d^2x}{dt^2} - 4\frac{dx}{dt} + 5x = 65\sin 2t$$

The complementary function is given by

$$\frac{d^2u}{dt^2} - 4\frac{du}{dt} + 5u = 0$$

The auxiliary equation is

$$m^2 - 4m + 5 = 0$$

$$m = \frac{4 \pm \sqrt{(16 - 20)}}{2}$$

$$= 2 \pm 1\sqrt{(-1)}$$

$$\text{the C.F. is } e^{2t}(C \cos t + D \sin t) \qquad \text{(i)}$$

To find the particular integral let $x = A \sin 2t + B \cos 2t$

$$\therefore \qquad \frac{dx}{dt} = 2A \cos 2t - 2B \sin 2t \text{ and } \frac{d^2x}{dt^2} = -4A \sin 2t - 4B \cos 2t$$

Substituting in the equation

$$(-4A \sin 2t - 4B \cos 2t) - 4(2A \cos 2t - 2B \sin 2t) + 5(A \sin 2t + B \cos 2t) = 65 \sin 2t$$

$$\therefore \qquad (A + 8B) \sin 2t + (-8A + B) \cos 2t = 65 \sin 2t$$

which is true for all values of t.

$$\therefore \qquad A + 8B = 65 \quad \text{and} \quad -8A + B = 0$$

$$\therefore \qquad A = 1, B = 8$$

$$\text{the P.I. is } \sin 2t + 8 \cos 2t \qquad \text{(ii)}$$

Combining (i) and (ii)

$$x = e^{2t}(C \cos t + D \sin t) + \sin 2t + 8 \cos 2t$$

Note that the particular integral in example 10 could be found in a similar way by considering $y = A \cosh x + B \sinh x$.

III. $f(x) = x^n$ where n is a positive integer

The derivatives of x^n involve lower powers of x and we consider $y = Ax^n + Bx^{n-1} + \ldots + Mx + N$ for the particular integral.

Example 12. Find the general solution of the equation

$$\frac{d^2y}{dx^2} + 16y = 16x^3$$

The complementary function is given by

$$\frac{d^2u}{dx^2} + 16u = 0$$

The auxiliary equation is

$$m^2 + 16 = 0$$

$$\therefore \qquad m^2 = -16, m = 0 \pm 4\sqrt{(-1)}$$

$$\text{the C.F. is } C \cos 4x + D \sin 4x \qquad \text{(i)}$$

To find the particular integral, let $y = Ax^3 + Bx^2 + Ex + F$

$$\therefore \qquad \frac{dy}{dx} = 3Ax^2 + 2Bx + E \quad \text{and} \quad \frac{d^2y}{dx^2} = 6Ax + 2B$$

Substituting in the equation

$$6Ax + 2B + 16(Ax^3 + Bx^2 + Ex + F) = 16x^3$$

This is true for all values of x; therefore, equating coefficients

x^3. $\quad 16A = 16 \qquad x^2. \quad 16B = 0,$

x. $\quad (16E + 6A) = 0 \qquad$ constant. $(16F + 2B) = 0$

$\therefore \qquad A = 1,\ B = 0,\ E = -3/8,\ F = 0$

and $\qquad$ the P.I. is $x^3 - 3x/8$ $\qquad$ (ii)

Combining (i) and (ii)

$$y = C\cos 4x + D\sin 4x + x^3 - 3x/8$$

When $f(x) =$ constant we let $y = C$ constant and the working is trivial.

Example 13. Solve

$$\frac{d^2y}{dx^2} - 9y = 20$$

$$\text{C.F. is } C\,e^{3x} + D\,e^{-3x}$$

To find the particular integral, let $y = C$

$$\therefore \qquad 0 - 9C = 20$$
$$C = -20/9$$

The complete solution is $C\,e^{3x} + D\,e^{-3x} - 20/9$.

Revision Questions 10.2

Complete the following statements	*Answer*	*Refer to*
1. The general solution of a second order equation contains . . . arbitrary constants.	**1.** two	Section 10.1
2. The auxiliary equation for $\frac{d^2y}{dt^2} + a\frac{dy}{dt} + by = 0$ is . . .	**2.** $m^2 + am + b = 0$	Section 10.4
3. When the auxiliary equation has the form $(m + 3)^2 = 0$ the solution of the corresponding differential equation is . . .	**3.** $(Cx + D)\,e^{-3x}$	Example 6
4. The general solution of the equation $\frac{d^2x}{dt^2} + a\frac{dx}{dt} + bx = f(t)$ has two parts: one is the complementary function, the other (i) . . . The complementary function is formed by (ii) . . .	**4.** (i) Particular integral. (ii) letting $f(t) = 0$ and solving the resulting equation.	Paragraph after Exercises 10.3

Exercises 10.4

Find the general solutions of the following equations:

1. $\dfrac{d^2y}{dx^2} + \dfrac{dy}{dx} - 6y = 12\,e^{3x}$

2. $\dfrac{d^2y}{dx^2} + 4\dfrac{dy}{dx} + 4y = 50 \sinh 3x$

3. $\dfrac{d^2x}{dt^2} - 2\dfrac{dx}{dt} + 2x = 10 \sin 2t$

4. $\dfrac{d^2x}{dt^2} + 9x = 81t^2$

5. $\dfrac{d^2x}{dt^2} - \dfrac{dx}{dt} - 12x = 50(\cos 3t + \sin 3t)$

6. Find the complementary function and particular integral and hence the general solution of the equation

$$\frac{d^2y}{dt^2} - 5\frac{dy}{dt} = e^{3t}$$

Check your answer by integrating the equation with respect to t and then solving the resulting first-order equation.

7. Show that the general solution of the equation

$$L\frac{d^2q}{dt^2} + R\frac{dq}{dt} + q/C = E$$

where L, R, C and E are constants such that $R^2 < 4L/C$, can be expressed in the form

$$q = A\,e^{-Rt/2L}\cos(\mu t - \alpha) + CE$$

where A and α are arbitrary constants and

$$\mu^2 = (4L - CR^2)/4L^2C.$$

8. Solve the equation

$$\frac{d^2y}{dx^2} - 6\frac{dx}{dy} + 8y = 6\,e^x$$

given that when $x = 0$, $y = 4$ and $dy/dx = 12$.

9. Solve the equation

$$\frac{d^2y}{dt^2} + 6\frac{dy}{dt} + 9y = 27t^2$$

given that when $t = 0$, $y = 3$ and $dy/dt = -5$.

CHAPTER ELEVEN

PARTIAL DIFFERENTIATION

11.1 Introduction

Up to now we have been dealing with the relative change between *two* related quantities. In many cases *more than two* quantities are interrelated. The pressure on an underwater swimmer varies not only with the depth but also with the density of the water (e.g. with its salinity). The volume of a gas varies both with the pressure and its temperature. The current in an electric circuit varies with both the applied voltage and the resistance of the circuit. The speed over the ground of an aircraft varies with the wind speed, the density of the air, its load and the thrust of its engines.

In considering more than two related quantities, we shall find that an entirely new study is not required but only an easy extension of the ideas developed so far together with a slight change of the notation.

Consider one of our early examples: the volume V of a right circular cylinder of radius r and height h, where $V = \pi r^2 h$, is a function of both r and h and can be written

$$V = V(r,h) \tag{11.1}$$

Figure 11.1*a* depicts the change in V when the radius r increases by a small amount δr, the height h remaining constant. Algebraically we have that

$$\begin{aligned}(V + \delta V)_{h \text{ constant}} &= \pi(r + \delta r)^2 h \\ &= \pi r^2 h + 2\pi r h \delta r + \pi h(\delta r)^2\end{aligned}$$

Now $$V = \pi r^2 h$$

$\therefore$ $$(\delta V)_{h \text{ constant}} = 2\pi r h \delta r + \pi h(\delta r)^2 \tag{11.2}$$

Note that using the functional notation in equation 11.1, $(\delta V)_{h \text{ constant}}$ could be written as $V(r + \delta r, h) - V(r,h)$.

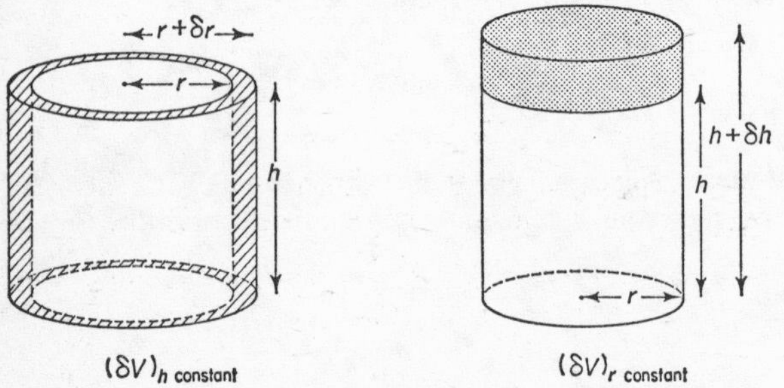

Fig. 11.1

From equation 11.2 we can obtain an expression for the relative change of V compared to the change in r, h being kept constant

$$\left(\frac{\delta V}{\delta r}\right)_{h\ \text{constant}} = 2\pi rh + \pi h\delta r$$

$$\therefore \qquad \underset{\delta r \to 0}{\text{limit}} \left(\frac{\delta V}{\delta r}\right)_{h\ \text{constant}} = 2\pi rh$$

The expression

$$\underset{\delta r \to 0}{\text{limit}} \left(\frac{\delta V}{\delta r}\right)_{h\ \text{constant}}$$

cannot be denoted by $\mathrm{d}V/\mathrm{d}r$ because we need to indicate that what we mean is the relative change in V compared to the change in r when r alone varies, or more shortly, the rate of change of V with respect to changes in r alone. The symbol used is

$\dfrac{\partial V}{\partial r}$ (read as 'curly dee vee by curly dee r', or 'partial dee vee by dee r')

If there is any possibility of misunderstanding which other variables are to be kept constant the suffix (or suffices) is retained.

$\partial V/\partial r$ is also known as the **partial derivative** of V with respect to r—'partial' because r varies alone. In this case

$$\frac{\partial V}{\partial r} = \left(\frac{\partial V}{\partial r}\right)_{h\ \text{constant}} = \underset{\delta r \to 0}{\text{limit}} \left(\frac{\delta V}{\delta r}\right)_{h\ \text{constant}} = 2\pi rh \qquad (11.3)$$

Using the functional notation 11.1

$$\frac{\partial V}{\partial r} = \underset{\delta r \to 0}{\text{limit}} \frac{V(r + \delta r, h) - V(r, h)}{\delta r} \qquad (11.4)$$

We can use our usual differentiation techniques, treating variables other than r as constants. Thus

$$\frac{\partial V}{\partial r} = \frac{\partial(\pi h)r^2}{\partial r} = (\pi h)2r = 2\pi rh \text{ (as before)}$$

Figure 11.1*b* depicts the change in V when the height h increases by a small amount δh, the radius r remaining constant. Algebraically we have that

$$(V + \delta V)_{r\ \text{constant}} = \pi r^2(h + \delta h)$$
$$= \pi r^2 h + \pi r^2 \delta h$$

Now $\qquad V = \pi r^2 h$

$$\therefore \qquad (\delta V)_{r\ \text{constant}} = \pi r^2 \delta h$$

From this we obtain an expression for the relative change of V as h changes, r being kept constant (or the rate of change of V with respect to h when r remains constant)

$$\frac{\partial V}{\partial h} = \left(\frac{\partial V}{\partial h}\right)_{r \text{ constant}} = \underset{\delta h \to 0}{\text{limit}} \left(\frac{\delta V}{\delta h}\right)_{r \text{ constant}} = \pi r^2$$

or

$$\frac{\partial V}{\partial h} = \frac{\partial(\pi r^2)h}{\partial h} = (\pi r^2) \,.\, 1 = \pi r^2 \qquad (11.5)$$

$\partial V/\partial h$ is called the partial derivative of V with respect to h.

Using the functional notation 11.1

$$\frac{\partial V}{\partial h} = \underset{\delta h \to 0}{\text{limit}} \frac{V(r,h + \delta h) - V(r,h)}{\delta h}$$

In general, if $f(x,y)$ is a function of x and y

$$\left.\begin{aligned} \frac{\partial f}{\partial x} &= \underset{\delta x \to 0}{\text{limit}} \frac{f(x + \delta x, y) - f(x,y)}{\delta x} \\ \frac{\partial f}{\partial y} &= \underset{\delta y \to 0}{\text{limit}} \frac{f(x,y + \delta y) - f(x,y)}{\delta y} \end{aligned}\right\} \qquad (11.6)$$

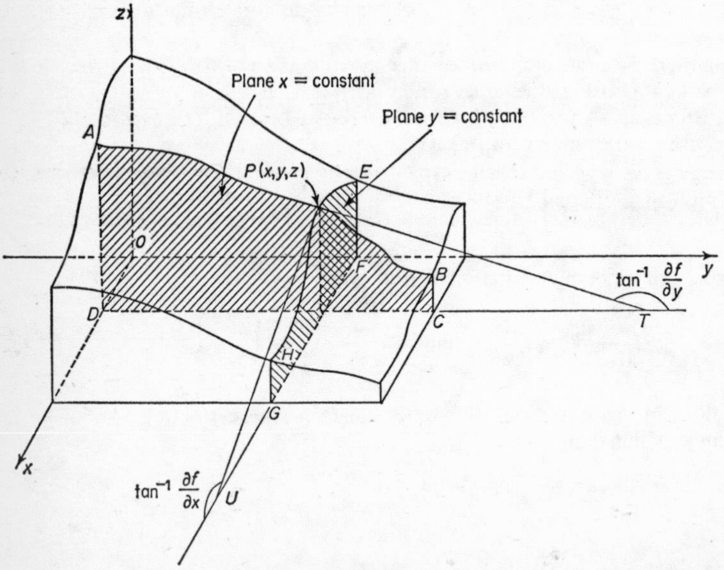

Fig. 11.2

A function $f(x,y)$ of two variables is another new idea and it is helpful, without being too rigorous, to give a geometrical interpretation. Let $z = f(x,y)$; then for each pair of values of x and y for which the function is defined there is a corresponding value for z, and these three values (x, y, z) can be represented in a three-dimensional figure by a point P (see Fig. 11.2).

As x and y vary, P will describe a surface such as $AEBH$. In the particular case when x is kept constant and y varied, P will describe a curve such as APB, and the value of $\partial f/\partial y$ will give the slope of the tangent to the curve at any point on it. In Fig. 11.2 the angle $\tan^{-1}(\partial f/\partial y)$ is obtuse because the value of z is decreasing as y increases.

Similarly, if y is kept constant and x varied, P will describe a curve such as EPH and the value of $\partial f/\partial x$ will give the slope of the tangent to the curve at any point on it.

Example 1. The cost of the electricity used by a domestic refrigerator is given by $C = kE^2/R$, where k is a constant, E is the voltage applied and R is the total resistance of the refrigerator. Find the rate of change of the cost C with respect to:

(i) changes in the resistance (due to varying temperature)
(ii) changes in the applied voltage (due to power cuts).

The rate of change of cost with respect to the resistance is given by

$$\frac{\partial C}{\partial R} = \left(\frac{\partial C}{\partial R}\right)_{E\text{ constant}} = \frac{\partial(kE^2)/R}{\partial R} = (kE^2)\,.-\frac{1}{R^2} = -\frac{kE^2}{R^2}$$

The rate of change of cost with respect to the applied voltage is given by

$$\frac{\partial C}{\partial E} = \left(\frac{\partial C}{\partial E}\right)_{R\text{ constant}} = \frac{\partial(k/R)E^2}{\partial E} = (k/R)2E = 2kE/R$$

Example 2. The rate of investment R_1 is given by the relation

$$R_1 = 15t + \frac{t^2 + 3000}{C}$$

where t is the time and C is the capital already invested. Find the rate of change of investment with respect to the capital invested at any one time.

The words 'at any one time' indicate that t is to be regarded as constant; therefore

$\left(\frac{\partial R_1}{\partial C}\right)_{t\text{ constant}}$ or simply $\frac{\partial R_1}{\partial C}$ is required

$$\frac{\partial R_1}{\partial C} = \frac{\partial\left(15t + \frac{t^2 + 3000}{C}\right)}{\partial C}$$

$$= \frac{\partial(15t)}{\partial C} + \frac{\partial[(t^2 + 3000)/C]}{\partial C}$$

$$= 0 + (t^2 + 3000)\,.(-1/C^2)$$

$$= -(t^2 + 3000)/C^2$$

Note that $\frac{\partial(15t)}{\partial C}$ is zero because $15t$ is regarded as a constant.

Example 3. A particle is projected vertically upwards from the surface of the earth. Allowing for the resistance of the air, it reaches a height h where

$$h = \frac{m^2}{2g}\ln(1 + u^2/m^2)$$

Find the partial derivatives of h with respect to both u and m.

When finding the partial derivative of h with respect to u, $m^2/2g$ is regarded as constant and only $\ln(1 + u^2/m^2)$ has to be differentiated by the function of a function rule (see section 4.6)

$$\frac{\partial h}{\partial u} = \frac{m^2}{2g} \cdot \frac{\partial \ln(1 + u^2/m^2)}{\partial u}$$
$$= \frac{m^2}{2g} \cdot \frac{1}{(1 + u^2/m^2)} \cdot \frac{2u}{m^2}$$
$$= u/[g(1 + u^2/m^2)]$$

When finding the partial derivative of h with respect to m both parts of the right-hand side can vary and we use the product formula of differentiation (refer to section 4.3).

$$\frac{\partial h}{\partial m} = \frac{\partial(m^2/2g)}{\partial m} . \ln(1 + u^2/m^2) + \frac{m^2}{2g} \cdot \frac{\partial \ln(1 + u^2/m^2)}{\partial m}$$
$$= \frac{2m}{2g} \ln(1 + u^2/m^2) + \frac{m^2}{2g} \cdot \frac{1}{(1 + u^2/m^2)} \cdot -\frac{2u^2}{m^3}$$
$$= \frac{m}{g} \ln(1 + u^2/m^2) - u^2/[gm(1 + u^2/m^2)]$$

Revision Questions 11.1

Complete the following statements	*Answer*	*Refer to*
1. $T = T(v, p)$ means that T is a function of . . .	**1.** both v and p.	Equation 11.1
2. Given that $T = T(v, p)$ $\left(\frac{\partial T}{\partial p}\right)_v$ is known as the . . .	**2.** partial derivative of T with respect to p (keeping v constant).	
3. Given that $T = 6v^3 - 3p$	**3.**	Examples 1 and 2
(i) $\left(\frac{\partial T}{\partial p}\right)_v = . . .$	(i) -3	
(ii) $\left(\frac{\partial T}{\partial v}\right)_p = . . .$	(ii) $18v^2$	
4. Given that $P = P(v, L)$ $\lim_{\delta v \to 0} \frac{P(v + \delta v, L) - P(v, L)}{\delta v} = . . .$	**4.** $\frac{\partial P}{\partial v}$	Equation 11.6
5. $\frac{\partial \sin(x^2 + y^2)}{\partial x} = . . .$	**5.** $2x \cos(x^2 + y^2)$	Example 3

Exercises 11.1

1. Given that $z = x^3y^2 + 2x^2 + 3y$, find both $\frac{\partial z}{\partial x}$ and $\frac{\partial z}{\partial y}$.

2. The power P required to propel a steamship is given by

$$P = 1000\, v^3L^2$$

where v is the speed and L the length of the ship. Find the rate of increase of the power with respect to the speed for a given ship.

3. The time T of oscillation of a clock pendulum is given by

$$T = 2\pi\sqrt{(L/g)}$$

where L is the length of the pendulum and g the acceleration due to gravity. Find the partial derivatives of T with respect to both L and g.

4. The specific gravity s of a body is given by the relation

$$s = \frac{W}{W - w}$$

Assuming that both W and w can vary, show that $W\frac{\partial s}{\partial W} + w\frac{\partial s}{\partial w} = 0.$

5. For a given mass of gas $T = pv/8$, where p is its pressure, v its volume and T its absolute temperature. Find $\left(\frac{\partial T}{\partial p}\right)_v$. By suitable rearrangements of the formula also find $\left(\frac{\partial p}{\partial v}\right)_T$ and $\left(\frac{\partial v}{\partial T}\right)_p$. Hence prove that $\left(\frac{\partial p}{\partial v}\right)_T \cdot \left(\frac{\partial v}{\partial T}\right)_p \cdot \left(\frac{\partial T}{\partial p}\right)_v = -1.$

6. The pressure p in an atmosphere is given by the expression

$$p = p_0 \, e^{-\frac{4z}{T}}$$

where p_0 is a constant, T is the absolute temperature and z is the height. Show that

(i) $\frac{\partial p}{\partial z} = -\frac{4p}{T}$ (ii) $\frac{\partial p}{\partial T} = \frac{4zp}{T^2}$

7. The surface area A of a right circular cone is given by the expression

$$A = \pi r\sqrt{(r^2 + h^2)} + \pi r^2$$

where r is the radius of its base and h is its height. Find the partial derivatives of A with respect to both r and h.

8. The pressure P at any point on a cylinder immersed in a steady stream of viscous fluid is given by

$$P = K - \rho V^2 + \rho V^2 \cos 2\theta$$

where K and ρ are constants, V is the speed of the fluid and θ is a variable angle. Find both $\frac{\partial P}{\partial V}$ and $\frac{\partial P}{\partial \theta}$.

9. At any point P on an ellipse centre C, the angle θ between the normal at P and the radius vector CP is given by

$$\theta = \tan^{-1}\frac{a^2 + b^2}{ab}$$

where a and b are the lengths of the semi-major and semi-minor axes respectively. Find both $\frac{\partial \theta}{\partial a}$ and $\frac{\partial \theta}{\partial b}$.

In Astronomy θ is known as *the angle of the vertical*, being the angle between the astronomical and geometrical zeniths, assuming the earth is spheroidal.

10. A publisher issues a book both in hardback form, which costs £1·20 to produce, and in paperback form, which costs £1·00 to produce. It is forecast that the numbers N_h, N_s sold will depend on the prices £h and £s, at which the respective editions are sold, where

$$0{\cdot}1\ N_h = 1000 - 450h + 100s$$
$$0{\cdot}1\ N_s = 4000 - 2260s + 220h$$

Show that his expected net revenue £R from the sales of this book is given by

$$0{\cdot}1\ R = -450h^2 + 320hs - 2260s^2 + 1320h + 6140s - 5200$$

Also show that when $h = 2{\cdot}00$ and $s = 1{\cdot}50$ then $\dfrac{\partial R}{\partial h} = 0 = \dfrac{\partial R}{\partial s}$. (These are part of the conditions for the net revenue R to be a maximum.)

11.2 Total Differential

We shall now consider the *total change* δV in the volume $V(r,h)$ of a right circular cylinder when *both* the radius r *and* the height h change simultaneously. Written without any suffices, δV is generally known as the **total differential,** and is equal to $V(r + \delta r, h + \delta h) - V(r, h)$, where δr and δh are the changes in the radius r and the height h respectively. To find δV, the change in V, we have

$$V = \pi r^2 h$$
$$V + \delta V = \pi[r^2 + 2r\delta r + (\delta r)^2](h + \delta h)$$
$$= \pi r^2 h + 2\pi rh(\delta r) + \pi h(\delta r)^2 + \pi r^2(\delta h) + 2\pi r(\delta r)(\delta h) + \pi(\delta r)^2(\delta h)$$

Ignoring products of two or more small quantities

$$V + \delta V \simeq \pi r^2 h + 2\pi rh(\delta r) + \pi r^2(\delta h)$$

However $\qquad V = \pi r^2 h$

Therefore by subtraction

$$\delta V \simeq 2\pi rh(\delta r) + \pi r^2(\delta h) \tag{11.7}$$

This is illustrated geometrically in Fig. 11.3. Comparing this with Fig.

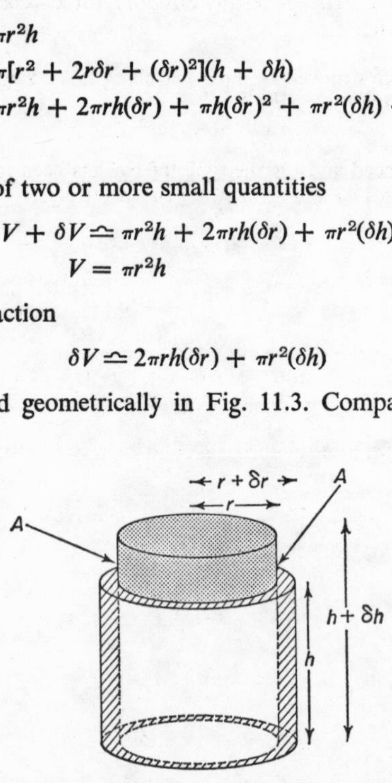

Fig. 11.3

11.1*a* and 11.1*b*, we have that the total change δV in V is given approximately by

$$\delta V \simeq \text{striped volume} + \text{dotted volume}$$

that is $$\delta V \simeq (\delta V)_h + (\delta V)_r$$

The circular strip A indicated in the diagram is the missing small volume of the second order of smallness.

Alternatively, referring back to the earlier results contained in equations 11.3 and 11.5—namely that

$$2\pi rh = \frac{\partial V}{\partial r} \quad \text{and} \quad \pi r^2 = \frac{\partial V}{\partial h}$$

and substituting these in equation 11.7—we have that

$$\delta V \simeq \frac{\partial V}{\partial r}\,\delta r + \frac{\partial V}{\partial h}\,\delta h \tag{11.8}$$

Thus we have linked the total differential δV—that is, the total change in V—with the separate small changes δr and δh and the two partial derivatives of V.

The equation 11.8 is true generally for any three related quantities. We shall verify it in another case.

Example 4. The distance s moved by a car travelling in a straight line with uniform acceleration a is given by

$$s = ut + \tfrac{1}{2}at^2$$

where u is the initial speed and t is the time the car has been travelling. Verify that for simultaneous changes δa and δt in a and t respectively

$$\delta s \simeq \frac{\partial s}{\partial t}\,\delta t + \frac{\partial s}{\partial a}\,\delta a$$

We have that

$$\begin{aligned} s + \delta s &= u(t + \delta t) + \tfrac{1}{2}(a + \delta a)(t + \delta t)^2 \\ &= ut + u(\delta t) + \tfrac{1}{2}(a + \delta a)[t^2 + 2t(\delta t) + (\delta t)^2] \\ &= ut + u(\delta t) + \tfrac{1}{2}[at^2 + 2at(\delta t) + a(\delta t)^2 + t^2(\delta a) + 2t(\delta a)(\delta t) + (\delta a)(\delta t)^2] \end{aligned}$$

Subtracting $s = ut + \frac{1}{2}at^2$ and ignoring second or higher orders of smallness

$$\begin{aligned} \delta s &\simeq u(\delta t) + at(\delta t) + \tfrac{1}{2}t^2(\delta a) \\ &\simeq (u + at)\delta t + (\tfrac{1}{2}t^2)\delta a \end{aligned} \tag{11.9}$$

Differentiating partially the relation $s = ut + \frac{1}{2}at^2$

$$\frac{\partial s}{\partial t} \equiv \left(\frac{\partial s}{\partial t}\right)_{u,a} = \frac{\partial[(u)t + (\frac{1}{2}a)t^2]}{\partial t} = u + at \tag{11.10}$$

$$\frac{\partial s}{\partial a} = \left(\frac{\partial s}{\partial a}\right)_{u,t} = \frac{\partial[(ut) + (\frac{1}{2}t^2)a]}{\partial a} = 0 + (\tfrac{1}{2}t^2)\,.\,1 = \tfrac{1}{2}t^2 \tag{11.11}$$

Substituting from equations 11.10 and 11.11 into equation 11.9

$$\delta s \simeq \frac{\partial s}{\partial t}\,\delta t + \frac{\partial s}{\partial a}\,\delta a \text{ (as required).}$$

In general, if z is a function of two variables x and y, say $z = f(x,y)$, then if both x and y vary by small amounts δx and δy the change δz in z is given by

$$\begin{aligned}\delta z = \delta f &= f(x + \delta x, y + \delta y) - f(x,y)\\ &= f(x + \delta x, y + \delta y) - f(x, y + \delta y) + f(x, y + \delta y) - f(x,y)\\ &= \frac{f(x + \delta x, y + \delta y) - f(x, y + \delta y)}{\delta x}\,\delta x\\ &\qquad + \frac{f(x, y + \delta y) - f(x,y)}{\delta y}\,\delta y\end{aligned}$$

If δx and δy are small then

$$\delta f \simeq \frac{\partial f}{\partial x}\,\delta x + \frac{\partial f}{\partial y}\,\delta y \quad \text{(refer to equation 11.6)}$$

Example 5. The profit P obtained by producing and selling a number N of articles is given by

$$P = 0{\cdot}02N^{3/2} - 30X - 0{\cdot}1NX^{1/2}$$

where X is the cost of producing and selling one article. Find the approximate change in the profit when X increases from 9 to 10 and N increases from 2500 to 2600.

The change in P is given by

$$\delta P \simeq \frac{\partial P}{\partial N}\,\delta N + \frac{\partial P}{\partial X}\,\delta X$$

We first find the partial derivatives of P with respect to N and X

$$\frac{\partial P}{\partial N} = \frac{\partial[0{\cdot}02N^{3/2} - (0{\cdot}1X^{1/2})N - 30X)]}{\partial N} = 0{\cdot}03N^{1/2} - 0{\cdot}1X^{1/2}$$

$$\frac{\partial P}{\partial X} = \frac{\partial[(-30)X - (0{\cdot}1N)X^{1/2} + (0{\cdot}02N^{3/2})]}{\partial X} = -30 - 0{\cdot}05N/X^{1/2}$$

$$\therefore \qquad \delta P \simeq (0{\cdot}03\sqrt{N} - 0{\cdot}1\sqrt{X})\delta N + (-30 - 0{\cdot}05N/\sqrt{X})\delta X$$

In this case we have that $X = 9$, $\delta X = 1$, $N = 2500$, $\delta N = 100$.

$$\begin{aligned}\therefore \qquad \delta P &\simeq (0{\cdot}03\sqrt{2500} - 0{\cdot}1\sqrt{9})\,.\,100 + (-30 - 0{\cdot}05\,.\,2500/\sqrt{9})\,.\,1\\ &\simeq (1{\cdot}5 - 0{\cdot}3)\,.\,100 + (-30 - 125/3)\\ &\simeq 120 - 30 - 42\\ &\simeq +48 \text{ units of profit}\end{aligned}$$

11.3 Application of the Total Differential to Error Calculations

The expression for the total differential which is given in equation 11.8 can be used to find approximately the total error in a result which is based on other, slightly inaccurate, values.

Example 6. A mound of coal is approximately in the shape of a cone of height h metres and radius of base r metres. The weight W of coal in the mound is taken to be

$$W = \tfrac{1}{3}\pi r^2 h\rho$$

where ρ is the average density of the mound. The height is found accurately to be 7 metres, the radius of the base is estimated to be 12 metres with a possible error of $\pm 0{\cdot}4$ metres and the density is estimated to be 0·8* tonnes per cubic metre with a

* Note that the density of the mound differs from the density of a lump of coal.

possible error of $\pm 0{\cdot}03$ tonnes per cubic metre. Find the greatest possible error in the estimate of the weight of coal in the mound.

The errors represent the greatest possible variations from the actual values; thus $(\delta r)_{max} = \pm 0{\cdot}4$, $(\delta \rho)_{max} = \pm 0{\cdot}03$. Using the expression for the total differential

$$\begin{aligned}\delta W &\simeq \frac{\partial W}{\partial r}\,\delta r + \frac{\partial W}{\partial \rho}\,\delta \rho \\ &\simeq \frac{\partial(\frac{1}{3}\pi h\rho)r^2}{\partial r}\,\delta r + \frac{\partial(\frac{1}{3}\pi hr^2)\rho}{\partial \rho}\,\delta \rho \\ &\simeq (\tfrac{1}{3}\pi h\rho)2r\,\delta r + (\tfrac{1}{3}\pi hr^2)\,.\,1\,\delta \rho\end{aligned}$$

From this result it can be seen that the maximum error in W is obtained by taking δr and $\delta \rho$ both positive or both negative. Substituting $h = 7$, $\rho = 0{\cdot}8$, $r = 12$, $\delta r = +0{\cdot}4$, $\delta \rho = +0{\cdot}03$

$$\begin{aligned}\delta W &\simeq \tfrac{1}{3} \times \pi \times 7 \times 0{\cdot}8 \times 2 \times 12 \times 0{\cdot}4 + \tfrac{1}{3} \times \pi \times 7 \times 12^2 \times 0{\cdot}03 \\ &\simeq 17{\cdot}92\pi + 10{\cdot}08\pi \\ &\simeq 88 \text{ tonnes}\end{aligned}$$

The formula 11.8 can be extended to cover the case of more than two variables. Suppose that the calculation of W depended on three other variables x, y, z; then

$$\delta W \simeq \frac{\partial W}{\partial x}\,\delta x + \frac{\partial W}{\partial y}\,\delta y + \frac{\partial W}{\partial z}\,\delta z$$

Example 7. The area of a triangular piece of land ABC is found by estimating from a map the lengths b and c of two of its sides and the size of the angle A between these sides. The length of b is 740 ± 7 metres, the length of c is 1025 ± 10 metres and the angle A is $53 \pm 0{\cdot}1°$. Find the maximum error which could be made in the calculation of the area S using the formula $S = \frac{1}{2}bc \sin A$

$$\begin{aligned}\delta S &\simeq \frac{\partial S}{\partial b}\,\delta b + \frac{\partial S}{\partial c}\,\delta c + \frac{\partial S}{\partial A}\,\delta A \\ &\simeq \tfrac{1}{2}c \sin A\,\delta b + \tfrac{1}{2}b \sin A\,\delta c + \tfrac{1}{2}bc \cos A\,\delta A\end{aligned}$$

The errors in b, c and A vary between the following limits

$$\delta b = \pm 7 \qquad \delta c = \pm 10 \qquad \delta A = \pm 0{\cdot}1 \times \frac{\pi}{180} \text{ radians*}$$

$$\begin{aligned}\therefore \quad (\delta S)_{max} &\simeq \tfrac{1}{2} \times 1025 \times \sin 53° \times 7 + \tfrac{1}{2} \times 740 \times \sin 53° \times 10 \\ &\quad + \tfrac{1}{2} \times 1025 \times 740 \times \cos 53° \times 0{\cdot}00174 \\ &\simeq 2865 + 2954 + 397 \\ &\simeq 6216\end{aligned}$$

The maximum error possible is about 6000 square metres.

Example 8. The amount E of gravitational energy which can be liberated as a cloud of gas slowly condenses to a sphere of radius R is given by the relation

$$E = \frac{GM^2}{R}$$

* Refer to section 4.2: $\dfrac{d \sin A}{dA} = \cos A$ if and only if the angle A is measured in radians.

where G is the universal gravitational constant. The radius R and the mass M of a star are measured with possible errors of ± 1 per cent and ± 2 per cent respectively. Find the greatest percentage error which could arise in calculating E, the gravitational energy liberated during the star's formation.

We note that if δx is the error in any quantity x then the percentage error in x is given by $(\delta x/x) \times 100$.

$$E = \frac{GM^2}{R} \qquad \text{(i)}$$

$$\delta E \simeq \frac{\partial\left[\left(\frac{G}{R}\right) M^2\right]}{\partial M}\,\delta M + \frac{\partial[(GM^2)/R]}{\partial R}\,\delta R$$

$$\delta E \simeq \frac{2MG}{R}\,\delta M - \frac{GM^2}{R^2}\,\delta R \qquad \text{(ii)}$$

Dividing equation (ii) by equation (i)

$$\frac{\delta E}{E} \simeq \left(\frac{2MG}{R}\,\delta M - \frac{GM^2}{R^2}\,\delta R\right) \Big/ \frac{GM^2}{R}$$

$$\simeq 2\frac{\delta M}{M} - \frac{\delta R}{R}$$

Multiplying both sides by 100 we have

$$\frac{\delta E}{E} \times 100 \simeq 2\frac{\delta M}{M} \times 100 - \frac{\delta R}{R} \times 100$$

that is, the percentage error in $E = 2 \times$ the percentage error in $M -$ the percentage error in R. The largest percentage error in E is therefore given by

$$(\%\text{ error in } E)_{\max} = 2 \times (+2\%) - (-1\%) = +5\%$$

or

$$(\%\text{ error in } E)_{\max} = 2 \times (-2\%) - (+1\%) = -5\%$$

Note that in this case opposite signs are taken for δR and δM because of the negative sign in the expression for $(\delta E/E) \times 100$. Note that example 14 in Chapter Three gives an alternative method, which can be used, in this case, by differentiating the logarithm of the original expression.

Further investigation of the use of the total differential is possible if the variables x and y are themselves dependent on another variable or another set of variables, but the work can soon become complicated. Consider the following.

Example 9. After a detailed survey of the number of accidents N occurring between a pedestrian and a motor vehicle in the centre of a town between 06.00 and 24.00 hours, it is found that an approximate expression for N is

$$kN = (Ax - 40x^2)(Ay - 300y^2) \qquad \text{(i)}$$

where k and A are constants, x and y the number of pedestrians and motor vehicles respectively. The numbers x and y are known to vary with the time t hours, where

$$\left.\begin{aligned} x &= C + a\,e^{-t/a}\left[1 - \cos\frac{2\pi(t-2)}{7}\right] \\ y &= D + b\,e^{-t/b}\left[1 - \cos\frac{2\pi(t-2)}{7}\right] \quad (6 \leqslant t \leqslant 24) \end{aligned}\right\} \qquad \text{(ii)}$$

a, b, C, and D being constants. Find the rate of change of the number of accidents with respect to the time.

It is possible to substitute in equation (i) the values of x and y given in the equations (ii), thus expressing N in terms of the constants and the time t. Then dN/dt can be obtained by ordinary differentiation techniques. The resulting expression for N is extremely complicated and it can be slightly easier to proceed as follows.

Since N is dependent on x and y

$$\delta N \simeq \frac{\partial N}{\partial x}\delta x + \frac{\partial N}{\partial y}\delta y$$

Dividing this equation throughout by δt

$$\frac{\delta N}{\delta t} \simeq \frac{\partial N}{\partial x} \cdot \frac{\delta x}{\delta t} + \frac{\partial N}{\partial y} \cdot \frac{\delta y}{\delta t}$$

In the limit as $\delta t \to 0$, because N, x, and y are all functions of the single variable t, we have that $\dfrac{\delta N}{\delta t} \to \dfrac{dN}{dt}$, $\dfrac{\delta x}{\delta t} \to \dfrac{dx}{dt}$, and $\dfrac{\delta y}{\delta t} \to \dfrac{dy}{dt}$. Therefore

$$\frac{dN}{dt} = \frac{\partial N}{\partial x} \cdot \frac{dx}{dt} + \frac{\partial N}{\partial y} \cdot \frac{dy}{dt} \qquad \text{(iii)}$$

Note that if x and y had both depended on two or more variables $t, u, \ldots$ then the limits of $\dfrac{\delta N}{\delta t}, \dfrac{\delta x}{\delta t}, \dfrac{\delta y}{\delta t}$ would have had to be expressed as $\dfrac{\partial N}{\partial t}, \dfrac{\partial x}{\partial t}, \dfrac{\partial y}{\partial t}$ giving the following expression

$$\frac{\partial N}{\partial t} = \frac{\partial N}{\partial x}\frac{\partial x}{\partial t} + \frac{\partial N}{\partial y}\frac{\partial y}{\partial t}$$

Even using the equation (iii) the work is too complicated to be within the scope of this book, as the reader can easily verify if he evaluates the four partial derivatives on the right-hand side of equation (iii).

Exercises 11.2

1. Rectangular boxes with square bases each have a volume V given by $V = x^2y$, where y, x, x are the lengths of three coterminous edges measured in metres. The boxes were originally made with $x = 0{\cdot}4$ metres and $y = 1{\cdot}2$ metres. Show that $\delta V = x(2y\delta x + x\delta y)$. Hence find the increase in the total volume of a 1000 boxes if x is increased to $0{\cdot}5$ metres and y is increased to $1{\cdot}3$ metres.

2. The speed of a car is given by $v = \sqrt{(u^2 + 2as)}$, where u is a constant, a is its acceleration and s is the distance travelled. Show that for small changes δa and δs in the acceleration and the distance travelled, the change δv in the speed is given by $\delta v = (s\delta a + a\delta s)/v$.

3. In order to find the distance across the mouth of a bay three surveying stations A, B and C are set up. Stations A and B are each on one of the headlands of the bay. The third station C is in a direct line, overland, with both A and B, and the angle ACB is found to be a right-angle. Pythagoras's formula is used to calculate the distance AB and α is the percentage error in both AC and BC. Show that α is also the percentage error in the calculation of AB.

4. A satellite of negligible mass is moving in an elliptical orbit of semi-major axis a astronomical units* with a period of P years about a planet of mass M. By Kepler's third law $M = a^3/p^2$, where M is measured in terms of our Sun's mass. The semi-major axis a is found to be 0·0040 astronomical units with an error of ±0·00003 and P to be 0·075 years with an error of ±0·0002. Find the greatest possible error in the calculation of M.

5. The density ρ of a gas is given by the expression $\rho = P\mu/RT$, where both μ and R are constants, P is the pressure and T the absolute temperature. Both P and T are measured to an accuracy of ±0·1 per cent. Find the greatest possible percentage error in calculating ρ using the formula given.

6. The time T of oscillation of a simple pendulum is given by the formula $T = 2\pi\sqrt{(L/g)}$, where L is its length and g is the acceleration due to gravity. Rearrange this formula to express g in terms of T, L and π. Hence find to two decimal places the possible errors in the calculated value of g if L is measured as 100 ± 0·1 cm and T as 2·000 ± 0·005 seconds.

7. The net revenue £R obtained when N units of an item are sold at a price £P is given by $R = NP - (750 + 0{\cdot}0001\,N^2)$. Find the approximate change in the net revenue when P increases from 1·00 to 1·05 and N decreases from 500 to 480.

8. The acceleration a of a piston is given by the equation

$$a = \frac{w^2r}{7}(4\cos\theta - 1)(\cos\theta + 2)$$

where r is a constant and w and θ are variables. Show that when the value of θ is 60°, $\dfrac{\delta a}{a} \simeq \dfrac{2\delta w}{w} - \dfrac{11\sqrt{3}}{5}\delta\theta$.

9. The power dissipation P along a blood vessel of length L and radius r is given by $P = Cf^2/r^4 + K\pi r^2 L$, where C and K are constants and f is the rate of flow of blood along the vessel. Find an approximate expression for the change in P when r and f both alter by small amounts δr and δf. Given also that $f^2 = \pi K L r^6/2C$ verify that the approximate change in P is $\gamma\delta f/r$ and find γ in terms of C, K, π, L.

11.4 Repeated Partial Differentiation

We have seen that given

$$V = \pi r^2 h$$

we can find the partial derivatives of V with respect to r and h; for example

$$\frac{\partial V}{\partial r} = 2\pi rh$$

This partial derivative is dependent on two variables and can itself be differentiated keeping either r or h constant. Thus there are two possible *second* partial derivatives obtainable from $\partial V/\partial r$

$$\frac{\partial}{\partial r}\left(\frac{\partial V}{\partial r}\right) = \frac{\partial(2\pi rh)}{\partial r} = 2\pi h$$

* An astronomical unit is the mean distance of the Earth from the Sun.

which is written more neatly as

$$\frac{\partial^2 V}{\partial r^2} = 2\pi h$$

and $$\frac{\partial}{\partial h}\left(\frac{\partial V}{\partial r}\right) = \frac{\partial}{\partial h}(2\pi rh) = 2\pi r$$

written as $$\frac{\partial^2 V}{\partial h\,\partial r} = 2\pi r$$

Similarly $$\frac{\partial^2 V}{\partial h^2} = \frac{\partial}{\partial h}\left(\frac{\partial V}{\partial h}\right) = \frac{\partial}{\partial h}(\pi r^2) = 0$$

$$\frac{\partial^2 V}{\partial r\,\partial h} = \frac{\partial}{\partial r}\left(\frac{\partial V}{\partial h}\right) = \frac{\partial}{\partial r}(\pi r^2) = 2\pi r$$

Note that $$\frac{\partial^2 V}{\partial r\,\partial h} = 2\pi r = \frac{\partial^2 V}{\partial h\,\partial r}$$

In some special cases these two second-order partial derivatives are not equal. In general they do have the same value.

Example 10. The surface area of a solid right circular cone is given by

$$A = \pi r\sqrt{(r^2 + h^2)} + \pi r^2$$

where r is the radius of its base and h its vertical height. Verify that

$$\frac{\partial^2 A}{\partial h\,\partial r} = \frac{\partial^2 A}{\partial r\,\partial h}$$

$$A = \pi r\sqrt{(r^2 + h^2)} + \pi r^2$$

$$\therefore \quad \frac{\partial A}{\partial r} = \pi\sqrt{(r^2 + h^2)} + \pi r \,.\, \tfrac{1}{2}(r^2 + h^2)^{-\frac{1}{2}} \,.\, 2r + 2\pi r$$

$$= \pi\sqrt{(r^2 + h^2)} + \pi r^2(r^2 + h^2)^{-\frac{1}{2}} + 2\pi r$$

$$\therefore \quad \frac{\partial^2 A}{\partial h\,\partial r} = \frac{\partial}{\partial h}\left(\frac{\partial A}{\partial r}\right) = \pi \,.\, \tfrac{1}{2}(r^2 + h^2)^{-\frac{1}{2}} \,.\, 2h + \pi r^2[-\tfrac{1}{2}(r^2 + h^2)^{-\frac{3}{2}}2h]$$

$$= \pi h(r^2 + h^2)^{-\frac{1}{2}} - \pi r^2 h(r^2 + h^2)^{-\frac{3}{2}} \qquad \text{(i)}$$

$$\frac{\partial A}{\partial h} = \pi r \,.\, \tfrac{1}{2}(r^2 + h^2)^{-\frac{1}{2}} \,.\, 2h$$

$$= \pi rh(r^2 + h^2)^{-\frac{1}{2}}$$

$$\therefore \quad \frac{\partial^2 A}{\partial r\,\partial h} = \frac{\partial}{\partial r}\left(\frac{\partial A}{\partial h}\right) = \pi h(r^2 + h^2)^{-\frac{1}{2}} + \pi rh[-\tfrac{1}{2}(r^2 + h^2)^{-\frac{3}{2}} \,.\, 2r]$$

$$= \pi h(r^2 + h^2)^{-\frac{1}{2}} - \pi r^2 h(r^2 + h^2)^{-\frac{3}{2}} \qquad \text{(ii)}$$

Comparing equations (i) and (ii) we see that $\dfrac{\partial^2 A}{\partial r\,\partial h} = \dfrac{\partial^2 A}{\partial h\,\partial r}$.

We shall assume that these two partial derivatives are equal in all succeeding work.

These partial derivatives occur in many of the mathematical equations used to describe physical situations—for example:

1. A long thin bar is being heated at one end. θ is the temperature at any point distance x from the end at time t. The temperature gradient along the bar is $\partial\theta/\partial x$ and $\partial^2\theta/\partial x^2$ is the rate of change of the temperature gradient along the bar. Assuming no heat losses into the surrounding medium

$$\frac{\partial^2\theta}{\partial x^2} = k\frac{\partial\theta}{\partial t}$$

This equation is known as the diffusion equation and also occurs in describing the transmission of current along an electric cable and in the study of the linear motion of a fluid.

2. If C is a country's capital stock then $\partial C/\partial t = I$ is the rate of net investment and $\partial^2 C/\partial t^2 = \partial I/\partial t$ is the rate of change of investment.

3. The gravitational potential V in any two-dimensional space unoccupied by matter is given by Laplace's Equation

$$\frac{\partial^2 V}{\partial x^2} + \frac{\partial^2 V}{\partial y^2} = 0$$

This also applies to electrical or magnetic potential in the absence of electric charges or of magnetic particles respectively.

4. Third and higher order partial derivatives can occur. The equation

$$EI\frac{\partial^4 y}{\partial x^4} + \frac{w}{g}\frac{\partial^2 y}{\partial t^2} = 0$$

arises in the study of transverse vibrations in a uniform beam.

Example 11. Show that $\theta = \frac{1}{k}\,e^{-ax}\sin(2a^2kt - ax)$ is a solution of the linear diffusion type of equation $\frac{\partial^2\theta}{\partial x^2} = \frac{1}{k}\frac{\partial\theta}{\partial t}$.

$$\frac{\partial\theta}{\partial x} = -\frac{a}{k}\,e^{-ax}\sin(2a^2kt - ax) + \frac{1}{k}\,e^{-ax}\cos(2a^2kt - ax)\,.\,(-a)$$

$$= -\frac{a}{k}\,e^{-ax}[\sin(2a^2kt - ax) + \cos(2a^2kt - ax)]$$

$$\frac{\partial^2\theta}{\partial x^2} = +\frac{a^2}{k}\,e^{-ax}[\sin(2a^2kt - ax) + \cos(2a^2kt - ax)] - \frac{a}{k}\,e^{-ax}$$
$$\times[-a\cos(2a^2kt - ax) + a\sin(2a^2kt - ax)]$$

$$\therefore\quad \frac{\partial^2\theta}{\partial x^2} = \frac{2a^2}{k}\,e^{-ax}\cos(2a^2kt - ax) \qquad \text{(i)}$$

$$\frac{\partial\theta}{\partial t} = \frac{1}{k}\,e^{-ax}\cos(2a^2kt - ax)\,.\,2a^2k$$

$$\therefore\quad \frac{\partial\theta}{\partial t} = 2a^2\,e^{-ax}\cos(2a^2kt - ax) \qquad \text{(ii)}$$

From the equations (i) and (ii) it can be seen that

$$\frac{\partial^2\theta}{\partial x^2} = \frac{1}{k}\frac{\partial\theta}{\partial t}$$

11.5 Maxima and Minima of a Function of Two Variables

One of the most useful applications of partial derivatives is to find largest or smallest values. In example 9 we saw that a simplified mathematical model of a traffic situation gave the number of accidents N, between a pedestrian and a motor vehicle, in terms of two variables, the number of pedestrians x and the number of motor vehicles y. This equation and ordinary common sense give two extreme cases when no accidents will occur ($N = 0$). They are when there are no pedestrians or no motor vehicles ($x = 0$ or $y = 0$) and when the numbers of pedestrians or motor vehicles is so large that a traffic jam occurs. In between these two extremes there must be some largest value of N. It is possible to find the maximum (or minimum) values of N given by the mathematical model.

In our earlier work on maxima and minima (see section 3.4) we were concerned with only one independent variable and hence $\mathrm{d}N/\mathrm{d}x = 0$ would give the values of x at the turning points which could be tested by considering the sign of $\mathrm{d}^2N/\mathrm{d}x^2$. In the present case a maximum or minimum value of N would depend on the values of *two* variables x and y. However, it can be shown (see Appendix Three) that the two values can be found by equating the *two* partial derivatives $\partial N/\partial x$ and $\partial N/\partial y$ to zero and solving simultaneously the resulting two equations in x and y. This gives the coordinates $(x_1, y_1), (x_2, y_2), \ldots$ of the stationary points. An extra test has now to be made to see if maxima or minima exist. The three second-partial derivatives are obtained and their values found at the stationary point. Then if

$$\left(\frac{\partial^2 N}{\partial x^2}\right) \cdot \left(\frac{\partial^2 N}{\partial y^2}\right) - \left(\frac{\partial^2 N}{\partial x\, \partial y}\right)^2 > 0$$

a maximum or a minimum exists according to whether $\partial^2N/\partial x^2$ (or $\partial^2N/\partial y^2$) is negative or positive respectively.

Example 12. Find the maximum value of the accident rate N given that $kN = (Ax - 40x^2)(Ay - 300y^2)$, where k and A are positive constants.

Firstly $\dfrac{\partial N}{\partial x} = 0, \quad \dfrac{\partial N}{\partial y} = 0$ gives

$$k\frac{\partial N}{\partial x} = (A - 80x)(Ay - 300y^2) = 0$$

$$k\frac{\partial N}{\partial y} = (Ax - 40x^2)(A - 600y) = 0$$

Solving these equations gives the four points $(0, 0)$, $(0, A/300)$, $(A/40, 0)$, $(A/80, A/600)$. The only one of practical interest is $x = A/80$, $y = A/600$.

Secondly $k\dfrac{\partial^2 N}{\partial x^2} = -80(Ay - 300y^2), \quad k\dfrac{\partial^2 N}{\partial y^2} = -600(Ax - 40x^2)$

$$k\frac{\partial^2 N}{\partial x\, \partial y} = (A - 80x)(A - 600y)$$

Therefore, at the point $x = A/80$, $y = A/600$

$$k\frac{\partial^2 N}{\partial x^2} = -80\left(A \,.\, \frac{A}{600} - 300 \,.\, \frac{A^2}{600^2}\right) = -\frac{A^2}{15}$$

$$k\frac{\partial^2 N}{\partial y^2} = -600\left(A \,.\, \frac{A}{80} - 40 \,.\, \frac{A^2}{80^2}\right) = -\frac{15}{4}A^2$$

$$k\frac{\partial^2 N}{\partial x\,\partial y} = \left(A - 80 \,.\, \frac{A}{80}\right)\left(A - 600 \,.\, \frac{A}{600}\right) = 0$$

Therefore, at the point $x = A/80$, $y = A/600$

$$\left(\frac{\partial^2 N}{\partial x^2}\right) . \left(\frac{\partial^2 N}{\partial y^2}\right) - \left(\frac{\partial^2 N}{\partial x\,\partial y}\right)^2 = \left(-\frac{A^2}{15k}\right)\left(-\frac{15A^2}{4k}\right) - (0)^2 > 0$$

and a maximum or a minimum exists.

Thirdly, because $\dfrac{\partial^2 N}{\partial x^2} = -\dfrac{A^2}{15k}$, which is negative, the point gives a maximum and not a minimum value, which is found by substituting in the original equation.

$$k \,.\, N_{\max} = \left[A \,.\, \frac{A}{80} - 40 \,.\, \frac{A^2}{80^2}\right]\left[A \,.\, \frac{A}{600} - 300 \,.\, \frac{A^2}{600^2}\right]$$

$$= \frac{A^4}{192\,000}$$

It is stressed that in this case the result given by the mathematical model is mathematically correct but because both x and y can vary with the time t the required values of x and y may, in practice, not always occur together.

Example 13. In exercises 11.1, No. 10, a publisher's net revenue £R was given by the expression

$$0{\cdot}1R = -450h^2 + 320hs - 2260s^2 + 1320h + 6140s - 5200$$

where £h and £s are the selling prices of the hardback and softback editions of a book. Find the values of h and s which will maximise his net revenue assuming the mathematical model to be correct.

Firstly, $\dfrac{\partial R}{\partial h} = 0$, $\dfrac{\partial R}{\partial s} = 0$ give the two equations

$$-900h + 320s + 1320 = 0 \qquad (1)$$

$$320h - 4520s + 6140 = 0 \qquad (2)$$

Multiplying equation (1) by 16 and equation (2) by 45 gives

$$-14\,400h + 5\,120s + 21\,120 = 0$$

$$14\,400h - 203\,400s + 276\,300 = 0$$

by addition

$$-198\,280s + 297\,420 = 0$$

$\therefore$ $s = 1{\cdot}50$

Substituting in equation (1) gives

$$-900h + 480 + 1320 = 0$$

$\therefore$ $h = 2{\cdot}00$

Secondly, we test if these values can give a maximum or a minimum. Differentiating

$$\frac{\partial^2 R}{\partial h^2} = -9000 \qquad \frac{\partial^2 R}{\partial s^2} = -45\,200 \qquad \frac{\partial^2 R}{\partial s\,\partial h} = 3200$$

$$\left(\frac{\partial^2 R}{\partial h^2}\right).\left(\frac{\partial^2 R}{\partial s^2}\right) - \left(\frac{\partial^2 R}{\partial h\,\partial s}\right)^2 = (-9000).(-45\,200) - 3200^2$$

$$= \text{positive}$$

Therefore $a = 1{\cdot}50$ and $h = 2{\cdot}00$ give a maximum or a minimum value of R.

Thirdly because $\dfrac{\partial^2 R}{\partial s^2}$ $\left(\text{and } \dfrac{\partial^2 R}{\partial h^2}\right)$ are negative there is a maximum and not a minimum value. Substituting $s = 1{\cdot}5$ and $h = 2$ in the expression for R we have that $R_{max} =$ 7250.

Therefore if the publisher sells the hardback edition of the book at £2·00 and the softback edition at £1·50 he should obtain a maximum net revenue of £7250.

Exercises 11.3

1. Given that $x = r \cos \theta$ and $y = r \sin \theta$ verify that

(i)
$$\sin \theta \frac{\partial^2 x}{\partial \theta^2} + \cos \theta \frac{\partial^2 y}{\partial \theta^2} = 0$$

(ii)
$$\cos \theta \frac{\partial^2 y}{\partial r\,\partial \theta} - \sin \theta \frac{\partial^2 x}{\partial r\,\partial \theta} = 1$$

2. Given that $r = \sqrt{(x^2 + y^2)}$ verify that

$$\frac{\partial^2 r}{\partial x^2} \times \frac{\partial^2 r}{\partial y^2} = \left(\frac{\partial^2 r}{\partial x\,\partial y}\right)^2$$

3. The cross-sectional area A of a water channel is given by

$$A = (9 - 2X + X \cos \theta)X \sin \theta$$

Find $\partial A/\partial X$ and $\partial A/\partial \theta$ and verify that when $X = 3$ and $\theta = 60°$ $\partial A/\partial X = 0$ and $\partial A/\partial \theta = 0$. Find also the values of the three second-partial derivatives of A and hence prove that the cross-sectional area of the water channel is a maximum when $\theta = 60°$ and $X = 3$.

4. In a resistance network the electric current is known to distribute itself so that the total heat H generated is a minimum. In a particular network two of the currents x and y are unknown and the heat generated is found to be

$$H = 10x^2 + 8xy + 5y^2 - 238x - 102y + 2023$$

Find the values of the unknown currents in the network by finding the values of x and y for which H has a minimum value. Verify that your values do in fact give a minimum value for H.

5. A distributor of margarine and butter finds that his total revenue £R per week is given by

$$R = 120x + 145{\cdot}5y - 2x^2 - 2{\cdot}5xy - 2{\cdot}25y^2$$

where x and y are the prices, in new pence, of margarine and butter respectively. Find the values of x and y which will maximise his total revenue, verifying that your values do give R a maximum value.

11.6 Problems

1. A silage tank is in the form of a right circular cylinder of height h and radius r, capped by a hemispherical dome. Its volume V and surface area A are given by

$$V = \pi r^2 h + \tfrac{2}{3}\pi r^3$$

and

$$A = 2\pi rh + 2\pi r^2$$

Verify that $\dfrac{\partial V}{\partial r} = A$ and that $\dfrac{\partial V}{\partial h} = \dfrac{r}{2}\dfrac{\partial A}{\partial h}$

2. The pressure p of a given mass of gas is given by

$$p = \frac{16T}{v - b} - \frac{3}{v^2}$$

where b is a constant, v the volume and T its absolute temperature. Express T in terms of v, p, and b. Hence prove that

$$\left(\frac{\partial T}{\partial v}\right)_p = (pv^3 + 6b - 3v)/16v^3$$

3. The centre of a conic section whose equation is $f(x, y) = 0$ can be found by solving simultaneously the two equations $\partial f/\partial x = 0$ and $\partial f/\partial y = 0$. Find the centre of the conic

$$8x^2 - 12xy + 17y^2 + 4x + 22y - 7 = 0$$

4. The zenith distance z of a star is given by

$$\cos z = \sin \delta \sin \phi + \cos \delta \cos \phi \cos H$$

where δ is its declination, H its hour angle and ϕ the observer's latitude. Find $\partial z/\partial H$ in terms of z, δ, ϕ, H. Given also that $\sin z \sin A = \sin H \cos \delta$, show that $\partial Z/\partial H = \sin A \cos \phi$.

5. A manufacturer wishes to make rectangular boxes open at the top, each one to have a volume of 108 cubic metres. In order to keep his costs as low as possible he wishes to minimise the surface area S of each box. The base of each is a rectangle x metres by y metres. Show that

$$S = xy + 216\left[\frac{1}{x} + \frac{1}{y}\right]$$

and hence find the values of x and y which will make S a minimum.

6. The temperature θ at time t at a point distance x from the end of a long thin bar is given by

$$\frac{\partial^2\theta}{\partial x^2} = \frac{1}{k}\frac{\partial\theta}{\partial t}$$

For all values of x and t, $\theta = \theta_0 e^{-\alpha x} \sin(nt - \alpha x)$ is a solution of the equation. Find an expression for α in terms of n and k.

7. The alternating current i in an electric circuit at time t is given by

$$i = \frac{E \cos pt}{R} \qquad (R \neq 0)$$

where p and E are constants, R is the resistance and t the time. For small changes δR and δt in R and t respectively show that

$$\frac{\delta i}{i} = -p(\tan pt)\delta t - \frac{\delta R}{R}$$

8. Due to the rotation of the earth a rocket fired vertically from the ground is deflected by an amount x where

$$x = \frac{gt^3v}{6r}$$

The values of t, v, r are measured to an accuracy of $\pm 0{\cdot}1$ per cent and the error in the value of g is negligible. Find the greatest possible percentage error in the calculation of x when using the formula.

9. A conic whose equation is $f(x, y) = 0$ can be a pair of straight lines. In this case the centre lies on the conic. Therefore the coordinates of the centre, which are given by solving simultaneously the equations $\partial f/\partial x = 0$ and $\partial f/\partial y = 0$, satisfy the equation $f(x, y) = 0$. Prove that the conic whose equation is

$$18x^2 - 33xy + 12y^2 + 15x - 10y + 2 = 0$$

is a pair of straight lines.

10. Given that

$$S = (6 - 5m - c)^2 + (2 - 4m - c)^2 + (4 - 4m - c)^2$$

find the pair of values of the variables m and c which make S a minimum. (This is a very simplified form of the problem of finding a line of 'best fit' to a number of points using the method of 'least squares'.)

11. (i) Given that $x = r\cos\theta$, $y = r\sin\theta$, evaluate the determinant

$$\begin{vmatrix} \dfrac{\partial x}{\partial r}, & \dfrac{\partial x}{\partial \theta} \\[2ex] \dfrac{\partial y}{\partial r}, & \dfrac{\partial y}{\partial \theta} \end{vmatrix}$$

(ii) Given that $x = r\sin\theta\cos\phi$, $y = r\sin\theta\sin\phi$, $z = r\cos\theta$, evaluate the determinant

$$\begin{vmatrix} \dfrac{\partial x}{\partial r} & \dfrac{\partial x}{\partial \theta} & \dfrac{\partial x}{\partial \phi} \\[2ex] \dfrac{\partial y}{\partial r} & \dfrac{\partial y}{\partial \theta} & \dfrac{\partial y}{\partial \phi} \\[2ex] \dfrac{\partial z}{\partial r} & \dfrac{\partial z}{\partial \theta} & \dfrac{\partial z}{\partial \phi} \end{vmatrix}$$

(These two determinants are examples of Jacobians which occur in later work, e.g. changing the variables in partial differential equations and double and triple integrals.)

12. The capacity q of an electric condensor formed from four concentric spherical shells of radii a, x, y, b respectively ($a < x < y < b$) is given by

$$q = \frac{ax}{x - a} + \frac{xy}{y - x} + \frac{yb}{b - y}$$

The radii x and y vary and a and b are fixed. Verify that q has a stationary point when $x = \dfrac{3ab}{2b + a}$, $y = \dfrac{3ab}{2a + b}$.

REVISION EXERCISES

1. In the theory of servomechanisms the period of oscillation T of a linear system is given by

$$T = 4\int_0^H \frac{dx}{\sqrt{(w_0^2H^2 - w_0^2x^2)}}$$

where w_0 and H are constants. Prove that $T = 2\pi/w_0$.

2. The amount of water Q discharged over a weir is given by

$$Q = 3BH^{\frac{3}{2}} - 0{\cdot}6H^{\frac{5}{2}}$$

Find the partial derivatives of Q with respect to B, the breadth of the weir, and H, the head of water.

3. The function $f(x)$ is given by

$$f(x) = a \cosh x + b \sinh x$$

where a and b are positive constants. Prove that if

(i) $a > b, f(x)$ has a minimum value of $\sqrt{(a^2 - b^2)}$
(ii) $a < b, f(x)$ has no maximum or minimum values

(Refer to Problems 4.11, No. 17.)

4. By using the sine and cosine formulae of spherical trigonometry, the zenith distance z, the hour angle H and the azimuth A of a star are found to be connected by the equations

$$\cos z = \sin \delta \sin \phi + \cos \delta \cos \phi \cos H$$

and

$$\sin z \sin A = \sin H \cos \delta$$

where δ, the star's declination, and ϕ, the observer's latitude, are constant. Show that

$$\delta z \simeq \sin A \cos \phi \, \delta H$$

5. Prove that (i) $\dfrac{d(\sin x)}{dx} = \sin (x + \pi/2)$, (ii) $\dfrac{d^2(\sin x)}{dx^2} = \sin (x + 2\pi/2)$, (iii) $\dfrac{d^3(\sin x)}{dx^3} = \sin (x + 3\pi/2)$. Deduce the value of $\dfrac{d^n(\sin x)}{dx^n}$, where n is a positive integer. What is the value of $\dfrac{d^n(\cos x)}{dx^n}$?

6. Find k given that

$$f(x) = \cos x \cosh x - 1 = kx^4 + \text{terms in } x^5, x^6 \ldots$$

The graph of $y = f(x)$ has a stationary value at $x = 0$. Determine whether it is a maximum, minimum or a point of inflexion.

7. Dieterici's equation (an alternative to Van der Waal's equation) states that the pressure p, volume v and absolute temperature T of a mass of gas are connected by the equation

$$p = \frac{RT}{(v-b)} \mathrm{e}^{-\frac{a}{vRT}}$$

where a, b and R are constants. Verify that both $\partial p/\partial v = 0$ and $\partial^2 p/\partial v^2 = 0$ for the critical volume and temperature v_c and T_c respectively, where $v_c = 2b$ and $T_c = a/(4bR)$. What is the value of p_c, the critical pressure, in terms of a, b and e?

8. Prove that the maximum volume of a rectangular parallelepiped with a fixed surface area is when it is a cube.

9. The parametric equations of a cycloid are $x = a(\theta + \sin\theta)$, $y = a(1 - \cos\theta)$, where a is a constant. Show that $s^2 = 8ay$, where s is the arc length measured from the point $\theta = 0$.

10. The range R of a particle projected from a point on a plane which is inclined at an angle α to the horizontal is given by

$$R = \frac{2u^2}{g} \cos\theta \sin(\theta - \alpha) \sec^2 \alpha$$

where the velocity of projection is u at an angle θ to the horizontal. Using the trigonometrical identity $2 \cos A \sin B = \sin(A + B) - \sin(A - B)$, find the maximum value of R as θ varies. Verify your result by differentiation.

11. A solid cylinder of radius a has a groove of semicircular section of radius $a/4$ cut round it. Find the volume of metal removed and the area of the surface of the groove.

12. In the kinetic theory of gases the average mean free path $\bar{x}$ of the molecules is given by $\bar{x} = \int_0^\infty Px\,\mathrm{e}^{-Px}\,\mathrm{d}x$, where P is a constant. Show that $\bar{x} = 1/P$.

13. Find the root mean square value of the function $a \cos(wx + \alpha)$ over the range $0 \leqslant x \leqslant 2\pi/w$, where a, w and α are constants.

14. The radial stress p_x and the circumferential stress p_y on a thick cylinder subject to fluid pressure are connected by the equations $p_x - p_y = 2a$ and $r\frac{\mathrm{d}p_x}{\mathrm{d}r} + p_x = -p_y$. Find expressions for p_x and p_y in terms of r and a, and b an arbitrary constant.

15. Given that $\frac{\mathrm{d}x}{\mathrm{d}y} = \left(\frac{\mathrm{d}y}{\mathrm{d}x}\right)^{-1}$ differentiate throughout with respect to x and show that $\frac{\mathrm{d}^2x}{\mathrm{d}y^2} = -\frac{\mathrm{d}^2y}{\mathrm{d}x^2}\Big/\left(\frac{\mathrm{d}y}{\mathrm{d}x}\right)^3$. Kepler's equation for the eccentric anomaly E states that $M = E - \mathrm{e}\sin E$, where M is the mean anomaly and $\mathrm{e} = 2{\cdot}718\ldots$ Find expressions for $\frac{\mathrm{d}E}{\mathrm{d}M}$ and $\frac{\mathrm{d}^2E}{\mathrm{d}M^2}$ and hence, using Taylor's Theorem, show that

$$\delta E \simeq \frac{\delta M}{1 - \mathrm{e}\cos E} - \frac{\mathrm{e}\sin E(\delta M)^2}{2(1 - \mathrm{e}\cos E)^3}$$

16. In a restricted Lorentz transformation in the theory of relativity the coordinates (x', y', z', t') and (x, y, z, t) are connected by the equations $x' = \beta(x - Vt)$, $y' = y$,

$z' = z$, $t' = \beta(t - xV/c^2)$, where $\beta = 1/\sqrt{(1 - v^2/c^2)}$. The components of velocity in the two inertial frames are

$$u = \frac{dx}{dt}, \qquad v = \frac{dy}{dt}, \qquad w = \frac{dz}{dt},$$

$$u' = \frac{dx'}{dt'}, \qquad v' = \frac{dy'}{dt'}, \qquad w' = \frac{dz'}{dt'}$$

Prove that

$$u' = \frac{(u - V)}{(1 - uV/c^2)}, \quad v' = \frac{v}{\beta(1 - uV/c^2)}, \quad w' = \frac{w}{\beta(1 - uV/c^2)}$$

(Hint: take differentials in the first set of equations; then $dx' = \beta(dx - Vdt)$, etc.)

17. Find μ_1' and μ_2', the first and second moments about the origin, of the probability function $p(x) = 1$ $(0 \leqslant x \leqslant 1)$. Show that the value of $M(a) = \int_0^1 e^{ax}\, dx$ is $\frac{1}{a}(e^a - 1)$. Expand $M(a)$ in a series of ascending powers of a and show that the coefficients of a and $a^2/2!$ in this expansion are equal to the values of μ_1' and μ_2'.

18. Given that $\int_0^\infty e^{-x^2}\, dx = \sqrt{\pi}/2$, show that $\int_0^\infty x^4 e^{-x^2}\, dx = 3\sqrt{\pi}/8$. From the kinetic theory the root mean square velocity of the molecules $(\bar{v}^2)^{\frac{1}{2}}$ is the square root of the integral

$$4\pi \left(\frac{m}{2\pi kT}\right)^{\frac{3}{2}} \int_0^\infty e^{-mv^2/2kT}\, v^4 dv$$

where k is the Boltzmann constant, T is the absolute temperature, m the mass of each molecule and v the speed of any molecule. Using the substitution $x^2 = (mv^2)/(2kT)$, show that

$$(\bar{v}^2)^{\frac{1}{2}} = \left(\frac{3kT}{m}\right)^{\frac{1}{2}}$$

19. The parametric equations of the curve known as the Tractrix are

$$x = \frac{c}{2} \ln \left[\frac{1 + \sin \theta}{1 - \sin \theta}\right] - c \sin \theta, \quad y = c \cos \theta \quad \left(0 \leqslant \theta < \frac{\pi}{2}\right)$$

Prove that the arc length s measured from the point $\theta = 0$ to any point θ is given by $s = c \ln (c/y)$. (Hint: first show that $\frac{ds}{d\theta} = c \tan \theta$.)

20. The depth of water x at any time t in a tank is given by

$$A\frac{dx}{dt} = B - C\sqrt{x}$$

where A, B and C are constants. Initially $x = 0$; show that

$$C^2 t = 2AB \ln \left(\frac{B}{B - C\sqrt{x}}\right) - 2AC\sqrt{x}$$

(Hint: let $x = y^2$.)

21. The two points P and Q lie on the lines L_1 and L_2. The coordinates of the points P and Q are respectively $(2, t, t - 1)$ and $(s, 2s + 1, 3s + 2)$, where s and t are variables. U, the square of the distance between the points P and Q, is given by

$$U = PQ^2 = (s - 2)^2 + (2s - t + 1)^2 + (3s - t + 3)^2$$

Find the shortest distance between L_1 and L_2 by finding the minimum value of U and hence of PQ $(= \sqrt{U})$. This is also the length of the common perpendicular to the lines L_1 and L_2.

22. The angles of a triangle are A, B and C. Prove that the maximum value of $\sin A \sin B \sin C$ is $3\sqrt{3}/8$. (Hint: remember that $A + B + C = \pi$ and eliminate C.)

APPENDIX ONE

BASIC THEOREM CONCERNING e^x

To prove that $[E(1)]^x = E(x)$ for all rational values of x.
Let a and b be any two constants. Then by definition

$$\frac{d[E(ax)]}{dx} = aE(ax) \qquad \text{(i)}$$

and

$$\frac{d[E(bx)]}{dx} = bE(bx) \qquad \text{(ii)}$$

with

$$E(0) = 1$$

Consider a new function $U(x)$, where $U(x) = E(ax) . E(bx)$. Let $x = 0$; then $U(0) = E(0) . E(0) = 1 \times 1 = 1$.

Also

$$\frac{dU(x)}{dx} = E(ax)\frac{dE(bx)}{dx} + \frac{dE(ax)}{dx}E(bx)$$

$$= E(ax)bE(bx) + aE(ax)E(bx) \quad \text{(from equations i and ii)}$$

$$= (a + b)E(ax)E(bx)$$

$$\therefore \quad \frac{dU(x)}{dx} = (a + b)U(x)$$

The solution of this equation is, by definition

$$U(x) = E[(a + b)x]$$

$$\therefore \quad U(x) = E(ax)E(bx) = E[(a + b)x] \quad \text{(with } E(0) = 1\text{)}$$

In particular, with $x = 1$

$$E(a)E(b) = E(a + b) \qquad \text{(iii)}$$

This result may be extended to n constants $a, b, c, \ldots p$, giving

$$E(a)E(b)E(c)\ldots E(p) = E(a + b + c + \ldots + p) \qquad \text{(iv)}$$

Let $a = b = c = \ldots = p = 1$, and equation iv becomes

$$E(1)E(1)E(1)\ldots E(1) = E(1 + 1 + 1 + \ldots + 1)$$

that is

$$[E(1)]^n = E(n)$$

Denoting the value of $E(1)$ by e, we have that

$$e^n = E(n) \text{ (when } n \text{ is a positive integer)}$$

Consider equation iv with q terms, where q is a positive integer, and let $a = b = c = \ldots = p/q$, where p/q is an arithmetical fraction in its lowest terms.

$$\therefore \quad E(p/q)E(p/q)\ldots \text{to } q \text{ terms} = E(p/q + p/q + \ldots \text{to } q \text{ terms})$$

$$\therefore \quad [E(p/q)]^q = E(p) = e^p$$

$$\therefore \quad E(p/q) = e^{p/q} \text{ (for any positive number)}$$

Finally, from equation iii, by putting $a = x$ and $b = -x$

$$E(x)E(-x) = E(x - x) = E(0) = 1$$

$$\therefore \quad E(-x) = 1/E(x) = 1/e^x = e^{-x}$$

$$\therefore \quad E(x) = e^x = [E(1)]^x \text{ (true for all rational values of } x\text{)}$$

APPENDIX TWO

AREA UNDER A GRAPH BY SUMMATION OF A SERIES

To find the area included between the graph of the function x^3, the axis of x and the ordinates $x = 0$, $x = b$. Referring to Fig. 5.1(a) and (b) the abscissae of the $(n - 1)$ points of intersection on the x-axis are

$$\frac{b}{n}, \frac{2b}{n}, \frac{3b}{n}, \ldots \frac{(n-1)b}{n}$$

The heights of the rectangles are the corrresponding values of x^3

$$\frac{b^3}{n^3}, \left(\frac{2b}{n}\right)^3, \left(\frac{3b}{n}\right)^3 \ldots \left[\frac{(n-1)b}{n}\right]^3, b^3$$

The area A consists of $(n - 1)$ rectangles and the area B of n rectangles

$$A = \frac{b}{n}\left[\frac{b^3}{n^3}\right] + \frac{b}{n}\left[\frac{2b}{n}\right]^3 + \frac{b}{n}\left[\frac{3b}{n}\right]^3 + \ldots + \frac{b}{n}\left[\frac{(n-1)b}{n}\right]^3$$

$$= \frac{b^4}{n^4}[1^3 + 2^3 + 3^3 + \ldots + (n-1)^3] \qquad \text{(i)}$$

$$B = \frac{b}{n}\left[\frac{b^3}{n^3}\right] + \frac{b}{n}\left[\frac{2b}{n}\right]^3 + \frac{b}{n}\left[\frac{3b}{n}\right]^3 + \ldots + \frac{b}{n}\left[\frac{(n-1)b}{n}\right]^3 + \frac{b}{n}\,.\,b^3$$

$$= \frac{b^4}{n^4}[1^3 + 2^3 + 3^3 + \ldots + (n-1)^3 + n^3] \qquad \text{(ii)}$$

The sum of the cubes of the first k natural numbers is given by

$$1^3 + 2^3 + 3^3 + \ldots + k^3 = \frac{k^2(k+1)^2}{4}$$

$$\therefore \qquad A = \frac{b^4}{n^4}\left[\frac{(n-1)^2n^2}{4}\right] \quad \text{and} \quad B = \frac{b^4}{n^4}\left[\frac{n^2(n+1)^2}{4}\right]$$

Because $A <$ Area under the graph $< B$

$$\frac{b^4}{n^4}\left[\frac{(n-1)^2n^2}{4}\right] < \text{Required Area} < \frac{b^4}{n^4}\left[\frac{n^2(n+1)^2}{4}\right]$$

$$\frac{b^4}{4}\left(1 - \frac{1}{n}\right)^2 < \text{Required Area} < \frac{b^4}{4}\left[1^2\left(1 + \frac{1}{n}\right)^2\right]$$

and in the limit as $n \to \infty$

$$\text{Required Area} = b^4/4$$

APPENDIX THREE

PROOF OF CONDITIONS FOR MAXIMA AND MINIMA OF A FUNCTION OF TWO VARIABLES

Before studying this appendix the reader is recommended to re-read the part of Chapter Eight between examples 14 and 15.

Taylor's Theorem (see equation 8.50) can be extended to the case of a function $f(x, y)$ of two variables. The form of the expansion is

$$f(x+h, y+k) = f(x, y) + \left[h\frac{\partial f}{\partial x} + k\frac{\partial f}{\partial y}\right] + \frac{1}{2!}\left[h^2\frac{\partial^2 f}{\partial x^2} + 2hk\frac{\partial^2 f}{\partial x\,\partial y} + k^2\frac{\partial^2 f}{\partial y^2}\right]$$

+ terms containing third and higher orders of h and k.

or

$$\delta f = f(x+h, y+k) - f(x, y) = \left[h\frac{\partial f}{\partial x} + k\frac{\partial f}{\partial y}\right] + \frac{1}{2!}\left[h^2\frac{\partial^2 f}{\partial x^2} + 2hk\frac{\partial^2 f}{\partial x\,\partial y} + k^2\frac{\partial^2 f}{\partial y^2}\right] + \ldots \quad \text{(i)}$$

The value of the function $f(x, y)$ is a maximum if its value is greater than any in its immediate neighbourhood for sufficiently small values of h *and* k. The geometrical model of $z = f(x, y)$ is a surface (see Fig. 11.2), and geometrically we are talking about a small peak. Also we are considering the immediate neighbourhood of the point so it is not necessarily the greatest value—that is, the top of the reigning peak—but can be the top of a small mound, even an anthill, on the surface. Similarly, for a minimum the value of $f(x, y)$ is smaller than any in its immediate neighbourhood for sufficiently small values of h *and* k. The geometrical picture is the bottom of a small hole.

The important thing is that $\delta f = f(x+h, y+k) - f(x, y)$ should have a constant sign. For sufficiently small values the terms of second or higher order in h and k can be neglected and the sign of δf depends on the sign of the terms in the first bracket $\left[h\frac{\partial f}{\partial x} + k\frac{\partial f}{\partial y}\right]$. The values of $\partial f/\partial x$ and $\partial f/\partial y$ are fixed, and as h and k change sign the value of δf will change sign. Therefore for δf to be constant in sign as h and k vary these terms must be zero. Therefore

$$\frac{\partial f}{\partial x} = 0 = \frac{\partial f}{\partial y} \quad \text{(ii)}$$

is a necessary condition for a maximum or a minimum.

It is interesting to note that the points which satisfy equation (ii) include also points which can be interpreted geometrically as points on a 'u' shaped horizontal ridge—tops of mountain passes and hollows enclosed on two or three sides by mountains but falling away on the other sides.

It now follows that

$$\delta f = \frac{1}{2!}\left[h^2\frac{\partial^2 f}{\partial x^2} + 2hk\frac{\partial^2 f}{\partial x\,\partial y} + k^2\frac{\partial^2 f}{\partial y^2}\right] + \ldots$$

and for sufficiently small values of h and k terms of third or higher order in h and k can be neglected and the sign of δf depends on the terms $h^2 \dfrac{\partial^2 f}{\partial x^2} + 2hk \dfrac{\partial^2 f}{\partial x\, \partial y} + k^2 \dfrac{\partial^2 f}{\partial y^2}$.

In the usual notation, let $r = \dfrac{\partial^2 f}{\partial x^2}$, $s = \dfrac{\partial^2 f}{\partial x\, \partial y}$, $t = \dfrac{\partial^2 f}{\partial y^2}$ all of which will be constant for a particular point. Therefore the sign of δf depends on the sign of

$$h^2 r + 2hks + k^2 t = \frac{1}{r}[h^2 r^2 + 2hksr + k^2 rt]$$

$$= \frac{1}{r}[(hr + ks)^2 - k^2 s^2 + k^2 rt]$$

$$= \frac{1}{r}[(hr + ks)^2 + k^2(rt - s^2)]$$

Now $(hr + ks)^2$ and k^2 are never negative; therefore if

$$rt - s^2 = \frac{\partial^2 f}{\partial x^2} \cdot \frac{\partial^2 f}{\partial y^2} - \left[\frac{\partial^2 f}{\partial x\, \partial y}\right]^2 > 0 \qquad \text{(iii)}$$

the sign of δf will depend on the (fixed) sign of r (or of t, since if $rt - s^2 > 0$ then rt must be positive and r and t must have the same sign). Thus if $r = \dfrac{\partial^2 f}{\partial x^2} \left(\text{or } \dfrac{\partial^2 f}{\partial y^2}\right)$ is negative there is a maximum point and if positive there is a minimum point.

If $rt - s^2$ is negative the sign of $[(hr + ks)^2 + k^2(rt - s^2)]$ can be positive or negative depending on the size of $(hr + ks)^2$ and there is no maximum or minimum.

If $rt - s^2 = 0$ the remaining term $(rh + sk)^2$ can be zero if $rh + sk = 0$ or $h/k = -s/r$, in which case the second-degree terms vanish and further investigation is necessary.

Summing up, for a maximum or minimum point

$$\frac{\partial f}{\partial x} = 0 = \frac{\partial f}{\partial y} \qquad \text{(ii)}$$

and

$$\frac{\partial^2 f}{\partial x^2} \cdot \frac{\partial^2 f}{\partial y^2} - \left[\frac{\partial^2 f}{\partial x\, \partial y}\right]^2 > 0 \qquad \text{(iii)}$$

If equations (ii) *and* (iii) are satisfied

$\dfrac{\partial^2 f}{\partial x^2}$ or $\dfrac{\partial^2 f}{\partial y^2} < 0$ gives a maximum point

$\dfrac{\partial^2 f}{\partial x^2}$ or $\dfrac{\partial^2 f}{\partial y^2} > 0$ gives a minimum point

When all the second-degree terms are zero further consideration of equation (i) is necessary but the work is lengthy.

SOLUTIONS

Exercises 1.1

1. (ii) 60π cm^2, (iii) $60{\cdot}01\pi$ cm^2.
2. $\delta V = -0{\cdot}999$ m^3, $\delta A = -3{\cdot}78$ m^2, No.
3. (i) -1, (ii) $+0{\cdot}01$, (iii) $+0{\cdot}0001$, (iv) $-0{\cdot}01$, (v) $+1$, (vi) $+0{\cdot}2001$, (vii) $-60{\cdot}1801\pi$
4. $12x\,\delta x + 6(\delta x)^2$, Yes. 6. In the answer to question 5 let $k = 6$, $v = x$.
7. (i) 1, (ii) -1, (iii) -9, (iv) -61, (v) -36π, (vi) $-244\pi/3$, (vii) -36π, (viii) $-244\pi/3$, $\delta A \equiv$ (v) and (vii), $\delta V \equiv$ (vi) and (viii).
8. $-5\,\delta N + 0{\cdot}000\,03\,N^2\,\delta N$. 9. $a\,\delta t + 3bt^2\,\delta t$.
10. Yes, by putting $s^2 = G$, $t = N$, $a = 5$, $b = -0{\cdot}000\,01$.
11. $0 \leqslant x \leqslant 1$ and $2 \leqslant x \leqslant 100$. 12. (i) $4a + 2h$, (ii) $-\dfrac{1}{a(a+h)}$, (iii) -4.

Exercises 1.2

1. (i) $24{\cdot}4\pi$, (ii) $24{\cdot}04\pi$, (iii) $24{\cdot}004\pi$, 24π.
2. (i) $-1{\cdot}569$, (ii) $-1{\cdot}597$, (iii) $-1{\cdot}600$. (iv) Because v decreases as p increases. (v) Not with any great assurance: a further step of 5 to $5{\cdot}0001$ gives $-1{\cdot}5999$ and indicates that the answer is possibly $-1{\cdot}600$.
3. (i) $200 - 0{\cdot}06t - 0{\cdot}03\delta t$, (ii) $200 - 0{\cdot}06t$.
4. $2kx\,\delta x + k(\delta x)^2$. 5. $\dfrac{L^5 w}{120EI}$. 6. k, 1.
7. (i) $3(x+1)^2$, (ii) $3(2x^3-1)^2$, (iii) $3\cos^2\theta$.

Exercises 1.3

1. speed $v = 4t^3 - 24t^2 + 36t$, acceleration $a = 12t^2 - 48t + 36$, $a = 0$ when $t = 1$ or 3, when $t = 1$ $v = 16$, when $t = 3$ $v = 0$.
3. $M = 2500$, $F = 300$. 4. $t = 10$, $C = 2240$.

Problems 1.15

1. (i) $24x^7$, $168x^6$, (ii) $-10x^{-3}$, $30x^{-4}$, (iii) $2x^{-\frac{2}{3}}$, $-\frac{4}{3}x^{-\frac{5}{3}}$, (iv) $3 + 2/x^2$, $-4/x^3$, (v) $-3/\sqrt{x^3}$, $9/2\sqrt{x^5}$, (vi) $3x^2 + 12/x^5 - 21/2\sqrt{x^5}$, $6x - 60/x^6 + 105/4\sqrt{x^7}$. (vii) $2/\sqrt[3]{x} - 20x^{-5} + 5$, $-2/3\sqrt[3]{x^4} + 100x^{-6}$.
2. (i) $3/\sqrt{y}$, (ii) $3/\sqrt{z}$, (iii) $-3/2\sqrt{p^3}$, (iv) not possible, (v) $3\sin^2\theta$, (vi) $1/2\sqrt{(3x)}$, (vii) $1/2\sqrt{(3x-2)}$, (viii) not possible at this stage, (ix) $-2(x+2)^{-3}$, (x) not possible at this stage.
3. $0{\cdot}0309/\sqrt[3]{P^2}$, $1/[15\sqrt[3]{(10P^2)}]$. 4. $v = 300 + 40t^{\frac{3}{2}}$, a $= 60\sqrt{t}$.
5. $q/4\pi\epsilon r^2$. 6. $-5kx^4 + 9kL^2x^2 - 4kL^3x$. 7. $-7C/2\sqrt{T^9}$.
8. $1{\cdot}241/W^{0{\cdot}27}$. 9. $\dfrac{\mathrm{d}P}{\mathrm{d}r} = -4f^2k/r^5 + 2K\pi rL$, $\dfrac{\mathrm{d}P}{\mathrm{d}L} = K\pi r^2$.
10. $x = 1/\sqrt{3}$ ($x = -1/\sqrt{3}$ is not within the given range of x).
11. (i) $-0{\cdot}0005$, (ii) $-0{\cdot}0007$. 12. $t = (a-c)/ack$ or $1/ck - 1/ak$.
13. $N = 100\sqrt{3M}$. 14. $s = 7kL^4/8$, $M = -90EIkL^3$, $S = -30EIkL^2$.
15. $H = 2k\pi r^2 + 2kV/r$.
16. $K = 3{\cdot}62 \times 10^{10}$ N cm; $-3{\cdot}82 \times 10^{-5}$ N cm^{-5}.

Exercises 2.1

1. $-\dfrac{dx}{dz} = 2x$. 2. $\dfrac{dx}{dy} \propto x^2$. 3. $-\dfrac{dx}{dt} \propto 1/x$.
4. $\dfrac{d(x^2)}{dt} = xy$. 5. $\dfrac{dx}{dt} = -kx\ (k > 0),\ x = C\,e^{-kt}$.
6. $-\dfrac{dx}{dy} = kx\ (k > 0),\ x = C\,e^{-ky}$.
7. $1 - 4x/1! + 4^2x^2/2! - 4^3x^3/3! + \ldots$
$1 + 3x/1! + 3^2x^2/2! + 3^3x^3/3! + \ldots$
$1 + x^3/1! + x^6/2! + x^9/3! + \ldots$
8. $\dfrac{d(v^2)}{dx} = -k(v^2 - a)\quad (k > 0),\ v^2 - a = C\,e^{-kx}$.
9. $\dfrac{dq}{dt} = -q/RC,\ q = k\,e^{-t/RC}$. 10. $\dfrac{d\theta}{dt} = k/r^2$, no.
11. $p = 300\,000\,e^{t/50}$, 366 000.

Exercises 2.2

1. $1/x$. 2. n/x. 3. $4/x$. 4. $-3/x$. 5. $1/2x$.
6. $-1/2x$. 7. (i) $1/\sqrt{z}$, (ii) $1/(2z)$. 8. (i) $1/p^4$, (ii) $4/p$.
9. (i) x^2, (ii) $1/x$, (iii) xy, (iv) x/y.

Exercises 3.1

1. All continuous.
2. Tangents $y = 3x - 3$, $y = 12x + 15$. Normals $3y + x - 1 = 0$, $12y + x + 110 = 0$.
4. $y = 12x$, $y = 12x + 27$. 5. $5y = x + 2$, $5y = -x + 3$.
6. Tangent $y = 2x - 4$, normal $2y + x + 8 = 0$.
8. (1, 1), $\ln(-\tfrac{1}{3})$ is not defined, $x = 1$. 9. $k = 0{\cdot}02$.

Exercises 3.2

1. $v = \sqrt{(gT/3w)}$. 2. $(-2, -30)$ and $(1, -3)$ minima, $(0, 2)$ maximum.
3. (0, 0) minimum, (6,432) horizontal point of inflexion.
4. (0, 0) minimum, $(-1, 1)$ maximum. 5. $wL^4/384EI$.
6. Yes, no, a series of points. 8. 1280, yes.
9. maximum $s = 250$ when $t = +5$.

Exercises 3.3

1. $-0{\cdot}224$ N/m. 2. 16π cm^2.

Problems 3.6

1. All zero. 4. $1{\cdot}4kv^{-1\cdot4}$. 5. 42.
6. Maximum profit £500 when $x = 500$, 305 to 680.
7. $f(0) = 0$ maximum, $f(2) = -16$ minimum.
10. $x = 2$ or $x = -2$, $x = -2$ is not acceptable because $\ln(-2)$ is not defined.
13. $A = 20x - x^2\ (0 \leqslant x \leqslant 20)$. 15. 33 m.p.h.
17. 31 104 cm^2 ($36 \times 72 \times 12$). 18. $X = 4$.

Exercises 4.1

1. (i) $-\text{cosec}^2 x$, (ii) $10\sec^2 5x$, (iii) $3\sec 3x \tan 3x$, (iv) $3\sin^2 x \cos x$, (v) $12\cos 4x$.
2. maximum $\sqrt{2}$, minimum $-\sqrt{2}$. 3. $-\sin(2x - 1)$.
4. $\cos(\sqrt{x})$. 5. $-\sin(z^2 - 1)$. 6. $\cos(\ln y)$. 7. $\cos(x^3 - 2x + 1)$.

Exercises 4.2

1. $4x^3 - 3x^2 - 1$.
2. $6x(x + 1)\,e^{2x}$.
3. $x^2(1 + 3 \ln x)$.
4. $3x^2 \cos x - x^3 \sin x$.
5. $\sqrt{x} \cos x + \sin x/2\sqrt{x}$.
6. $-3x^2 + 2x - 3\sqrt{x}/2 + 1/2\sqrt{x} + 1$.
7. $e^{2x}\,(2 \sin x + \cos x)$.
8. $-e^{-2x}(2 \cos x + \sin x)$.
9. $(3x^2 - 2x + 1) \ln x + (x^2 - x + 1)$.
10. $5x(x \cos 2x + \sin 2x)$.
11. $e^x(1 + x) \sin x \cos x + x\,e^x(\cos^2 x - \sin^2 x)$.
12. $2x\,e^x \ln x + (x^2 - 1)\,e^x \ln x + (x^2 - 1)\,e^x/x$.
15. maximum s when $r = 2\,e^{0\cdot5}$.

Exercises 4.3

1. $x^2(2x - 3)/(x - 1)^2$.
2. $-4x/(x^2 - 1)^2$.
3. $(2 - 2 \ln x)/x^2$.
4. $5\,e^x(x - 2)/x^3$.
5. $2\,e^{2x}(x^2 - x + 1)/(x^2 + 1)^2$.
6. $[-3(x^2 - x + 1) \sin x - 3(2x - 1) \cos x]/(x^2 - x + 1)^2$.
7. $(-x^4 + 2x^3 + 3x^2 - 4x + 2)/(x^2 + 1)^2(x - 1)^2$.
8. $5(2 + \cos x)/(2 \cos x + 1)^2$.
9. $[x(x - 1) \cos x - \sin x]/(x - 1)^2$.
10. $(x^3 - x^2 + x + 1)\,e^x/(x^2 + 1)^2$.
11. $(2 \sin x\, e^x)/(1 + \sin 2x)$.
12. $e^x(1 + \sin x \cos x)/\cos^2 x$; alternative form $e^x(\sec^2 x + \tan x)$.
13. $\dfrac{dp}{dv} = \dfrac{2a}{v^3} - \dfrac{RT}{(v - b)^2}$, $\dfrac{d^2p}{dv^2} = \dfrac{2RT}{(v - b)^3} - \dfrac{6a}{v^4}$, $p = a/27b^2$.
14. $\sqrt{(200r/R)}$.
15. maximum $p = k/4R$ (when $z = R$).

Exercises 4.4

1. $\cos 2x$.
2. $e^{2x}(2 \sin x + \cos x)$.
3. $-e^{-x}(\cos x + \sin x)$.
4. $\sec x(\sec^2 x + \tan^2 x)$.
5. $-\operatorname{cosec} x(\operatorname{cosec}^2 x + \cot^2 x)$.
6. $4 \sin^3 x \cos x$.
7. $3 \sin x/\cos^4 x$.
8. $2 \sec^2 x \tan x$.
9. $2 \tan x \sec^2 x$.
10. $-\sin x\, e^{\cos x}$.
11. $\sec x \operatorname{cosec} x$.
12. $(2 \cos^2 x + \sin^2 x)/2\sqrt{\cos^3 x}$.
13. $-(2 \sin^2 x + \cos^2 x)/2\sqrt{\sin^3 x}$.
14. $10(2x - 1)(x^2 - x + 1)^9$.
15. $(3x^2 - 2)/[2\sqrt{(x^3 - 2x)}]$.
16. $2x \sec^2 (x^2)$.
17. $\tan^2 x + 2x \tan x \sec^2 x$.
18. $\sin x \cos x + x(\cos^2 x - \sin^2 x)$.
19. $-3 \sin^2 (1/x) \cos (1/x)/x^2$.
20. $-\sin 3x\, e^{\cos 3x}$.
21. $2x \sin 3x + 3(x^2 - 1) \cos 3x$.
22. $2x \cos (3x + 1) - 3x^2 \sin (3x + 1)$.
23. $[2x \tan x - (x^2 - 1) \sec^2 x]/\tan^2 x$.
24. $[-3(x^2 + 1) \operatorname{cosec}^2 3x - 2x \cot 3x]/(x^2 + 1)^2$.
25. $12x(1 + x^2)^2/(1 - x^2)^4$.
26. $m \cos mx \cos nx - n \sin mx \sin nx$.
27. $m \sin^{m-1} x \cos^{n+1} x - n \sin^{m+1} x \cos^{n-1} x$.
28. $4 \cot x/(1 + \cos^2 x)$.
29. $e^{\sqrt{\cos x}} - x \sin x\, e^{\sqrt{\cos x}}/2\sqrt{\cos x}$.
31. $0{\cdot}024$ m^3/min.
32. $-0{\cdot}028$ rads/sec.
33. (i) -5 m^2/min, (ii) $-5/32\pi$ m/min.
35. $E = q/(4\pi e r^2)$, $-q/(1728\pi e)$.

Exercises 4.5

1. $-y/2x$.
2. $(y^2 - 1)/(1 - 2xy)$.
3. $(4 + y\, e^{xy})/(10y - x\, e^{xy})$.
4. $(y \sin xy - 2xy)/(1 + x^2 - x \sin xy)$.
5. $\dfrac{dy}{dx} = -\dfrac{1}{2}$, $\dfrac{d^2y}{dx^2} = \dfrac{5}{8}$.
6. $(4x - 5y - 1)/(1 + 5x - 4y)$, $(\frac{3}{2}, 1)$, $(-\frac{7}{2}, -3)$.

Exercises 4.6

1. $\dfrac{dy}{dx} = \dfrac{2t}{3}, \dfrac{d^2y}{dx^2} = \dfrac{2}{9}$.
2. $y = 1 - x^2$, no, the curve corresponding to the x, y equation includes the other but is larger.
3. $\dfrac{dy}{dx} = (t^2 - 1)/2t$, $x^2 + y^2 = 1$, $y = \sqrt{(1 - x^2)}$, $y = -\sqrt{(1 - x^2)}$.
4. $t = 1\tfrac{1}{2}$ s, $\tan^{-1}(2{\cdot}4)$.
5. $\tan\theta$.

Exercises 4.7

1. $\cos^x x[\ln(\cos x) - x\tan x]$.
2. $x^{\cos x}\left[\dfrac{\cos x}{x} - \sin x \ln x\right]$.
3. $x^{x-2}\left[\dfrac{x-2}{x} + \ln x\right]$.
4. $-\dfrac{2}{(x^2 - 4)}\sqrt{\dfrac{x+2}{x-2}}$.
5. $\dfrac{-3x}{(1 - x^4)}\left(\dfrac{1 - x^2}{1 + x^2}\right)^{\frac{3}{4}}$.
6. $\dfrac{1 - x^2}{(x^2 + 1)^2 - x^2}\left[\dfrac{x^2 + x + 1}{x^2 - x + 1}\right]^{\frac{1}{2}}$.
7. $2 \times 3^{2x+3} \ln 3$.
8. $10^x \ln 10$.
9. $1/(x \ln x)$.
10. $(1 + 2\ln x)/(x \ln x)$.

Problems 4.11

1. $AC/CB = (I_1/I_2)^{\frac{1}{3}}$.
3. $\sin^{-1}\left(\dfrac{c}{a}\right)^{\frac{1}{3}}$.
4. $0{\cdot}6\%$.
5. $x = 0{\cdot}58l$.
6. $s = 110$.
7. (i) $-13{\cdot}9$ m/s, (ii) $11{\cdot}18$ m/s.
8. $y^2 = 4ax$, $y = 2\sqrt{(ax)}$, $y = -2\sqrt{(ax)}$, yes all equal to $1/t$.
9. maximum $i = 3\sqrt{3}/2$ when $t = \pi/3p$, minimum $i = -3\sqrt{3}/2$ when $t = 5\pi/3p$.
11. (i) $f^n(x) = \dfrac{(-1)^n 2^n n!}{(2x + 3)^{n+1}}$ (all n), (ii) $f^n(x) = \dfrac{(-1)^n(n - 2)!}{x^{n-1}}$ $(n > 2)$.
12. $\dfrac{dn}{d\theta} = -kn$, $n = 46{\cdot}0\,e^{-k\theta}$.
13. (i) $1 + x + x^2/2! + x^3/3! + \ldots + x^n/n! + \ldots$, (ii) $0{\cdot}9048$, (iii) $a = -1$, $b = +\tfrac{1}{2}$.
14. Maximum $F = \dfrac{16k}{25\sqrt{5a^4}}$.
16. $+0{\cdot}6\%$.
18. $5R(1 - 1/T)/2T$.
19. (i) $x = 1$, (ii) $x = 2$, (iii) $x = 2$.

Exercises 5.1

1. $\dfrac{x^{10}}{10}, \dfrac{4x^{\frac{11}{4}}}{11}, -3x^{-\frac{1}{3}}, \dfrac{3}{5}x^{\frac{5}{3}}, \dfrac{2}{7}x^{\frac{7}{2}}$.
2. $-1/x$, $-1/x^4$, $-4/\sqrt{x}$, $-12/\sqrt[3]{x^7}$, $\ln|x|$.
3. $\tan x$, $-\cot x$, $-\operatorname{cosec} x$, $\sec x$, $6\sin x - 5\cos x$.
4. $(\tfrac{4}{3}x^3 - x^2 + x)$, $\left(\dfrac{11x^2}{2} + \dfrac{3}{x} - \dfrac{3}{x^2}\right)$.
5. $3\tan x + 2\cos x$.
6. (i) $1/(3 + x)$, $\ln|3 + x|$, $x \neq -3$, (ii) $1/(x - 5)$, $\ln|x - 5|$, $x \neq 5$, (iii) $2/(2x + 3)$, $\tfrac{1}{2}\ln|2x + 3|$, $x \neq -\tfrac{3}{2}$, (iv) $-1/(5 - x)$, $-\ln|5 - x|$, $x \neq 5$, (v) $3\cos 3x$, $\tfrac{1}{3}\sin 3x$, all x, (vi) $-5\sin 5x$, $-\tfrac{1}{5}\cos 5x$, all x.
7. $v = 3t^2 - 4t + 6$, $s = t^3 - 2t^2 + 6t$.
8. $v = \sqrt{(12s^{\frac{3}{2}} + 4)}$, $s = 4$.
9. $\theta = 15 + 85\,e^{-x}$.
11. $7000 + 3n + 0{\cdot}2n^2$.
12. $S = S_1 + C\ln\left(\dfrac{T}{T_1}\right)$.

Exercises 5.2

1. (i) $\frac{1}{5}$, (ii) $\frac{1}{5}$, (iii) $\frac{1}{5}$.
2. (i) e − 1, (ii) $(e^2 - e^{-2})/2$, (sinh 2), (iii) $(1 - e^{-8})/4$.
3. (i) $4\frac{2}{3}$, (ii) $\frac{3}{8}$, (iii) $\frac{3}{8}$.
4. (i) $\ln \frac{3}{2}$, (ii) $\ln \frac{3}{2}$, (iii) ln (1/4).
5. (i) 1, (ii) 1, (iii) $\sqrt{2}$.

Exercises 5.3

1. 24.
2. $68\frac{1}{3}$.
3. $58\frac{1}{3}$.
4. $\sqrt{2}$.
5. 2.
6. $\ln \frac{5}{2}$, $\ln \frac{5}{2}$.
7. $\frac{11}{6}$.
8. $20\frac{5}{6}$.
9. $21\frac{1}{3}$.
10. (−2, −26), (0, 0), (5, 65).

Exercises 5.4

1. 8320 joules.
2. 0·375 joules.
4. $250\sqrt{2}$ joules.
5. $4{\cdot}19 \times 10^8$ joules.

Exercises 5.5

1. $3 + 305\alpha$.
2. 13.
6. (i) $u/2$, (ii) $2u/3$.
7. $I_1/\sqrt{2}$, $I_2/\sqrt{2}$.
9. R.M.S. is $\frac{1}{2}\sqrt{\frac{3}{2}}\,I_0^2R$, mean value is $\frac{1}{2}I_0^2R$.
10. $\bar{p} = \dfrac{9{\cdot}45(5 - 3k)}{5}$, $k = \frac{5}{7}$.

Exercises 6.1

1. (i) $-\cos(x + b)$, (ii) $\sin(x + b)$, (iii) e^{x+b}, (iv) $(x + b)^{n+1}/n + 1$, (v) $\ln|x + b|$, (vi) $\tan(x + b)$.
2. (i) $-\dfrac{1}{a}\cos(ax + b)$, (ii) $\dfrac{1}{a}\sin(ax + b)$, (iii) $\dfrac{1}{a}e^{ax+b}$, (iv) $\dfrac{(ax + b)^{n+1}}{a(n + 1)}$, (v) $\dfrac{1}{a}\ln|ax + b|$, (vi) $\dfrac{1}{a}\tan(ax + b)$.
3. (i) $-\frac{1}{3}\cos(3x + 2)$, (ii) $-\frac{1}{2}\sin(4 - 2x)$, (iii) $-\frac{1}{2}e^{1-2x}$, (iv) $\frac{1}{3}(2x + 3)^{\frac{3}{2}}$, (v) $-\dfrac{(5 - 2x)^{15}}{30}$, (vi) $\frac{1}{3}\ln|3x - 1|$, (vii) $\frac{1}{2}\ln|2x + 1|$, (viii) $-\ln|1 - x|$, (ix) $\frac{1}{2}\cot(1 - 2x)$, (x) $-\sec(1 - x)$.
4. $-\cos(x^2 - 1)$.
5. $2(x^3 + 1)^{\frac{3}{2}}/9$.
6. $-\frac{1}{2}\ln|1 - x^2|$.
7. $(\ln x)^4/4$.
8. $\frac{2}{3}\sqrt{(x^3 - 3x + 1)}$.
9. $-\frac{1}{3}e^{-x^3}$.
10. $\frac{1}{2}\sin(x^2 - 2x + 5)$.

Exercises 6.2

1. e^{x^3}.
2. $\dfrac{-1}{13(x^2 + 3)^{13}}$.
3. $\dfrac{2(x^3 + 5)^{\frac{3}{2}}}{3}$.
4. $\frac{1}{2}\sin(x^2 - 3)$.
5. $\frac{1}{3}\tan(x^3 + 1)$.
6. $-2\cos\sqrt{x}$.
7. $\frac{1}{2}(x^2 + 4) - 2\ln(x^2 + 4)$.
8. $\frac{2}{5}(x + 7)^{\frac{5}{2}} - \frac{28}{3}(x + 7)^{\frac{3}{2}} + 98(x + 7)^{\frac{1}{2}}$.
9. $-1/\ln x$.
10. $2\ln|\ln x|$.
11. $-\frac{1}{3}\ln|\ln x|$.
12. $\frac{1}{6}\sin^6 x$.
13. $-2\sqrt{\cos x}$.
14. $-\frac{1}{2}\cos^2 x$.
15. $\frac{1}{3}(x^2 - 2x + 3)^{\frac{3}{2}}$.
16. $\frac{1}{3}\ln|x^3 + 6x - 1|$.
17. $\ln(1 + \sin^2 x)$.
18. $\frac{1}{6}$.
19. $\frac{1}{6}$.
20. $\frac{1}{6}$.
21. $\frac{1}{5}(\ln 2)^5$.
22. $\frac{1}{3}\ln\left(\dfrac{3e + 1}{4}\right)$.
23. $\ln\left(\dfrac{1 + \sqrt{2}}{2}\right)$.
24. $16\frac{13}{15}$.
25. $5\frac{1}{3} - 8\ln 2$.
26. $23\frac{11}{15}$.
27. 2e(e − 1).
28. $\frac{1}{3}\ln(\frac{8}{5})$.
29. e(e − 1).

Exercises 6.3

1. $\frac{1}{3}x\,e^{3x} - \frac{1}{9}\,e^{3x}$.
2. $-(2x + 1)\cos x + 2\sin x$.
3. $(1 - x)\sin x - \cos x$.
4. $(x + x^2)\ln x - \left(x + \frac{x^2}{2}\right)$.
5. $(x^2 - 2)\sin x + 2x\cos x$.
6. $(x^2 - 2x + 2)e^x$.
7. $(2 - x - x^2)\cos x + (2x + 1)\sin x$.
8. $\frac{x^3}{3}\ln x - \frac{x^3}{9}$.
9. $\frac{x^4}{32}\,[8(\ln x)^2 - 4\ln x + 1]$.
10. $e^{2x}(2\sin x - \cos x)/5$.
11. $e^{-x}(3\sin 3x - \cos 3x)/10$.
12. $-(\sin 2x\sin x + 2\cos x\cos 2x)/3$.
13. $\sin x\tan x + \cos x$, $(\sec x)$.
14. $\frac{1}{2}\left(1 - \frac{2}{e}\right)$.
15. (i) $\frac{1}{8}$, (ii) $\frac{1}{2}$.
17. $6 - 2e$, $6 - 2e$.
18. $1 - 2/\pi$.
19. $4\ln 2 - 2$.
20. $\frac{5\ln 5}{2} - \ln 2 - \frac{3}{2}$.

Exercises 6.4

1. (i) $2\ln\left(\tan\frac{x}{4}\right)$, (ii) $\frac{3}{2}\ln|\sec(\frac{2}{3}x)|$, (iii) $4\ln\left|\sin\frac{x}{4}\right|$, (iv) $-\frac{5}{3}\ln\left|\tan\left(\frac{\pi}{4} - \frac{3x}{10}\right)\right|$
(v) $a\ln\left|\sec\frac{x}{a}\right|$.

2. (i) $-\frac{\cos^3 x}{3}$, (ii) $\frac{\sin^5 x}{5} - \frac{\sin^7 x}{7}$, (iii) $\sin x - \frac{2}{3}\sin^3 x + \frac{\sin^5 x}{5}$,
(iv) $\frac{\sin^4 x}{4} - \frac{\sin^6 x}{6}$, (v) $\frac{1}{3}\sec^3 x - \sec x$, (vi) $-\text{cosec}\, x$.

3. (i) 0, (ii) 0, (iii) 0, (iv) $-\frac{4}{9}$, (v) π, (vi) $\frac{\pi}{4} - \frac{5}{4}\sin(\pi/5)$.

4. $(1 - \ln 2)/2$.
5. $(1 + \ln 2)/2$.
6. $\frac{8}{3}$.
8. $\frac{1}{7}$.
9. $\frac{12}{35}$.
10. $(4\pi - 3\sqrt{3})/192$.

Exercises 6.5

1. $(4\pi - 3\sqrt{3})/24$.
2. $2(\sqrt{2} - 1)$.
4. $3(\sqrt{3} - 1)$.
5. $(\sqrt{3} - 1)/16$.
6. $\left(\frac{\pi}{6} + 1 - \frac{\sqrt{3}}{2}\right)$.
7. $(6\pi + 9\sqrt{3})/8$.
8. 1.
9. $\frac{1}{2}$.
10. $(\pi - 2)/2$.

Exercises 6.6

1. $(x^2 - \ln|x^2 + 1|)/2$.
2. $(3x^2 - 4x + 3\ln|2x + 1|)/2$.
3. $5\ln\left|\frac{x + 2}{x + 3}\right|$.
4. $\ln\left|\frac{(2x - 1)^2(x + 1)}{x^3}\right|$.
5. $\ln\left|\frac{3x - 1}{x + 3}\right| + \frac{1}{x + 3}$.
6. $x^2 + 3x + 2\ln\left|\frac{x - 5}{x}\right|$.
7. 0.
8. $2 + \ln(\frac{3}{2})$.
9. $\ln\frac{4}{5}$.
10. $-\frac{1}{2}\ln 2 + \ln(2\sqrt{3} - 1) - \frac{\pi}{24}$.
11. $\ln\frac{5}{3} + \frac{1}{\sqrt{2}}\tan^{-1}(2\sqrt{2})$.
12. $\frac{1}{4}\ln 3$.

Exercises 7.1

1. 10.
2. $\ln 2 + 3\frac{3}{4}$.
3. $1\frac{7}{8}$.
4. $\frac{61}{216}$.
5. $32\frac{7}{64}$.
6. $\frac{17}{12}$.
7. 3π the curve is a semicircle.
8. 8a.
9. $2\sqrt{2}$.

Exercises 7.2

3. $A = 2\pi ad$. 4. $\pi(\ln 2 + \frac{15}{16})$. 5. $16\pi/3$. 6. $12\pi a^2/5$.
7. $2\pi(\sqrt{2} + 1)/15$.

Exercises 7.3

1. $(\pi h^3 \tan^2 \alpha)/3$. 2. $\pi^2/2$. 3. 108π. 4. $10{\cdot}8\pi$.
5. $1{\cdot}094 \times 10^{12}$ km^3.

Exercises 7.4

1. $\frac{1}{4}$ the way up the axis from the base.
2. $\frac{1}{3}$ the way up the axis from the base.
3. $\bar{x} = \bar{y} = 4a/3\pi$.
4. $2a/3$ along Ox from the vertex.
5. $7a/5$. 6. $39a/100$.

Exercises 7.5

1. $Ma^2/3$, $a/\sqrt{3}$. 2. $M2a^2/3$, $\sqrt{2}a/\sqrt{3}$. 3. $M2a^2/5$, $\sqrt{2}a/\sqrt{5}$.
4. $M(b^2 + c^2)/3$, $\sqrt{(b^2 + c^2)}/\sqrt{3}$. 5. $M4a^2/3$, $2a/\sqrt{3}$.
6. $Mr^2/2$, $r/\sqrt{2}$. 7. $M3r^2/10$, $\sqrt{3}r/\sqrt{10}$.
8. (i) Ma^2, a, $Ma^2/2$, $a/\sqrt{2}$. 9. $Ma^2/6$, $a/\sqrt{6}$.

Exercises 7.6

1. $M5a^2/4$. 2. $Mb^2/3$, $M(a^2 + b^2)/3$. 3. $Ma^2/2$, $M3a^2/2$.
4. $M[(3a^2 + h^2)/12]$. 6. $M[(12a^2 + 3h^2)/80]$. 7. $0{\cdot}067$ kg m^2.

Exercises 7.7

1. $k(1 - 4\,\mathrm{e}^{-3})/9$, $3/(1 - \mathrm{e}^{-3})$. 2. 0, $(4 - \pi)/\pi$, $(4 - \pi)/\pi$.
3. $A(1 - 3\,\mathrm{e}^{-2})/4$, $A(1 - 5\,\mathrm{e}^{-2})/4$. 4. 300 h, 100 h.
5. $\theta(\mathrm{e} - 2)/(\mathrm{e} - 1)$. 6. $(\mathrm{e} - 2)/(\mathrm{e} - 1)$, $(2\mathrm{e} - 5)/(\mathrm{e} - 1)$.

Exercises 8.1

1. $1\frac{1}{4}$, $1\frac{1}{3}$, $\frac{5}{13}$.
2. $\cosh(A + B) = \cosh A \cosh B + \sinh A \sinh B$.

10. $V_3 = \dfrac{V_1 + V_2}{(1 + V_1V_2/c^2)}$.

Exercises 8.2

3. (i) $2 \sinh x \cosh x$, (ii) $3 \sinh(3x - 1)$, (iii) $3 \tanh^2 x \operatorname{sech}^2 x$, (iv) $\sinh x + x \cosh x$, (v) $\dfrac{-2 \cosh x}{(1 + \sinh x)^2}$, (vi) $\coth x$, (vii) $\sinh x\, \mathrm{e}^{\cosh x}$, (viii) 1.
5. $A = [w \tanh(\alpha^2 L/2)]/\alpha^2$, $\beta = -w/\alpha^2$.
6. $(\mathrm{e}^{t \ln 64} - 1)/(\mathrm{e}^{t \ln 64} + 1)$.

Exercises 8.3

1. $\ln 3$, $\ln 5$, $\ln \sqrt{3}$. 2. $\ln \{[(1 + \sqrt{(1 + x^2)})]/x\}$.

3. (i) $\dfrac{3}{\sqrt{(1 + 9x^2)}}$, (ii) $\dfrac{5}{\sqrt{(25x^2 + 10x)}}$, (iii) $\dfrac{2}{(-4x^2 + 12x - 8)}$, (iv) $\dfrac{-1}{x\sqrt{(x^2 + 1)}}$, (v) $\dfrac{1}{2\sqrt{(x^2 - x)}}$, (vi) $\dfrac{1}{(x^2 - 2x)}$.

6. (i) 1/250, (ii) 1/100.

Exercises 8.4

7. $\rho = -\dfrac{(1 + x^2)^2}{4x}$.

Exercises 8.5

1. $27ay^2 = 4(x - 2a)^3$, semi-cubical parabola. 2. $\rho = c \sinh t$.

Exercises 8.6

1. (i) $x - x^2/2 + x^3/3 - x^4/4 + \ldots$,
   (ii) $1 - x^2/2! + x^4/4! - x^6/6! + \ldots$,
   (iii) $\ln a - x/a - x^2/2a^2 - x^3/3a^3 - \ldots$
2. $1 + x^2/2! + x^4/4! + \ldots$, $c + x^2/(2!c) + x^4/(4!c^3) + \ldots$, parabola $y = c + x^2/2c$.
3. $1 + ax + a^2x^2/2! + a^3x^3/3! + \ldots$
4. (i) $x + x^3/3 + 2x^5/15$, (ii) $x - x^3/3! + x^5/5!$, (iii) $1 + x^2/2! + 5x^4/4!$
5. $2x^2/2! - 2^3x^6/6! + 2^5x^{10}/10! - 2^7x^{14}/14! + \ldots$
6. $\frac{1}{3}$. 7. $1/60$. 8. $2(x + x^3/3 + x^5/5 + \ldots)$ $(-1 < x < 1)$.
9. (i) 1, (ii) $\frac{1}{2}$, (iii) -1, (iv) 2. 10. $k = 1/15$.

Exercises 8.7

1. $5/6$. 2. $1/6$. 3. -1. 4. Does not exist.
5. $\dfrac{na^2}{(n-2)}$. 6. 1. 7. 1.
9. $x = 0$ maximum, $x = 1$ horizontal inflexion, $x = 4/7$ minimum.
10. $f(\pi/2) = 1$ maximum, $f(-\pi/2) = -1$ minimum, $f(0) = f(\pi) = f(-\pi) = 0$ horizontal inflexion.
11. $c = 0{\cdot}021$ minimum, $0{\cdot}500$ maximum, $0{\cdot}979$ minimum.
12. $0{\cdot}0543$.

Exercises 9.1

1. (i) $\frac{2}{3}\tanh^{-1}\left[\dfrac{\tan(x/2)}{3}\right]$ or $\frac{1}{3}\ln\left[\dfrac{3 + \tan(x/2)}{3 - \tan(x/2)}\right]$, (ii) $\frac{1}{4}\ln(5 + 4\cosh x)$, (iii) $-\dfrac{\sqrt{(4 + x^2)}}{4x}$, (iv) $\sqrt{(x^2 + 4)}$, (v) $\frac{1}{2}\ln(1 + \tanh\theta)$, (vi) $\dfrac{x}{2}\sqrt{(9 + x^2)} + \dfrac{9}{2}\sinh^{-1}(x/3)$, (vii) $\frac{1}{3}(x^2 - 4)^{\frac{3}{2}}$, (viii) $(\sinh^{-1} x)^2$, (ix) $\ln\left[\dfrac{1 + \tanh(x/2)}{2 + \tanh(x/2)}\right]$.
3. $1{\cdot}13$. 4. $s = c\sinh(x/c)$.
5. $\sqrt{(x^2 - 9)}$. 6. $[(3\sqrt{2} - \sqrt{10})/3]$.
7. $V = 35\pi/32$, $\pi(8\ln 2 + 15)/16$, $\pi(8\ln 2 + 15)/8$.
8. $(\pi - 2)/\sqrt{2}$.

Exercises 9.2

1. $\cosh^{-1}\left(\dfrac{x+2}{3}\right)$. 2. $\sinh^{-1}\left(\dfrac{x-3}{2}\right)$. 3. $\sinh^{-1}\left(\dfrac{x-1}{5}\right)$.
4. $\sin^{-1}\left(\dfrac{x-5}{3}\right)$. 5. $\frac{1}{3}\sinh^{-1}\left(\dfrac{3x-1}{2}\right)$. 6. $\frac{1}{4}\cosh^{-1}\left(\dfrac{4x+3}{3}\right)$.
7. $\frac{1}{2}\sin^{-1}\left(\dfrac{2x+3}{5}\right)$. 8. $3\sqrt{(3 + 2x - x^2)} + \sin^{-1}\left(\dfrac{x-1}{2}\right)$.
9. $\frac{1}{3}\sqrt{(9x^2 - 6x - 3)} + \cosh^{-1}\left(\dfrac{3x-1}{2}\right)$.
10. $\frac{3}{2}\sqrt{(4x^2 + 20x + 34)} - 2\sinh^{-1}\left(\dfrac{2x+5}{3}\right)$.

Exercises 9.3

1. $I_4 = \int x^4 \sin x\,dx$, $I_{23} = \int x^{23} \sin x\,dx$, $I_0 = \int \sin x\,dx$.

2. $I_{2,3} = \int_0^{\pi/2} x^2 \cos 3x \, dx$, $I_{4,2} = \int_0^{\pi/2} x^4 \cos 2x \, dx$, $I_{0,4} = \int_0^{\pi/2} \cos 4x \, dx$,
$I_{3,0} = \int_0^{\pi/2} x^3 \, dx$, $I_{0,0} = \int_0^{\pi/2} dx$.
3. $I_{1,1} = \int_0^1 (1 - x)\, x \, dx$, $I_{3,4} = \int_0^1 (1 - x)^3 x^4 \, dx$, $I_{0,12} = \int_0^1 x^{12} \, dx$,
$I_{23,0} = \int_0^1 (1 - x)^{23} \, dx$, $I_{0,0} = \int_0^1 dx$.
4. (i) $I_{3,1}$, (ii) $I_{4,7}$, (iii) $I_{12,0}$, (iv) $I_{0,9}$.
5. $(n - 1)I_n = (n - 2)I_{n-2} - \cos x \operatorname{cosec}^{n-1} x$.

Exercises 9.4

1. (i) $15\pi/4096$, (ii) $16/3003$, (iii) $128/150\,15$, (iv) $1/120$, (v) $63\pi/512$, (vi) $35\pi/128$, (vii) $128/315$, (viii) $8/15$.
2. $-(\cos x \operatorname{cosec}^3 x + 2 \cot x)/3$.
3. $(2 \ln 2 - 1)/4$.
4. $(52 - 15\pi)/60$.
5. $1/630$.
6. $x[(\ln x)^3 - 3(\ln x)^2 + 6 \ln x - 6]$.
7. $(e^{\pi/2} - 1)/2$.

Exercises 9.5

4. $5\pi^2/32$.

Exercises 9.6

1. 2.
2. Does not exist.
3. $\frac{1}{2}$.
4. $\pi/4$.
5. $\pi/9$.

Exercises 9.7

1. 4.
2. 6.
3. -1.
4. Does not exist.
5. π.
6. 4.
7. 4.
8. $\cosh^{-1} 2$ or $\ln (2 + 2\sqrt{3})$.
9. Does not exist.
10. Does not exist.

Exercises 9.8

1. 3·1416.
2. 1·107.
4. 1·120.
5. 19 900 m².

Exercises 10.1

1. $x = 2(1 - \cos 2t)$.
2. $V = \dfrac{abV_1}{(b - a)}\left[\dfrac{1}{x} - \dfrac{1}{b}\right]$.
3. $x = 4N$.
4. $t = \dfrac{1}{k} \ln 2$.
5. $v = \dfrac{g}{k} + C\,e^{-kt}$.
7. $46\frac{2}{3}$°C.
8. $s = g(e^{-kt} + kt - 1)/k^2$.
11. $x = \dfrac{10(1 - e^{5kt})}{(1 - 2\,e^{5kt})}$.
12. $t = [k^{\frac{3}{2}}(\pi + 2)]/(2\mu^{\frac{1}{2}})$.
13. $v = -u \ln (1 - kt) - gt$, $s = \dfrac{u}{k} \ln (1 - kt) - ut \ln (1 - kt) - \frac{1}{2}gt^2 + ut$.

Exercises 10.2

1. $y = (x + C)\,e^{-2x}$.
2. $y = x^4 + C/x$.
3. $y = \sec x \tan x + C \sec x$.
4. $y = \ln x + C/\ln x$.
5. $y = (x^2 + C)\,e^{x^3}$.

Exercises 10.3

1. $C\,e^{-3x} + D\,e^{-4x}$.
2. $C \cos 4x + D \sin 4x$.
3. $(Cx + D)\,e^{-4x}$.
4. $C\,e^{-t/2} + D\,e^{3t}$.
5. $e^{-x}(C \cos 3x + D \sin 3x)$.
6. $C\,e^{5t} + D\,e^{-5t}$ or $C \cosh 5t + D \sinh 5t$.
7. $e^{3t}(C \cos 5t + D \sin 5t)$.
8. $C\,e^{-4x} + D$.
9. $-e^{-t} \sin 3t$.
10. $\sqrt{2}\,e^{-3x} \sin (4x - \pi/4)$.

Exercises 10.4

1. $y = C\,e^{-3x} + D\,e^{2x} + 2\,e^{3x}$.
2. $y = (Cx + D)\,e^{-2x} + 26 \sinh 3x - 24 \cosh 3x$,
   or $(Cx + D)\,e^{-2x} + (e^{3x} - 25\,e^{-3x})$.
3. $x = e^t(C \cos t + D \sin t) + 2 \cos 2t - \sin 2t$.
4. $x = C \cos 3t + D \sin 3t + 9t^2 - 2$.
5. $x = C\,e^{4t} + D\,e^{-3t} - 2 \cos 3t - \frac{8}{3} \sin 3t$.
6. $y = C\,e^{5t} + D - \frac{1}{6}\,e^{3t}$.
8. $y = 3\,e^{4x} - e^{2x} + 2\,e^{x}$.
9. $y = (2t + 1)\,e^{-3t} + 3t^2 - 4t + 2$.

Exercises 11.1

1. $\dfrac{\partial z}{\partial x} = 3x^2y^2 + 4x,\quad \dfrac{\partial z}{\partial y} = 2x^3y + 3$.
2. $\dfrac{\partial P}{\partial v} = 3000\,v^2L^2$.
3. $\pi/\sqrt{Lg},\ -\pi\sqrt{(L/g^3)}$.
5. $v/8,\ -8T/v^2,\ 8/p$.
7. $\dfrac{\pi(2r^2 + h^2)}{\sqrt{(r^2 + h^2)}} + 2\pi r,\ \dfrac{\pi r h}{\sqrt{(r^2 + h^2)}}$.
8. $-2\rho V + 2\rho V \cos 2\theta,\ -2\rho V^2 \sin 2\theta$.
9. $\dfrac{b(a^2 - b^2)}{(a^4 + 3a^2b^2 + b^4)},\ \dfrac{a(b^2 - a^2)}{(a^4 + 3a^2b^2 + b^4)}$.

Exercises 11.2

1. $0{\cdot}112$ m^3.
4. $\pm 3{\cdot}16 \times 10^{-7}$.
5. $\pm 2\%$.
6. $\pm 5{\cdot}92$ cm/s^2.
7. $+$£7.
9. (i) $\delta P = \dfrac{2Cf}{r^4}\,\delta f + \left(-\dfrac{4cf^2}{r^5} + 2K\pi rL\right)\delta r$, (ii) $\gamma = \sqrt{(2\pi kLC)}$.

Exercises 11.3

3. $\dfrac{\partial A}{\partial X} = (9 - 4X + 2X \cos \theta) \sin \theta,\quad \dfrac{\partial A}{\partial \theta} = (9X - 2X^2) \cos \theta + X^2 \cos 2\theta$,

   $\dfrac{\partial^2 A}{\partial X^2} = \sin \theta\,(-4 + 2 \cos \theta),\quad \dfrac{\partial^2 A}{\partial \theta^2} = (2X^2 - 9X) \sin \theta - 2X^2 \sin 2\theta$,

   $\dfrac{\partial^2 A}{\partial \theta\,\partial X} = \cos \theta(9 - 4X) + 2X \cos 2\theta$.
4. $x = 11\frac{1}{2},\ y = 1$.
5. $x = 15,\ y = 24$.

Problems 11.6

2. $T = \left(p + \dfrac{3}{v^2}\right)(v - b)/16$.
3. $x = -1,\ y = -1$.
4. $\dfrac{\partial z}{\partial H} = \dfrac{\cos \delta \cos \phi \sin H}{\sin z}$.
5. $x = y = 6$.
6. $\alpha = \pm\sqrt{(n/2k)}$.
8. $\pm 0{\cdot}5\%$.
10. $m = 3,\ c = -9$.
11. (i) r, (ii) $r^2 \sin \theta$.

Revision Exercises

2. $\dfrac{\partial Q}{\partial B} = 3H^{\frac{3}{2}},\ \dfrac{\partial Q}{\partial H} = \dfrac{9}{2}\,BH^{\frac{1}{2}} - 1{\cdot}5H^{\frac{3}{2}}$.
5. $\sin (x + n\pi/2),\ \cos (x + n\pi/2)$.
6. $k = -\frac{1}{6}$, maximum.
7. $p_c = a/(4e^2b^2)$.
10. $u^2/[g(1 + \sin \alpha)]$.
11. $v = \pi a^3(3\pi - 1)/48,\ A = \pi a^2(2\pi - 1)/4$.
13. $a/\sqrt{2}$.
14. $p_x = a + b/r^2,\ p_y = -a + b/r^2$.

15. $\dfrac{\partial E}{\partial M} = \dfrac{1}{(1 - \mathrm{e}\cos E)}, \dfrac{\partial^2 E}{\partial M^2} = \dfrac{\mathrm{e}\sin E}{(1 - \mathrm{e}\cos E)^3}.$
17. $\mu_1' = \frac{1}{2}$, $\mu_2' = \frac{1}{3}$.
21. $s = \frac{2}{3}$, $t = \frac{11}{3}$, minimum value of PQ is $4/\sqrt{3}$.
22. Maximum value when $A = B = C = \pi/3$.

INDEX